Restless China

Restless China

Edited by
Perry Link
Richard P. Madsen
and
Paul G. Pickowicz

ROWMAN & LITTLEFIELD PUBLISHERS, INC.
Lanham • Boulder • New York • Toronto • Plymouth, UK

Published by Rowman & Littlefield Publishers, Inc.
A wholly owned subsidiary of The Rowman & Littlefield Publishing Group, Inc.
4501 Forbes Boulevard, Suite 200, Lanham, Maryland 20706
www.rowman.com

10 Thornbury Road, Plymouth PL6 7PP, United Kingdom

British Library Cataloguing in Publication Information Available

Library of Congress Cataloging-in-Publication Data Available
ISBN 978-1-4422-1510-8 (cloth : alk. paper)
ISBN 978-1-4422-1511-5 (pbk. : alk. paper)
ISBN 978-1-4422-1512-2 (electronic)

∞™ The paper used in this publication meets the minimum requirements of American National Standard for Information Sciences Permanence of Paper for Printed Library Materials, ANSI/NISO Z39.48-1992.

Printed in the United States of America

Contents

Acknowledgments

First drafts of all but one of the chapters in this book were discussed at a conference in November 2011 at the Chinese University of Hong Kong (CUHK). We are extremely grateful for the leadership of Professor Hsiung Ping-chen, who, as dean of arts and humanities and director of the Research Institute for the Humanities at CUHK, generously provided funding and local arrangements for the conference. Special thanks also to Professor Hsiung's staff, especially May Cheung, Dr. Abraham Chan, Charlotte Li, and Terence Chan, who together set the gold standard for professionalism and hospitality. The chapter drafts benefited greatly from thoughtful and constructive comments from scholars based in Hong Kong, including CUHK professors Choi Chi Chung, Anthony Fung, Ying Him, Katrien Jacobs, Desmond Hui, Ann Huss, Puk Wing Kin, Jack Qiu, Lin Chuan, Wu Fengshi, and Xue Yu—as well as James Lee, dean of the School of Humanities and Social Science, Hong Kong University of Science and Technology.

We are grateful for funding from two endowed chairs at the University of California—the Chair in Modern Chinese History at the University of California, San Diego, and the Chancellorial Chair for Teaching Across Disciplines at the University of California, Riverside, and to Cambridge University Press for permission to include Yunxiang Yan's "Food Safety and Social Risk in Contemporary China," which originally appeared in the *Journal of Asian Studies* 71, no. 3 (August 2012).

Special thanks, too, to Li Huai, whose deft eye has captured the photograph for the book's cover, and to our editor Susan McEachern, whose support and good judgment has been unstinting through all three of our joint projects: *Unofficial China* (1989), *Popular China* (2002), and now *Restless China*.

The Editors

Restless China

An Introduction

Perry Link, Richard P. Madsen, and Paul G. Pickowicz

This book is the third installment of a collaborative enterprise by the three editors that began twenty-five years ago. The history of this quarter-century-long endeavor reminds us not only of the enormous changes in China but also of evolution in the ways scholars have tried to understand it. Our project began around 1987, when China was in the first stages of its reform and opening, in the initial throes of economic transformation and what people at the time called "cultural fever." State socialist structures were partially giving way to a market economy in a process that was liberating but also unsettling to ordinary citizens. New opportunities were opening up, but inequality and insecurity were increasing. Restrictions on freedom of speech had been partially lifted, and contact with the outside world was steadily increasing, leading to passionate debates among intellectuals about how Chinese culture should change and how its political system should be reformed. Once confined to studying about China from the outside through the clouded lenses of official media and refugee interviews, Western scholars were now increasingly able to travel to China, to engage with Chinese intellectuals, and to see at least part of China from the inside.

Many at the time had a reasonably good picture of the changes that were or were not taking place in Chinese economic and political structures as well as an awareness of what some leading Chinese intellectuals were saying about the changes, but there was very little understanding of what ordinary citizens thought or how climates of opinion and moral values might be changing. Thus, we assembled a group of scholars to begin to explore popular culture in China. This yielded the first volume in this series, *Unofficial China*, which was mostly written just a few months before the Beijing Spring of 1989 and published just a few months after the Tiananmen massacre on June 4. The book did not predict the mass movements of 1989, but, in retrospect, it did present unique clues to the subterranean currents that led to that crisis.

1

The book explored value changes among Chinese youth and small entrepreneurs, the emergence of new forms of religious practice and old forms of ethnic discrimination, transformations in gender relations and family life, and the development of new media for mass communication. These were topics that hardly had been touched in the scholarly literature but that have since emerged as major objects of study. The authors of our chapters came from many different disciplines, including literature, history, sociology, anthropology, and political science. Since the terrain they were exploring was so new, they could not fall back on the standard methods of their disciplines. Instead, they creatively opened themselves to cross-fertilization across academic boundaries.

A dozen years later, the political system remained rigid and repressive, but China had undergone an economic takeoff and was experiencing perhaps the fastest rate of economic growth of any society in history. The emerging market economy had become deeply integrated into the global market, and one could see the effects of globalization everywhere. But it was still difficult to see the meaning that these changes had for ordinary people. Thus, we organized a second conference to explore new ways to understand the many, various, and often ambiguous meanings that ordinary Chinese were giving to their conflicted political economy. In 2002, this effort produced a second book, *Popular China*. More than in the previous volume, we focused on different reactions to the widening inequalities that came with the new globalizing market economy. Chapters spanned the whole range of social strata, including successful young urbanites, laid-off workers, farmers, migrant laborers, and even beggars. There was, necessarily, a chapter on popular reactions to pervasive corruption, and several chapters explored the widening sphere of private consumption and recreation, from house decoration to basketball fandom. Other chapters dealt with newly developing identities. We published one of the first essays on an emerging homosexual culture in China, and many of the others analyzed some aspect of changing gender relationships, including domestic violence. Finally, there was even more emphasis than in the first volume on new forms of media, from cheap tabloid journals to glossy women's magazines to satirical sayings circulated by word of mouth.

Once again, authors in the second volume represented a full range of academic disciplines in the humanities and social sciences. But once again, academic disciplines knew no borders. The emerging forms of popular culture were too elusive to be pinned down by most standard research methodologies, and to develop adequate ways of comprehending them, we recognized the need for all the cross-disciplinary help we could get. Furthermore, there was a significant change in the array of authors in the second volume. They represented a wider range of academic generations, from senior scholars to new PhDs. Although only one of the authors in the first volume was Chinese, almost half in the second volume were.

Neither the first nor the second volume claimed to portray a complete picture of Chinese popular culture. The immense—and rapidly increasing—diversity of China would have rendered that impossible. We simply offered glimpses of interesting new trends, and many of these glimpses have stimulated new research among a younger generation of scholars.

Now, another decade has passed, and many of those developments in popular culture that were barely visible in 2002 have not only become clearly manifest but are leading to unforeseen new consequences. China's economic growth has made it the second-largest economy in the world. Its level of economic inequality exceeds even that of the United States. Marxist ideology has almost completely collapsed and is being replaced by a combination of materialism and assertive nationalism. The vast migration of labor from countryside to city has continued apace. The pressures of a hypercompetitive market economy are ripping apart the traditional family. Political corruption has reached new heights. The political system is even more rigid but perhaps more brittle than a decade ago. There seems to be enormous popular pride in the ascension of China to the rank of a global superpower and general satisfaction in the material benefits that the poor as well as the rich have been gaining from an expanding economy. But there is also great restlessness, anger about structural injustice and political corruption, and a search for new forms of spirituality and ethics to replace a collapsing moral order. The time has come, we think, to take our explorations of Chinese popular culture to a new level.

The collapse of socialist ideals, which began in the late Mao years and by now is all but total, has led to what scholars both inside China and outside have sometimes referred to as a "values vacuum." Accustomed, for better or worse, to a powerful public ideology, people find when it disappears that they still need some kind of ethical belief system for use in daily life both as a guide to their own decision making and as a basis for assuming how others in their society will conduct themselves. In China's booming economy of recent times, moneymaking and materialism have filled the space to become the most conspicuous public values, and these values have been satisfying, but only up to a point. When pursuit of materialism gives rise to patterns of unscrupulous behavior and social injustice and when these patterns sometimes rest on special access to power, people look for something better. Fundamental notions of right and wrong are too deep in Chinese culture to allow people to feel comfortable with a formula that says that "only money counts" no matter how it is attained. In several ways, Chinese people today struggle with such questions as, What norms can we agree on? How can we put them into action? and What do we want it to mean, in the early twenty-first century, to *zuoren* (be a good person)?

A related set of underlying questions concerns Chinese identity. What does it mean, in the emerging new China, to be Chinese? Since the early 1990s, the government has stressed one version of Chinese nationalism: China, the Party-state, is "rising"; it can project power in its region, exert influence at the United Nations, host a spectacular Olympics, and so on. Nationalist sentiment in the populace has sometimes lagged behind this but in some cases has also gone further, taking on more aggressive and chauvinistic forms. In any case, the new nationalism has, like moneymaking, been one of the Chinese answers to the question, What can we believe in today? But, like moneymaking, it succeeds only up to a point. It is too thin to be an ethical guide to daily life or a complete answer to the question, What is it to be Chinese? A proud, secure twenty-first-century China needs something more substantial, more in line with its traditional dignity, to be the answer to that question. A significant weakness in the government-sponsored version of nationalism is that it stresses only the macrolevel, the level of the Party-state. But what does it mean to be a citizen? How can ordinary people also be twenty-first-century Chinese? The dramatic spread of the Internet and of notions of *weiquan* (supporting rights) have brought these questions much more into play than they were a decade ago, when we published *Popular China*.

These questions that concern values and identity have given rise to what we are calling "restlessness." It is important to see them as a weighty underside of the Chinese economic juggernaut that has been so eye-catching to the world but also important to see that the restlessness is not monolithic. It has many varieties that differ by region, social class, ethnicity, gender, and subculture. As in our earlier books, here we offer samples, not an exhaustive catalog. We do not predict that the restlessness amounts to a volcano that is headed for eruption. The restless energy could play out in a number of ways. It is worth noting, though, that people high in the Chinese government are among those who have noticed the ground-level ferment. Beginning in 2010, the government's expenditures on domestic *weiwen* (stability maintenance) have been exceeding its budget for national defense. Restlessness at the bottom, in other words, has been a factor in restlessness at the top.

The following chapters are grouped in four thematic clusters, the first of which we call "Legacies." One of the main points of the first three chapters is that the restlessness of the present day is connected in various ways to legacies of the Mao era. It is crucial, they suggest, to locate the stresses and strains of today in the broader context of long-term patterns associated with the history of state socialism in China. In chapter 1, Jeremy Brown demonstrates the links between present and past by looking at car crashes, fires, floods, and train wrecks. He asserts that Mao-era legacies, especially tensions between development and safety, and disputes related to power and privilege still shape how the Party handles accidents today. Citizens now have easy unofficial access to breaking news about shocking accidents, but the Party still seeks to conceal, falsify, and contain. The resulting tension creates restlessness. Anxious citizens ask, Is there any place in China where people can feel safe? Why are officials reluctant to report the truth about accidents and determine responsibility? X. L. Ding explores the theme of legacies in chapter 2 by arguing that even the wealthiest Chinese—major winners in the era of reform and opening—feel profoundly restless and insecure. Capitalists have vast sums of money but, just as in the Mao era, are not trusted by the Party-state and have no real political power. Ding's study of business culture reveals that rich capitalists are almost entirely dependent on political patrons. Their money might get them out of legal messes, but it cannot trump the political power of the Party-state bureaucracy. Restless red capitalists, vividly aware of the legacies of the Mao era, are terrified of losing everything. Consequently, they are obsessed with schemes designed to get themselves, their families, and their money out to safe havens in North America and elsewhere. In chapter 3, Paul Pickowicz deals with the issue of legacies by examining the wicked culture of joke telling. Restless Chinese love to tell political jokes. Pickowicz was surprised, however, to discover that young, educated urban dwellers—including Party members—are especially fond of irreverent political jokes set in the former Soviet Union. China is not mentioned in these jokes, but the barbs and jabs they contain are easily applied to the Chinese case. Hypocrisies, abuses, and corrupt practices associated with the Soviet Union in the twentieth century seem all too relevant to conditions in restless China in the early twenty-first century. Globalization and transnational currents are important research topics, but we know far too little about distinctively socialist cross-border cultural experiences that still link places like Russia and China.

Our second thematic cluster is "A New Electronic Community," arguably the hottest research topic in contemporary Chinese studies. These chapters accept the premise that new cultural developments need to be understood in the context of Mao-era legacies, but they also argue that the Internet culture functions today in China as a fresh and extraordinarily important game changer. The Party's ability to control the flow of information has been drastically reduced. In chapter 4, Perry Link and Xiao Qiang cite examples to show that the Internet has generated a healthy if sometimes contentious dialogue about individual and group identities. Who are "we"? Netizens increasingly question the notion that love of country entails love of Party. True, the state is also a player in the new Internet culture. It regulates, preaches, censors, and filters in an effort to control the spread of information in ways that serve the power interests of the Party. But netizens are actively creating new languages and new conceptualizations. "Cyberassembly" is now a potent force in restless China, and increasingly the state is forced to respond to cyberopinion and even make policy adjustments. State leaders are acutely aware that resentment and distrust of officialdom is a major characteristic of Internet culture. In chapter 5, Yang Lijun offers an intriguing microscopic view of evolving Internet culture by focusing on China's most famous blogger, a young man whose blog has attracted an astounding 570 million visits. Some say that the Internet made Han Han; others say that Han Han made the Internet. Yang not only analyzes the controversial content of Han Han's posts, which include criticisms of ultranationalism, money worship, corruption, and environmental degradation, but also, perhaps more important, engages with the complex views of Han Han's legions of fans and detractors. Yang argues that Han Han's broad appeal has much to do with his unpredictable, "free-spirit" persona. At a time when many Chinese intellectuals have abdicated their time-honored critical responsibilities, Han Han has surfaced as a new-style nonelite Chinese "public intellectual" whose activities frustrate Party bureaucrats. In chapter 6, Shuyu Kong offers a second case study of new electronic communities by looking at television programming. She focuses on a reality show called *Are You the One?* This phenomenally popular dating program features twenty-four stylish young women peppering a single young man with ego-deflating questions. Kong wants to know why this apparently silly program is so amazingly popular and what it tells us about the complicated identities of the young and the restless. By analyzing the social issues broadcast on television screens and the highly emotional online audience responses that follow each episode, Kong identifies a new form of civic engagement, a phenomenon she calls public communication of lifestyle politics. Young people are terrified of "failing," and their passionate discussions of jobs, recreation, fashion, self-improvement, and friends are easily transformed into political matters.

Our third cluster is simply called "Values." Given all the moral confusion that has accompanied globalization, rapid economic development, staggering social transformation, and disorienting cultural shifts (including the Party's unceremonious abandonment of Maoism and traditional socialist ideology), many ordinary citizens are desperate to encounter ideas and practices that give meaning to their lives. Richard Madsen argues in chapter 7 that many citizens, including rural dwellers, have turned restlessness and alienation into cultural creativity by engaging in exciting and invigorating grassroots religious activities. His field research points to a mysterious, hot, even holy creativity that is able to break through the stifling cracks of ice-cold bureaucratic life. Indifferent to the state and its priorities, restless citizens find deep meaning in the colorful, nonstandardized, spontaneous, bottom-up, and unpredictable dimensions of popular religious expression and formations that include faith-healing cults, Pentecostal Christian communities, and many others. Madsen argues that China is not morally empty and is not "individualized." It is more useful to see China as "decentered." The demise of a one-size-fits-all center has given rise to myriad sparks of creative energy that reside beyond the center. In chapter 8, David Moser expands on this theme by looking at the ever-growing numbers of "urban Buddhists," also referred to as "weekend Buddhists." Many of these people are highly successful white-collar professionals who are engaged in a search for meaning and identity. They are almost "invisible" because their participation is largely informal, idiosyncratic, and personal, taking place outside the framework of temple rituals. Indeed, many are cyber-Buddhists who are redefining the meaning of Buddhism in the Internet age. They "shop" for masters, and they switch sects on a regular basis. Their activities explain why Buddhism is the largest and fastest-growing religion in China. Some believers embrace Buddhism to solve concrete personal problems (including serious health issues), others are trying to find a deeper spiritual realm, while still others are looking for a cooler lifestyle image. In chapter 9, William Jankowiak continues our examination of values by exploring a moral issue that preoccupies tens of millions of restless Chinese: Precisely how does one go about finding a life partner? He argues that love and sex are not just emotional problems; they are ethical problems as well. The early post-Mao period was still dominated by what Jankowiak calls a "courtship culture," but since the early 1990s, this mode has been replaced by a confusing and complicated informal "dating culture." Young people are kissing earlier, sleeping together sooner, and having more dating partners than ever before, but few know exactly why. When it comes to finding a life partner, the challenge is not figuring out how to play the game; the challenge is figuring out what game is being played. Restless happiness, joy, and contentment are often accompanied by restless disappointment, regret, and anger.

Our final thematic cluster is "Global Standards." These chapters take very seriously the notion that the leaders of post-Mao China value globalization and very much want to preside over a China that is integrated into world and regional systems. It is well known that they want China to meet global standards when it comes to education, trade, finance, scientific research, athletic competition, and space travel. But it is equally apparent that in many important fields, the regime has neither the will nor the ability to meet these global standards and that its failure to do so generates both restlessness and fear among citizens. In chapter 10, Su Xiaokang and Perry Link discuss the troubling problem of environmental degradation in China, the Party's failure to embrace relevant global standards, and the tragic consequences of that neglect. The pursuit of economic growth without calculation of environmental costs has led to catastrophic air and water pollution, depletion of farmlands, mountains of garbage, and water shortages. We know that wealthy businessmen are obsessed with sending their money abroad, but in this chapter, Su and Link show that anxious rich people and Party elites alike also send their families abroad for reasons of health. Meanwhile, China produces one-quarter of the world's carbon emissions, its urbanites have twice as much lead in their blood, and in a single year (2007), at least 350,000 of its people died of air pollution. In chapter 11, Hsiung Ping-chen continues the discussion by looking at global standards in the important field of education. In this case, leaders have made it clear that they want China's top universities to be ranked on a par with Harvard and Oxford and have devoted vast sums of money to various education-related "megaprojects." The result has been disappointing because of a fundamental tension between Party standards and global standards. Student and faculty netizens complain about political control, breaches of academic ethics, embezzlement of research funds, and low campus morale. In brief, academic freedom does not prevail, and China's drive to meet world standards in education falls far short of what has been achieved in South Korea, Taiwan, Japan, Singapore, and Hong Kong. In chapter 12, Yunxiang Yan asserts that China's globalizing and modernizing leaders also claim that they want the quality of the nation's food supply to meet world standards. But wave after wave of food safety scares have raised grave concerns at home and abroad about dangerous additives, adulterated foods, counterfeit foods and medicines, trade in sick or dead animals, and contamination by pesticides, chemical fertilizers, hormones, and steroids. In the most alarming cases, poisonous chemicals are deliberately added to increase profits. Yan argues that food safety panics have led to widespread distrust of food sellers and the food industry. As in the 1950s, elites have access to special, safer food supplies. Market forces have developed rapidly, but social trust has declined. As one restless citizen put it, "You never know what is inside a package of food. Anything is possible."

Our final cluster, "Global Standards," brings *Restless China* full circle. The desire of Chinese elites and ordinary citizens to reach world standards in such areas as environmental regulation, higher education, and food safety are intimately connected to and complicated by the issues discussed in our first three clusters, namely, the legacies of the Mao era, new-age cyberassembly, and the search for new ethical moorings. Will "moneymaking" remain the dominant value, or will it be constrained and on occasion even trumped by broader and more pressing ethical concerns?

Part I

Legacies

ONE

When Things Go Wrong

Accidents and the Legacy of the Mao Era in Today's China

Jeremy Brown

Cross the street and get hit by a bus.[1] Successfully board a bus, only to be incinerated when flammable materials carried by another passenger suddenly ignite.[2] Test your luck on the subway instead, but the signal system is malfunctioning and your carriage collides with an oncoming train.[3] Shanghai residents can be forgiven for feeling anxious when they wake up and get ready to walk out the door in the morning. Maybe it would be better to stay in bed, but then you realize that your high-rise apartment building could be engulfed in flames and that the local fire department has no hoses or ladders long enough to reach your eighteenth-story flat.[4] And even if you do manage to survive the fire and are rushed to a hospital where expert surgeons can treat your wounds, what if a new blaze breaks out next to the operating room and the doctors run away, leaving your sedated body on the gurney? All of these things have happened in Shanghai in the past four years, including the improbable events of August 24, 2011, when a patient under anesthesia at Shanghai's Number 3 People's Hospital died on the operating table after everyone else in the room fled thick smoke coming from a fire in an adjoining room.[5] Is there anywhere in today's China where people can feel safe and go about their lives without worrying about terrible accidents?

Fears about accidents exist on two levels. First is the pervasive concern that anyone could be killed or maimed at any moment. The second, deeper anxiety is that if an accident does occur, the authorities will mis-

11

handle the aftermath by covering it up and denying compensation and justice to the victims. Top Communist Party leaders are acutely aware of both levels but have been unable to either reduce accidents or prevent official mishandling after they occur. Authorities in Party center are especially worried that accidents and other "sudden crises" (*tufa shijian*), such as protests and natural disasters, could threaten the Party's efforts to maintain social stability and build a harmonious society.[6]

The collision between two high-speed trains near Wenzhou on July 23, 2011, killing forty people and injuring 192, confirmed the fears of top leaders in Beijing. Five days after the Wenzhou crash, on the same day that Premier Wen Jiabao visited the disaster site, an editorial on the front page of *People's Daily* tried to send the message that the Party understood widespread anxiety about accidents and would not tolerate safety lapses. "China wants development, but it does not want a bloody GDP [gross domestic product]" (*Zhongguo yao fazhan, dan bu yao daixie de GDP*), the editorial intoned. "We should mobilize all social forces, resolutely win the war of production safety, and make great efforts to achieve scientific and safe development."[7] Skeptical readers could say, "I told you so" exactly two months later, when two subway trains collided on Shanghai's Metro Line 10, injuring 290 people. China's GDP was still dripping blood.

China has had a bloody GDP ever since the Communists came to power in 1949. The difference today is that more people know about it, thanks to intrepid Internet reporting combined with digital images and videos taken by private citizens carrying smart phones. During the Mao Zedong era (1949–1978), industrial, traffic, and mining accidents claimed many lives and affected hundreds of thousands of families, but the toll remained secret. Newspapers were extremely selective and cautious in reporting accidents. They were more likely to celebrate the sacrifices of heroic "martyrs" such as Lei Feng, who died when he was accidentally crushed by a falling pole in 1962, than to investigate the causes of crashes, fires, and explosions. Newly available sources from the Mao period, however, reveal that horrifying accidents were common. More important, archival documents show how Party officials dealt with, mishandled, covered up, and attempted to prevent accidents in the 1950s, 1960s, and 1970s. This Mao-era legacy shapes how the Party handles accidents today. To build on Timothy Cheek's metaphor of "Living Maoism" as "the software that runs on the hardware of China's physical and human geography" during the reform period,[8] the Communist Party uses a fundamentally Maoist "operating system" to handle accidents in the twenty-first century—like Windows 8, the system has been updated and looks shiny, but it has the same bones as Windows 95.

Like passersby, scholars can be tempted to rubberneck and finger-point at accident scenes. It helps to remember that deadly accidents happen everywhere, not only in China. How they unfold in particular places reveals problems, pressures, and patterns that are unique to different societies. In the United States, for example, between fifteen and twenty-five children die each year when they are left unattended in overheated cars.[9] And even though window-blind cords strangle one child each month in the United States, manufacturers have been hesitant to transition to safer cordless blinds, citing high costs.[10] These facts help us understand certain aspects of American society today: some parents become incomprehensibly distracted, and some corporations put profit ahead of safety.

Looking at accidents in contemporary China can be similarly revealing. The Party's handling of accidents shows how the patterns and practices of the Mao period, especially tensions between development versus safety and disputes related to power and privilege, have endured and evolved in the reform period. Enduring legacies of the Mao era include a counterproductive accident reporting system that encourages cover-ups and repression of accident victims. In recent years, these problems have been exacerbated by new opportunities to make massive profits by taking big risks. It is no wonder, then, that people in China are more worried about accidents than ever.

PRODUCTION SAFETY, OR PRODUCTION VERSUS SAFETY?

Between February and June 1950, twenty-three workers at a pair of mines in Hunan were killed or injured by floods, fires, and cave-ins. According to *People's Daily*, capitalist mine owners were directly responsible for the accidents. They "only cared about making money and did not care about mine safety."[11] Putting profits ahead of safety and recklessly pursuing production were leftover vestiges of the old society, China's new leaders proclaimed. Many of the factories and mines the Communists had seized from the Japanese and Nationalists between 1945 and 1949 had "bad safety equipment and bad safety systems." The Communists promised that things would be different in the new society. They pledged to protect workers by eliminating the evils of capitalist- and imperialist-style workplaces. Accidents would be prevented thanks to a "safe production" (*anquan shengchan*) regime imported from the Soviet Union.[12]

The new safety system established in the early 1950s combined rewards for preventing accidents with punishments for allowing them to happen. It also included strict reporting guidelines to ensure that higher-ups in the bureaucracy knew about accidents as soon as they occurred. China's current safety regime, codified in the Production Safety Law of 2002 and accident reporting rules passed in 2007 and overseen by the State Administration of Work Safety (SAWS; established in 2005) and the State Administration of Coal Mine Safety, is the direct descendant of the Soviet-inspired system of the 1950s. Savvy translators at SAWS gave their organization an innocuous name in English, but its Chinese name—the one that really matters—is a throwback to the "safe production" language of the early Mao years: State Safe Production Supervision and Management Headquarters (*Guojia anquan shengchan jiandu guanli zongju*).

Reports and Labels

In January 1951, the Tianjin Labor Bureau complained that only twenty factories had submitted their accident reporting forms on time in the previous year, causing inaccuracies in record keeping. Any time a "major accident" (*zhongda shigu*) happened, meaning at least one death or five injuries, the factory was required to inform the labor bureau by telephone or telegraph within thirty minutes. Factories then had to fill out forms that indicated the names and ages of dead and injured workers, the "type" of accident ("for example, carbon monoxide poisoning, explosion, fire, electrocution, etc.," the paperwork helpfully offered), the cause of the accident, details about rescue efforts, handling the aftermath (*shanhou chuli*), and what measures had been taken to prevent accidents in the future (*fangzhi duice*). Even if a factory made it through a month without any deaths or injuries, it was still supposed to submit a written report of "no accidents" to the labor bureau by the third day of each month.[13]

By 1970, the categories had changed, but the requirement to submit detailed and timely accident reports had not. A "major accident" referred to three or more deaths, while the "especially major" (*tebie zhongda*) label was reserved for accidents that killed ten or more people. Instead of the three examples provided in 1950, people filling out forms twenty years later had to choose the "accident type" from a precise list of twenty-two grisly possibilities, ranging from "(2) vehicle injury (including crowding, crushing, collision, overturning, etc.)" to "(19) boiler and pressurized container explosions." And in a reflection of the charged political atmosphere of the Cultural Revolution, the paperwork included a space for deaths and injuries attributed to "political accidents caused by class enemies committing sabotage."[14]

An "especially major" accident in China today does far more damage than an "especially major" one did in 1970. According to regulations that went into effect in June 2007, an accident classified as "especially major" kills at least thirty people, severely injures at least 100 people, or causes direct economic losses of at least 100 million yuan (US$15.72 million). Other accident categories include "major" (ten to twenty-nine deaths), "rather large" (three to nine deaths), and "average" (one or two deaths).[15] What was a "major" accident in 1950 is now merely "average."

Reporting requirements have also become more complex and convoluted. Instead of the phone call or telegram within thirty minutes, the "relevant person" at the scene of an accident today must report to the person in charge of the work unit "immediately." That "person in charge" (*fuzeren*) then has one hour to report to the county- or district-level safe production department. When he picks up the phone to call his superiors, the official in charge is already in big trouble. He knows that he is likely to be blamed and punished for any accident that occurs in his jurisdiction. It has been that way since 1950, when administrative leaders, bureau directors and deputy directors, managers, and department heads were deemed "responsible" for all accidents caused by negligence. Officials who kept accident numbers low would be rewarded.[16] Today, the postaccident penalties for leaders "who did not carry out their safe production management duties" get harsher according to the severity of the accident: "especially major" accidents call for a fine of 80 percent of the official's salary, while "major," "rather large," and "average" accidents lead to fines of 60, 40, and 30 percent, respectively. On top of that, officials in charge are also subject to criminal charges and intra-Party discipline.[17]

Profit versus Safety

That is how the Party's accident prevention and reporting system looks on paper. How has it worked in practice? More often than not, making money and meeting production quotas have trumped accident prevention, especially during intense pushes for rapid industrialization, such as the First Five-Year Plan and the Great Leap Forward. During the Leap, as Frank Dikötter writes, "failure to fulfill a target could cost a manager his career, while violation of labour safety attracted a mere slap on the wrist."[18] In the Mao era, punishment for safety breaches, if it came at all, was usually delayed until the next political movement, when the masses were encouraged to expose and criticize official negligence.

Overloaded vehicles and boats are a clear example of the temptation to seek greater profits or surpass quotas by circumventing safety rules. Sell another ticket or make less money by staying at capacity? Sneak a few extra boxes on board or risk missing a quota? On June 29, 1974, the eleven-person crew of the *Ganzhong* (*Loyal Jiangxi*) decided to allow 136 passengers on the riverboat, which had a capacity of 120. They also stored more than 2,000 kilograms of firewood, fruit, and luggage on top of the ship's canopy, making the vessel extremely top-heavy. The *Ganzhong* encountered a sudden storm as it made its way down the Gan River from Wan'an to Ganzhou. When strong winds caused the boat to list to one side, panicked passengers made the problem worse by all rushing to the other side. The boat capsized, killing ninety-three people. The postaccident report circulated by the Jiangxi Revolutionary Committee criticized leaders for paying more attention to fulfilling production tasks and tons transported per kilometer than to safety work. It also blamed General Cheng Shiqing, the former provincial Party Secretary who had been arrested in disgrace in 1972 in the aftermath of Lin Biao's death, for acting as Lin's representative in Jiangxi by putting "profits in command."[19]

Pursuit of profits motivated a rural school transportation company in Gansu to overload a small van with sixty-two children, one teacher, and one driver on November 16, 2011. The van, originally meant to carry nine people, had all of its seats removed in order to cram in as many kindergartners as possible. On a foggy morning, the van collided with a coal delivery truck, killing eighteen children and two adults and injuring dozens more. Lu Huadong, head of the Qingyang Municipal Education Bureau, explained that the region was poor and had a limited education budget. Lu also said that authorities had told transport operators to stop overloading kindergarten buses, but they "just ignored our request for the sake of profit."[20] After the crash, the victims' mourning family members were assembled in a guesthouse, where more than 130 county and township cadres "comforted" them and engaged in "stability control." Two cadres were assigned to each family and were present when anyone from outside the guesthouse met with the grieving parents.[21] Local authorities seemed to be devoting more attention and resources to preventing protests than to addressing the problem of overcrowded vehicles.

Overloaded buses are unsafe because they are difficult to turn, slow down, and evacuate. They are also more likely to blow up. On July 22, 2011, a double-decker sleeper bus in Henan raced through the night with forty-seven passengers on board—twelve over capacity. Only eight people were on board when the bus started its journey in Shandong, but it gradually filled up along the way. According to a *Caixin* report, "Bus conductors regularly solicit passengers from outside the stations," overloading buses because they "operate on low profit margins." Passengers who board buses on the side of the road stow their luggage quickly, never getting close to the security screening machines installed in many bus stations. Flammable chemicals stored in the sleeper bus's luggage compartment exploded around 4 a.m., causing a massive conflagration that killed forty-one people.[22] News about this "especially major" accident was quickly overwhelmed by coverage of the high-speed train collision outside Wenzhou the next day, even though the bus disaster killed one more person than the train crash did.

Cover-Ups and Lies

Fatal accidents involving overloaded buses happen with alarming regularity in China, but perhaps because the buses are mostly crammed full of impoverished rural people, they do not grab headlines the same way the high-speed train crash did. China's high-speed trains are expensive to ride and serve major cities, so most passengers are upper-middle-class urbanites who carry smart phones capable of recording video and uploading blog entries and Weibo messages. This is how the images and videos of excavators destroying and burying parts of the damaged trains circulated like wildfire on the Internet after the Wenzhou crash, sparking outrage that the Party was trying to cover up the accident. Journalist Zhu Fangqing posted a photograph of at least four excavators dumping train parts in a huge pit along with the comment, "Do you fucking think that Chinese people are all idiots?" (*ni ma yiwei guoren dou shazi?*).[23]

When asked to explain the buried carriages, hapless Railway Ministry spokesperson Wang Yongping said that he had been told that the train wreckage was used to stabilize muddy ground. Wang then uttered the infamous words, "Whether you believe it or not, I believe it anyway" (*Zhiyu ni xin bu xin, wo fanzheng xin le*). Netizens followed up with more than three million send-ups of Wang's exhortation to have blind faith in the Party ("The Chinese Football Association says: China will qualify for the World Cup in 2014. Whether you believe it or not, I believe it anyway").[24] Wang may have been the only person in China who believed the words coming out of his own mouth. Outraged observers suspected that officials were hiding something because the Party has openly attacked an epidemic of covering up and lying about accidents in recent years.

Hiding accidents has been a problem ever since the Communists implemented their "safe production" system in the 1950s. The policy mix of rewards, punishments, and stringent communication guidelines was designed to ensure that no accident went unreported. But in practice, the system encouraged cover-ups. This was painfully clear to Cao Yongjia, a longshoreman in Shanghai. At 3 a.m. on September 22, 1956, Cao slipped, and a heavy bag of salt fell on his left leg.[25] He told his coworkers that it hurt, but nobody suggested that he seek medical attention, so he rested on the dock for an hour. When Cao's boss appeared and gave the workers instructions for their next job, Cao limped over and pointed out that his kneecap seemed like it was dislocated. "It can't be dislocated," Cao's boss said. "If it were, you wouldn't be able to walk." Cao struggled to complete his next task, and at the end of the shift he showed his leg to a safety officer who said, "It's not red or swollen. Do you want to report a work injury?" Cao's boss quickly jumped in, saying, "If you want to report it, go ahead." Cao hesitated. "I thought that since the safety officer said it wasn't red or swollen, if I reported a work injury, they would say I was just trying to get time off," he recalled.

Cao went home to sleep, but his leg pain woke him up, so he called the phone number the safety officer had given him. When nobody answered after three tries, Cao went to his boss's home. His boss said, "I'm sure it hurts, but it can't be dislocated." He ordered Cao to show up for work the next day, saying that he would be assigned light tasks and that "the team will do its best to take care of you." When Cao got home, his team's union leader and another coworker were waiting for him. They told him the same thing his boss had: come to work tomorrow, and the team will look after you.

Cao kept working until early October, but his leg felt worse and worse. He finally asked his boss for three days off and said he wanted to formally report a work injury. His boss denied him the time off, saying that Cao's family could not afford it, and then claimed that it was too late to make an injury report. "He meant," Cao recalled, "that work injuries had to be reported within twenty-four hours." Before Cao left, his boss added one more thing: if you see the district director, walk slow and try not to limp. "He was afraid the director would ask me why I was limping," Cao wrote.

Cao Yongjia limped along until March 1957 until his leg pain made it impossible to work at all. He racked up medical costs shuttling between various doctors. When he stopped by the Shanghai Port Authority safety office in May to once again try to report a work injury, the officer brushed him off, asking, "Why didn't you report it back when you got hurt? This is an old injury." We know about Cao's case because during the Hundred Flowers Movement in 1957, he was emboldened to write a letter requesting that the authorities recognize that his injury was caused by a work accident and demanding compensation for his medical costs. Prompted by whistle-blowers such as Cao, a Port Authority work team interviewed forty-one workers who were on "illness leave" and discovered that ten of them had been injured in work accidents that had never been reported.[26]

Why were managers so disinclined to report injuries, and why did workers go along with the ruse? When the foot of a thirty-three-year-old worker named Liao was crushed by a loom in June 1956, he could not work for five days. But his team had been praised as an "advanced unit," so to maintain the honor, his accident went unreported. In order to gain and protect honors and rewards, supervisors told workers who got hurt that they would be assigned light work or granted them "illness leave" instead of "work injury leave." And practically everyone who worked around the port had heard the erroneous claim that if more than twenty-four hours had elapsed since an accident occurred, it could not be reported as a work injury. Clever managers had found a way to use stringent reporting rules to prevent reports from ever getting made. The pressure on Shanghai longshoremen to go along with hiding and mischaracterizing injuries was subtle but clear. Cai Gaode's leg was crushed by a bag of corn, but he was "afraid of causing disunity in his team," so he did not formally report a work injury and ended up paying a doctor twenty yuan out of his own pocket.[27]

Lies about their legs made life difficult for Cai Gaode and Cao Yongjia, but their troubles were piddling when considered in the context of the Communist Party's overall track record of concealing and falsifying information about accidents. When a small earthen dam failed in rural Hunan in 1954, one man named Li fished eighty bodies out of the river before losing count. A few days later, Li was outraged when officials announced that only three people had died in the dam breach. Li had lost trust in the Party for good. "It's all a series of lies from their mouths!" he said.[28]

Twenty-one years later, Li would not have been surprised about the cover-up of a much larger disaster, but he had no way of knowing about it. In August 1975, the massive Banqiao and Shikumen dams in Henan collapsed along with more than fifty smaller dams. Deadly walls of water sped downstream, killing as many as 230,000 people in Henan and neighboring Anhui.[29] Tens of thousands were swept to their deaths by the first waves, and many others died of disease and famine when they were stranded in the floodwaters in the weeks that followed. The dams were overcome by heavy rainfall when a typhoon stalled over Henan, but the disaster was man-made. Engineers had built the dams to withstand only fifty- or 100-year floods, even though records from the Ming dynasty showed that flooding on a similarly massive scale had taken place during the Wanli reign.[30] They had gambled and lost—much like Japanese nuclear engineers who failed to build Fukushima Daiichi to withstand an earthquake-tsunami one-two punch, even though the historical record showed that such an event had occurred in the past and was likely to happen again.[31]

Because Japanese citizens living near Fukushima in March 2011 knew that something terrible was happening at the nuclear plant, many chose to evacuate. In 1975, by contrast, hundreds of thousands of Henanese villagers were given no warning that the huge dams might collapse. And after the flooding, an information blackout kept victims in the dark. In response to an emergency telegram from the leaders of Zhumadian prefecture about the dam failures, Party center dispatched a "comfort team" led by Vice Premier Ji Dengkui on August 11, 1975. Zhang Guangyou, a Xinhua journalist, accompanied the delegation to Henan. Zhang was already friendly with Ji Dengkui, so he asked the Politburo member how he should report on the disaster. Ji replied, "Central leaders have decided that there will be no reports or information released to the public about the flooding. Not only should there be no open reporting, but the disaster conditions in particular need to be kept secret."[32] Zhang wrote many internal reports to central leaders, including one in which he estimated that the number of people who drowned in the immediate aftermath of the dam failures was between 30,000 and 40,000, but he followed orders and issued no public reports about the disaster.[33] *Henan Daily* published at least two vague articles about heroic rescue efforts,[34] but everyone else in China remained in the dark.

As more scholars plumb archives from the Mao period and as more people such as Zhang Guangyou write about their experiences, more horrific accidents that have been covered up for years are coming to light. For example, in February 1977, an auditorium fire on Chinese New Year's Eve at a Xinjiang Production and Construction Corps settlement killed 694 people, most of them children.[35] A child set off a firecracker that ignited a pile of months-old wreaths left over from Chairman Mao's memorial service (no one wanted to be accused of disrespecting Mao's memory, so the desiccated wreaths were never removed from the stage). The auditorium's ceiling was made out of reeds covered by a layer of bricks. After the reeds caught fire, the bricks collapsed, and people inside were unable to evacuate because half of the main exit and all of the other windows and exits had been bricked over earlier in the 1970s. After the disaster, officials enforced an information lockdown, and nothing was openly published in China about the fire until retired Xinjiang-based journalist Gao Dong's article appeared in 2010.

Given that top officials in Beijing have been complicit in concealing accidents such as the Henan dam failures of 1975 and the Xinjiang fire of 1977, it is unsurprising that local officials continue to ignore directives against covering up or submitting false reports about accidents. In Guangxi's Nandan county, for example, mining accidents killed 259 people in 2000, but officials reported only fifty-seven deaths.[36] In the spring of 2011, a rash of cover-ups in which mine bosses concealed corpses and went into hiding led central authorities to draw up even harsher penalties for lying about accidents.[37] The new rules mandated that leaders who cover up and send false reports should be fined 100 percent of their salary. Their work units can be fined millions of yuan, depending on the severity of the accident and whether the cover-up hindered rescue efforts and worsened the disaster.[38]

Will the tougher rules be effective in stamping out cover-ups? Not likely. As journalist Wang Dapeng has perceptively noted, concealing accidents is a "rational choice" (*lixing xuanze*) for local officials. When a major accident occurs in an official's jurisdiction, he is already in a lose-lose situation. He will be disciplined and fined for having allowed an accident to happen and will also be punished if he is found to have hidden or lied about the accident. Smart officials successfully cover up accidents or tweak the death count to eight or nine (just below the cutoff for a "major accident"), thereby saving their own skin and maybe even earning praise from superiors for promoting safe production.[39] Officials have been making the same "rational choice" to hide accidents ever since the 1950s, for today's combination of rewards and punishments is an updated version of the "safe production" regime implemented in the early years of the People's Republic.

What has changed since the 1950s is that the potential rewards for skirting safety regulations have become far greater. Today, officials stand to earn millions of yuan in cash for colluding with corrupt mine bosses, as X. L. Ding shows in chapter 2 in this volume, whereas Mao-era cadres could garner a coveted label as an "advanced unit" for fraudulently claiming an accident-free year. The cost of getting caught is also far greater today than it was during the Mao period. Tough new regulations from Beijing may be telling local officials not to lie, but the message they are actually hearing is "Don't get caught." What happens, though, when officials themselves are personally caught up in an accident? The answer sheds light on power and privilege in contemporary Chinese society.

POWER AND PRIVILEGE

"Students, sit down! Don't move! Let the leaders leave first!" No other words better capture the widely held belief that Chinese officials care more about themselves than about the greater good. According to witnesses, the shrill order was screamed by a female voice in the early evening of December 8, 1994, after a stage light ignited a curtain at the Friendship Hall in Karamay, Xinjiang.[40] The fire spread rapidly, and the one open exit was quickly blocked by the bodies of people trying to flee (the other exits were locked tight, and the person in charge of the keys was nowhere to be found after the fire started).[41] Of the 325 people who died in the fire, 288 were children.[42]

Save Yourself

The deeper that one digs into the Karamay fire, the worse Chinese officials look. No one has dug deeper than documentary filmmaker Xu Xin, whose monumental six-hour documentary about the disaster intersperses lengthy interviews with grieving parents with gut-wrenching footage of the fire and its aftermath.[43] Local schoolchildren packed the auditorium to watch their star classmates perform a song-and-dance routine for an inspection team of education officials from the Xinjiang Uyghur Autonomous Region. The students and teachers waited for hours because the leaders were late coming from a lunch banquet. When they finally made their way to their seats in the front rows, many appeared red-faced and drunk. It was bad enough that officials ran out of the auditorium without bothering to help evacuate the children, but the actions of the deputy Party secretary of the Karamay Education Bureau, who was intimately familiar with the auditorium's layout, rise to especially galling heights of callousness. She locked herself alone in a washroom that could have held thirty people, ignoring the terrified cries of children who were seeking refuge. After she emerged unscathed, she bragged about her survival instincts.[44]

That nearly 300 students died while officials saved their own lives has become a compelling morality tale that pits selfish power holders against the youngest, most powerless members of Chinese society. This explanation seems especially convincing when it comes from parents who lost kids in the fire. Children depend on adults to keep them safe and to lead them away from danger. Protecting them is the "collective responsibility" of all of China's government bodies and adult citizens, according to the

PRC's Child Protection Law.[45] They count on grown-ups to make sure that hot stage lights are kept a proper distance from flammable curtains (the lights were closer than safety regulations allowed), to keep emergency exits unlocked, to properly equip and train firefighters (the first trucks that arrived at the auditorium had empty water tanks and no tools that could pry open doors), and to take immediate action when given stern warnings by fire safety inspectors (who had pointed out numerous safety violations at the Friendship Auditorium on three separate occasions between 1992 and 1994).[46]

One detail that has rarely been pointed out amid the justifiable outrage about Karamay's "powerful officials versus powerless children" narrative was that among the cadres sitting in the front rows on December 8, 1994, the highest-ranking ones perished in the fire. Of the twenty-three members of the provincial-level education inspection team, seventeen died, and five suffered severe burns. None of the sixteen Karamay municipal education officials in the auditorium died.[47] The local cadres, who had attended many meetings in the auditorium and knew which exits were unlocked and which washrooms offered refuge, were the first to escape.[48] Not only did they abandon hundreds of terrified children, but they left their superiors behind. The Xinjiang officials, some of whom may have been drunk,[49] had to fend for themselves in an unfamiliar environment. "Power" played a role in determining who survived the inferno, but for the men and women in the front rows, local knowledge was far more important than administrative rank.

The Karamay municipal cadres were not the first Chinese Communist officials to put their own survival above the safety of others. On February 27, 1966, thirteen people drowned when their leaky, overloaded boat capsized on the way to a reservoir construction project in rural Guangxi.[50] Shen Yingxuan and Hua Yueshan, members of a Four Cleanups work team in Luzhai county, found an old abandoned boat that they thought they could use to transport villagers to a reservoir work site. Shen boarded the dilapidated craft once and was barely able to keep it afloat by constantly bailing out water but never ordered repairs or told anyone to stop using it. When Hua Yueshan saw the wobbly boat in action, he and other village officials decided to walk to the work site instead.

After the accident, enraged family members of victims confronted officials on the Four Cleanups work team, saying, "You study the works of Chairman Mao every day and are supposed to care about the masses, so why weren't you together with the masses? You knew the boat was dangerous and wouldn't take it yourself, so why didn't you stop the masses from using it?" One villager who lost his daughter and daughter-in-law in the accident was so despondent that he tried to kill himself. The cadres who encouraged locals to use the unsafe boat were transferred away to engage in self-criticism but were given "appropriate work to do" because "their work should not be completely halted by self-criticism." This was a light slap on the wrist compared with the punishment meted out to negligent officials in Karamay who were deemed criminally responsible for the fire's high death toll. Thirteen of them received prison sentences ranging from four to seven years.[51]

Special Treatment

Around 2 p.m. on July 24, 2010, Zhu Jihong went to the toilet, slipped, fell, and hit the back of his head really hard—so hard, in fact, that he fractured his skull and his brain began to hemorrhage. Zhu was transferred to a hospital, but he lost consciousness. Two days later, he died. What an unfortunate way to go, we might think, especially after learning that Zhu was a twenty-nine-year-old in the prime of his life who was working overtime on a Saturday and had just finished an Internet chat with his girlfriend before heading to the toilet. But we would not have known about Zhu's demise had he not been an official. After Zhu Jihong died "in the line of duty," he was named an "Outstanding Party Member" by the Jiangyang District Party Committee of Luzhou, Sichuan. This entitled his family to a condolence payment of 4,000 yuan from the organization department of the District Party Committee plus a 5,000-yuan grant from the district union.[52] It also prompted online ridicule. Netizens asked, "Does falling in the toilet during lunch hour count as 'in the line of duty?'" and "Is chatting with your girlfriend 'work?'"[53]

One wonders what Zhou Enlai would have thought about Zhu Jihong's death. It might have reminded him of how upset he was back in 1949, just weeks before the founding of the People's Republic. That's when Li Weihan, United Front minister, fell in a toilet at Zhongnanhai and broke his hip. Li was a Hunanese who had deep, long-standing connections with Zhou Enlai. During the 1920s, Li studied in France, where he worked together with Zhou Enlai to found the Communist Party of Chinese Youth in Europe. In the summer of 1949, he was in Beijing to help choose the membership of the new Political Consultative Conference—the PRC's first constitutional convention.

On the evening of August 19, 1949, Li Weihan and his wife joined Mao Zedong and Jiang Qing in Zhongnanhai for an outdoor film screening. Tong Xiaopeng, another United Front official who had served as Zhou Enlai's secretary in the 1940s, was also there with his wife. During the movie, Tong got up to go to a nearby, unlit toilet. Fumbling in the darkness, Tong fell into a hole in the floor, quickly jumped out, and finished urinating. Zhongnanhai was undergoing extensive renovations, and it turned out that repair workers had pulled up floorboards around the toilet the previous day. Tong headed straight to head bodyguard Wang Dongxing and told him, "Your workers are fixing the toilet but didn't cover it up with a board or lock the door, so I fell in." A few moments later, they heard Li Weihan crying out from the toilet. He had fallen into the hole and broken his hip and could not get himself out. It took months for him to fully recover.[54]

Eleven days after Li broke his hip, Wu Yunpu, who headed the administrative section of Party Center's General Office, sent a report about the accident to Yang Shangkun and Zhou Enlai. Wu wrote that he "should take the primary responsibility" for his department's "slipshod work" and noted that Li Weihan's injury was a major setback to the important tasks confronting the Party. Even though he was not personally on the scene when the incident occurred, Wu pointed out, he had to take responsibility because his directionless leadership had led to a situation in which nobody made reports or inspections.[55]

If Wu Yunpu thought that his self-debasement would satisfy Li Weihan's old comrade Zhou Enlai, he was sorely mistaken. In his handwritten comments on Wu's report, Zhou blasted Wu Yunpu and his colleagues. "It is evident from this report and from the self-criticism meeting that the administrative section is severely disorganized, unsystematic, undisciplined, and anarchic," Zhou wrote, "In his report, Comrade Wu Yunpu was unable to solve the problem in terms of the system and the organization. Who was actually responsible for the accident? Wu Yunpu says he was, but he did not give a reason." Zhou compared the staff in the General Office's administrative section to a "sheet of loose sand," saying that it was unclear who was reporting to whom. "Criticizing yourself and handling the matter this way will not improve your work," Zhou went on. "It reveals Comrade Wu Yunpu's incompetence in administration and shows that his unorganized and anarchic thought is still very serious."

Zhou was just getting started. His friend from his days in Paris had been badly hurt, and now he was going to spread the pain around. After reaming Wu Yunpu, Zhou tore into Yang Shangkun, who was director of the General Office. "After Comrade Yang Shangkun got this report, he did not deal with it or notice any problems; he just sent it on up," Zhou fumed. "This also confirms his severely bureaucratic work style and a perfunctory attitude of not using his brain." Zhou "really could not tolerate" that he had been looking into the accident ever since it happened and had brought it up multiple times, even holding meetings to discuss it, only to have such a pathetic report land on his desk. He ordered Yang Shangkun, Wu Yunpu, and Wang Dongxing to do a new self-criticism together to "determine their own punishment" and to propose how to rectify the organization and set up a new system to improve their work.

We know that the editors of Mao's manuscripts left out material that they thought would make him look bad.[56] Why would cautious censors include Zhou's harsh tirade in the first release of the premier's collected manuscripts in 2008? Probably because the exchange shows how serious he was about meting out responsibility and properly running a bureaucracy in the immediate lead-up to the founding of the People's Republic. But Zhou's obsession with Li Weihan's toilet spill also shows how accidents were handled differently depending on the rank and stature of the people involved. Would Zhou have followed up so insistently if, say, a low-ranking bodyguard had fallen or if the toilet had been outside the gates of Zhongnanhai? The premier's many admirers might answer that it was only natural for Zhou to pay special attention to a preventable injury suffered by someone he had known for so long and for him to want the central leadership compound to be particularly safe. But it is precisely what appears "natural" that is most revealing about how a society works. It seemed natural that top Communist leaders deserved special treatment, and that is exactly what they received when they were personally involved in accidents or tried to skirt safety regulations.

Vice Premier Chen Yi wanted to swim in peace. Was that too much to ask? But no, the lifeguards had to yell at him to get back on his boat when he jumped in the lake at the Summer Palace in Beijing in 1957. Summer Palace staff were vigilant about preventing anyone from entering the water outside of the designated swimming zone. Chen Yi was outside the zone, so he got shouted at like everyone else. This must have miffed the vice premier, who was not accustomed to people telling him what he could not do. After the incident, a "verbal order from the higher levels" was transmitted to Summer Palace facilities management "to not strictly manage swimming in non-swimming areas," according to section head Yang Degong, who wrote a letter to the Beijing municipal parks director in July 1957.[57] Like Shanghai longshoreman Cao Yongjia, Yang was encouraged to complain by the widespread venting of grievances during the Hundred Flowers Movement.

In rather passive-aggressive fashion, after receiving the order from on high, Summer Palace workers "relaxed all types of work, and more and more people swam in non-swimming areas." As a result, Yang wrote, seven people had died outside the swimming zone in 1957. On July 7, Zhang Jiarong, a twenty-year-old assistant technician at a research institute, drowned after he jumped off his boat for a swim. After the tragedy, Zhang's work unit wrote to the Summer Palace demanding the implementation of a better safety system. The day after Zhang died, the body of an eight-year-old from the Summer Palace Elementary School was pulled out of the lake. In the following two weeks, three others drowned.

"These accidents could have been prevented if they had happened in the swimming area," Yang Degong pointed out. "This year, nobody has drowned in the swimming area." Yang was asking for permission to go back to strict enforcement of the nonswimming zone. His letter subtly implies a direct causal chain starting with Chen Yi being ordered to get back on his boat and ending with seven preventable deaths. We have no evidence that Chen Yi personally intervened, but it is easy to imagine his expressing annoyance to an assistant, who then took it on himself to tell

Summer Palace lifeguards to back off and let a guy enjoy the water. Summer Palace staff simply accepted the order and stopped patrolling rather than requiring skilled swimmers to pass a test before allowing them to enter deeper water or insisting that lives would be in danger if they were not permitted to do their job properly. This suggests that fears of offending powerful leaders profoundly affected workers' decisions about safety and reasonable risk. A similar dynamic prompted someone to yell, "Let the leaders leave first" in Karamay on December 8, 1994. The phrase continues to resonate in today's China—Pi San's darkly satirical 2011 animated short *Little Rabbit, Be Good*, for example, features screaming bunnies engulfed in flames who are told, "Don't move, let the leaders leave first!" at a meeting about "Constructing a Harmonious Forest." This resonance suggests that the problem of prioritizing deference to leaders over broader public safety has not gone away.[58]

Outrage at the Arrogance of the Privileged in the 2000s

What if Yang Degong, head of facilities at the Summer Palace in 1957, had a blog or Weibo? Would he have been able to expose the "verbal order from the higher levels" to relax safety work, thereby swaying public opinion enough to save seven people from drowning? I doubt it. Chen Yi was so high up that the only way openly to criticize him would be to wait for a Maoist political movement. Yang was able to make indirect insinuations because of the Hundred Flowers Movement, and Chen would later be subjected to brutal attacks during the Cultural Revolution (for leading the so-called February Countercurrent of 1967, not for causing people to drown). Since the Party disavowed Maoist campaigns in the late 1970s, top central leaders have become untouchable. Factional infighting is the only thing that might bring them down or shunt them aside. Critical online comments about a leader of similar stature today— say, Jia Qinglin, who has stuck around on the Politburo Standing Committee in spite of widespread rumors of his personal involvement in corruption scandals—would be quickly censored.[59]

It is possible, however, to expose and criticize lowlier members of China's privileged classes today. As Perry Link and Xiao Qiang show in their discussion of the Wenzhou train crash (see chapter 4 in this volume), Internet activism can push the Party to change the way it handles an accident. On the evening of October 16, 2010, a drunk twenty-two-year-old named Li Qiming plowed his car into two female students at Hebei University in Baoding, killing one and injuring the other. After angry onlookers blocked his path, he apparently thought it would be a good idea to say, "Sue me if you dare, my dad is Li Gang." Witnesses heard the remark and investigated online, and soon millions of people knew that Li Gang was the deputy director of a district Public Security

Figure 1.1. **"Let the leaders leave first!" is yelled as a fire engulfs a meeting about "Constructing a Harmonious Forest."** *Source:* **This reference to the Karamay fire of 1994 is from** *Xiaotu guaiguai* **(Little rabbit, be good), directed by Pi San, 2011,** *Beijing Huxiang donghua youxian gongsi,* **http://youtu.be/rnw5Bvx SDmM.**

Bureau in Baoding and that Li Qiming was trying to use his father's position to weasel his way out of trouble.[60]

If Li Qiming had kept his mouth shut on campus and waited until he arrived at the police station to quietly mention his father's identity, it is doubtful that the event would have sparked such public outrage, and Li might have even been able to get off lightly. But since the accident had gone viral online, the authorities had to show that they were taking the matter seriously. Father and son made tearful apologies on television. A few months later, Li Qiming was given a six-year prison sentence, and his father paid 460,000 yuan in compensation to the dead student's family.[61] This punishment was severe enough to stem off a new round of online vitriol, but it still protected the Party's own: Li Qiming will be able to rebuild his life after he gets out of prison, and Li Gang is surely finding ways to refill his bank account. Authorities were likely satisfied at how everything played out—better for people to let off steam online and make thousands of jokes with "My dad is Li Gang" as the punch line than for something genuinely explosive to happen. It must have been a relief to officials that the accident at Hebei University did not unleash something similar to what happened in the Anhui city of Chizhou in June 2005.

It was the kind of minor accident that happens every day on the crowded streets of Chinese cities. A car bearing Jiangsu plates hit and knocked over a twenty-two-year-old student named Liu Liang.[62] Liu asked that the car's owner, businessman Wu Junxing, take him to the hospital to make sure he was not injured. Wu responded that Liu should compensate him for scratching the paint on his car. In the scuffle that ensued, Liu damaged the vehicle's side-view mirror. This prompted Wu to tell his two burly bodyguards to beat up Liu Liang. What is the big deal, Wu yelled, "I'd only have to pay a few hundred thousand in compensation for beating someone to death." Wu Junxing may not have been kidding. As X. L. Ding shows in chapter 2 in this volume, it is indeed possible to get away with murder by paying several hundred thousand yuan. Such matters, however, are generally handled quietly after the fact, not blurted out as public threats. Wu's remark outraged the crowd of onlookers who had gathered to watch the melee. When Wu and his bodyguards tried to leave, motorcycle taxi drivers surrounded the car and would not let the outsiders get away. Someone called the police.

Things took a turn for the worse when two patrolmen arrived on the scene. The police arranged to have Liu Liang sent to the hospital and told Wu Junxing and his bodyguards to get out of their car, but they had locked themselves in and refused to budge. The angry crowd wanted to see the rich businessman and the muscle heads cuffed and put in the back of the patrol car. What they saw instead—an officer getting in Wu's car and driving it to the neighborhood police station with the offenders still inside—made them suspect that the police were siding with moneyed arrogance rather than with the bullied masses of Anhui. A throng of 2,000 Chizhou residents proceeded to the police station. What they saw there confirmed their misgivings: as a police officer yelled at the crowd to disperse, one of Wu's bodyguards ostentatiously carried his scary-looking knife out of the car. As more people gathered, they heard various versions of what had happened, none of which made them happy: "A student has been killed! A big boss said that killing someone from Anhui would only cost him 300,000!"

The crowd first attacked the car with the Jiangsu plates, trashing and overturning it. After about 10,000 people had gathered, the main target of their anger shifted to the police, who had seemingly protected the bad guys. This looked to the crowd like collusion between state power and jerks who thought their wealth put them above the law. What happened next was what scholar Yu Jianrong calls a "social venting incident" (*shehui xiefen shijian*).[63] People pushed a patrol car in front of the police station's front door and set it on fire and threw rocks and firecrackers at the building. Two other official vehicles were torched, and a nearby department store was looted. It was not until just before midnight, about ten hours after the initial accident, that 700 police officers regained control of Chizhou. The car-versus-pedestrian accident that led to the riot was not nearly as severe as Li Qiming's violent joyride through the Hebei University campus, but the disorder that followed gave Party leaders more to worry about than rueful "My dad is Li Gang" jokes.

HANDLING ACCIDENTS

It is no coincidence that an accident sparked the Chizhou riot. Accidents in today's China bring social tensions and anxieties to the fore. They heighten grievances about inequality and unfairness. They exacerbate feelings of insecurity and helplessness. It is stressful to go to work or school worrying that something beyond your control could smash into you at any moment. But do not worry, the drafters of the PRC's Sudden Crisis Response Law might say. "Our country has quite a few natural disasters and accidental catastrophes."[64] If an unfortunate accident does occur, we will "handle" it according to the relevant regulations. Does the Party's record of handling accidents provide solace for people stressed out by fears of explosions, fires, and bridge collapses? In some ways, the Party's post–June Fourth obsession with preventing social disorder has worsened the pain of accident victims and their families. When accidents happen, the post-1989 tendency to value stability above all has been superimposed on such Mao-era legacies as prioritizing production over safety, cover-ups and lies, and protecting higher-ups. The result is that victims' well-meaning attempts to seek answers, justice, and compensation are likely to be met with repression.

The most revelatory moment in Xu Xin's *Karamay* is footage of a speech delivered by Zhou Yongkang on December 22, 1994, two weeks after the fire. Zhou, who was deputy Party secretary of the China National-al Petroleum Company at the time, had been sent to Karamay to transmit Party center's instructions about how to handle the aftermath of the fire. The central theme of Zhou's visit was that "stability should overwhelm everything else" (*wending yadao yiqie*, a phrase that Deng Xiaoping coined in February 1989 and reemphasized after the Beijing massacre). Zhou's speech was so over the top that if you were given a transcript without knowing what it was, you might think it was a piece of satire written by Han Han. In fact, if you read what Han Han posted on July 26, 2011, about the Wenzhou train crash before censors deleted it, Zhou Yong-kang's speech will give you shivers.[65]

All of us cadres, Zhou said, must "draw a lesson from painful experi-ence and investigate how not to allow the more than 300 victims to have shed their blood in vain." The Party's top priority was for "stability to overwhelm everything else," Zhou continued. Invoking the memory of the fire's victims, Zhou said, "I believe that all of the little boys and girls in their graves would hope for Karamay to be stable. We depended on stability to build this oil base in the Gobi and to achieve today's [level of] development and lifestyle." What was the best way to comfort the dead children, Zhou asked? "We should all say whatever words are conducive to stability and unity," he said grimly. "We should all do whatever things are conducive to stability and unity. Be steadfast in opposing whatever words and deeds are not conducive to stability and unity."[66]

After Zhou Yongkang's speech, grieving family members who demanded justice or compensation beyond what the Party was willing to offer were labeled troublemakers who were harming "stability and unity." Some were detained for weeks, and others were put under surveillance by state security agents. As for Zhou Yongkang, his career really took off after his handling of the aftermath of the Karamay catastrophe. He became the minister of land and resources in 1998, served as Party secretary of Sichuan province, and was promoted to minister of public security in 2002. Beginning in 2007, Zhou became the Politburo

Figure 1.2.   Zhou Yongkang tells cadres in Karamay on December 22, 1994, that they must emphasize "stability" (*wending*) in handling the aftermath of the auditorium fire that killed 288 children and thirty-seven adults. *Source:* Screen shot from *Kelamayi* (Karamay), directed by Xu Xin, 2010, distributed in North America by dGenerate Films.

Standing Committee member in charge of law enforcement and headed the Stability Maintenance Leading Small Group.

NOTES

1. "Gongjiaoche zhuangsi qiche laoren" (Public bus kills elderly cyclist in collision), *Jiefang niuwang*, August 22, 2011, http://www.jfdaily.com/a/2278611.htm.
2. "Shanghai jingfang cheng gongjiao huozai xi chengke xie yiran wupin shangche suozhi" (Shanghai police say that passenger carrying flammable materials caused bus fire), *Zhongguo wang*, May 6, 2008, http://www.china.com.cn/city/txt/2008-05/06/content_15073819.htm.
3. This accident on September 27, 2011, injured 290 people, but there were no fatalities.
4. At least fifty-eight people died when a high-rise on Jiaozhou Road caught fire on November 15, 2010.
5. "Shoushushi qihuo zhi mazui bingren siwang 6 ming yihu renyuan cheli" (Surgery room catches fire, causing death of anesthetized patient; 6 doctors and nurses evacuated), *Xinmin wang*, October 25, 2011, http://news.sina.com.cn/s/2011-08-25/095723048984.shtml?c=spr_sw_bd_maxthon_society.
6. In August 2007, the National People's Congress passed a "Sudden Crisis Response Law" (*Tufa shijian yingdui fa*) that addresses four types of crises: natural disasters, accident disasters, public health incidents, and security incidents. *Renmin ribao* (*People's Daily*, hereafter abbreviated as RMRB), November 1, 2007, 16.
7. RMRB, July 28, 2011, 1.
8. Timothy Cheek, *Living with Reform: China since 1989* (New York: Zed Books, 2006), 52.
9. Gene Weingarten, "Fatal Distraction: Forgetting a Child in the Backseat of a Car Is a Horrifying Mistake. Is It a Crime?" *Washington Post*, March 8, 2009, http://www.washingtonpost.com/wp-dyn/content/article/2009/02/27/AR2009022701549.html.
10. Andrew Martin, "A Debate over Window Blinds," *New York Times*, April 21, 2011, B1.
11. RMRB, June 17, 1950, 2.
12. RMRB, June 24, 1950, 6.
13. Letter from Tianjin shi renmin zhengfu laodong ju with attachments, January 26, 1951, author's collection (hereafter abbreviated as AC). The reporting regulations, including the requirement to inform superiors about a major accident within thirty minutes, were circulated nationwide in RMRB, May 4, 1950, 1.
14. Hubei sheng geming weiyuanhui jihua weiyuanhui, *Guanyu jin yi bu zuohao zhigong shangwang shigu tongji gongzuo de tongzhi* (Circular on improving the compilation of statistics about worker accident injuries and deaths), December 18, 1970, circulated by Hubei sheng Xiangfan shi geming weiyuanhui shengchan zhihuizu on April 18, 1971, AC.
15. Zhonghua renmin gongheguo guowuyuan, *Shengchan anquan shigu baogao he diaocha chuli tiaoli* (Regulations on reporting, investigating, and handling production safety accidents), 2007, http://www.gov.cn/ziliao/flfg/2007-04/19/content_589264.htm.
16. RMRB, August 5, 1950, 2.
17. Clause 38 of Zhonghua renmin gongheguo guowuyuan, *Shengchan anquan shigu baogao he diaocha chuli tiaoli*.
18. Frank Dikötter, *Mao's Great Famine: The History of China's Most Devastating Catastrophe, 1958–1962* (New York: Walker & Co., 2010), 269–70.
19. Jiangxi sheng geming weiyuanhui, *Pizhuan sheng jiaotong ju, sheng gongan ju "Guanyu 'Ganzhong' hao kelun fasheng chenmo zhongda shigu de chubu diaocha baogao"* (Transmitting the provincial Transport Bureau and Public Safety Bureau's "Prelimi-

nary investigation report on the '*Ganzhong*' passenger boat sinking major accident"), *Gangefa* (1974) 54 *hao*, August 17, 1974, AC.

20. "Kindergarten Chairman Detained over Fatal School Bus Accident in NW China," *Xinhua*, November 17, 2011, http://news.xinhuanet.com/english2010/china/2011-11/17/c_131253764.htm.

21. "Dangdi 'bao hu' anfu yu'nanzhe jiashu" (Local authorities "assigned to households" to comfort families of victims), *Xin Jing bao*, November 18, 2011, A20, http://epaper.bjnews.com.cn/images/2011-11/18/A20/xjb20111118A20.pdf.

22. Jiang Xinjie and Cui Zheng, "Highway Bus Fire in Henan," *Caixin Online*, August 5, 2011, http://english.caixin.cn/2011-08-05/100287860.html.

23. Zhu Fangqing's Weibo, July 24, 2011, http://www.weibo.com/1460681635/xge3BnRfk, cited in "Shinkansen Expert Satoru Sone: Unbelievable China is Disassembling and Burying Train Carriages," *Shanghaiist*, July 26, 2011, http://shanghaiist.com/2011/07/26/satoru-sone-shinkansen.php.

24. Wu Jie, "Zhiyu ni xin bu xin, wo fanzheng xinle: Tiedao bu fayanren yulu cheng wangluo liuxingyu" (Whether you believe it or not, I believe it anyway: Railway Ministry spokesperson's quote becomes catchphrase online), *Xiandai kuaibao*, July 27, 2011, feng 8, http://kb.dsqq.cn/html/2011-07/27/content_110509.htm.

25. The following paragraphs are from Cao Yongjia's letter of June 18, 1957, Shanghai Municipal Archive, C1-2-2379.

26. Zhongguo haiyuan gonghui Shanghai qu weiyuanhui, "Shanghai gongwuju suoshu ge danwei yinman gongshang shigu de qingkuang baogao" (Report on concealing work injury accidents in each unit of the Shanghai Port Authority), July 26, 1957, Shanghai Municipal Archive, C1-2-2379.

27. Zhongguo haiyuan gonghui Shanghai qu weiyuanhui, "Shanghai gongwuju suoshu ge danwei yinman gongshang shigu de qingkuang baogao."

28. Denise Chong, *Egg on Mao: The Story of an Ordinary Man Who Defaced an Icon and Unmasked a Dictatorship* (Toronto: Random House Canada, 2009), 70.

29. A former People's Liberation Army journalist who was purged after the Tiananmen massacre in 1989 published the first article in English about the dam failures. Using a pseudonym, the journalist wrote that 85,600 people died because of the dam breaches but also noted that dam critics in the 1990s estimated that the disaster killed 230,000. Yi Si (pseudonym), "The World's Most Catastrophic Dam Failures: The August 1975 Collapse of the Banqiao and Shimantan Dams," in *The River Dragon Has Come! The Three Gorges Dam and the Fate of China's Yangtze River and Its People*, comp. Dai Qing (Armonk, NY: M. E. Sharpe, 1998), 28.

30. Yi Si, "The World's Most Catastrophic Dam Failures," 37.

31. Evan Osnos, "The Fallout: Seven Months Later: Japan's Nuclear Predicament," *The New Yorker*, October 17, 2011, 48, 61.

32. Zhang Guangyou, "Mudu 1975 nian Huaihe da shuizai" (Seeing the great Huaihe flood of 1975 with my own eyes), *Yanhuang chunqiu* 1 (2003): 14.

33. For the text of Zhang's 1975 report about the death toll, see Zhang Guangyou, "Mudu 1975 nian Huaihe da shuizai," 20.

34. Yi Si, "The World's Most Catastrophic Dam Failures," 34.

35. Gao Dong, "697 ren sangsheng de Xinjiang 61 tuanchang huozai" (697 people died in a fire at Xinjiang's number 61 military farm), *Yanhuang chunqiu* 8 (2010): 62–63. In a subsequent blog post, Gao corrected the death toll to 694. See Gao Dong, "Yi shi jiqi cengceng lang" (One stone stirred up waves upon waves), *Gao Dong (Chang Anru) de boke*, November 7, 2010, http://blog.sina.com.cn/s/blog_6729469e0100me1y.html.

36. Yuan Fang and Sun Shuhan, "Yi nian shigu sunshi liangqianyi?" (Are annual damages from accidents really 200 billion?), *Nanfengchuang* 8 xia (2002): 29.

37. Guowuyuan anquan shengchan weiyuanhui bangongshi, "Guowuyuan anweihui bangongshi guanyu Heilongjiang sheng Jixi shi Didao qu Guifa meikuang '4.26' deng liu qi manbao chibao huangbao shigu de tongbao" (State Council Safety Office circular on the Guifa coal mine in the Didao district of Jixi municipality in Heilongjiang province "April 26" accident and five other cases of concealing, late reporting, or

false reporting of accidents), *Guojia anquan shengchan jiandu guanli zongju, Guojia mei-kuang anquan jiancha ju gonggao* 6 (2011): 22–24.

38. Guojia anquan shengchan jiandu guanli zongju, "Guojia anquan jianguan zong-ju guanyu yinfa shengchan jingying danwei manbao huangbao shigu xingwei chachu banfa de tongzhi" (SAWS directive on investigating and punishing the concealment and falsification of accidents by production units), *Guojia anquan shengchan jiandu guanli zongju, Guojia meikuang anquan jiancha ju gonggao* 7 (2011): 27–30.

39. Wang Dapeng, "Zhongyang zhengfu daji shigu manbao" (The central govern-ment attacks the concealment of accidents), *Nanfeng chuang* 23 (2008): 20–21.

40. Although the first published claim that someone at the front of the auditorium yelled "Let the leaders leave first!" appeared in January 1995, the phrase did not become a well-known stand-in for critiques about official privilege until it reappeared online in articles and blog posts commemorating the tenth anniversary of the fire in December 2004. See Liu Dong and Liu Guangniu, "Renhuo meng yu huo—Kelamayi "12.8' can'an de jingshi" (A man-made disaster worse than fire—The wake-up call of the Karamay tragedy of December 8), *Zhongguo qingnian bao*, January 10, 1995, re-printed in *Henan jiaoyu* 5 (1995): 39; "Kelamayi dahuo zhong 'rang lingdao xianzou' cheng lishi shangba" ("'Let the leaders leave first' in the Karamay fire has become a historical scar), *Beifangwang*, December 9, 2006, http://news.enorth.com.cn/system/2006/12/09/001485603.shtml.

41. Liu Dong and Liu Guangniu, "Renhuo meng yu huo," 38–39.

42. Jin Ling, "Leijiu Kelamayi" (Crying for Karamay), *Shehui gongzuo* 3 (1995): 8. An official poster released after the fire listing the names of those who "sacrificed them-selves in the line of duty" (*yingong xisheng*) provides a slightly lower death toll: 323 dead, of whom 284 were elementary and middle school students, seventeen were teachers, and twenty-two were officials and other people. Zhonggong Kelamayi shi weiyuanhui, Zhonggong Xinjiang shiyou guanli ju weiyuanhui, Kelamayi shi renmin zhengfu, Xinjiang Shiyou guanli gu, *Fugao* (Death notice), December 29, 1994, repro-duced and transcribed on Chen Yaowen's blog, April 5, 2007, http://chenyaowen.blshe.com/post/943/36122.

43. *Kelamayi* (Karamay), directed by Xu Xin, 2010, distributed in North America by dGenerate Films, http://dgeneratefilms.com/catalog/karamay.

44. The deputy Party secretary's actions outraged many of the parents of dead children who were interviewed by Xu Xin in *Kelamayi* and were also detailed in an indignant report by two Beijing journalists who went to Karamay to cover the story and published at least three articles in *Zhongguo qingnian bao* in December 1994 and January 1995. Liu Dong and Liu Guangniu, "Renhuo meng yu huo."

45. Peng Zhiyong, ed., *Xuesheng anquan shigu anli xuanbian* (Selected case studies of student safety accidents) (Chongqing: Chongqing daxue chubanshe, 2008), 259.

46. Liu Dong and Liu Guangniu, "Renhuo meng yu huo."

47. "12 yue 8 ri: Rang Kelamayi ren xincui" (December 8: A day that breaks the hearts of people in Karamay), *Jiancha ribao*, September 2, 2008, http://www.jcrb.com/zhuanti/fzzt/nwya/rwwz/200809/t20080902_68792.html.

48. Chen Yaowen makes this point in "Chidao de baodao: Kelamayi '12.8' teda huozai shigu jiemi" (Tardy report: Uncovering the secrets of the Karamay "December 8" especially major fire accident), pt. 1, February 5, 2007, *Chen Yaowen—Siji de yang-guang didai*, http://chenyaowen.blshe.com/post/943/15192.

49. *Kelamayi*, directed by Xu Xin.

50. This and the following paragraph are based on Guangxi qu dangwei, *Pizhuan Liuzhou diqu siqing zongtuan dangwei guanyu Luzhai xian Danzhu gongshe fasheng chen-chuan yansi shisan ren de yanzhong shigu de baogao* (Transmitting the Liuzhou district Four Cleanups headquarters party committee's report about a serious accident in Danzhu commune, Luzhai county, in which a boat sank and thirteen people drowned), *Guifa* (66) 37 *hao*, March 12, 1966, AC.

51. RMRB, October 13, 1995, 3.

52. "Luzhou Jiangyang quwei zhuishou Zhu Jihong 'Youxiu gongchandangyuan' rongyu chenghao" (Jiangyang district party committee of Luzhou bestows the honorable title of "Outstanding Party Member" on Zhu Jihong), *Sichuan zaixian*, July 30, 2010, http://sichuan.scol.com.cn/lzxw/content/2010-07/30/content_1070871.htm?node=948.

53. Chen Zhangcai, "Wuxiu shi shang cesuo shuaidao shenwang gongwuyuan 'yingong xisheng' yin zhengyi" (The "sacrifice in the line of duty" of a civil servant who died in a fall while using the toilet during lunch break sparks controversy), *Huaxi dushi bao*, August 16, 2010, 15,http://www.wccdaily.com.cn/epaper/hxdsb/html/2010-08/16/content_223349.htm.

54. Tong Xiaopeng, *Shaoxiao lijia laoda hui: Tong Xiaopeng huiyilu* (I left home when I was young and returned when I was old: Tong Xiaopeng's memoir) (Fuzhou: Fujian renmin chubanshe, 2000), 348, cited in Yin Zhijun, "Zhou Enlai yanchu 'Li Weihan dieshang shijian,'" (Zhou Enlai dealt severely with the "Li Weihan injury incident"), *Shiji* 1 (2009): 39.

55. This and the following two paragraphs are from "Dui Li Weihan dieshang shijian chuli baogao de piyu" (Written remarks on a report about the handling of the incident of Li Weihan injuring himself in a fall), September 2, 1949, *Jianguo yilai Zhou Enlai wengao*, vol. 1 (Beijing: Zhongyang wenxian chubanshe, 2008), 336–38.

56. For a discussion of the type of material that was omitted from Mao's officially vetted manuscripts, see Michael Schoenhals, "Why Don't We Arm the Left? Mao's Culpability for the 'Great Chaos' of 1967," *China Quarterly* 182 (2005): 277–300.

57. This and the following two paragraphs are from Beijing shi yuanlin ju yiheyuan guanli chu, "Guanyu benyuan Kunming hu bennian lianxu fasheng yansiren shigu de huibao" (Report on the continuous occurrence of drownings in Kunming lake at the Summer Palace this year), July 27, 1957, Beijing Municipal Archive, 98-1-344.

58. *Xiaotu guaiguai* (Little rabbit, be good), directed by Pi San, 2011, copyright Beijing Huxiang donghua youxian gongsi, http://youtu.be/rnw5BvxSDmM.

59. Richard McGregor, *The Party: The Secret World of China's Communist Rulers* (New York: Harper, 2010), 7–8. To see what I mean about censorship, compare a biography of Jia Qinglin from inside the Great Firewall (http://baike.baidu.com/view/1791.htm) to one hosted outside the wall (http://zh.wikipedia.org/wiki/贾庆林).

60. "Dang bei renrou he taofa chengwei guan'erdai de mingyun" (Being subjected to a human flesh search and crusaded against become the fate of a second-generation official), *Yan Zhao dushi wang*, October 18, 2010, http://news.yzdsb.com.cn/system/2010/10/18/010749427.shtml.

61. Bai Mingshan and Yue Wenting, "Hebei daxue jiaotong zhaoshi an xuanpan: Li Qiming bei panxing 6 nian" IHebei University traffic accident verdict announced: Li Qiming sentenced to 6 years), *Souhu xinwen*, January 30, 2011, http://news.sohu.com/20110130/n279161518.shtml.

62. The account of the Chizhou riots is from Cheng Meidong, ed., *Toushi dangdai Zhongguo zhongda tufa shijian* (Perspectives on major sudden crises in contemporary China) (Beijing: Zhonggong dangshi chubanshe, 2008), 188–96, and Wang Jilu, "Anhui Chizhou daza qiangshao '6.26' shijian quntixing shijian diaocha" (Investigation into the "June 26" mass beating, smashing, looting, and burning incident in Chizhou, Anhui), *Nanfang dushi bao*, July 1, 2005, http://www.chinaelections.org/newsinfo.asp?newsid=5852.

63. http://chinadigitaltimes.net/2010/03/yu-jianrong-于建嵘-maintaining-a-baseline-of-social-stability-part-5.

64. From a government spokesperson's response to journalists' questions about the Sudden Crisis Response Law, RMRB, October 31, 2007, 10.

65. The point of Han Han's post was to satirize government responses to the train crash that implied that Chinese people should be quietly thankful for material progress and grateful that things are not even worse. "The train from Shanghai to Beijing used to take a whole day," Han wrote. "Now you're there in five hours (as long as there's no lightning). Why aren't you grateful? What's with all the questions?" and

"We could be more authoritarian than North Korea. We could make this place poorer than the Sudan. We could be more evil than the Khmer Rouge. Our army's bigger than any of theirs, but we don't do any of that. And not only are you not thankful, but you want us to apologize! As if we've done something wrong?" The translation is from ChinaGeeks, July 28, 2011, http://chinageeks.org/2011/07/han-han-the-derailed-country.

66. *Kelamayi*, directed by Xu Xin.

TWO

"The Only Reliability Is That These Guys Aren't Reliable!"

The Business Culture of Red Capitalism

X. L. Ding

In 2011, it was reported that China is experiencing a "third wave of cross-border migration." The first two waves were made up of poor college students and technical professionals, but this new wave is made up of rich entrepreneurs. Those applying to migrate to North American countries and Australia must own net family assets above US$1.5 million (10 million RMB in the exchange rates in effect at the beginning of this new migration wave). For those who were targeting Hong Kong and Singapore, two popular migration destinations, the wealth thresholds were even higher.[1]

According to data collected on the Chinese side, in 2008–2009 there were more applicants than any other country for the US EB-5 investor migrant visa (through which any foreigner who invests between $500,000 and $1 million and creates at least ten domestic jobs from that investment gets a green card). The same was true for PRC investor migrants into Canada.[2]

More alarming still, a nationwide survey report revealed in May 2011 that almost 60 percent of the Chinese mainland citizens with disposable family assets above $1.5 million had completed cross-border migration procedures or were considering doing so. In the superrich category of owning assets of $15 million, 27 percent had already become—and 47 percent were trying to become—investor migrants.[3] When asked why they wanted to give up their PRC citizenship, one of the most frequently cited concerns was safety—safety of their wealth and that of themselves, including the family.[4]

The news reporting in China about the third wave of migration caused a nationwide outcry. It seemed as if China's most wealthy and talented citizens were voting no-confidence with their feet. When picked up by the English-language press, the news reports have further attracted wide international attention.[5] The new rich's departure suggests that the social environment for native entrepreneurs has worsened, a phenomenon seemingly contradictory to the global perception of a prosperous and rising China.[6]

The Communist Party has been making gestures to assure Chinese entrepreneurs that all is well. In the fall of 2012, Liang Weng'en, the richest individual in China on both the *Forbes* and the *Hurun* list for 2011, was a delegate to the Eighteenth National Party Congress.[7] Liang is the chairman of the construction machinery maker Sany Heavy Industry Co., Ltd, and personally owns an estimated wealth of $9.3 billion. This appears to be a positive message from Beijing to assure the Chinese business class that the mainland still is and will continue to be a good place to make money and that Deng Xiaoping's principle "Getting rich is glorious!" will not be reversed.

However, as numerous comments made by PRC observers online have pointed out, the political fate of Liang Weng'en for the near future is hard to predict. The annual rankings of the richest individuals in China are popularly nicknamed by Chinese residents a *shazhu bang*, meaning "a list of pigs to be slaughtered," for many of those who were once in the upper echelon of these lists have been picked up by the Chinese authorities for punishment, either in detention, in prison, or in exile.[8] The sense of vulnerability, victimization, and anxiety has been so profoundly planted in the hearts and minds of countless businesspeople in China over the years that a single event, such as Liang Weng'en's participation in the National Party Congress, can hardly uproot the widely shared mood of insecurity. We need to explore and explain the reasons for such a generally shared mood.

THE MECHANISM DRIVING CHINA'S RED CAPITALISM[9]

China studies scholars share the observation that the blended type of red capitalism since the 1980s has had a crucial element; namely, the businessman in the Chinese mainland, if he himself is not from a Communist Party-state official's family, must forge a special relationship with a powerful officeholder in order to make his business operation viable. The profitability of such a relationship is well understood, and the parties to this relationship will split the gains under the table in one way or another.[10] But, as a popular saying suggests, "there is no free lunch"—this type of special relationship also has intrinsic risks that are far less explored. Let us start with a real example.

A Hotel Business Case[11]

In a midsize city in central China, at the intersection of highways leading to a World Cultural Heritage Site, the best-located hotel in town is owned by the city government administration (formally called the logistics administrative bureau), which appointed a man nicknamed Da Biezi to be the top manager of the hotel. The city administration uses the standard "contractual responsibility regime" to define the relationship between itself and Da Biezi: at the beginning of each year, the contract specifies a certain amount of financial returns generated from the hotel business that the manager must hand over to the city administration, and he retains the rest of the net profit for himself. So the entire hotel business carries little risk, in that the city administration guarantees loans from local state bank branches to cover maintenance and renovation costs, and the manager has full discretionary power to decide on room rates, staff wages, and benefits. The more business revenue generated, the more the manager earns.

The manager is clever enough to see that there are plenty of opportunities in the day-to-day running of the hotel for him to gain more at the expense of the nominal owner. For example, he can negotiate a better contract every year to hand over a smaller amount of business returns to the city administration, he can take a sizable amount of kickbacks from the maintenance and renovation contractors, he can hire relatives and cronies to staff the hotel and the three affiliated restaurants, and he can entertain his buddies while shifting the costs to the operational cost accounts. He is said to have done all this regularly. The key for his successful maneuvering is that he forges a special relationship with the deputy mayor, who oversees all the city government's logistics and business affairs, including the determination of the terms and conditions of contracting out the hotel to Da Biezi.

Da Biezi, understandably, treats the deputy mayor very well: he upgrades a hotel segment to the quality of a presidential suite for the boss's regular use free of charge (the published rate for the suite alone was nearly 3,000 RMB per night in 2002–2003, more than the deputy mayor's two-month salary); he reimburses many invoices and receipts for the boss, who cannot get reimbursed legitimately from the government accounting office; he presents luxury gifts to the boss on memorable days of the year; he organizes trips to tourist attractions for the boss's family and friends; and he, most considerately, hires and pays for young, pretty prostitutes to serve the boss frequently. That is how he gets the contract renewed every time on his favorable terms and conditions.

With the domestic tourism market growing at a spectacular rate, both the manager and the deputy mayor see the hotel business as a cash cow, for most of the tourists visiting the World Cultural Heritage Site need to stay there. Both men intend to keep the hotel business in their own hands, and conflict between the two becomes unavoidable. The deputy mayor has the upper hand, of course; he decides not to renew the contract for Da Biezi and makes instead an offer to a closer friend. Da Biezi begs the deputy mayor's continued patronage by reminding the official of how much he has "*jingong*" (meaning the tribute a vassal offers to a ruler) to him but in vain. Afterward, he sends a registered letter to the Chinese Communist Party's disciplinary commission at a level higher than the city administration, in which there are photos of the deputy mayor being served by prostitutes. Da Biezi has installed spy cameras in the presidential suite, the VIP rooms of the hotel's massage center, and karaoke lounge. When the deputy mayor is entertaining with the prostitutes arranged by Da Biezi, high-quality photos are being taken secretly. This opens a series of investigations into the deputy mayor's misconduct and corruption, and eventually he is sentenced to twelve years in prison. But Da Biezi gets in trouble, too: the deputy mayor also reports on his financial wrongdoings and the stealing of large amounts of public money from the city-owned hotel, leading Da Biezi to a seven-year prison sentence.

Common Ingredients

This hotel business case is not at all unusual, and it contains a few central ingredients we see in many other, more famous cases as well. First, public property of great potential commercial value is controlled by a public official. He can delegate it to virtually anyone to manage, and he can decide how much the manager should pay for using the public property in generating private or semiprivate financial returns (this type of manager is not the same as a standard state-owned-enterprise cadre). However, in practical terms, the public official does not need to take responsibility for intentionally or unintentionally failing to stop the manager from stealing public property.[12]

Second, there are plentiful opportunities and thus strong incentives for the public official to collude with the manager to abuse the public property, including the financial returns therefrom, in order to maximize their own personal gains. That is the widely known pattern in all economic reforms starting with state socialist systems, which a Chinese popular saying describes as *jianshou zidao*, meaning a custodian-turned-thief.

Third, this custodian–outsider collusion in systematic theft (which may last for years and evolve over time) is not protected by any formal, lawful regime of rules and regulations. Therefore, both parties to the relationship have to design measures for self-protection to prevent the other side from breaking the under-the-table arrangement at any moment. So a series of secret war preparations is under way from the very beginning of the collusion.

Fourth, in this war game, in which often "defense is played out as offense and vice versa," the two parties are not on a level playing field. The public official can mobilize a variety of state resources to defeat the manager; for example, the local industry and commerce bureau, which has the authority to investigate all business activities and issue minor to midlevel administrative penalties to the business owner or manager; the local public health bureau, which can conduct regular or sudden hygiene inspections in the hotel and its affiliated restaurants and then place heavy fines on them; the local transportation bureau, which can work on a road repair project in front of the premises for weeks or even months to hurt the business; the local labor affairs office, which can deny the eligibility of employment for some people hired by the hotel business complex; and, finally, the local police and the court, which can put the manager into detention or jail and eventually ruin his business or even his entire career and life. This list is by no means exhaustive: such problems look more or less "legitimate" in the PRC legal and regulatory context. There are many more problems that can be created for businesses by powerful officeholders—and not only for the business manager himself but also for his family members and relatives. The section below on the legal front illustrates a few of the mafia-like techniques at the disposal of powerful officials.

In comparison, the business manager has little chance to rely on those state resources in confronting the public official. So, finally, the manager must resort to alternate measures, mostly forms of blackmail, to prepare for the worst possible scenarios. The most commonly employed tactics include the secret photographing, videotaping, or proof-copying of the public official when he is taking bribes, performing criminal business transactions, or enjoying illegal sex. For instance, the "Red Mansion" in the coastal city of Xiamen, Fujian province, was constructed by Lai Changxing exactly for such purposes. When he ran the largest smuggling ring in China in the 1990s, he routinely arranged high-class prostitution services for powerful officials, sometimes with gambling as well, and instructed his men to secretly take photos of the scene.[13] In another major corruption case, Liu Zhihua, the deputy mayor of the Beijing municipal government in charge of urban development, was arrested in June 2006 and received a death sentence with a two-year suspension. His downfall was triggered by a video sent from Hong Kong to the central Party disciplinary authorities in Beijing. His enemies in land deal conflicts managed to have videotaped him and prostitutes in bed in a Hong Kong hotel room.[14] Individuals who were close to his circle said that Liu Zhihua had been quite prudent in comparison with his infamous predecessor Wang Baosen in taking such entertainment arrangements; he had turned down many similar offers on the Chinese mainland in order to control risks but in the end was trapped overseas. The senior vice mayor of Beijing, Wang Baosen, was well known for his playboy lifestyle; he shot himself in April 1995 after his scandal was leaked out bit by bit, a scandal that was later proven to be a hundreds-of-millions-of-dollars embezzlement scheme. [15]

WHERE TO HIDE "BLOODSTAINED MONEY"? [16]

In the booming Chinese economy, the hotel business in general is not a particularly lucrative industry except for the minority of five-star hotels with special operational prerogatives. When we turn our lens to more profitable business sectors, we will be able to identify more realistic and heavier risks and worries rooted in the realities of the PRC business world. The coal mining industry is a proper illustration for such fat-profit sectors: China has the largest coal mining industry in the world, a signifi-cant portion of the richest people in China are owners or managers of coal mines, and China has the highest rate of coal mining accident deaths in the world. [17] Following is an example of how mine owners make their profits.

A Resource-Rich Area for Mining [18]

The Inner Mongolian region is a vast mining area in northern China. The locals tell us that in a county-level jurisdiction in the region, not far from the place we are visiting, the population in fiscal year 2009 has already enjoyed a per capita gross domestic product (GDP) comparable to that of Singapore and Hong Kong. The sources of the new wealth come almost entirely from the local coal mining industry. For potentially valu-able new coal mining sites, it is mainly the bosses of the county-level government who make the final decision about to whom the license of commercial exploration is granted. The top two bosses in the government hierarchy—the Communist Party secretary and the head of the civil ad-ministration—dictate the process, and the rest of the bureaucracy has little opportunity to approve or kill a permit once approved by the top two officials.

. After a license is given to an investor, he himself is responsible for raising the initial capital to conduct the preliminary exploration for test-ing the likely quality and quantity of the coal deposits. If the mine depos-its that are tested are poor or small, the investor loses the money and walks away empty-handed. If the deposits are commercially viable to extract, the investor will be able to run the business for the first year and claim the income. The key to making continuous profits is the granting of a license to extract the coal after the initial testing period. Because the initial exploration may end up with the total loss of the starting capital by the investor, the local government would not normally ask the investor to pay substantial fees for getting a license. Once it is proven that the coal deposits are good for commercial extraction, the local government can raise the fees. And if the coal deposits turn out to be profitable for longer-term exploration, the local government can change the terms and conditions of the license when it expires, often annually.

Thus, it is a life-and-death struggle for the investor turned mine manager to obtain a license continually, for the more he sees the potential exploitability of the coal mine, the more he will put his money into the digging and supporting of facilities such as roads and equipment, and eventually the more he will lose if he fails to get a license reissued at a reasonable fee level. This author asked the local government officials how often coal mine managers had lost licenses over the years. They said that over the past nine to ten years, they did not see anyone in their prefecture who was rejected for a renewal. After I asked why the investor-managers had been so lucky, I received the following explanation.

To ensure the extension of a license, the coal mine investor-manager has to allow the top officials in the local government to share the private profits in one way or another. This can be through secret payments on a regular basis, company stocks, villas or luxury apartments, luxury automobiles, or constant financial support for the officials' kin or mistresses living or studying abroad. Such profit-sharing schemes usually allow the top officials to take away one-third to one-half of the business returns from the coal mining operation. In addition to the lion's share for the top two officials who have the power of final approval or rejection, the investor-manager also needs to show his "deep appreciation" to a number of bureaucrats in the local government who are in charge of numerous regulatory offices.

The coal mine investor-manager is the one who takes all sorts of risks up front, and the top local officials—who are really business partners in the mining operations despite no or insignificant financial investment made out of their pockets—are behind the scenes to make sure the business operation can continue should something bad happen. The most commonly documented bad things concerning coal mining are conflicts between mine exploitation and farmers in the surrounding area, whose land and agricultural activity may be destroyed;[19] heavy pollution that hurts nearby communities; unlawful labor practices, such as using the mentally disabled or underaged as workers;[20] and, most of all, underground accidents that get workers trapped or killed. The latter two sorts of events can lead to criminal investigations and penalties for coal mine owner-managers, for they often hire thugs to kidnap the mentally disabled or use organized crime to cheat poor, illiterate peasants into mining. When terrible accidents happen, falsifying the accident records, underreporting the deaths, destroying the corpses, threatening the victims' families, and so forth all rely on the maneuvering and protection of the local government bosses, the police, and the mafia as well. Thus, the huge wealth generated from the coal mining industry has for years been characterized by critical Chinese intellectuals as "bloodstained GDP." The main beneficiaries themselves know this very well.

Over the past number of years, more sophisticated mine owner-managers have come up with new methods to distance themselves from the most risky operations. They are far less directly involved in using the mafia to kidnap or force poor individuals into mining, and they also try hard to not have direct dealings with the coal mine workforce. Instead, they sign contracts with *laowu* (literally, "labor affairs," and, more accurately, "job placement") companies that collect laborers and assign them to particular mine sites. In case workplace injuries and deaths happen, the coal mine owner-manager pays to the *laowu* company boss, who will use soft and hard means combined to handle the financial compensations and regulatory-legal matters. The range of financial compensation for a worker killed by mine accidents is around 100,000 to 200,000 RMB. The *laowu* company boss calculates this amount by the annual salaries of a worker in the locality times ten to twenty years. Thus, the coal mine owner-manager would be far less likely to be held responsible for such terrible accidents. Much of the huge wealth from running coal mining is still bloodstained, but the coal mine owner-manager's hands look cleaner.

In part because private and semiprivate owners and managers of small to medium-size coal mines—the primary source of labor abuses and underground accidents in the country's mine industry[21]—understand well the risks and dangers intrinsic to their moneymaking venture, they are more reluctant than ordinary rich businesspeople to put their financial assets into the state bank system under their own names. In case very bad things happen, their bank deposits could be frozen first and later taken away by the regulatory and legal institutions to pay the injured or dead workers' families. Therefore, their most common practice is to purchase luxury apartments and villas or to hide financial assets far away from their hometown or workplace.

Beijing is the largest metropolitan area near the main coal mining regions in northern China, and every high-grade property agency there can tell you how large a percentage of its customers are coal mine owner-managers and how often they pay cash in millions of RMB for multiple-unit purchases. In late 2008, a government official overseeing the coal mining industry in a small county, Puxian, in Shanxi province was found to have secretly purchased thirty-eight apartment units in Beijing and on Hainan island, worth over $25 million. This amount was only a small part of his total family assets. From 1999 to late 2008, he, along with his family as the behind-the-scenes owner of a coal mine in the county, had made a fortune of at least $57 million.[22] Even the Hong Kong property market, which was already at the top of the world's price scale, has in recent years begun to be under the sway of these superrich from the mainland.[23]

"IN OUR COUNTRY NO ONE CAN USE THE LAW AS A SHIELD!" [24]

Both ordinary types of businesses like the hotel case and more dangerous types like coal mining depend on manipulating the legal system. This system, especially the police, [25] is the primary coercive source of protection and punishment in the business community. Many seasoned observers of contemporary China agree that in the past three decades, the legal system has made important progress, but it is still subject to political interference from the Party-state at high levels and to personal manipulation from local government officials. As Jerome Cohen neatly summarizes, "So that's the situation today thirty years after [the beginning of the reform]: Great progress in terms of legal norms. You have a legal system, but it's not a credible rule of law system, and that's not merely an academic matter for China. It could be a matter of the greatest importance and it certainly will have an impact on the evolving economic crisis [begun in 2008]." [26]

Police and Power

According to what I have learned throughout the course of thirteen years of fieldwork in different parts of China since the late 1990s, the industrial sectors of mining, entertainment and hospitality, transportation (including both long-distance bus and taxi services), construction, and real estate are far more likely to be interfered with by police officers because of the nature of the business activity in these sectors and the regulatory frameworks imposed on them by the government. [27] To ensure ongoing profitability, the owners and senior managers of these business entities must first pay protection fees regularly to the chief and core officers of the local police branch. These police officers often become hidden owners or big stakeholders (*gangu*, investing not only cash but also coercive power) of the businesses. In the late 1990s, an empirical survey done in several urban areas in the northeastern region revealed that more than half the police chiefs of the police substations (*paichusuo*, the lowest level of the police system) and above were already wealthy enough to have sent their children to Japan, South Korea, and the West to attend college and university and also to own high-grade real estate property. The whole northeastern region at that time was suffering economic hardships largely because of the closure of many outdated industrial plants of the standard state-owned-enterprise type. The survey findings suggest that most of these petty police chiefs accumulated wealth through illegitimate or even criminal means. Seizing a job in the local police force was regarded widely as seizing a golden ring: after having successfully passed all the formal procedures of police recruitment, a young man still had to pay around $10,000 to $15,000 to the petty police chief as a "gift of gratitude" in order to go on duty, assuming that policing duty means assuming extrasalary income channels. Without paying a proper gift of gratitude, the young police officer might be left on a waiting list for half a year.[28]

In natural resource–rich and economically prosperous areas, the local police force's chance to get rich is truly spectacular. After the infamous case of kidnapped and forced labor in a brick-making factory in Hongdong county, Shanxi province in 2007, the anticorruption staff that was sent down from the central authorities in Beijing to the locality found that the petty police chief Liu Linzhong had kept about $53 million in financial assets in banks. Three years later, when a couple of police officers in the same county were murdered, investigations into the crime accidentally discovered that the couple had left a family fortune in the millions and that their three children were studying abroad. In both cases, the police officers' accumulated wealth was equal to their legitimate aggregate salaries of 100 to 1,000 years.[29]

Law enforcement personnel's involvement in unlawful moneymaking has multifaceted detrimental impacts on the nation's general business environment. When a conflict of interest occurs between a law enforcer and a businessman, often the former resorts to coercive power to retaliate against the latter. In case of a dispute between two businesses, the side that has special access to the law enforcement staff might prevent justice from being delivered. In both situations, the outcome is dictated by the law of the jungle instead of the rule of law.[30]

The Law as Servant of Power

To explore the ramifications of the legal institutions' malfunctioning in China's red capitalism today, we need to revisit two legal traditions interwoven in the "socialist legal system with Chinese characteristics" that has been emphasized since the early 1980s. There is an old saying that "If you have enough money, you can hire the devil to push the millstone for you!" (*youqian nengshi gui tuimo*). This is an expression of the power of money in legal disputes.[31] Some may argue that in contemporary Western societies, especially in the United States, the outcome of legal disputes is also affected by how much money you have in hiring the most capable legal team. But the main difference between the old Chinese legal practice and the contemporary Western legal procedure is that in the former the money goes illegally to the governmental bureaucrats who manipulate the legal process against the established norms and procedures,[32] and in the latter the money goes to the law firms who know best how to play games under the law in accordance with the established procedures to help the resourceful client avoid trouble.

The second legal tradition was illustrated vividly by a question-and-answer session in the early 1980s when several young Chinese journalists had a brief exchange with one of the Communist revolutionary elders,

Peng Zhen, chairman of the National People's Congress, who had been jailed and tortured in the Cultural Revolution of 1966–1976. The revolutionary elder just declared that after the horrible Cultural Revolution, in which numerous individuals had suffered so much, the Communist Party now was committed to building a good legal system in China in which the law would govern every activity in society. The young journalists were excited and asked the senior leader to clarify: "Will the law govern the Communist Party's activity? Who is to overrule when the two unfortunately get into conflict?" Peng Zhen thought for a while and replied with apparent sincerity, "That is a tough question and I cannot give a generalized answer. Under the specific conditions in our country, sometimes it is the law that is above the Party, but sometimes it is the Party that is above the law."[33]

So now we may be able to draw a rough hierarchy to designate the interrelations among the three forces of law, money, and power playing out in the sorts of cases under discussion here. First, there are laws—the rules, norms, and procedures written on paper. If the two sides in a legal contention are equal, the laws would by and large determine the outcome. If one side has much more money and knows to whom the money should be best distributed in proper amounts and methods, then the outcome would predictably be in favor of the big-money side regardless of the laws on paper. If the third type of force—the executive power of Party-state bureaucrats—plays into the process, then both the laws on paper and the big-money side in the litigation would most likely be defeated.

When Peng Zhen made his comment, perhaps he had in mind some important political issues concerning the Party-state's major policies and programs, which of course could hardly be challenged in the court under a one-party regime. But the Party-state regime would be a ghostlike structure without the millions of high-level, midlevel, and petty officials and officers staffing it. As far as the middle- and low-ranking members of the Party-state machinery are concerned, they themselves are the Party, the state, and the system. And their manipulation of the legal system for their private interests is based on the same political principle that Wu Bangguo, the current chairman of the National People's Congress, has reemphasized: "The Western model of a legal system cannot be copied mechanically in establishing our own," meaning, in China's legal system, the laws are used to reinforce the Party-state, not to constrain it.[34] This simplified hierarchy of "money above laws" and "bureaucratic power above both money and laws" serves as the background for our next case study.

A Business Dispute–Related Murder Case[35]

On March 17, 2006, three brothers—Yuan Baojing, Yuan Baoqi, and Yuan Baoseng—were executed in the city of Liaoyang, Liaoning province, and their close relative Yuan Baofu was sentenced to death with a two-year suspension. This case shocked the general public because of several extraordinary features. Yuan Baojing was a young billionaire known for his huge success in the stock market and merger-and-takeover operations. The brothers were charged with the paid murder on October 4, 2003, of Wang Xing, who once was their business partner and then turned to be an adversary. Wang Xing was not an ordinary businessman; he had been the head of the powerful criminal police section in the city of Liaoyang before taking up a business career. During the summer and autumn of 2005 when in police custody, Yuan Baojing reported that he had hard evidence on high-level corruption and crime. At the request of a senior provincial Party official, he had purchased $30 million of stocks in Hong Kong for the official's wife. He also reported that this senior Party official was deeply involved in illegal drug trafficking and fake banknote transactions. This senior official had asked Yuan to use his company to do money-laundering for his illegal and criminal gains at the rate of 30 percent service charges; that is, for each 10 million RMB of "dirty money" washed clean, Yuan was paid 3 million yuan by the senior official.

Yuan Baojing made this attempt with the understanding that under the PRC Supreme Court's rule, if a prisoner reports a serious criminal act and helps public prosecutors uncover the crime, the prisoner will be rewarded with a significant reduction in his penalty. But shortly after Yuan Baojing made the report, the executions were carried out. The Yuan brothers' family members quickly revealed that the reported senior Party official was the secretary of a provincial committee of politics and law (*zhengfawei shuji*), the top bureaucrat overseeing the entire legal system in the province. They suggested that someone very powerful in that province wanted to see Yuan Baojing dead.[36] The defense lawyers for the Yuan brothers and several independent law professors questioned key aspects of the alleged murder case, such as the police's use of torture to obtain the Yuan brothers' confessions, unclear linkages between the accused payers/organizers of the murder and the accused killer, controversial findings from laboratory examinations of the alleged gun and bullet used in the murder, and so forth. These law professionals commented that if capital punishment were to be based on such an unsound foundation, the message conveyed would be truly terrifying. Despite this, the executions went ahead quickly. Many critical questions have pointed to the special backgrounds of Wang Xing and the unnamed senior Party official, the boss of a provincial committee of politics and law.[37]

Many Laws, No Protection

On March 3, 2011, the Ministry of Foreign Affairs spokesperson Jiang Yu said that in China, "no one can use the law as a shield!" This now world-famous quotation, despite having been ridiculed by many inside and outside China, is a rarely seen official public statement that is both honest and realistic. Jiang Yu was saying that there were no rights under the law to protect dissidents who might have been inspired by the Arab world protests in the spring of 2011 to challenge the Chinese regime.[38] Yet when looking into the middle and low levels of contemporary Chinese society, it appears that laws on paper cannot function as a shield to protect any legitimate rights, even those that have nothing to do with a regime-challenging agenda. Let us visit two more recent cases to illustrate this point. A naturalized American scientist, Hu Zhicheng, came back to China in 2004 using his technical expertise to set up a business. After a dispute with a company based in the city of Tianjin, Hu Zhicheng was jailed for seventeen months and then released because of a lack of hard evidence to formally incriminate him. But since late April 2010, when the case against him was formally dropped, Hu Zhicheng has been banned from taking a flight back to his home in California, and no PRC legal authorities have officially explained to him why. Hu Zhicheng's own explanation is based on a generalized observation: "Chinese companies often cultivate influence with local officials and thus may rally law enforcement and a malleable legal system to their side when deals go awry. . . . He feels outmatched by a well-connected local company, having lived outside China for so long and having failed to cultivate the contacts Chinese prize for smoothing business. 'I'm used to the US and following the laws,' Hu Zhicheng said. 'Clearly China is a different place.'"[39]

Countless individuals in business circles in China can tell you of similar experiences, and what most of them have experienced or observed is surely more unreasonable and horrible because of their PRC citizen status. American citizenship at least allows Hu Zhicheng to ask for consular help, and that is certainly a central consideration for most of the applicants for foreign legal status from the PRC.

The social realities of "many laws, little protection" in contemporary China have led to another characteristic situation: the efforts of the "yellow road" (*huang dao*, the business circles) to reach out toward the "white road" (*bai dao*, Party-state officials and officers), and/or the "black road" (*hei dao*, the underground society). A businessman will be labeled as *hei-bai tongchi*, or "green lights through traffic to both the black and white worlds." But in numerous localities, businesspeople either have few channels to get connected to the truly powerful officials and officers or have found them to be too expensive or unreliable for helping frequently encountered business troubles. Thus, special relations with the mafia turn out to be a strategic alternative for the businessperson who does not come from an official's family background.[40] Mafia protection of business is a worldwide phenomenon, but it is particularly well established in places where the formal legal system is fragile.[41] In such places, not only dubious commercial operations but also those that are doing lawful transactions need the mafia's special care. Recently, the "sweeping black-society organizations away" campaign in the city of Chongqing received global attention.[42] During the eight-month period from mid-2010 to early 2011, some 5,000 individuals of alleged mafia affiliation were taken away by the police through the classical style of mass movement "anti–this-or-that bad elements," a standard practice copied from the Maoist era. One does not have to accept the Chongqing police authorities' justification for the Maoist campaign in which so many individuals were arrested in such haste—and "the faster, the better." Even if a portion of the arrested were really mafia members, one has to raise the question of why. Why had so many businesspeople in Chongqing turned to the mafia for help? This is a clear indication of the failure of the official law enforcement institutions in providing a clear, transparent, fair, and reliable environment for normal business.[43]

MAD IN THE PRC BUSINESS WORLD

This chapter selects one mechanism of the dynamics of the PRC's red capitalism to illustrate the root of worry, fear, and anxiety in private and semiprivate business circles. It is public knowledge that in China one needs to develop special connections with powerful and resourceful Party-state bureaucrats to advance one's business interest.[44] Yet these types of connections are intrinsically contaminated with high risks. Both parties to the special relationship, in which interests and benefits are exchanged informally and unlawfully, are repeatedly reminded of the rational, realistic calculation that "If someday something goes wrong, I have to utilize this or that means to protect myself." Thus, a down-to-earth type of negative opportunism is built into the relationship between private businessmen and public officials from the start and is in play most of the time. The iron law of damage prevention and self-protection drives both parties to prepare for the worst possibilities. In the majority of the cases I have read over the past ten years or so, one side of the relationship would sell out the other side to its advantage if the price looked adequate. Under the PRC's formal and informal rules of the game, protective measures can readily become killing bullets. Red capitalism's built-in mechanism of public power exchangeable for private profit has led to a MAD business climate: weapons of mutually assured destruction. In my interviews with experienced journalists on economic and legal issues in China, more than occasionally I am reminded that in reading news reports and legal materials on business and legal disputes, "Don't trust too much what the official tells you, and don't trust too much what the business-man tells you either; nobody's hands are completely clean."[45] A simple translation: "The only reliability is that these guys are not reliable!"

At the beginning of this chapter, I brought up the question of why so many Chinese businesspeople have moved or try to move overseas in a time when their motherland appears to be the top star in the world econ-omy and when financially struggling residents of many developed coun-tries look with envy at Chinese tourists' spending power.[46] This seeming-ly perplexing phenomenon ought to be examined through multiple lines of development in mainland China in recent years. It is closely related to economic and societal factors, such as the increased cost of production in the coastal areas, the policy of *guojin mintui* (meaning that the state sector advances at the expense of the private sector), formal and informal tax burdens, the poor quality of education, and the lack of social security entitlements.[47] All these factors deserve comprehensive treatment in sep-arate empirical studies. By being focused on the "culture of business," this chapter aims to show why, even though China is "booming" in so many ways, so many people in the business community still feel nervous and insecure about the future. In summary, the main arguments are that businesspeople's relations with the Party-state authorities are always laced with distrust, and this leads to the need to anticipate ways to gain leverage over their partners who may later turn into enemies with the weapon of inside information. This creates pervasive insecurity about the future, causing businesspeople to launder money, ship it overseas, and prepare to flee overseas themselves.

To place what this chapter has illustrated into a wider comparative context, we can observe a rather persistent pessimistic outlook on the part of the entrepreneurial class for the future under other Communist regimes, even those that did undertake noticeable economic reforms. For instance, in the spring of 1921, the new Communist government in Rus-sia, under the growing pressure of nationwide economic hardship, was forced to introduce the capitalist-like New Economic Policy (NEP). But the Russian peasantry, who had just been treated as semi–slave laborers by the Communist government's coerced grain collection scheme, did not trust that the NEP would last for long. Even many Communist Party members believed that the NEP was designed as a trap for the business-minded folks. Thus, the top leader, Lenin, and his senior associates ac-knowledged that the peasants were like frightened sparrows and could hardly be cheated once more by the same Communist government.[48]

It appears that a considerable number of the Chinese business class also act like frightened sparrows in large part because of the repeated instances of major figures in their cohorts being arrested or forced to run away. Taking a wider view across a vast range of industries and areas, we see clearly that the sense of vulnerability among the PRC business community is a reflection of a multifaceted and multilayered institutional complex. Much more still needs to be done to assure the entrepreneur class that for legitimate business adventurers, their homeland is not a land with too many land mines. To start with, the top leadership in Beijing must work sincerely, as numerous PRC observers and scholars on the legal and economic policy fronts have proposed,[49] to remove the dual swords over the PRC legal processes, a profoundly complex black box on which this chapter's three-level analysis can throw only a bit of light: that the written law can be easily overruled by bribery, and then bribery can be arbitrarily overruled by bureaucratic power. Once the PRC authorities begin to pay decent respect to the laws and courts established by themselves in the first place, the domestic business community's confidence in their motherland's future will be built up step-by-step. The two territories of Hong Kong and Singapore serve as good examples in this regard: they have not developed a Western-style political system, yet both have adopted a functional and predictable legal system more or less compatible with the common-law tradition, capable of providing a fair level of property rights protection and curbing severe abuses of human rights. Largely (but not entirely) because of these qualities, the two have recently become the highly attractive migration destinations for mainland Chinese businesspeople.

During the period of late 2010 through early 2012, there was a widely circulated popular satirical saying (*shunkouliu*) on the Chinese mainland:

> Chinese capitalists in the Mao era fall into two groups: those whose property has been confiscated and those whose property is to be confiscated soon.
>
> Chinese capitalists in the Deng era fall into two groups: those who have been jailed and those who are to be jailed soon.
>
> Chinese capitalists in the Jiang era fall into two groups: those who have been admitted into the Party and those who are to be admitted into the Party soon.
>
> Chinese capitalists in the Hu era fall into two groups: those who have migrated overseas and those who are to migrate soon.

This satire is, of course, laced with a certain degree of exaggeration. For instance, the Jiang Zemin era of 1989–2002 was not such a golden age for native Chinese capitalists; at most, one can say only that the native capitalists were grouped into two: a tiny number being admitted into the Communist Party and a large number being promised to have a chance to obtain Party membership in the uncertain future. Nevertheless, the satire is a powerful expression of the widespread perception within business circles and beyond. The post–Hu Jintao leadership needs to make enormous efforts to change the social realities that have given birth to such popular perceptions.

NOTES

The data for this chapter come from research conducted by Yang Feng, a research student at the Social Science Division, Hong Kong University of Science and Technology, in late 2011. He used primarily the published domestic sources from the Chinese mainland rather than overseas media reports. After a list of thirty-five rich and super-rich individuals was compiled, Yang Feng did cross-checking to reduce possible errors. In spite of this, some details are still open to controversy. For instance, the reports on the problems with Mr. Rong Zhijian's business activities in Hong Kong appear to have little if any connection with the PRC authorities. Nevertheless, this list collected from widely circulated reports on the Chinese mainland serves as an indicator of how vulnerable a PRC citizen could be after his or her name appeared on the lists of the superrich. What is absent in this data set is equally if not more illuminating: we do not see anyone in the families of top PRC leaders—in office, retired, or passed away—although there has been much domestic and international reporting on their spectacular self-enrichment and ostentatious lifestyle. The full data set can be obtained by request from the author.

1. Xin Shaowen, "Disanbo yiminchao: Rencai de liushi?," *Nanfengchuang Biweekly* (Guangzhou), no. 9 (2011): 49–50.

2. Xin Shaowen, "Disanbo yiminchao," 49.

3. Li Ying, "Disanbo yiminchao qiaoxian, touziyimin caifuguanli shangji texian," *Xianggang shangbao* (Beijing: CFI.cn), May 23, 2011, 1.

4. Li Ying, "Disanbo yiminchao qiaoxian, touziyimin caifuguanli shangji texian," 1.

5. Ed Zhang, "Super-Rich Want to Leave Mainland: Half Those with Assets of More Than 10 Million Yuan Are Considering Emigration, Survey Finds," *South China Morning Post*, November 1, 2011; Yuan Ye, "Most of the Mainland's Rich People Want to Migrate, the USA and Hong Kong Are the Top Choices," http://www.VOANews.com, November 1, 2011.

6. The author's interview with the senior reporters of the *Nanfengchuang Biweekly*, September 20, 2011.

7. See the top news story in *Huaxia shibao* (Beijing), September 26, 2011, 1.

8. See the data set referred to in this chapter's notes for the superrich PRC businesspeople who were in various degrees of trouble after their names had appeared on the lists.

9. Although scholars use differing terms to describe the blended type of capitalism in Dengist China, the basic characteristics of that brand of capitalism are commonly observable, and the reader can obtain a good review of these in Yasheng Huang, *Capitalism with Chinese Characteristics: Entrepreneurship and State during the Reform* (Cambridge: Cambridge University Press, 2009).

10. David L. Wank, *Commodifying Communism: Business, Trust, and Politics in a Chinese City* (Cambridge: Cambridge University Press, 1999), chap. 5.

11. I collected information on this case first in the summer of 2005 and then updated some details in the autumn of 2006. The personal identities are slightly altered.

12. In the first major corruption case disclosed in 2012, Tang Chengqi, a senior official in the city of Nanchang, Jiangxi province, allocated an aggregate of several hundred millions of RMB in public assets in three operations to help his cronies' businesses and caused a total loss of 284 million RMB to the public accounts. A large part of his personal illicit gains of 39 million RMB came from the deliberate misuse of public funds. See Hu Jinwu, "Nanchang yuan shiwei changwei Tang Chengqi shouhui 3901 wan yuan, yisheng pan sihuan," Xinhua News Agency, January 29, 2012.

13. Oliver August, *Inside the Red Mansion: On the Trail of China's Most Wanted Man* (Boston: Houghton Mifflin, 2007).

14. "Beijing yuan fushizhang Liu Zhihua shoushen," *Xinhua fazhi* (Beijing: Xinhua Wang), October 15, 2008. The part of the case about Hong Kong videos was learned in December 2008 in Beijing in my discussion with two senior state television reporters.

15. "Wang Baosen anjian jiben ziliao," *Zhengyi wang* (Beijing: Zhongguo jiancha ribao she), November 29, 2000.

16. The term "bloodstained money" has been applied to profits from a number of business spheres in China, and the coal mining industry stands out among them. See Tim Wright, *The Political Economy of the Chinese Coal Industry: Black Gold and Blood-Stained Coal* (London: Routledge, 2012).

17. Tom Holland, "Reliance on Coal Spells More Disasters," *South China Morning Post*, February 6, 2008.

18. I collected the following information when accompanying for a week in the summer of 2010 a small group of local government officials who were the members of an anticorruption team at the prefectural rank. They were on a public relations program.

19. On May 10, 2011, a herdsman named Morigen was brutally run over by truck drivers of a mining company in the Inner Mongolian region, and his death caused large-scale local protests. On October 20, 2011, a similar incident occurred in the same region in which herdsman Zorigt was killed by a fuel truck when he was defending his grazing land. See conflicting reports by the PRC official bodies and the local Mongolian residents compiled by the New York–based Southern Mongolian Human Rights Information Center and published on its website at http://www.smhric.org.

20. To abduct mentally handicapped people and then sell them to mining and other heavy-duty and dangerous workplaces has been a mafia-like business enterprise in poor rural areas in China, see Brian Spegele, "Chinese Police Free Thirty Held as Slaves in Kilns," *Wall Street Journal*, September 8, 2011, 5.

21. According to a widely cited study, in 2003 coal output in China was 35 percent of the world's total, but the accidental deaths from coal mining in China were 80 percent of the world's total (Yang Yiyong and Li Hongmei, "Dui Zhongguo kuangnan de zhidu fengxi," *Zhongguo jingji shibao*, April 15, 2005). During that period, coal mining deaths in China were reported to be around 5,000 to 6,000 per year, but researchers in China believe that this was underreported by a large margin, and the actual figures could be two to five times more. Many accidental deaths were covered up by a combination of coercive and financial means. It has been so difficult to close down small and medium-size coal mines because so many local officials and police officers were involved in their operations. See Gady Epstein, "Beijing Dispatch: The Price of Corruption," *Forbes*, October 2009, and Sharon LaFraniere, "Graft in China Covers Up Toll of Coal Mines," *New York Times*, April 11, 2009.

22. The Hao Pengjun case is now well known in China. I first learned of the case from Dr. Dong Yanbin, a legal scholar originally from Shanxi province.

23. Ed Hammond, "Expensive Home Prices Soar in Asia," *Financial Times*, September 21, 2011, 4.

24. This is a slightly rephrased translation of the famous quotation by the PRC Ministry of Foreign Affairs spokesperson Jiang Yu from March 3, 2011. See the context of this realistic, honest statement in "Jiang Yu's Greatest Quips," *Sinostand: Culture, Politics and Business of China*, April 3, 2011.

25. In the summer of 2011 when I gave a talk on "comparative perspectives on social stability and social management" in a major city in Guangdong province, I expressed that in China, almost all the provincial police chiefs are now promoted to standing committee member status in the provincial Party committee, a significant sign of the police force's relative weight in the Party-state system. A local official who was once a police officer reminded me, "Shortly after the establishment of our People's Republic of China, Premier Zhou Enlai taught us already: 'You *gongan xitong* [police force] and the People's Liberation Army are the two great pillars of our *zhengquan* [regime]. The stability of our *zhengquan* is half dependent on your police force!'"

26. Jerome Cohen, "Thirty Years of Chinese Legal Reform," *Wall Street Journal*, December 4, 2008.

27. See a review of some major problems in the construction industry in X. L. Ding, "The Quasi-Criminalization of a Business Sector in China," *Crime, Law and Social Change* 35, no. 3 (April 2001): 177–201.

28. My interviews with local journalists on economic affairs in the cities of Changchun, Jilin province, and Harbin, Heilongjiang province, in early 2000. The survey was not published.

29. The data come from the same source on the Hao Pengjun case.

30. In some of the cases I have collected recently, there appears to be a regular pattern that the local police force and the local mafia are bridged in large part by local mining company bosses: they jointly run the "conflict management" affairs in the locality. For instance, in Hengshan county bordering Shaanxi province and the Inner Mongolia region, the local mafia *kandao dui* ("the team of choppers") did their work of violently attacking small-business owners or ordinary residents under the cover of a "security service company." It was formally supervised by the public security bureau of the county government, but the real chief was a coal mine company owner. This mine owner drove a vehicle with a police license plate, and he and the public security bureau chief were joint operators on illegitimate arrangements (Liu Lichun, "Shaanxi 'kandao dui' shangren an gaopo, meilaoban jingche guakao gongan ju," *Xibu wang*, April 30, 2010).

31. This trend in "money can buy anything" in the legal system is reflected in the "managed outcome" (*baiping*) of homicide crimes at the county level and below that I have been informed of in the fieldwork. The lowest cost for someone who was found directly responsible for the murder of a person to walk away from punishment was around 50,000 RMB in rural towns in Hainan in the mid-1990s. The price was up to some 700,000 MB in the early to mid-2000s in a mine resource–rich area in Shaanxi province ("Shaanxi Tongguan gongan juezhang deng 20 duo ming jingcha canyu hei shehui," *Liaowang Weekly*, Beijing, April 22, 2008).

32. Legally sentenced to be in prison, government bureaucrats can therefore live outside prison through bribing local police and prison officers. The People's Supreme Prosecutorial Office, in its sporadic inspections on receiving complaints from localities, has verified 1,300 such cases in 2004 and 555 such cases in 2010. See the brief mentioning of the inspections and two recent cases in the city of Jiangmen, Guangdong province, and similar incidences in other localities in "Haiyou duoshao fuxing tanguan xiaoyao jianwai?," *Guangzhou ribao*, September 30, 2011; *Xi'an wanbao*, October 5, 2011; and *Dahe bao*, Zhenzhou, October 29, 2011. In late 2011, the top prison administrator in Hunan province, Liu Wanqing, was punished for accepting 17 million RMB in illicit payments in exchange for manipulating prison laws and regulations to help jailed officials go free. The top prison administrators of Sichuan and Zhejiang provinces, Li Wenhua and Tian Feng, were also punished a bit earlier on the same charges. See "Sheng Jianyu juzhang shouqian fangren yitiaolong," *Zhidai zhoubao* (Guangzhou), no. 1 (2012).

33. There are a few slightly different versions of this exchange. My translation here is based on what I had been told formally at a routine political study meeting in Beijing in the spring of 1984.

34. Mark O'Neill, "Right to Defense Vital to Judicial System," *EJ Insight, Hong Kong Economic Journal*, October 3, 2011, 2.

35. Wang Jiayao and Xing Xuebo, "Yuan Baojing nan bei wuzui shifang," *The 21st Century Economic News* (Beijing), August 20, 2004, 1–2; "Yuan Baojing guxiong sharen an shimo," *Meiri xinbao* (Tianjin), March 31, 2006, 1–3. Shortly after the conclusion of the Yuan brothers' case, I learned much from reflective discussions at the Chinese University of Politics and Law in Beijing; the chief defense lawyer was a professor there, and Yuan Baojing was a graduate of that university.

36. In the big underground banking case of Wu Ying that took place in the city of Dongyang, Zhejiang province, we see a similar pattern. Wu Ying was accused of running an investment fund of 770 million RMB outside the state financial system, taking deposits from the locals, and issuing loans to private businesses at interest rates

higher than the state banks. She has been in detention since 2007, when she was twenty-seven years old. During the interrogations, she reported to the public prosecutors that she had offered large sums of cash to powerful government officials and state bank managers to keep the underground financial operation running. After she confidentially submitted two lists of more than ten names of the officials and bank managers taking huge amounts of money from her in exchange for a reduction in her sentence, a dozen or so local officials sent a joint petition to the court demanding that she be sentenced to death. After the first trial of Wu Ying, in which a death penalty was announced, the case was generating nationwide discussion and debate, and the public was crying for the disclosure of the involved officials' names. The group of local officials, who are unnamed still, made a second petition to the higher court to urge the execution of Wu Ying. Her father told journalists that those officials wanted to kill her so that the truth would be buried forever. See "longcong-和讯财经微博-@曹盛洁：吴英父亲吴永正在接受采访时透露," http://t.hexun.com, January 20, 2012. See also a summary of the controversy over this case in Hai Tao, "Feifa jizi? Cong Sun Dawu tuxing dao Wu Ying sixing," http://www.VOAnews.Chinese.com, January 26, 2012. For a general review of the case from a financial regulation perspective, see Cai Yu, "Will Wu Ying Be Sentenced to Death for Borrowing Money?," *China Entrepreneur Magazine* (Beijing), January 30, 2012. Finally, on April 20, 2012, the Chinese supreme court overturned the death sentence and sent the case back to the Zhejiang Provincial Court, which resentenced Wu Ying to death with a two-year reprieve, which is usually commuted to a life sentence after two years.

37. When Chinese reporters tried to ask the relatives of the Yuan brothers about the identity of the boss, they did not give the name in public (based on the conversations I heard in Beijing in the summer of 2008).

38. To sense how extremely nervous the Party-state apparatus has felt about the Arab Spring's influence on the Chinese citizenry, see the court proceeding over Zhu Yufu, a Hangzhou resident who was immediately arrested by the police in early March 2011, in "Dissident Tried over Skype Messages, Poem," Associated Press, January 31, 2012.

39. Charles Hutzler, "AP Exclusive: US Scientist Trapped in China," Associated Press, September 30, 2011.

40. A clarification seems to be needed here. Not all members of the huge Party-state officialdom of many millions can provide sufficient protection for their family members and close relatives when their business ventures run into trouble. The number one official in a locality (i.e., *yibashou*) and those who are in charge of the "politics and law committees" and of the Party organization departments appear to be the most effective protectors.

41. Arnold J. Heidenheimer, Michael Johnston, and Victor T. LeVine, eds., *Political Corruption: A Handbook* (New Brunswick, NJ: Transaction Publishers, 1990), pp. 305–374.

42. John Garnaut, "Show Them the Money, Old China," *Sydney Morning Herald*, March 26, 2011.

43. This is basically the explanation from well-tempered law professionals; see the public letter by He Weifang of the Peking University Law School on his sina.blog, April 12, 2011. My interviews with the businesspeople who either are based in the city of Chongqing or have commercial interactions with the city's marketplaces often use the phrase *"hei da hei"* (one black society hits another black society), or *"dahei chi xiaohei"* (the big black society eats the small black society) to characterize the "sweeping away" campaign.

44. See an insightful examination of the uneasy relationship between bureaucracy and business in post-1989 China in Minxin Pei, *China's Trapped Transition: The Limits of Developmental Autocracy* (Cambridge, MA: Harvard University Press, 2006), chap. 4.

45. This observation is widely believed to be realistic in relation to owners of private and semiprivate businesses in China, as reflected in the popular saying of the business class's *yuanzui* (i.e., the original sin). Yet my fieldwork and reading of count-

less cases also show that it is applicable to large numbers of senior and midlevel managerial cadres of publicly owned firms and government officials. I have discussed part of this in X. L. Ding, "The Informal Asset Stripping of Chinese State Firms," *The China Journal*, no. 43 (2000): 1–28. In early 2012, two PRC legal organizations published a research brief: in 2011, at least eighty-eight senior managers of major state firms were legally punished for severe crimes of corruption. On average, each of them had taken 33.8 million RMB illegally (around US$5.2 million), a threefold increase over the previous year. See "2011 nian Zhongguo qiyejia fanzui baogao" (Report on the criminal cases committed by China's state-owned-enterprise managers in year 2011)," *Fazhi ribao* (Beijing), January 15, 2012. Thus, more and more PRC commentators emphasize that it is the general political economy environment that should be taken as the root cause rather than the "moral quality or mistakes" of individual people, as previously stressed by the official propaganda.

46. Arvind Subramanian, *Eclipse: Living in the Shadow of China's Economic Dominance* (Washington, DC: Institute of International Economics, 2011); Gao Fei, "Eighty Percent of Mainland Chinese Tourists Go Abroad in the Holiday Season Just for Big Shopping," *Hong Kong Economic Journal*, January 27, 2012, A11.

47. I have briefly discussed some of the policy problems in my recent public lecture collection; see Ding Xueliang, *Zhongguo moshi: Zancheng yu fandui* (The Chinese model: For and against) (Hong Kong: Oxford University Press, 2011), chaps. 10 and 11. For a recent example of private businesspeople's personal struggle, see David Barboza, "Entrepreneur's Rival in China: The State," *New York Times*, December 7, 2011.

48. Louis Fisher, *The Life of Lenin* (New York: Phoenix Press, 2001), chap. 40.

49. This based on what I learned from a number of small and large discussion panels and seminars in which I participated during 2006–2008 when I was working for the Carnegie Endowment for International Peace's joint program in Beijing and the three widely noted major meetings in Guangzhou and Beijing in which I was involved in 2010: the Times Weekly Economic Forum, the Thirty Anniversary of the Resolution on the CCP History, and the Annual Caijing Economic Conference.

THREE

Political Humor in Postsocialist China

Transnational and Still Funny

Paul G. Pickowicz

A guy stood in the middle of the street and cursed, "Khrushchev's an idiot!"
As a result, he was sent away for twenty-two years. Two years for cursing a
state leader. Twenty years for leaking a state secret.

There are many ways to handle individual and group restlessness. One way is to have a good laugh about our discomforts and anxieties. During a prolonged stay in China in 2010, I was struck by people's tendency to resort to humor as a way of handling their frustrations and worries. Sometimes I was passive and simply listened to jokes that people wanted to tell. Sometimes I was more proactive and asked people if they had heard any good ones. Before long, I concluded that jokes, especially political jokes, circulate quite widely in contemporary China but that many aspects of this type of humor are poorly understood by students of Chinese culture and society. I decided to collect, transcribe, and translate Chinese-language jokes that had been brought to my attention. In many respects, it was a field research project. I was assisted by students and young academics who not only fed me a steady stream of jokes but also sat with me and tried to explain precisely why they think the jokes are so funny. Translating the jokes was a challenge because I very much wanted the English versions to be as funny as the original Chinese versions. My informants gave high marks to all the jokes discussed in this chapter.

I was particularly struck by one genre: jokes that are set in the former Soviet Union from the time of Lenin to the age of Gorbachev. Let us call them jokes about socialist societies. I should note at the outset that I am not using the term "socialist" in any grand theoretical sense; rather, I am using it to refer specifically to state socialist environments. The jokes amount to utterances and observations that are critical of what people have experienced as state socialist and "Communist" systems—critical from an "internal" perspective.

My interest in the Soviet joke does not mean that Chinese jokesters are timid about telling political jokes that refer specifically to China.[1] For instance, when I did a Chinese-language search on Google/Hong Kong for "Anti-Cultural Revolution jokes" (*fan wenhua da geming xiaohua*) on October 9, 2011, a total of 1,520,000 items appeared. The purpose of this chapter, however, is to take a close look at the Soviet joke and its role in restless China.

By the end of my stay in China, I had amassed eighty jokes of this sort. With the Soviet Union long gone, I wondered, why do the young, urban, educated, and restless Chinese I encountered in Shanghai, including Communist Party members, think these jokes are so funny? Of what relevance are these jokes in the brave new world of consumer frenzy in early twenty-first-century China? My first instinct was to say that these jokes are a safe way to blow off a little steam. No one can charge that Chinese socialist leaders or socialist institutions are being subjected to direct critical humor since Chinese leaders and China are almost never mentioned. At one level, the jokes merely laugh out loud about the failed Soviet Union. But at another level, the jokes clearly involve the possibility of displacement and invite substitution. The jokes tell of Lenin, Stalin, Khrushchev, Brezhnev, and Gorbachev, but these names can easily be read as Mao Zedong, Hua Guofeng, Deng Xiaoping, Jiang Zemin, Hu Jintao, and Xi Jinping. Indeed, the temptation to substitute is almost impossible to resist. The problems and issues discussed in the jokes are associated with the former Soviet Union, but restless jokesters in China, many of them closet wise guys, seem to be vividly aware that many of the same, age-old problems that plagued the former Soviet Union exist in present-day China.

Early on in my research, I wondered about the question of authorship. Who crafted these Chinese-language jokes? How are we to understand authorship? Are the jokes recycled versions of jokes that were circulated in the Soviet Union itself? Or are the jokes crafted by Chinese people in the Chinese language for an exclusively Chinese audience? Some of the young people with whom I discussed the jokes were certain that these jokes were "Made in China" for a decidedly Chinese audience, though it proved to be impossible to identify specific "authors." But that is the nature of jokes. It is hard in a global cultural setting to know where a joke originated. That is precisely the point. Jokes get passed around informally by word of mouth, and in the process they change and adapt to particular needs and purposes. They even cross borders. These days, jokes about the former Soviet Union, like everything else, can be found on the

Chinese-language Internet and then get spread around and altered in ways that seem appropriate to restless netizens. But even on the Internet, Chinese jokes are virtually never linked to an "author." A Chinese-language Google/Hong Kong search I conducted on October 9, 2011, for the term "Anti-Soviet jokes" (*fan Sulian xiaohua*) yielded 2,170,000 results.

In the end, I concluded that the issue of authorship is of little or no significance. These days we constantly talk about "global," "transnational," and "cross-border" phenomena. These jokes might actually be a fascinating example of cross-border, transnational, and postsocialist cultural production in which authenticity of authorship is not important at all. Instead, we might be talking about a case of global cultural "recycling." Some or most of the jokes may well have originated in the Soviet Union or Eastern Europe and then gotten translated into Chinese somewhere along the line by someone.[2] Some may have originated in China. So what? In an important sense, it does not matter who created them. The point is that they are circulating very widely in China and are definitely "out of control." The question is, Why do such jokes circulate so widely in restless China? One rarely hears jokes about the former Soviet Union told in the United States. So why are they popular in China?

LEADERS AND AUTHORITY FIGURES

All of this raises the question of precisely how one should approach or categorize the Chinese-language joke about the Soviet Union. At the outset, it seemed to me safe to say that a fairly high percentage of these jokes, like the one told at the beginning of this chapter, poke fun at, mock, and even insult socialist state leaders and authority figures. Many of these jibes are crude and direct. One such joke concerns a visit by Brezhnev to Poland:

> On the eve of Brezhnev's visit to Poland, Polish officials ordered a famous artist to do a monumental oil painting titled "Brezhnev in Poland" as a gift. The artist was unhappy, but he took the job because he felt he had no choice. When a high-level official stopped by to pick up the painting, he was shocked. The painting depicted a man and a woman flirting on a luxurious bed, with the Kremlin visible through a window. "What the hell is this? Who's this woman?" the official asked angrily.
> "That's Brezhnev's wife," the artist responded.
> "Then who's the guy?"
> "That's Brezhnev's secretary."
> "So where's Brezhnev?"
> "Brezhnev's in Poland," the artist answered.

Many things are going on in this joke. First, jokes as crude as this one, especially jokes that contain sexual content, are not common among those

I collected. The main point, of course, is that Brezhnev is a fool, despite all his apparent power. It is great fun taking him down a few notches. The secondary point is that it is hilarious to imagine that the wives of top Party leaders sleep around behind the backs of their husbands. The joke also reveals that the Soviet Union was deeply resented by ordinary people in its client states.

A similarly crude joke involves the endless tours of inspection undertaken by state leaders who want to have their pictures in the paper in order to demonstrate that they are actually doing something. In this case, it is Gorbachev, the reformer, who is on the road:

> One day, when Gorbachev was on a visit to a collective farm, he spotted a bunch of pigs. He went over to have his photo taken with the pigs. An assistant immediately recorded the following caption for the photo: "Gorbachev together with pigs." But he felt this was a little bit off, so he made a change: "Pigs together with Gorbachev." But he still felt it wasn't quite right, so he made one final change: "The third one from the left is Gorbachev."

Again, the big-shot leader looks like an idiot because he has no idea that the caption writer is struggling to find a way to identify Gorbachev in a dignified way. The befuddled aide looks like an incompetent and bungling flunky who does not know how to make apparent the difference between the great Communist leader and a pig.

Other Chinese jokes about the Soviet Union that poke fun at leaders are more nuanced. Of particular interest is the type of joke that insists that it is top state leaders who have the least amount of belief in socialist ideology. The higher the leader, the less likely he or she is actually to believe in socialism or Communism. That is, they preside over a self-styled socialist state, but they and their family members do not take socialist thought and values at all seriously. This type of joke often involves comments on the lavish lifestyles enjoyed by senior leaders. Educated young people I encountered in Shanghai howled about this one:

> After Brezhnev became secretary-general of the Soviet Communist Party, he invited his mother to leave the countryside to visit Moscow. After his mother arrived, Brezhnev did everything he could to make a good impression: a beautiful house, a fancy car, the best furniture, and so forth. After doing all this, he asked the old lady if everything was all right. She replied, "Son, all this is really wonderful. But what will you do if the Communists come?"

The underlying assumption is that in the matriarch's mind, there is no connection between her son and the Communists. Indeed, she has a very low opinion of Communists and Communism. The jokesters are delighted because the blatant hypocrisy of the leadership class is revealed.

The notion that the most senior leaders embrace a puzzling and convoluted ideological outlook when it comes to managing a socialist state,

one that differs from the politically correct posture of many Party under-
lings, is repeated in many of the Chinese-language jokes about the former
Soviet Union. In the following scenario, the distinction between top leaders and ambitious bureaucrats is brought to light:

> During a Soviet Party Congress, the Chair suddenly said, "Those com-
> rades who think socialism is good, please sit on the left hand side of the
> auditorium. Those comrades who believe capitalism is good, please sit
> on the right." The great majority sat on the left, while a minority sat on
> the right. But there was one guy who remained in the middle and
> didn't move. The Chair said, "Comrade, what about it? Have you made
> up your mind about which is better, socialism or capitalism?" The man
> responded, "I think socialism is good, but the way I live is capitalist."
> The Chair then said with excitement, "Well in that case, come on up!
> You belong up here on stage!"

The politically correct majority is dull and predictable. The sober realist
minority is too frank. The person who babbles double-talk about having
it both ways is the one who will rise.

Some of the jokes that express contempt for the highest echelon of
leaders contain very little information that is place or time specific. In
these cases, it is especially easy to read the jokes as commentaries on
present-day Chinese restlessness. Here is one vivid example:

> The Soviet postal system printed a set of stamps featuring all the for-
> mer leaders, but after one month the postal authorities made an urgent
> announcement prohibiting the use of these stamps. The reason? People
> sending out letters didn't know which side of the stamps to spit on.

Not surprisingly, these types of directly applicable jokes about leaders
also take up the issues of corruption and special privilege:

> A worker said, "We have already achieved Communism!"
> Someone asked, "Why do you say that?"
> The worker responded, "We have put into practice the principle of
> 'From each according to his ability, to each according to his need.'"
> The other guy said, "What!?"
> The worker then explained, "You don't get it? Our leaders wantonly
> take whatever they need, while we workers toil to the best of our abil-
> ity!"

In this case, the joke works because of its successful use of irony. There
has been a willful distortion of the utopian goals associated with the
Communist society of the future, a distortion that draws attention to
what many citizens understand to have been the real outcomes of the
socialist revolutionary process.

Indeed, the Chinese-language jokesters repeatedly underscore the notion that senior leaders have no sincere interest in socialist or Communist
ideology. In this tale, political insiders simply cannot imagine that there
is any elite who takes socialist ideology seriously:

> When Brezhnev gave a report at the Twenty-third Congress of the Soviet Communist Party, he asked, "Are there enemies among us here today?" One guy answered, "Yes, there's one. He's in row 4, seat 18."
> Brezhnev asked, "How do you know he's an enemy?"
> The guy responded, "Because Lenin said the enemy never sleeps. Looking out over the crowd here, I see that he is the only person who hasn't fallen asleep."

Again, the irony is powerful. Lenin, of all people, is invoked to make the case that total lack of interest in ritual political displays is the norm among top leaders; thus, there is good reason to be suspicious of anyone who takes socialist sloganeering seriously. In fact, the whistle-blower is correct. It is quite logical for him (and system insiders) to regard as an enemy anyone who really takes socialist and Communist values seriously. The existence of "real" socialist revolutionaries would pose a threat.

HUMAN RIGHTS

A fair number of Chinese-language jokes set in the former Soviet Union raise the question of human rights abuses in traditional state socialist systems. Of course, it is very much the case that early twenty-first-century China no longer falls completely into the category of "traditional" socialist systems, at least as far as economic development is concerned. But as Jeremy Brown has pointed out in chapter 1 in this volume, many important legacies of the state socialist system continue to constitute bedrock features of present-day China. Restless anxiety about serious problems in the human rights area is one of those features.

Some of the jokes attack the problem rather directly and with considerable effectiveness. In this case, the joke refers directly to the appeals of political joke telling in state socialist societies:

> A prosecutor in the Internal Affairs Department of the People's Personnel Ministry was returning to his office after a day of investigative work when he suddenly burst out into hysterical laughter for no apparent reason. A colleague across the way thought this was strange and asked, "What's so funny?"
> "Oh boy!" the prosecutor replied as he used a handkerchief to wipe away tears of laughter. "It's an incredibly funny joke!"
> "What is it? Tell me!" the colleague said.
> "Are you crazy!" the prosecutor said, "I just gave a guy five years of hard labor for telling this joke!"

Once again, mind-boggling hypocrisy is on display. The offending joke is obviously right on target. Even this state insider agrees. But the freedom of speech required to retell the joke does not exist.

Another example that touches on freedom of speech is more indirect and perhaps even more effective:

> An American and a Soviet are having a conversation.
> The American: "I dare to stand outside the White House and yell 'Down with Reagan!' Do you dare to do anything like that?"
> The Soviet: "What's so daring about that?!"
> After the conversation ended, the Soviet took off, stood outside the Kremlin, and yelled, "Down with Reagan!"

The interesting twist here is that the joke proves there is no freedom of speech but does so by revealing that some citizens are in denial about that basic fact.

A similarly nuanced joke raises an even broader question about "freedom." Like the Reagan joke, the narrative is located in an international context:

> When Rabinovich was on a fact-finding mission to a capitalist country, he sent a telegram back to his unit: "I choose freedom!" His unit immediately called a meeting of Party representatives for the purpose of denouncing Rabinovich and disposing of the matter. But during the meeting, Rabinovich suddenly appeared! Everyone was stunned! Rabinovich was miffed and said, "Extremely interesting. So this is how you view freedom!"

The joke is highly effective because listeners in present-day China, like Rabinovich's comrades, simply assume at the outset that he defected during his trip. The comrades are embarrassed but not surprised. Although they are Party insiders, they understand "freedom" to mean life in a capitalist society. This reminds us of Chinese President Xi Jinping's desire to have his daughter enroll at Harvard. Why are the universities in China not good enough for her? Like the joke about the sleeping delegates, the insiders (all of them shameless hypocrites) simply cannot imagine that there is a true believer who regards socialist/Communist society as a realm of "freedom."

Of additional interest is the sort of human rights joke that links absence of a basic human right (in this case, freedom of speech) to complaints about unacceptably low standards of material life. In this joke, the main concern of the protestor is not human rights abuses but, rather, low standards of living:

> Outside the Lubyanka headquarters of the Soviet KGB. A frustrated guy was walking along muttering to himself, "No soap, no batteries, no socks . . ." Another guy, who seemed to be a plainclothes policeman, approached him and whispered, "Citizen comrade, if you continue to slander our great socialist nation in this way, I'll have no choice but to hit you on the head with the handle of my pistol!" The pitiful guy took a look at the plainclothes cop and continued talking to himself, "See what I mean? We don't even have bullets!"

Of course, it is possible to reason that this joke is hard to apply to the early twenty-first-century Chinese case because of the higher standards of living and greater levels of material abundance that exist for many in China today. Nonetheless, the joke still works because it reminds people of a time not so long ago when there were chronic shortages in China, it does not deny that there are many people in China today who do not have access to the new abundance, and it underscores the ongoing problem of human rights violations. The message delivered by state operatives is clear: those who protest any sort of problem are candidates for threats and punishment.

SURVIVAL STRATEGIES

It is important not to fall into the trap of thinking that all jokes about the Soviet Union currently circulating in restless China express contempt for senior leaders or register righteous indignation about human rights violations. A significant number of jokes come close to suggesting that large numbers of nonelites in state socialist societies, in sharp contrast to the ruling class (that has no illusions about the nature of the system), have to some degree been successfully "brainwashed." This elitist and rather disturbing suggestion begs the following questions. Is the system really capable of "brainwashing" people? Or do ordinary people merely pretend to be fully socialized? Or do ordinary people prefer to live in a perpetual state of denial as part of a conscious or subconscious survival strategy?

The following is a short-and-sweet example of this type of joke. The biblical reference is interesting, and so too is the use of the present tense:

> Question: "What country are Adam and Eve from?"
> Answer: "Well, they have nothing to wear, they have to split an apple, but they think they're living in paradise. They've got to be Soviets!"

This is a case in which the third part of the joke ("they think they're living in paradise") is the one that relates most easily to present-day China. The phenomenon of mass denial is also at the heart of the following query:

> Question: "Which aspect of the sixth sense of Soviet citizens is the most developed?"
> Answer: "The sense of feeling highly satisfied!"

A related joke suggests that all citizens will be fully programmed and thoroughly self-disciplined in the Communist utopia of the future:

> Question: "When we realize Communism, will there still be policemen?"
> Answer: "Of course not. By that time, all our citizens will know how to arrest themselves."

That is to say, there might still be some grumbling in the supposedly utopian future and thus a need to place people under arrest, but transgressors will be fully capable of identifying and punishing themselves.

Some of the jokes about denial and brainwashing are located in a global context:

> Question: "Why was the decision made to buy so much grain from Western countries?"
> Answer: "Because it's important to understand that the greatest short-coming of capitalism is overproduction!"

A related one hints that brainwashing may also involve isolating people from external sources of information and thus keeping them in a state of ignorance:

> A socialist, a capitalist, and a Communist made an appointment to get together to chat. The socialist arrived late and explained, "Sorry, I had to wait in line to buy some sausages."
> The capitalist asked, "What do you mean by 'wait in line'?" The Communist asked, "What do you mean by 'sausages'?"

These types of jokes betray more than a bit of condescension of the part of some Chinese political jokesters. The joke assumes that people "in the know" are not so easily kept in a state of ignorance, nor are they easily fooled by socialist propaganda that insiders themselves do not believe. But such "in the know" people show little sympathy for those who are in total denial or have been brainwashed.

Still, keeping oneself uninformed and ignorant does not guarantee survival. There is such a thing as being too stupid and thus unwittingly exposing oneself to danger. In the following example, an embittered old lady puts her foot in her mouth in this version of a "Polish joke":

> After World War II ended, an old Polish peasant woman often gazed at photos displayed along the street. Every time she looked, she insisted that a certain person looked just like her grandson.
> Someone said, "What are you talking about?! That's Comrade Stalin."
> Old Lady: "Who the hell is he?"
> Response: "He kicked the Nazis out of Poland!"
> Very agitated, the old lady asked, "Will he be able to kick out the Russians too?"

In her mind, there is no difference between the Nazis and the Communists. They are both unwelcome invaders. And once again there is evidence of Eastern European resentment of Soviet overlords. One wonders whether Chinese listeners ever apply such jokes to tense relations between Hans and the many non-Hans (Tibetans, Uyghurs, and so on) who live under Han rule.

One of the most interesting categories of Soviet jokes is about people who are well informed about realities, who have no illusions about the nature of the system, but whose instinct for survival trumps all else. One example is the type of joke that refers to the brand of caution exercised by people who do in fact have a deep understanding of the system:

On a Moscow subway car.
A: "Good day my dear fellow citizen."
B: "Good day!"
A: Excuse me, but may I ask whether you are a KGB comrade?"
B: "No, I'm not."
A: "Are you a former KGB comrade?"
B: "No."
A: "Among your relatives and close circle, are there any KGB comrades?"
B: "None."
A: "In that case, please move your foot. You're stepping on my toes."

Others are motivated by outright fear. The following joke, which deals directly with the fears that nonelites have about the repressiveness of the system, also includes the familiar global comparison:

Brezhnev and US President Carter were at a meeting in Switzerland. During a break, both men were rather bored. They began to make comparative remarks about whose bodyguards are more loyal. Carter went first. He called in one of his bodyguards, opened one of the windows on the twentieth floor, and said, "John, jump out the window!" Crying, John responded, "How can you do this Mr. President? I have a wife and a kid!" When it was his turn, Brezhnev used a booming voice to call in his own bodyguard, "Ivan, jump out the window!" Without saying a word, Ivan headed toward the window. Carter jumped up, grabbed him, and said, "Are you crazy?! If you jump, you'll die!" Ivan struggled to get away, saying, "Let go of me you bastard! I have a wife and a kid!"

In both cases, the main concern is the welfare of the wife and child. In the US case, according to the logic of the joke, survival requires defiance of the president, while in the Soviet case, survival dictates unfailing submission to even the absurd demands of authority figures. Those who exercise extreme caution, including Party insiders, try their best to cover all bases:

The Party branch secretary asked, "Comrade, do you have an opinion about this question?"
Answer: "Yes, I have an opinion. But I don't agree with my own opinion."

In the world of jokes about the former Soviet Union, even the highest leaders openly acknowledge that the system depends on fear and the threat of reprisal. In this case, the comparative framework involves a developing nation rather than an advanced capitalist state:

During Brezhnev's visit to India, a huge throng of Indians went to the airport to greet him. He asked Indira Gandhi, premier at that time, "What method did you use to get so many people to come to the airport to welcome me?"

Gandhi responded, "Everyone who comes to the airport gets a five-rupee reward." Later, when Gandhi made a visit to the Soviet Union, many tens of thousands of Soviets were standing along the roadside on the way to Moscow to welcome her.

So, she asked Brezhnev, "What method did you use to get so many people to come out to welcome me?" He replied, "Anyone who fails to show up to greet you will be fined five rubles!"

Disincentives rather than incentives are the norm. Threats of retaliation cause people to conform. An interesting underlying assumption embedded in the first part of the joke is that Brezhnev simply assumes that Indian people do not have the slightest interest in greeting him. He is baffled about the appearance of so many people. In short, he lacks self-confidence, and that knowledge is satisfying to the restless Chinese listener.

An even more compelling "survival" joke involves the ability of people who understand the system and are basically hostile to it, mastering ingenious ways to manipulate and game the system in order to survive and to achieve personal goals. This example also comments on the tense relations between police (agents of the state) and ordinary (seemingly powerless) people:

An old-timer was strolling along and carelessly stumbled into a river by the side of the road. He screamed out for help. Two cops heard everything but ignored the situation, moving along chatting and laughing as if nothing had happened. The desperate old-timer came up with an idea and suddenly shouted out, "Down with Brezhnev!!" The two cops were shocked and immediately jumped down the embankment, dragged out the old-timer, and put him in handcuffs.

In some of the jokes, personal survival sometimes involves a clear inability or lack of desire to express compassion for others who are at risk. In the following example, ordinary people are invited to define "happiness":

An Englishman, a Frenchman, and a Soviet were chatting. The Englishman said, "The greatest happiness is going home on a winter's night, putting on a pair of woolen pants, and sitting by the fire." The Frenchman said, "You English are too stiff. The greatest happiness is being on a vacation in the Mediterranean with a lovely blond and having a grand time with each other before parting amicably." The Soviet said, "The greatest happiness is when someone knocks on my door in the middle of the night and says, 'Constantine, you are under arrest,' and I say, 'You are mistaken. Constantine lives next door!'"

In this pathetic scenario, it does not matter what happens to one's friends and neighbors as long as one's own survival is not threatened. Social conscience does not exist. Indeed, a scenario involving the victimization of another person instead of "me" is defined as the "greatest happiness."

Another "survival strategy" joke takes up the issue of job security. Once again, the person highlighted in the joke is "in the know." He understands the basic nature of the system. But he does not want to do anything that will undermine his fundamental, low-level economic security:

> Rabinovich works in Moscow. His job is to stand in a watchtower and look off into the distance. When he sees that the Communist society of the future has arrived, he is supposed to send out a signal to herald the grand event. An American tries to recruit him to work for America instead. He is asked to send out a signal the next time a big economic crisis is about to happen. Rabinovich answers, "I'm not interested. I want a steady job!"

Since Communist society will never arrive, his job is secure. Furthermore, he is certain that an economic crisis will take place in the near future; thus, his term of employment in the new job might be brief. In short, it is in his own interest to work for an apparently self-perpetuating system that he knows is bankrupt.

THE DYSTOPIAN, THE SURREAL, AND THE ABSURD

Perhaps the most intellectually challenging type of Soviet joke requires the jokester to play with and twist language by taking deadly serious terminology to absurd extremes. This type of creative use of language is discussed in detail in chapter 4 in this volume. In certain cases of this sort, the reasoning is logical, but somehow the conclusion is profoundly nonsensical. Here is one such example, the only Soviet joke I found in which China is directly mentioned:

> Question: "Will money exist in the Communist society of the future?"
> Answer: "The Yugoslav revisionists say it will. The Chinese dogmatists say it will not. But when one looks at it from the point of view of dialectics, yes, there will be money, but not everyone will have it!"

Presto! The vision of a Communist utopia has been converted at once into a confusing dystopia. And in this case, a cruelly stratified society of a few "haves" and many "have-nots" is immediately relevant to conditions in present-day China , notwithstanding the painful reference to a time during the mid-Mao era when Chinese ideologists were saying that a utopian society in which there is no need for money was on the horizon.

Speaking of horizons, other jokes about the advent of the perfect Communist society play amusing word games with the sort of conceptual language frequently found in the ideological propaganda of high socialist states. In this case, gullible citizens ask innocent questions in order fully to comprehend utopian promises:

> A speaker told everyone that Communism had already appeared on the horizon. So someone in the audience asked him a question: "What do you mean by *horizon*?" The speaker responded, "The horizon is an imaginary line, the line where the sky and the land meet in the distance. But as you move toward it, it moves further away from you."

The speech amounts to dystopian double-talk. The purpose of the speech is to declare that the good society will arrive very soon, but knowingly or unknowingly the speaker, an insider, has indicated that the Communist heaven will never arrive. Listeners are free to reach their own conclusions.

Speaking of heaven, the subject of the Roman Catholic conception of heaven is treated openly in another joke that refers to the Communist utopia. The context is an imagined meeting between Brezhnev and the pope:

> Brezhnev had a question for the pope: "How come people believe in the heaven of the Catholic Church but don't believe in the heaven of Communism?" The pope responded, "It's because we have absolutely never allowed anyone to see our heaven!"

In this case, a top leader is actually admitting that no one believes in the promise of a Communist utopia. It is the pope who advises the Soviet leader not to make reckless claims about the extent to which present reality has anything to do with a vague promise about the utopian realm of the future.

A related joke goes so far as to make the miseries of the present a scientific prerequisite for the realization of a (dys)topian future:

> The home of a Soviet man was being broken into all the time by thieves. Deeply depressed, the man asked his neighbor, "When will the day arrive when our things aren't stolen from our homes?" The neighbor said, "Just wait until the day Communist society arrives. Things will no longer be stolen then."
> "Why?"
> "Because by the end of the socialist stage, everything will have been stolen already."

Like the joke about "dialectics" discussed earlier, this joke redefines and mangles the Marxist-Leninist sociohistorical stage of "socialism" in a way that conforms to the life experiences of nonelites.

A final group of dystopian jokes can be described only as surreal in the way they play with the static conceptions and paradigms familiar to educated people who live in state socialist settings, including China. The first one requires a bit of contemplation before the humor sets in:

> One day an archaeologist suddenly discovered a Stone Age cave. There was a slogan on the wall right by the entrance: "Long live the slave system, the brilliant future of all mankind!"

Again, the jokester is having serious fun with standard Marxist-Leninist "scientific" terminology. From a Marxist point of view, the transition from prehistoric modes of living to slave society was in fact a progressive step forward in the march of history. By this sound logic, prehistoric people had every reason to look forward with great enthusiasm to the arrival of slave society. The more subtle point, however, is that the Stone Age slogan is no less bizarre to subjects of a state socialist regime than slogans about capitalist (i.e., "prehistoric") society inevitably giving way to a liberating socialist (i.e., "slave") society. Naive citizens are asked to accept the weird notion that slavery can be better than what came before it. In joke after joke, the scientific pretenses of socialist theory are lambasted by wise-guy jokesters:

> Question: "Is Communism a science or an art?"
> Answer: "Of course it's an art. If it were a science, they would have experimented on a rabbit first."

These sorts of short, Orwellian sound-bite jokes can leave the listener with a sense of short-term confusion and disorientation. Note the following account of the realm of the (sur)real:

> "Why were you jailed the first time?"
> "I opposed Ivanovich."
> "Why were you jailed a second time?"
> "I supported Ivanovich."
> "Who are you?"
> "I am Ivanovich."

In such jokes, the main speaker is locked into a mode of glaring self-contradiction:

> Question: "What's the main advantage of the Soviet system?"
> Answer: "Its ability to successfully overcome difficulties that don't exist in other social systems!"

The same holds true in the following example:

> Question: "Rabinovich, are you a regular reader of our newspapers?"
> Answer: "Of course! Otherwise, how would I know about the happy life we enjoy today?"

What he no doubt meant to say is "how could he know *so much*" about the happiness of the present day, but it comes out as "how could he know *anything at all*" about the alleged happiness of today. This sort of intentionally sloppy use of language is also a factor in the following one-liner:

> The slogan of the Artillery Academy: "Our target: Communism."

This joke works much better in Chinese than in English since the word *mubiao* can mean "goal," "aim," or "target." When it is read as "target," it seems like the goal of the people running the Artillery Academy is not to achieve Communism but to open fire on it.

The following joke heads in a similar, mind-warping direction:

"Do you think there's a possibility America will go Communist?"
"It's possible. But if that happens, where will we buy our grain?"

On the one hand, the socialist subject is confident that America will have a Communist revolution but is equally certain that American capitalism is far superior to Soviet socialism, at least when it comes to the production of basic foods.

Equally surreal is a longer story suggesting that even low-level insiders are uncertain about the identity of the "real" leaders of the socialist state. The following example, deeply appreciated by young Chinese I encountered, is both bizarre and vivid:

When Gorbachev was still general secretary, he stepped out of his office one day to run some personal errands. He thought his driver was going too slow and urged him several times to hurry up. But there was a big traffic jam, and Gorbachev remained frustrated. Finally, Gorbachev suddenly took control of the wheel by force, pushed the driver into the back seat, and drove the car himself. He wove back and forth, creating great chaos. A local cop called the head of traffic control to report the situation. The head angrily questioned the local cop on the scene.
Head: "Did you get a good look at the troublemaker?"
Cop: "Yes, I did."
Head: "So why didn't you arrest him?"
Cop: "I don't dare."
Head: "Why?"
Cop: "He's a very high official."
Head: "How high?"
Cop: "I don't know. But I can tell you this: Gorbachev is his driver!"

In thematic terms, many of the jokes fall into multiple categories. This one, for example, could just as easy be placed under the heading of "survival strategies" because neither the cop nor his boss is going to do anything risky.

THE AUDIENCE FOR TRANSNATIONAL SOVIET JOKES

The issue of the audience for Chinese-language Soviet jokes is very important. Who is the target audience? Is it the same audience that is addicted to Han Han's blog (discussed in chapter 5 in this volume) or to the *Feicheng wurao* reality show (treated in chapter 6)? Why does the audience for this type of humor think it is funny? And what do the jokes mean? That is, what do they tell us about restless China?

First, we must acknowledge that there are many kinds of humor and many audiences. The audience for the type of *xiangsheng* stand-up acts studied by Perry Link is not necessarily the same as the audience for present-day political humor.[3] We need to take into account that Link studied the early 1950s, while the Soviet jokes discussed here are best appreciated in their distinctively early-twenty-first-century context. It would be a mistake, for instance, to assume that everyone in China likes political jokes or to suggest more specifically that appreciation and understanding of overtly political humor about the former Soviet Union is universal.

For one thing, it is clear that appreciation of this kind of humor requires a basic knowledge of socialist terminology and the history of Communist party-states, including the twentieth-century histories of both the People's Republic and the Soviet Union. Without such knowledge, it is hard to make connections and fully appreciate certain ironies and absurdities. Most high school graduates (especially urban graduates) and virtually all college graduates have been exposed to these basics.

After considering this issue for a time and discussing the nature of this humor with people in China, I came to the conclusion that the main audience for political jokes about the former Soviet Union is comprised of relatively young, well-educated, cosmopolitan, urban people in general. But it is tempting to single out Party members in particular. A significant portion of the audience for this type of political humor, it seems to me, is in fact comprised of rank-and-file, low-level Party members and educated non-Party people who have a bit more than the usual amount of knowledge of socialist concepts and the histories of state socialist nations, China included.

In fact, the more I thought about it, the more I realized that most of the jokes I collected were supplied to me by young, well-educated people, a number of whom are Party members. Many of these people adored the jokes I collected. On other occasions, I witnessed small groups, including family gatherings, engage in joke sharing. Some of those present were Party members, and some were not, but all appreciated the humor.

Of course, the argument could be made that China is not really a socialist nation; thus, jokes about the former Soviet Union could not possibly have much meaning or resonate with the daily lives of nonelites. But it might be more accurate to say that present-day China "is" and "is not" socialist. In the economic sphere, clearly, the new market-oriented dispensation stands in sharp contrast to the pervasive shortages and stagnation associated with the traditional socialist economies of both China and the Soviet Union. But it was not so long ago that there were long lines, scarcity, and rationing in China. Thus, the jokes about chronic shortages intentionally serve to remind people in present-day China about the recent past and discourage empty-headed nostalgia for the "good old days" of high Maoism. There is very little that is "new left" about the criticism contained in these political jokes.

In the political realm, clearly, there are many affinities between the present situation and life under Mao and Deng Xiaoping. This is where the issue of legacies and continuities comes in. There is broad consensus among scholars of China (both inside and outside China) that China has serious problems in the age of "opening and reform." Too often, the tendency is to blame the problems on developments that are "new," "global," and "reform" related, developments that seem to have nothing to do with the early history of the PRC or the history of socialist development in the Soviet Union. But the popularity of the jokes suggests that many of the problems that plague the political sphere today are directly related to the ongoing "legacies" of the Stalin and Mao eras. There are many in China who want more human rights and a pluralistic political system that values accountability. Indeed, it is easy to find young Party members in China who disapprove of one-party rule (and the political legacies of the Stalin and Mao eras) and say privately but openly that they favor a multiparty political arrangement that features free elections and a free press. If Taiwan can elect its own leaders and hold them accountable, why, they say, cannot the mainland do the same?

THE IMPACT AND RELEVANCE OF SOVIET JOKES: STATE VIGILANCE AND REASONS FOR PESSIMISM

Chinese-language Soviet jokes are widely popular in China and can be easily found on numerous websites. But what about their impact? They document restlessness and disaffection among certain kinds of Chinese citizens, but what role do they play in the larger cultural arena? It is hard to know with any degree of certainly. One might say that they are relatively harmless and do little more than allow the restless to blow off a little steam. That is, they constitute no threat and do not appear to be part of a larger and more politically charged counterculture movement. But opponents of this view will complain that we dismiss this type of popular cultural form at our own peril. By dismissing the political joke, they would say, we are giving the Party/state too much credit for its ability to maintain its political dominance. Our research should emphasize the agency of nonelites and the ability of "bottom-up" social forces to create pressure for change. But critics of the "bottom-up" school will insist that real change comes only from the very top and that placing much emphasis on popular social forces is misguided and naive, a type of analysis that assigns too much agency to "society."

This debate will not be settled here in our discussion of irreverent jokes about the former Soviet Union that circulate in China. It might be useful, however, to take note of Arthur Waldron's recent essay on the ways in which state-sponsored academics in China have talked about the collapse of the former Soviet Union and the corresponding lessons that need to be learned by current Party leaders.[4] Citing recent authoritative reports commissioned by the Central Party School and other like-minded institutions, Waldron shows that important Party elites in China believe that the failure of the Soviet Communist Party "to maintain a comprehensive dictatorship" is what caused the collapse of the Soviet Union. The Party needs to adhere, they say, to the "wrongly-maligned model of dictatorship of Joseph Stalin." Both Khrushchev and Gorbachev headed in a disastrous direction when they attempted to make the system "humane" by promoting a "humanitarian, democratic socialism" (*rendao de minzhu de shehuizhuyi*). Waldron quotes a Chinese study published in 2000 to the effect that

> this Khrushchev, who had called Stalin "my very own father" and "the greatest genius of humanity, teacher and leader," in order to accommodate the demands of certain unreliable people, made an all-out attack on Stalin in front of a party meeting, calling him "a murderer," "a bandit," "a criminal," "a professional gambler," "an autocrat," "a dictator," "a bloody fool," "an idiot" and so forth. The effect was to negate the whole period of Stalin's rule. . . . But at that moment, the Chinese Communist Party, under the leadership of Mao Zedong, stood up, and powerfully refuted these demented words. . . . The lessons of that period of history are still fresh in our memories.

Another study mentioned by Waldron, published in 1999 by the Chinese Academy of Social Sciences, argues that Gorbachev followed the same path to no good end. According to Waldron, these analysts concluded that in 1988 Gorbachev advocated the mistaken idea of "humanistic and democratic socialism" and thus proposed the idea of "division of power and the catastrophic decision to allow a multi-party system." The result was that when the "party released its grip on power, all sorts of conflicts and disorders arose."

One cannot help but notice the pivotal place of "Stalin" in these studies. One of the state-sponsored Chinese studies states that "the disorders of the 1980s and 1990s in the Soviet Union and Eastern Europe all have a conspicuous characteristic, which is that they were all set in motion by negation of and attacks on 'the Stalin model.'" Further on, the analysts argue that "the lesson of the collapse of the Soviet Communist Party and the Soviet Union is a very sad one. The sudden and fundamental political change was started by criticizing the Stalin model, thereby giving the practice of socialism a bad name."

Waldron is surely correct when he states that "in China saying anything negative about Stalin can very easily be understood as criticism of Mao. Even today, Stalin has never been criticized in China." Later, Waldron asserts that "Mao is China's Stalin; discrediting him undermines the founding myths of the party and state." It follows then that criticizing Stalin and the Stalin system and all its ongoing legacies is tantamount to criticizing Mao and the Stalinist modes that he and his collaborators put in place in China. It seems reasonable to assume that Chinese-language jokes about the Soviet Union are understood by insiders and outsiders alike as criticisms of leaders and key aspects of the inherited and deeply rooted "system."

WHAT WOULD IMPRISONED NOBEL LAUREATE LIU XIAOBO SAY? THE VOICE OF OPTIMISM

What would Liu Xiaobo say about the culture of jokes and jokesters in postsocialist China? Let us ask him. Although Liu has never discussed in any detail the genre of jokes about the Soviet Union, he did write an interesting essay in 2006 titled "Political Humor in a Post-Totalitarian Dictatorship."[5]

For openers, Liu thinks that jokes are very important. He is interested mainly in what he calls "*egao*" humor, a form that uses parody, "twisted meanings," and "odd juxtapositions" to generate an "air of absurdity." Liu especially likes irreverent *egao* humor because it undermines the monopoly on "public expression" once enjoyed by intellectual and political elites. In short, there is a democratic quality to it. In the realms of music and literature, he says, with considerable justification, that Cui Jian and Wang Shuo were pioneers of the sort of *egao* expression that is more sarcastic and insulting than it is angry.

Liu observes that there is a debate about such humor in restless China, a debate that in some ways corresponds to the debate in scholarly circles outside China about "agency" and where it resides in the march of history. Some, he states, argue that while humor of this sort destabilizes "pretentious Communist jargon" and "subverts official ideology," it also deepens mass cynicism. "They are afraid," Liu says, "that something that debunks the sacred and subverts authority, but does nothing more, is only destructive, not constructive. If such a trend spreads out of control, the price of sweeping out pompous authority will be creation of a moral wasteland." Liu acknowledges that there is some validity to this perspective. In a place like postsocialist China, *egao* humor "is a symptom of spiritual hunger and intellectual poverty." "People can get drunk laughing at one political joke after another that tells about suffering, darkness, and unhappiness," Liu suggests. "One could even say that the laughter *egao* induces is a heartless kind, something that buries people's senses of justice and their normal human sympathies." This comment reminds one of the thrust of the joke mentioned earlier about "Constantine's next-door neighbor."

But Liu Xiaobo is inclined to side with those on the other side of the debate. He is more optimistic about the long-term impact of cold and cynical political humor. "I see political humor as an important and widespread form of popular resistance in post-totalitarian society," he asserts. "It played a similar role in the Soviet Union and Eastern Europe." It seems, then, that we are talking about something more significant than what James Scott calls "weapons of the weak," that is, forms that snipe at authority from the periphery of society but remain marginalized nonetheless and have little ability to generate substantive change.[6]

Referring to Bakhtin's notion of "cultural carnival," Liu considers the possibility that jokes are in fact "heartless" and "vulgar" but at the same time express "authentic feeling" and feed "real creativity." "In dictatorships," Liu argues, "where control of daily life relies importantly on fear, it is especially important for rulers to maintain the threat that a solemn public atmosphere implies. It is an atmosphere that makes official rule seem fixed, legitimate, even sacred." But when Bakhtin's "carnival" is in evidence, "the people at the grassroots, accustomed to their place at the receiving end of scoldings, suddenly become 'fearless.'" They use "parody, mockery, ridicule, and insolence" to "vent their sentiments." Most important of all, Liu reminds us that "satire of what is wrong implies that something else is right; it tears things down for the sake of rebirth." He concludes that the benefits of dark humor "outweigh the costs."

At the end of his essay, Liu Xiaobo makes the interesting point that the deadly serious and decidedly "not funny" writings of intellectual dissidents in the former Soviet empire made an impressive impact precisely because of the groundwork laid by irreverent jokesters. "Some people say that political humor tore the Iron Curtain down," Liu notes. "This may be giving it a bit too much credit, but there can be no doubt that [grim, unfunny, dissident] truth-telling and [very funny, irreverent] joke-making have worked hand-in-hand to dismantle post-totalitarian dictatorships." Political jokes proved that "people's consciences were still alive," and they "exposed the rot of post-totalitarian dictatorship for everyone to see, and made it plain that, sooner or later, the political decay would lead to an avalanche-like collapse of the dictatorship." It is important to understand, Liu maintains, "how far-reaching the corrosive effects of political humor can be."

Liu Xiaobo's optimism about the future knows no bounds. "In China," he asserts, "political jokes have already been making it clear for some time now that the legitimacy of the dictatorship is unsustainable; this means that an end, when it comes, will not be so much of a shock. People will be able to take it more easily in stride, and this will have the benefit of reducing anxieties and lessening the likelihood that people will seek violent revenge." Because jokes have been allowing people to blow off steam, nonelites "will have less accumulated anger to deal with."

This outlook brings to mind one of the relatively few Soviet jokes currently circulating in restless China that makes mention of violence. Note that the joke deals with the very last, reform-minded Soviet leader and has nothing to do with shortages. Instead, it deals with control:

> After Gorbachev issued an order restricting access to alcoholic beverages, the only way a person could get alcohol was to wait in a long line at an officially authorized store. A guy from Moscow was very frustrated while waiting in line and suddenly exploded: "I'm not going to wait in line anymore! I'm going to the Kremlin and take out Gorbachev!!" Then he turned around and left. But a short time later he was back. Someone asked, "You took him out already?" The guy said, "What the fuck! The line over there is even longer than the line here!"

It is quite impossible to refrain from chuckling. There is no violence after all. But, as Liu Xiaobo points out, "the grins of the people are the nightmares of the dictators."

NOTES

1. Here is an example of a recent critical joke that is set in China.

> During a recent police crackdown on prostitution, a cop was interrogating a hooker:
> Cop: "What's your name?"
> Hooker: "You call me seven times a day, and you're asking me my name?"
> Cop: "So, Zhang Xiaohong, where do you work?"
> Hooker: "You go there seven times a week, and you're asking me where I work?"
> Cop: "So, Zhang Xiaohong, how long have you been working at Passion Club?"
> Hooker: "You came in on the first day, and you're asking me when I started working?"
> Cop: "So, Zhang Xiaohong, in the year you've been working at Passion Club, how many clients have you had, and who are they?"
> Hooker: "How many people are there in the government? You're asking me?"

Here is another example of a recent political joke set in China:

> Listen to this. Just now a Taiwan friend told me, "I am going to vote tomorrow morning. We'll know who will be President by the evening." I didn't know how to respond to him. Though there's no real communication barrier between us, I felt awkward standing in front of him. All I could say in response was, "You guys are pretty backward. If we had a vote tomorrow morning, we would know the result tonight."

2. I shared my translations of all eighty Chinese jokes with Robert Edelman, a prominent Soviet history specialist who does cutting-edge research on popular culture and who traveled frequently to the former Soviet Union. He reported that he had heard Russian-language variations of fifteen of the eighty jokes.

3. See Perry Link, "The Crocodile Bird: *Xiangsheng* in the Early 1950s," in *Dilemmas of Victory: The Early Years of the People's Republic of China*, ed. Jeremy Brown and Paul G. Pickowicz (Cambridge, MA: Harvard University Press, 2007), 207–31.

4. See Arthur Waldron, "Chinese Analyses of Soviet Failure: Humanitarian Socialism," Jamestown Foundation, *China Brief*, no. 11, May 27, 2010.

5. See Liu Xiaobo, "From Wang Shuo's Wicked Satire to Wu Ge's *Egao*: Political Humor in a Post-Totalitarian Dictatorship," in *No Hatred, No Enemies*, ed. Perry Link, Tien-chi Martin Liao, and Liu Xia (Cambridge,. MA: The Belknap Press of Harvard University Press, 2012), 177–87.

6. James Scott, *Weapons of the Weak: Everyday Forms of Peasant Resistance* (New Haven, CT: Yale University Press, 1985).

Part II

A New Electronic Community

FOUR

From Grass-Mud Equestrians to Rights-Conscious Citizens

Language and Thought on the Chinese Internet

Perry Link and Xiao Qiang

Control of information has always been an important tool of governance for the Chinese Communist Party (CCP). In the 1950s, the Xinhua ("New China") News Service built a hierarchical system in which people were provided information by rank: the higher a person's rank, the more and better information he or she got. At the lowest levels of the system, where news reports were public and open, content was strictly controlled so that the CCP never appeared, either directly or indirectly, in an unfavorable light. At the highest levels, where only a handful of top leaders had access, reports were much more realistic, and "problems" were addressed more factually. These two extreme levels—and all the intervening levels as well—were unified by the principle that the purpose of dispensing information is to serve the power interests of the Party: the top leaders need to know how things really stand, so they get straight information. The "masses" need to be channeled into obedience, so they get information that assists in the channeling. People in the middle get an appropriate mixture of the two.

This system remained stable for five decades as different media—newspapers, magazines, bulletin boards, loudspeakers, radio, and television—shifted in prominence as technology advanced. Whatever the medium, the government's various policing agencies always found ways to adapt and maintain control. But the Internet has proven different. It is the first medium in the history of the People's Republic of China that the

CCP has not been able fully to control. The struggle to tame it is ongoing, and the story's end has not yet been written, but already the Internet has made changes that seem destined to last.

The Internet is not exclusively the tool of "netizens," as independent-minded Web users are called. Government authorities also use the Internet to monitor public opinion and to "guide" it as they see necessary. Netizen opinion often resists government repression but not always. Many Web users passively accept government guidance (often without even knowing that they are doing so), and some ultranationalist netizens actually chastise the government on issues such as being insufficiently aggressive toward Japan, Taiwan, or the United States. Freer expression on the Internet makes a variety of things more possible.

In any event, when a news item pops up in Chinese society today, it is often reported first on the Internet by eyewitnesses using cell phones or computers. Internet police can try to block such messages, but in many cases, especially if events are large or dramatic, they cannot. Links on the Internet flash forward too quickly. Moreover, citizen reports, because they are undoctored by censors, have better credibility with the public than the official media have. Hence, the official media feel two kinds of pressure: to catch up in the speed of reporting and to catch up in credibility. Reporters in the liberal sectors of the official media—such as at *Southern Weekend*—tend to welcome this kind of competition because it helps them to be the kind of honest reporters that in any case they want to be. (Some reporters work as official journalists during the day and unofficial bloggers in the evenings.) This pattern, by which news reports originate on the ground and seep upward, represents a severe challenge to the hierarchical control of information that had been in place for the five decades when the Xinhua News Service enjoyed a monopoly on news reporting.

But supplying news is only one of the Internet's functions and only one of its challenges to the CCP's power. The Web also allows people, to an extent far beyond what had been possible before, to express their opinions in public. Many choose to use pseudonyms on the Web, but once they have expressed themselves, they often find that they are not alone. Other netizens concur, and a kind of cyberassembly becomes possible. In regular (noncyber) Chinese society, the CCP prohibits the formation of organizations that it does not control or could not easily control if it wished. But in cyberspace, groups easily form around issues and in some cases continue to operate as different issues come and go. Netizens can apply the pressure of "assembled" opinion even though, in the physical world, they remain atomized in front of computer screens. Such pressure can be very effective. It can lead to policy changes, to reparations for victims, and even to apologies and resignations by miscreant officials. The leverage works not because officials care much about popular approval or disapproval for its own sake. It works largely because officials want to avoid a "bad record"—something that can leave them vulnerable to rivals in power struggles or as potential scapegoats for higher officials. (For some of the ways in which this kind of official jockeying works, see chapter 2 in this volume.)

One other of the challenges that the Internet brings to the CCP might, in the end, prove the most potent of all. This is new "netizen language" that is arising. Originally appearing as back talk and sarcasm, netizen language has developed some new forms—new words, new characters, and even new grammar—in part to avoid Internet censorship but in part, too, as ways for people who have grown up with the Internet to assert their distinctive identities. Largely invented by young gadflies, a surprising number of these terms have begun to spread widely. Liberals, ultranationalists, and even the *People's Daily* have used them.

This raises a fairly profound question: Will new language lead to new thinking? Linguists and cognitive scientists since Benjamin Whorf in the late 1930s have debated questions such as this, but one group that has never doubted the strong connection between language and thought is the CCP. In the Mao era, people were obliged to recite prescribed language in order to show that their thinking was "correct." The obvious assumption was that right language induces right thinking. Today, Mao is gone, but the CCP's assumptions about linguistic ritual as a tool to forge conformity remain in place. People are still trained to believe, for example, that *dang* (党, "Party") and *guo* (国, "nation") are inseparable or at least close enough that *aiguo* (爱国, "patriotism") and *ai dang* (爱党, "love of the Party") need not be distinguished. In official language, *wo-dang* (我党, "our Party") implies "the Party of everyone." This makes it especially significant that, in today's Internet lingo, terms like *guidang* (贵党, "[your] honorable Party") are beginning to be used in a way that puts sarcastic distance between the speaker and the Party. As this kind of usage spreads, it begins to raise questions of national identity. If netizens are tossing out "Party = country," what are they replacing it with? What does it mean today to be "Chinese"?

EXAMPLE: A TRAIN WRECK

On July 23, 2011, two high-speed trains collided on a bridge near Wenzhou in Zhejiang province. Four carriages fell from the bridge, forty people died, and nearly 200 were injured. Within hours, backhoes and bulldozers were beginning to bury the fallen carriages.

The first report of the accident came at 8:47 p.m. in a tweet from a passenger's mobile phone: "Help! Train D301 has left the tracks near the Wenzhou South Station. The carriage is filled with the wailing of children! No rail personnel are in sight! Save us!"[1] A barrage of further tweets began to flow onto microblog sites. Netizens began to compile lists of the names of people who had died. When these lists hit the Web, the government begin publishing its own lists. Officials first said that lightning was the cause of the accident but later said that a signal switch had failed. The CCP's Department of Propaganda issued the following order:

> All media outlets are to promptly report information released from the Ministry of Railways. No journalists should conduct independent interviews. All subsidiaries including newspapers, magazines and websites are to be well controlled. Do not supply links to articles about the development of high-speed trains. Do not publicize people's reflections.[2]

A number of reporters rushed to the scene anyway. Wang Yongping, a spokesman for the Ministry of Railways, arrived as well and tried to calm things down at a noisy news conference the next day, July 24. Someone at that session asked why the railcars had been buried so quickly. Wang answered that "they were buried to facilitate rescue" and then, in the face of hostile incredulity, added that "you can believe it or not believe it, but I, anyway, believe it."[3] This arbitrary comment led a netizen to take a poll on Sina Weibo (China's version of Twitter) that asked, "Why do you think the railcars were buried?" Among the first 63,000 people to respond, only 2 percent accepted official explanations, while 98 percent said "to destroy evidence."[4]

Another questioner at Wang Yongping's news conference asked why it happened that workers sifting through the wreckage found an infant girl who was still alive, long after the search for survivors had officially been called off. Wang responded, "I can only say that this was a miracle." Wang's use of the word *qiji* (奇迹, "miracle") was especially unfortunate because government officials had used this very word to describe China's high-speed trains themselves. Only weeks earlier, Wang himself had said that "China's high-speed trains are a living miracle wrought by the Chinese people under the leadership of the Communist Party of China."[5]

Perhaps Wang's earlier use of "miracle" had slipped his mind, but in any case netizens noticed—and pounced. In cyberspace, the sentence "It's a miracle" went viral, as did that other of Wang's ill-considered sentences, "You can believe or not, but anyway I do." Both sentences were used sarcastically in contexts that had nothing to do with the train crash. Suddenly, in the face of anything ridiculous, one could say, "It's a miracle!" or "Anyway, I believe it," and other netizens would get the joke. Is Osama bin Laden still walking around on the bottom of the sea? "It's a miracle!" "Anyway, I believe it!" and so on. On July 26, the *Apple Daily* in Hong Kong ran a headline that read, "Train gets through, but no rescue needed—What the *hell*?!" The headline coursed through the mainland blogosphere, and a few days later, on July 31, the *Southern Weekend* ran a headline that read, "One Hell of a 'Miracle'!!!"[6]

As public pressure mounted, the government sought stability by offering monetary payments to the injured and the bereaved, sometimes in return for "contracts" specifying that they remain quiet. The government's budget of only 172,000 yuan for this purpose met with derision on the Internet. Within days, it was raised to 500,000 yuan, then again to 915,000 yuan.[7] But the sarcasm persisted.

Such virulent popular response calls for explanation. Why should something like a train crash resolve so quickly into a matter of "victim" and "victimizer"? Why could an accident not be simply an accident? And why does public resentment seem reflexively to zero in on officials? (The Zhejiang train wreck is only one of many examples of this kind. For other examples, see chapter 1 in this volume.) It is hard to explain such a pattern without postulating that deeper and more perennial feelings are at play. Resentment and distrust of officials apparently lie dormant or just simmer along until an incident pops up to trigger an outburst. Chinese police themselves have noted the phenomenon. In their analysis of "mass incidents" (demonstrations, marches, and so on), they distinguish between two kinds of protesting crowds. One kind, called "groups whose direct interests have been harmed," are family, friends, or coworkers of the victims or people who have some other kind of personal connection to them. The other category is "groups whose direct interests have *not* been harmed." These are bystanders to an incident but people who are moved to protest because of their general pent-up resentments and who take the side of ordinary people against the authorities almost automatically. For the authorities, this second group is often a bigger problem than the "directly interested" group because its numbers are much greater. Netizens who piled on after Wang Yongping said "It's a miracle!" were overwhelmingly in the "direct-interest-not-harmed" category. One blogger captured this point by writing that "when a country is so corrupt that a mysterious 'lightning strike' can cause a train crash . . . none of us is an outsider. China is a train traveling through the lightning storm . . . and we are all passengers."[8]

In the blogosphere, the issue of the train wreck resonated with other recent reports and escalated into broad questions of governance and the fate of the nation. A welter of songs, jokes, and commentaries made it clear that people were asking not only "What's gone wrong?" but also "Who is China?" and "What should China be?" Li Chengpeng, a well-known blogger, wrote that

> those fallen carriages are no longer just a train; they symbolize the Chinese state. This state is a "miracle" machine. It needs to crank out miracles, one after another, in order to certify its "superiority." It does this because it knows that in a country where very few people have seen a real ballot box, where Web users often read that "the page you are seeking does not exist," where most farmers cannot explain the difference between a prosecutor and a court, and where people learn

all about the glorious founders of the Party but are forbidden from emulating those virtues by founding a party themselves, only the miracle of unending GDP [gross domestic product] growth can certify superiority.[9]

GOVERNMENT CONTROL OF THE INTERNET

The Internet arrived in China in 1987, and the first network on a college campus appeared at Tsinghua University in 1991. The first international connection, between the Beijing Electro-Spectrometer and Stanford University's Linear Accelerator, came in 1994.[10] Through much of 1995, the government barely noticed the Internet but in January 1996 discovered it to be a "problem" and ordered that users register with Public Security before going online. "Each time?," people began asking—and soon the order proved impossible to monitor. During 1997, college students were beginning to go online in significant numbers, and by 2001 a considerable amount of Internet commerce—which the government wished to encourage—had appeared as well.

Over the next decade, use of the Internet grew exponentially, as did government efforts to control it. In 2007, more than 50 million Chinese were regularly reading blogs and were posting—on average—ten posts per person per day on public bulletin boards.[11] In July 2011, official surveys counted 317,680,000 blogs in the country[12] and showed that about 58 percent of the readers were under thirty years of age.[13] As of early 2012, the government counted 513 million Internet users in China and 900 million users of mobile phones. Most Web use is for entertainment, social networking, and commerce. Netizens who follow politically sensitive issues—train wrecks and the like—are a minority whose numbers have been variously estimated between 10 million and 50 million. But they are a growing minority, and they are melding into the mainstream. They include young Party members, like those who crack "anti-Soviet jokes" of the kind that Paul Pickowicz analyzes in chapter 3 in this volume, as well as officials and their family members. New expressions that are invented on the Internet also tend to jump off the Web and into gossip and banter at dinner parties and in other informal contexts. The same official who hews to orthodox language on the job can indulge in the new lingo during off-hours. People have become accustomed to this kind of split existence and switch back and forth easily, with no sense of contradiction. The most common new Internet terms have spread to gaming, fashion, sport, travel, and nearly every aspect of life.

The authorities have taken note. In a January 2007 speech, President Hu Jintao said that "whether we can cope with the Internet is a matter that affects the development of socialist culture, the security of information, and the stability of the state."[14] Four years later, when social networking on the Web proved to be an effective tool in overthrowing dictators during the "Arab Spring," Hu gave another speech in which he stressed that Internet control must be sharply accelerated and, in particular, the "virtual society" to which it has given rise "guided" toward "healthy directions." [15] There is no sign that Hu had any new ideas about how exactly to achieve greater control; to the police, therefore, the message likely came across as "do more intensely what you are already doing." The organs that bear primary responsibility for Internet control are the Party's Department of Propaganda, which is in charge of content guidelines, and the Information Office of the State Council, which is in charge of websites. Both command bureaucracies that extend from the central to the provincial, county, and municipal levels, but these bureaucracies can be unwieldy. Local officials who seek to repress a local story can find that authorities in neighboring jurisdictions or at higher levels, with their different power interests, may not support them.

In any case, a number of Web control tactics have been standard at all levels. We summarize them here in five categories.

1. *Regulations, surveillance, and social pressure.* Since 1996, the government has issued a steady stream of rules about what can and cannot be put on the Internet and who can put it there. Some rules have been unenforceable—such as prohibitions of pseudonyms, which hundreds of millions of people use every day. But rules about content often *can* be enforced. Internet police monitor the Web, deliver warnings and threats to violators, and sometimes close down a website if disobedience persists. Adapting a method of social control from China's imperial past, authorities hold entire groups responsible for the transgressions of a single member; when one error can lead to the closing of a whole website, users have an incentive to monitor and restrain one another—becoming, in effect, one another's police. Authorities provide hotlines for anyone who is willing to report the misbehavior of anyone else, and such snitching is made palatable by calling it "patriotic." In public campaigns, political dissent is lumped together with pornography (on the grounds that both are "unhealthful"), and this, too, can serve to make prohibitions seem more reasonable. The stated reason for closing a website can be to purge the Internet of sex while the actual reason is to block comment on the Dalai Lama, the Falun Gong, or the overseas activities of the offspring of top leaders.

2. *Self-censorship induced by threats.* For many years, China has led the world in the number of writers in its prisons. [16] But these numbers— normally two or three dozen at any time—are still tiny in comparison to the much larger effect of self-censorship. Authorities understand that people who sense danger or who even just imagine it will curb themselves voluntarily. Official phrases like "you yourself know what you are doing wrong" and "you alone will bear the consequences" are purposefully vague in order to maximize the range within which people watch

what they say. In 2007, authorities introduced two animated cartoon figures to the Internet. Their names—Jingjing and Chacha—are an obvious
attempt to make the word *jingcha* (警察, "police") seem playful. The two
cartoon-police pop up on computer screens and provide links through
which users can ask questions about which words are legal and which
are not and also can report any "unhealthful" posts that they might notice. But these mechanical functions are only secondary to Jingjing's and
Chacha's main mission. One police officer in Shenzhen, in a moment of
candor, acknowledged that "their main function is to intimidate, not to
answer questions."[17]

3. *Word filters.* Induced self-censorship has always been the CCP's
main censorship device, but it has not been enough to keep the lid on the
troublesome Internet, for which authorities have found that word filters
are necessary. Filters spot and delete "sensitive" terms. There are thousands of such terms, and they constantly grow in number on updated
lists. They include words like "truth," "dictatorship," and "human
rights"; dates like "June Fourth" (the date of the Beijing massacre in
1989); and personal names that include, interestingly, those of top Communists, such as Hu Jintao, as well as top anti-Communists, such as Hu
Ping.

Netizens play perpetual cat-and-mouse games to circumvent the filters. "June Fourth," for example, can be rewritten as "May 35th" or just
"535." For a time, the democracy manifesto called *lingba xianzhang* (零八
宪章, "Charter 08") was written as *linba xianzhang* (淋巴县长, "lymph-
node magistrate") until police decided that reference to lymph-node
magistrates had to be banned as well. In late February 2011, after police
banned *molihua* (茉莉花, "jasmine") in order to quell the notion of a Jasmine Revolution in China, some netizens, in a cunning countermeasure,
started using *lianghui* (两会, "two meetings") to stand for "Jasmine."
Lianghui is the standard abbreviation in CCP jargon for the huge meetings every year in March of the National People's Congress and the Chinese People's Political Consultative Conference. To ban *lianghui* on the
Internet would be to throw the planning for the two meetings into chaos,
and netizens knew that authorities could not do this.

4. *A firewall.* From the point of view of China's rulers, foreign countries are a main source of "sensitive" or "unhealthful" material on China's Internet. Accordingly, in the late 1990s, they conceived a Golden
Shield Project whose goal has been to keep undesirable material out. The
project, implemented in 2003, soon acquired the nickname the "Great
Firewall." Activists resent it intensely, and the tech-savvy among them
use virtual private networks and other means to "jump" it. Once on the
other side, they can gather information and bring it back inside, where, if
the information is interesting, it often spreads rapidly. But this is not to
say that the Great Firewall is ineffective. It still blocks much material, and
it creates a psychological wall along with the technical wall. Many netiz-

ens, content with the variety that already exists within the wall and knowing the dangers of getting caught jumping it, just stay inside.

But it is a serious error to suppose that freethinking comes only from outside the wall. In recent years, the principle that "it is wrong to send people to prison for their words" has gained considerable ground in Chinese netizen opinion, and most of the examples that have established this point are of protesters whose actions and imprisonments have been reported entirely *inside* the firewall. Most netizens have not needed the examples of internationally known dissidents in order to reach their conclusions.

5. *Guiding.* Broadly speaking, the duties of Internet police are of two major types: repression of dissenting speech and encouragement of "correct" speech. The latter function has a history in CCP politics that predates the Internet era. In Mao's day and well into the Deng Xiaoping era, the Party's Propaganda Department issued periodic bulletins that specified which ideas and terms should be "stressed" in the media.[18] People in "political study" meetings in Mao's day were obliged to show that they had mastered certain linguistic formulas. Today's Internet police are subtler but in essence aim at a similar result: in a process called *yindao* (引导, "guiding"),[19] they enter websites in the guise of ordinary users and post pro-government opinion.[20] Beginning in 2004, people were offered the opportunity to do this on a freelance basis for pay,[21] and soon thereafter these people earned the sarcastic sobriquet *wumao dang* (五毛党, "fifty-cent party") because they were believed to be paid fifty cents for each post they put up. Netizens invented the word *wao* and a new character to go with it in their honor (figure 4.1).

Figure 4.1. *Wao*

The "fifty-cent" initiative has not fared too well. Pro-government postings have become so repetitive and mechanical that Web users have little trouble spotting them. Fifty-centers succeed in correcting factual errors, but their efforts to reverse Internet opinion on issues like the Zhejiang train wreck have been overwhelmingly futile. Their postings even run the risk of undermining opinion that might be genuinely pro-government because they make any pro-government post subject to the suspicion that it was done for hire. Internet police at the local level are sometimes aware that their efforts are largely futile but continue routinely to pour fifty-cent posts onto the Internet just to show their higher-ups that they are doing their jobs. Satire of *wumao* has spread so much that in recent years the term has come to mean any regime apologist of any kind. Someone who says that the railcars in Zhejiang had to be buried in order to help with the rescue effort is a *zifei wumao* (自费五毛, "self-paid fifty-center"). Henry Kissinger, when he writes fulsome praise of Communist leaders, is a *yang wumao* (洋五毛, "foreign fifty-center").

It would be a mistake, however, to conclude that the regime's "guiding" as a whole has been a failure. The education system in a broader sense—in schools, the state media, and elsewhere—has had much success in shaping the thinking of young people. The Internet is making inroads, but they are still only inroads.

INTERNET LANGUAGE

One reason that citizen inroads have reached further on the Internet than in other media is that linguistic innovations have helped the Internet seem like a new, open realm. All human languages constantly evolve, of course, and in principle there is nothing new in having new terms appear on the Chinese Internet. But their production and spread there have been especially rapid—in part because of the need to evade word filters and other forms of censorship. (We should note the irony that the government's repression has indirectly increased the number of items that the government needs to repress.) Internet language has nurtured new subcultures in which style and camaraderie have become values in their own rights, and in which "cyberassembly" has emerged. The populations of these subcultures are primarily but not entirely the young.

New linguistic terms have come about in a number of different ways:

By double meanings. Some of the new terms grow from temporary code words that netizens have used in order to evade word filters. The term *zhengfu* ("government"), for example, counts as "sensitive," and efforts to skirt it have given rise to a number of new terms. One of these is *tianchao* (天朝, "heavenly dynasty"), which, besides avoiding filters, delivers the mischievous suggestion that the government is hardly modern. Another term for the regime, even more sly, is *Xi Chaoxian* (西朝鲜, "West Korea"; implicitly understood as West *North* Korea). The name "Mao Zedong" can get caught in a filter, too, so people use terms like *taizu* (太祖, "original emperor") for Mao or, even less respectfully, *larou* (腊肉, "cured meat") because Mao's corpse continues to lie, impervious to rot, in Tiananmen Square. The CCP's Department of Propaganda is referred to as the *zhenlibu* (真理部, "Ministry of Truth").

By sound. The words *fan zui* (犯罪, "commit crime") can startle the police, so people write 饭醉 ("drunk on rice") instead. A *guanliyuan* (管理员, "administrator"), who peers at what you are doing, can be rewritten as a 灌狸猿 ("watered weasel ape") (figure 4.2, upper left). The Xinhua

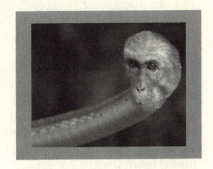

Figure 4.2. **Watered weasel ape (upper left); monkey snake (upper right); grass-mud horse (lower left); an invented Chinese character for "grass-mud horse" (lower right).**

News Service is the CCP's *hou she* (喉舌, "throat and tongue—mouth-piece"), or in other words, its 猴蛇 ("monkey snake") (figure 4.2, upper right). With the revival of "red culture" in Chongqing by its neo-Maoist mayor, Bo Xilai, netizens dubbed the city *Xihongshi* 西红柿, ("tomato"), a pun on 西红市 ("western red city"). Bo's surname literally means "thin," so netizens sometimes refer to him as *buhou Xilai* (不厚熙来, "not-thick Xilai"). China can be *chai ne* (拆呢, "demolish!") where the pun on the English word "China" carries the added zest of mentioning the wide-spread popular complaint about well-connected entrepreneurs who forcibly *chai* ("demolish") people's homes in order to build developments. Another way to refer to China has been *Jingdezhen* (景德镇), a city in Jiangxi famous for its porcelain—which is called, in English, "China." When codes become as indirect as this, they are a headache for Internet police, especially because they constantly shift.

One of the most famous Internet puns is *caonima* (草泥马, "grass-mud horse"), which, with a shift only of tone, can mean "fuck your mother" (see figure 4.2 for the animal and the invented Chinese character). Characters like this one (and the one noted for *wao* above) are playful novelties that circulate among the relatively small groups who enjoy such jokes. But the term *caonima* as a spoken word has a much broader range, reaching to many kinds of people both on and off the Internet. In a famous photograph, the artist Ai Weiwei leaps into the air, stark naked except for a stuffed-animal grass-mud horse that he holds over his genitals, where it *dang zhongyang* (挡中央, "blocks the center") (figure 4.3). And what exactly is blocking the center? The grass-mud horse, of course—so viewers are invited to imagine the full sentence *caonima dang zhongyang* (肏你妈,党中央, "up your mother's, Party Central"). The elegance of Ai's art is that he can produce this thought in viewers' minds without uttering a single syllable. To Internet police he can say, "You said it, not me."

Another widespread term is *héxiè* (河蟹, "river crab"), a near homonym of *héxié* (和谐, "harmony"). The Hu Jintao regime, in its public rhetoric, has put great stress on *hexie shehui* (和谐社会, "harmonious society"). By recasting the phrase as "river crab society," netizens invoke the image of the crab in Chinese folklore as a bully that sidles sideways. They use *hexie* as a verb as well as a noun. When a website is closed down or a computer screen goes blank, victims say, "I have been river-crabbed!," that is, "harmonized!" An image of a river crab wearing three watches (figure 4.4) has spread widely on the Web. This is satire of Jiang Zemin, who was Hu Jintao's predecessor as China's president and who chose to

Figure 4.3.   Ai Weiwei blocking Party Central with a grass-mud horse. Photo courtesy of Ai Weiwei.

Figure 4.4. River Crab

call his unique contribution to Marxist thought *sange daibiao* (三个代表, "the three represents"). With a twist, netizens made this *dai sange biao* (戴 三个表, "wearing three watches"). The river crab—the sideslipping bully—wears all three watches, that is, does all three "representings."

By shortening and lengthening. Young people writing on the Internet sometimes pull Chinese characters apart and string them out. *Hao* (好, "good"), for example, can be written as 女子 or *shu* (树, "tree") as 木又寸. Such usage, like others, may have originated to foil filters, but it has also evolved into a pattern that signals group identity. Older people can, to be sure, read messages that are strung out in this way but generally cannot do it as easily as the very cool young can. In other cases, Internet language compresses things. Another way to refer to Mao, for example, is *mao* (耄), a character that is properly pronounced in the fourth tone and means "extremely old" or "confused" but that, of course, can also be seen as *lao Mao* (老毛, "old Mao"). Another example of shortening is *xiudang* (修党, "repair Party"), where *xiu* is a phonetic contraction of *shiyou* (柿油, "persimmon oil"). *Shiyoudang* ("persimmon oil party"), in turn, is a homonym for *ziyoudang* ("freedom party") when pronounced in Wu and other southern dialects that do not use the retroflex initials of northern Mandarin. (In chapter 8 of his famous work "The True Story of Ah Q" (1922), the eminent modern writer Lu Xun described people who misunderstood "freedom party" as "persimmon oil party.") Today, *xiudang* refers to liberal intellectuals and others who would establish an independent political party if they could.

By borrowing. Many new Internet words are borrowed from English, Japanese, or other non-Chinese languages. Either sound or metaphor can be borrowed. *Chugui* (出柜, "come out of the closet—be openly gay") borrows a metaphor, while *fensi* (粉丝, "fans," meaning supporters, not air fans) borrows sound. The English word "hold" has been given the Chinese complement *zhu* (住) to produce "hold-*zhu*," meaning "control" or "be on top of." The term *egao* (恶搞) originated in Japanese video game culture, later spread to Taiwan, and then, when it reached the mainland

Chinese Internet, blossomed into a wide range of meanings. *E* is "evil" or "wicked," and *gao* is a colloquial and highly flexible word whose meanings range across "do," "make," and "work on" but often carry a somewhat negative flavor, rather like "mess with" in English. Depending on context, *egao* could be translated variously as "satire," "debunk," "parody," "skewer," "lampoon," "mock," "expose," "tear down," "upset," "invert," "dismantle," or "make fun of."

In addition to individual words, whole phrases—sometimes fairly long ones—can become standard in expressing second-level or even third-level meanings. We saw examples above in Wang Yongping's gaffes "It's a miracle" and "You can believe or not, but anyway I believe it." Another recent example is the phrase *wo zai ye buxiangxin aiqing* (我再也不相信爱情), which literally means "I will never believe in love any more" but has a much more general sense of "Now I've seen it all!" or "I'm totally disillusioned." (In US politics, if Dennis Kucinich announced his support of the Tea Party, one might say *"wo zai ye buxiangxin aiqing."*) In November 2011, Hu Zhanfan, a chief editor at the *Guangming Daily*, was appointed to head CCTV. Netizens unearthed a comment that Hu had made that "some news workers conceive themselves not as propagandists, but as professional journalists; this is a fundamental error of identity." Copying Hu's grammar and substituting other vocabulary, netizens posted sentences like "Some television viewers conceive of themselves not as receptacles of propaganda but as thinking persons; this is a fundamental error of identity," "Some people conceive of themselves not as grateful minions of the state, but as taxpayers; this is a fundamental error of identity," and "Comrade Hu Zhanfan conceives of himself not as a slave, but as a director of a television station; this is a fundamental error of identity." An informal online competition ensued to see who could deliver the most clever satire. The pattern itself acquired the nickname "Zhanfan formula."

The linguistic innovations have involved even grammar. When police summon people for interviews about dissident activity, they use the euphemism *he cha* (喝茶, "have tea"). The contribution of the police to the new usage was only vocabulary, not grammar. But on the Web, the passive marker *bei* (被) is added to create the sense of "suffer tea-drinking." A sentence like *wo zuotian bei he guo yici cha* (我昨天被喝过一次茶), literally "yesterday I was tea-drinked," actually means "the police called me in for interrogation yesterday." Here the grammatical innovation lies not only in the unconventional use of *bei* but also in the switch of *he cha* from an intransitive to a transitive verb: *he cha* is now something that party A can *do to* party B.

Some of the linguistic innovations that circulate on the Internet are confined largely to subcultures. "I have been tea-drinked" means something only to people who have interacted with the police over political issues or who know people who have. Gay and lesbian culture, to take another example, uses a special jargon that has arisen in part from resistance to censorship but also from interaction with gay and lesbian culture in Hong Kong, Taiwan, Japan, and the West. *Lazi* (拉子), which long has meant "lesbian" in Taiwan, came to the mainland Internet as *lala* (拉拉), while a more literal *leisibian* (蕾丝边, "lesbian") entered from English. "GL" (written in English letters) means "girls' love" and "BL" "boys' love." For centuries in China, *ji* (鸡, "chicken") and *ya* (鸭, "duck") have meant female and male sex workers, respectively, but now, with the Internet, we have *e* (鹅, "goose"), which can cater to either sex. There are many other examples.

But the most common of the new Chinese Internet phrases transcend subcultures and have spread from the Internet into other media and into general oral use. *Gei li* (给力, "gives power"), which spread first on the Internet, now has a very wide range of uses. A netizen who finds a way to "jump the firewall" might say, "This is really *geili*! Now I can watch YouTube!" A boring class in school could be "*bugeili*" ("not power-giving")—a real drag. A boss who hands out bonuses might be called "really *geili*!" Cool moves in video games, spiffy new dresses, and calisthenics that remove fat from one's abs all have been called *geili*. Another Internet term that has spread to society, *keng die* (坑爹, "killing me"), is used for things that are shockingly deceptive or fraudulent. For example, "The CCTV news tonight was all about Libya again, and not a word about the explosion in Jiangxi—*keng die*!" *Niubi* (牛屄, "cow cunt") originally meant "nonsense!" but later, used ironically, went viral to mean something like "fantastic!" or "frigging awesome!" A motorbike that can carry three people and still zip along is *niubi*.

DOES NEW LANGUAGE GIVE RISE TO NEW THOUGHT?

It is beyond the scope of this chapter to argue a position on the controversial Whorf hypothesis that holds, to put it simply, that the language a person speaks tends to determine the way a person thinks. Critics of Whorf have claimed that, at least sometimes, causality goes the other direction because thought can precede language and causes it to be what it is. But for the purposes of this chapter, the "direction of influence" question does not matter. China's new Internet lingo might give rise to new thinking, new thinking might create new Internet lingo, or both. What matters (for the purpose of this chapter) is only how the new "language + thought" relates to other systems of "language + thought" in Chinese society. On this question, the contrasts are sharp and the implications potentially far-reaching.

For years, scholars of the politics of language in contemporary China have observed a distinction between the "official" and "unofficial" levels of language.[22] Formal political Chinese has generally been more stan-

dardized and abstract and more influenced by Western-language grammar and vocabulary than has ordinary Chinese on the streets and in
home life, which has been more flexible, idiomatic, and concrete and has
deeper roots in Chinese culture. In the late Mao years, official Chinese
also took on a greater air of artificiality than it had had before. It became a
sort of public "language game" that people were obliged to play in order
to get certain things done, even as the game grew increasingly distant
from inner motives and feelings.

Now, in the Internet age, both the official and the unofficial kinds of
the Chinese language have grown in ways that make it useful to speak of
two major kinds of each. Within the official language, there is now an
important distinction between the traditional variety that appears in the
People's Daily and elsewhere (where *wodang* [我党], "our Party," often
caiqu cuoshi [采取措施], "take measures," and so on) and a "new officia-
lese" that appears in outlets like the *Global Times*, where the texture of
language is much closer to colloquial, unofficial patterns, but the rhetoric
as a whole is still "official" in the sense that it hews closely to guidelines
of the Department of Propaganda. The appearance of this new branch of
the official language can be seen in considerable measure as a response to
the rise of the Internet. Authorities have realized that if they want credibility with an Internet-savvy generation inside their country—to say
nothing of an international readership—they need to sound less rigid and
doctrinaire. Part of the effort to fashion "smart propaganda" in the new
age has been to adopt Internet lingo. On November 10, 2010, a lead headline in the *People's Daily* used *geili* as a verb: "Jiangsu *geilis* as a 'Power-
culture Province.'" During an unusual blizzard in southern China in the
winter of 2008, Wang Yang, the governor of Guangdong, gave a speech in
which he sought to assuage popular anger over rail stoppages. Wang
complimented netizens for being "well informed, thoughtful, and enthusiastic" and peppered his speech with trendy neologisms. He said he was
"willing to *guan shui* [灌水, "irrigate—rap on"] with you . . . [and] as for
the imperfections in our decisions and our work, we are happy to see you
pai zhuan [拍砖, "slap bricks—let it fly"].[23]

Within unofficial language, the "new branch" is primarily the Internet
language that we have been considering in this chapter, and the question
before us is how much it might be giving rise to new thought and culture.
Chinese activists have argued about whether Internet repartee is a mere
safety valve. Does it just let people blow off steam so that, once relieved,
they can more easily fit back into the status quo? Sometimes resistance
does seem little more than a fun game: Xinhua reports won't tell what
really happened? Okay, we will. You close us down for doing so? Okay,
we'll jump around and find another way. You keep doing it? Okay, we'll
satirize you as a bunch of crotchety river crabs. The "safety valve" theory
holds that this kind of resistance, which is almost recreational, may be

cathartic but does not really affect the way people think and behave in the offline world.

But others have argued that Internet sarcasm has deeper effects. Once it catches on, they say, it tends to spread. Satire of things like bullying and corruption naturally extend just as far as the problems themselves extend—which is very far indeed, potentially into every corner of society. There, in those myriad corners, satire can begin to rot the foundation on which bullying and corruption rest and "prepare the ground" for more significant change. One can even hope that regime change, when it eventually arrives, will be more likely to be peaceful than violent insofar as the ground for it has been softened. If we view you only as a quirky river crab, we will not be utterly shocked to see you depart the scene and will feel little need to hack you in half with a cleaver as you go.[24]

Figure 4.5. *Pimin*, or "fart people."

An important shift takes place when sarcastic terms spread into general use: they come increasingly to lose their sarcastic bite and to seem just like normal terms. To refer to China's ruling circles as *tianchao* (天朝, "heavenly dynasty") began as biting satire, but once it spread and became standard, the sarcasm drained away, and it turned simply into a way of saying "government." Similarly, *pimin* (屁民, "fart people"), rooted in the bitter comment that powerful people view ordinary people as mere farts, became just another way to say *laobaixing* (老百姓, "ordinary folk") (see the invented character, figure 4.5). But the seemingly innocuous process by which sarcastic terms are normalized can have profound consequences. It converts the terms from the relatively narrow role of expressing resistance to the much broader one of conceiving how the world normally is. When *tianchao* is used specifically as a jab at the regime, it is a tool with a purpose and can be countered with a return jab. But when it reflects and expresses normality, much more is at stake. The question of an alternative worldview emerges.

"CYBERASSEMBLY" ON THE INTERNET

Worldviews that differ from the official one are not new in the People's Republic of China. They certainly preceded the Internet. In the past, though, such views were almost entirely confined to private spaces—either to the privacy of individual minds or to small groups that were beyond public earshot. People who share alternative worldviews have not been allowed to hold public assemblies. The Internet, though, allows people to "meet" without meeting physically. Through online consultation, they can do many of the things that physical assemblies do in a free society: debate issues, argue over the wording of petitions and manifestos, sign statements, vote in polls, and bring public pressure to bear on specific issues—all while each sits separately in front of his or her computer screen.

Traditionally, when Chinese police have controlled physical assemblies, their techniques have been of three kinds: driving people out of a shared space, confining people within a shared space, or mingling within the shared space to audit and manipulate what happens there. Of these three activities, only the third works for cyberassemblies. Police audit chat rooms and try to "guide" opinion. But the other two kinds of traditional technique are largely ineffective. Breaking meetings up physically cannot work because people are already dispersed physically. The alternative of boxing them in physically does not work very well either. It used to be that authorities could close the gates to university campuses during politically "sensitive" times and that, because the whole campus was confined by walls, students and others could not get out. But this technique is obviously useless in blocking cyberassemblies. In cyberspace, the rapid forwarding of links can create "meetings" that no physical barrier can block.

Cybermeetings resemble physical meetings in some ways that have politically important implications. They are, first of all, autonomous assemblies that usually originate from the bottom up. Let us look at an example. On June 23, 2011, netizens discovered microblogs by a twenty-year-old beauty named Guo Meimei, who, as she flaunted expensive handbags and spiffy cars, claimed to be the "commercial general manager" at the Red Cross Society of China. After this netizen-discovered story went viral on the Internet, China's official media began to discuss it, too, and eventually it reached the international media. Netizens not only broke the story but drove public opinion on it, step-by-step. Online "assemblies" large and small denounced Guo Meimei, excoriated the Red Cross Society of China (to whom donations fell sharply despite the group's denial of any connection to Guo), raised suspicions about the entire world of philanthropy in China, and eventually decried the general decline in ethical norms in Chinese society as a whole.[25] The Guo Meimei case flared quickly but also receded quickly, and in such cases it is hard to say that it left behind an enduring "cyberorganization." In other cases, though, it is clear that online campaigns have indeed given birth to organizations. They have survived the issues that originally brought them together and have sometimes led to action in the outside (noncyber) world.

For example, on March 9, 2011, netizens in Nanjing noticed that workers had begun transplanting the stately French plane trees that line Northern Peace Boulevard in the city. Originally, there had been 900 of these trees, and forty had already been transplanted in order to make way for a new Line Three of the Nanjing subway. Someone posted data on the Internet showing that in 2006, when trees had been transplanted in order to build Line Two, 80 percent had died. Netizens took photos of the threatened trees and sent them to Huang Jianxiang, a famous Nanjing blogger. Huang formed a "Nanjing Plane Tree" microblog group, which attracted 8,000 members within hours.[26] Physically, this "group" was scattered throughout the Nanjing area and indeed across the country. Some of those who lived nearby stepped out of cyberspace and took to the streets, tying green ribbons around trees, taking more photos to put onto the Web, and delivering letters to the Nanjing Subway Authority. By March 17, more than 14,000 people had forwarded links about Huang Jianxiang's plane-tree group, and word had spread even to Taiwan, where Qiu Yi, a Taiwan legislator, took note and posted a strongly worded protest on Huang's blog. Qiu wrote that the trees not only meant something to Nanjing citizens but also were symbols of the spirit of Sun Yat-sen. Speaking as a ranking member of the Guomindang, Qiu expressed his "deepest protest" of the transplantation plan. Journalists in Taiwan began to follow up, and on March 20 the deputy mayor of Nanjing announced that the tree-moving project had been canceled.[27]

NEW IDENTITY ON THE INTERNET?

When netizens like the Nanjing plane-tree activists win a battle, they sometimes win more than the issue itself. Their cyberassembly can lead to personal relationships that endure both online and offline and that can be reactivated when new issues arise. Like assemblies in the physical world, cyberassemblies can lead to notions of personal identity as well. If I "am one of" the Nanjing plane-tree group, this becomes part of who I am, just as I might be a Buddhist, a Nanjing person, or a Chinese.

In addition to making new identities possible, Internet culture has subjected others, like national identity, to reimagination. What is it to be Chinese today, and how does netizen culture affect the question? The CCP has always offered a ready answer to the question of Chinese identity and has stressed it in the schools and the media: to be Chinese is to stand with the CCP. People have been trained for decades to take the terms "Party" and "country" as essentially coextensive. To depart the Party is to be not only politically incorrect but un-Chinese as well.

On the Internet, however, these axioms are being drawn into question, and alternative answers to the national identity question are beginning to appear. The terms *wodang* ("our Party") and *woguo* ("our [CCP-led] state"), which we have noted above, have come in for some satiric distancing. A few years ago, a netizen with a sly sense of humor began using the terms *guidang* (貴党, "your [honorable] Party") and *guiguo* (贵国, "your [honorable] state"). *Gui*, originally meaning "noble" or "expensive," has long been prefixed to nouns as a polite way to say "your": *guixing* (贵姓, "your honorable surname"), *gui furen* (贵夫人, "your esteemed wife"), and so on. *Guiguo* has also, for a long time, been an established term to mean "your country" when people from different countries are talking to each other in a formal way. But now, in some circles on the Internet, *guiguo* has taken on the sarcastic meaning of "*your* state" — the state that belongs to you rulers, not to me. The topic of "What is *guiguo*?" has popped up in Internet chat rooms. In one of these, in October 2010, a netizen wrote, "It turns out that this *guo* is not our *guo*, but the *guo* of a certain *dang*. This fact makes the terms *guiguo* and *guidang* appropriate." A few months later, another anonymous netizen was blunter: "It means I'm not going to dance with you bunch of SOBs anymore."[28]

As with other new usages on the Internet, the use of *gui* in this sarcastic meaning has "traveled" from term to term. In addition to *guiguo*, we now also have *guizhengfu* (贵政府, "your esteemed government"), *guiwai-jiaobu* (贵外交部, "your esteemed Foreign Ministry"), *guichao* (贵朝, "your esteemed dynasty"), and so on. As price inflation arrived during 2011, netizens also began to play on the ambiguity by which *gui* also means "expensive." *Guiguo* began to take on the second meaning of "inflation-ridden country" or "overpriced country" — in which housing, fuel, medical care, education, and access to political power all require too much money.

But if netizens are putting ironic distance between themselves and *guiguo*, the question arises of what, after the distancing, they *do* identify with at the national level. What *is* it, in the new day, to be Chinese? This is a big question, and the answers that are beginning to appear are only tentative.

Consider *pimin* (屁民, "fart people"), the playful tag that has come to stand in opposition *guiguo*. The *pimin* usage originated from an incident on October 29, 2008, when Lin Jiaxiang, a fifty-eight-year-old Communist Party official, was eating and drinking in a local restaurant and asked an eleven-year-old girl where the men's room was. For Lin, it was not enough that the girl point the way. He wanted to be shown right to the door. Once there, he grabbed the girl and tried to force her into the men's room. She escaped and ran to her parents. Her father confronted the would-be molester, and an argument ensued during which Lin pointed at the father and yelled, "I was sent here by the Ministry of Transportation! My rank is the same as your mayor's! You people are farts to me!

You wanna take me on?! You wanna test what I can do to you?!" Unfortunately for Lin, the exchange with the father was caught on surveillance camera and leaked to the Internet, where it went viral.[29] Lin eventually was fired, and "fart people" became a standard term. Gradually, it morphed into a term of pride. Fart people became "us," netizens and ordinary people, the ones on the receiving end of abuse, the ones who have no vote, the ones who empathize and identify with one another—the ones who, in short, form the polar opposite of *guiguo*.

The imbalance in power between *guiguo* and *pimin* is sometimes highlighted by the satiric use of *bei* (被), the usage we noted above in connection with "suffering tea-drinking." *Bei* originally meant "quilt" or, as a verb, "cover" but has also been used as a marker for "suffering (an action)." It has been useful in translating the passive voice from Western languages. Using *bei*, an English sentence like "my wallet has been stolen" can be rendered in Chinese as *wo de pibao bei tou le* (我的皮包被偷了). Now, as we noted above, *wo bei hexie le* (我被和谐了, "I have been harmonized") has become a standard quip when censors strike. The role of *bei* in the phrase is important. It signals that I suffered the action; it happened *to* me; it did not arise in any way from my volition. This "involuntarily passive" implication has led to a range of other sarcastic uses. One is *bei xingfu* (被幸福, literally "happiness-ified"). In the Mao era, it was said that the Great Leader *mou xingfu* (谋幸福, "sought happiness") for the people, but to be on the receiving end, then as now, is *bei xingfu*. Similarly, we are *bei manyi* (被满意, "made to be satisfied"). We look at the officials who "represent" us and see ourselves as *bei daibiao* (被代表, "suffering representation"). In each case, the point is that the "esteemed country" *acts on* the "fart people," not the other way around.

Guiguo, pimin, bei hexie, and other terms of this kind have some powerful implications. They imply that the twenty-first-century answer to the question "What is it to be Chinese?" does not have to be the formula China = CCP and that there is a terrain on which people can explore alternative answers to questions of identity. Terms that suggest other ideas—ones that contain *min* (民, "people"), for example—are becoming more salient. *Pimin* ("fart people") is sarcastic and as such does not provide a concept with which people will identify for long. But another word containing *min* is *gongmin* (公民, "citizen"), and it, too, has been spreading on the Internet. *Gongmin* is dignified. Like *pimin*, it establishes a distance between citizen and Party-state, but unlike *pimin*, it can be the basis of a new concept of national identity. *Gongmin* are people who have *quan* (权, "rights").

Talk on the Internet of rights of various kinds—the "right to know," the "right to express," the "right to monitor [officialdom]," and others—has been steadily increasing in recent years. In September 2011, Li Yan, a student at the Tsinghua University Law School who was doing research on the overlap of responsibilities of three government ministries (the

Ministries of Land and Resources, of Education, and of Science and Technology) and whose requests for information had been turned down, filed a lawsuit against the ministries on the basis of her "right to know."[30] For months after the high-speed train crash in Zhejiang and citing the same "right to know," netizens flooded the Ministry of Railways with demands that they publicize their lists of the names of victims. In October 2011, a Google search for the combination of the phrases "right to know" and "high-speed train" produced 3,750,000 results, which is at least some indication of how large numbers of people were conceiving the issue. In short, a restlessness is afoot within the Internet and its related subcultures, and language on the Internet reflects some changed modes of thinking.

INTERNET DISCOURSE IN PERSPECTIVE

The opening of space on the Internet for expression of authentic public opinion and the use of that opinion to bring pressure to bear on the state-run media and on officials who make decisions have already become established patterns in China. It is unlikely that they can be dislodged. A number of events in 2011 alone—the Guo Meimei Red Cross scandal, the Zhejiang train wreck, the crushing to death of toddler Wang Yue,[31] waves of netizens making the journey to visit blind activist Chen Guang-cheng at his home in Shandong province,[32] and others—show how the mechanisms by which people can be heard and can exert pressure are not only in place but almost regular and predictable as well.

Meanwhile, government efforts to repress this pattern are becoming less effective. Government budgets for policing the Internet have doubled several times since the late 1990s, but the numbers of computer users and cell phone users have grown even faster, and it is becoming clear that the police cannot keep up. For government leaders, the cost–benefit ratio of repression has grown ever higher. Some analysts of the Chinese Internet are predicting that the day will come when China's rulers judge that the results are no longer worth the costs. They might just back off and let the Internet go. (Their alternative of unplugging the entire Internet, although technically possible and although authorities did do this in Xinjiang for ten months during 2009–2010, would be difficult. Such a radical solution would cause turmoil in commerce as well as in politics.)

If the CCP were to set the Internet free, it could still rely on the other powerful tools at its disposal—police, surveillance cameras, informers, thugs, obedient courts, and prisons—to try to stay on top politically. Still, this would mark the collapse of its control of information, which, as we noted at the outset, has for decades been a vital strut to its power. The fact that China's rulers, at least so far, have worked hard to control the Internet shows that they themselves see how important the issue is. A free Internet would mean that the CCP, held to account by independent news reports, would have to argue from the truth—and that requirement, authorities realize, would present major new difficulties for them. In any case, the question of what will happen on the Internet is a source of uncertainty in China. One side is hopeful and the other apprehensive, and no one is confident.

NOTES

1. Li Jia (李佳), "Dong che shigu fa diyitiao qiuzhu weibo nühai cheng jiu pa huoche baozha" (动车事故发第一条求助微博女孩称就怕火车爆炸, In the first micro-blog after the train crash, a girl says she fears the carriage will explode), *Beijing Youth Daily*, July 28, 2011, http://chinadigitaltimes.net/chinese/2011/07.

2. "Directives from the Ministry of Truth: Wenzhou High-Speed Train Crash," *China Digital Times*, July 25, 2011, http://chinadigitaltimes.net/2011/07/directives-from-the-ministry-of-truth-wenzhou-high-speed-train-crash.

3. Liaoning Satellite TV, as shown on tv.sohu.com (辽宁卫视 《说天下》), July 25, 2011, http://tv.sohu.com/20110725/n314468330.shtml.

4. "Poll: 98% Say Wenzhou Train Buried to Destroy Evidence," *China Digital Times*, July 25, 2011, http://chinadigitaltimes.net/2011/07/poll-98-say-wenzhou-train-buried-to-destroy-evidence.

5. "Wang Yongping: China's High-Speed Trains Are a Living Miracle Wrought by the Chinese People under the Leadership of the Communist Party of China" (王勇平：中国高铁是中国人民在中国共产党领导下创造的人间奇迹), Xinhuanet.com, July 7, 2011, http://news.xinhuanet.com/video/2011-07/07/c_121637457.htm.

6. "One Hell of a 'Miracle'!!!" (他妈的"奇迹"), *Southern Weekend*, July 31, 2011, A23.

7. "Media Reveal Internal Information behind the 'Leap' of the Compensation Standards of High-Speed Railway Crash Incident" (媒体揭露动车事故赔偿标准实现"三级跳"内情), *Zhengzhou Evening News*, August 17, 2011, http://news.ifeng.com/mainland/special/wzdongchetuogui/content-3/detail_2011_08/17/8462344_0.shtml.

8. Tania Branigan, "Chinese Anger over Alleged Cover-Up of High-Speed Rail Crash," *Guardian Media Group*, July 25, 2011, http://www.guardian.co.uk/world/2011/jul/25/chinese-rail-crash-cover-up-claims.

9. Li Chengpeng "This Is a Miracle," *China Digital Times*, July 25, 2011, http://chinadigitaltimes.net/chinese/2011/07.

10. PC World, "A Brief History of the Internet in China," May 17, 2004, http://www.pcworld.idg.com.au/article/128099/china_celebrates_10_years_being_connected_internet?pp=2&fp=2&fpid=1.

11. Zhu Huaxin et al., "Analysis on Internet Public Opinion in China, 2007," in *Society of China: Analysis and Forecast 2008* (Beijing: Social Sciences Academic Press, January 2008), 236.

12. China Internet Network Information Center, "The 28th Statistical Report," http://www.cnnic.cn/research/bgxz/tjbg/201107/P020110721502208383670.pdf, 24.

13. China Internet Network Information Center, "The 28th Statistical Report," 15–16.

14. "Hu Jintao Asks Chinese Officials to Better Cope with the Internet," *People's Daily*, January 24, 2007, http://english.peopledaily.com.cn/200701/24/eng20070124_344445.html.

15. "Zhazhashishi tigao shehui guanli kexuehua shuiping, jianshe Zhongguo tese shehuizhuyi shehui guanli tixi" (Solidly raise the scientific level of societal management and establish a system of societal management with Chinese characteristics), *People's Daily*, February 20, 2011, http://politics.people.com.cn/GB/1024/13959222.html.

16. Committee to Protect Journalists, "2011 Prison Census: 179 Journalists Jailed Worldwide," December 1, 2011, http://www.cpj.org/imprisoned.

17. "Image of Internet Police: Jingjing and Chacha Online," *China Digital Times,* January 22, 2006, http://chinadigitaltimes.net/2006/01/image-of-internet-police-jing jing-and-chacha-online-hong-yan-o%C2%BAae%C2%A5%E2%84%A2aaio%C2%BAa.

18. See Michael Schoenhals, ed. and trans., "Selections from *Propaganda Trends,* an Organ of the CCP Central Propaganda Department," *Chinese Law and Government* 24, no. 4 (1992).

19. It is a sweet irony but utterly coincidental that the Chinese word *guiding* (规定, "stipulate"), when spelled in *hanyu pinyin,* is the same as the English word "guiding."

20. The intervention of Chinese government agents on domestic websites is a different project from their apparent work in cyberattacks on computers overseas. The latter topic is beyond the scope of this chapter.

21. CCP Department of Propaganda, Hefei, Anhui province, "Guanyu Nanchang, Changsha, Zhengzhou xuanchuan wenhua gongzuo de kaocha baogao" (Investigative report on propaganda and cultural work in Nanchang, Changsha and Zhengzhou), May 24, 2006.

22. For example, James H-Y. Tai, *Syntactic and Stylistic Changes in Modern Standard Chinese in the People's Republic of China since 1949* (Washington, DC: United States Information Agency, 1977); Michael Schoenhals, *Doing Things with Words in Chinese Politics: Five Studies* (Berkeley, CA: Center for Chinese Studies, 1992); Ji Fengyuan, *Linguistic Engineering: Language and Politics in Mao's China* (Honolulu: University of Hawaii Press, 2004); and Perry Link, *An Anatomy of Chinese: Rhythm, Metaphor, and Politics* (Cambridge, MA: Harvard University Press, 2013).

23. Quoted in Liu Xiaobo, "Imprisoning People for Words and the Power of Public Opinion," in *No Enemies, No Hatred: Selected Essays and Poems* (Cambridge, MA: Harvard University Press, 2012), 219.

24. Liu Xiaobo makes this argument well in "From Wang Shuo's Wicked Satire to Hu Ge's *Egao*: Political Humor in a Post-Totalitarian Dictatorship," in *No Enemies, No Hatred,* 177–87.

25. See Edward Wong, "An Online Scandal Underscores Chinese Distrust of State Charities," *New York Times,* July 3, 2011, http://www.nytimes.com/2011/07/04/world/asia/04china.html?_r=1.

26. Zhu Fulin, "Huang Jianxiang huyu wenhuaquan zhengjiu bei fa de Nanjing wutongshu (黄健翔呼吁文化圈拯救被伐的南京梧桐树, Huang Jianxiang calls on cultural circles to rescue Nanjing plane trees from cutting), *Nanjing Morning Post,* March 14, 2011, http://city.ifeng.com/cshz/nj/20110314/48492.shtml.

27. Yu Renfei, "Nanjing shiwei shuji: Ru baohu shengming ban baohu wutongshu" (南京市委书记：如保护生命般保护梧桐树, Nanjing Party secretary: Protect the French plane trees as we protect our lives), *Nanjing Morning Post,* March 23, 2011, http://city.ifeng.com/cshz/nj/20110314/48492.shtml.

28. SunQ, "Why Is Celestial Empire Called 'Honorable State(guiguo)'?" (大家为啥称天朝为"贵国"？), July 25, 2009, http://www.daibei.org/celestial-why-everyone-said-to-your-country.html.

29. "Lin Jiaxiang and the China Web Vigilantes," *China Digital Times,* November 22, 2008, http://chinadigitaltimes.net/2008/11/lin-jiaxiang-and-the-china-web-vigilantes.

30. "Qinghua nüsheng qisu sanbuwei xinxi gongkai yiweizhe gongmin jiandu zhengfu chao mai le yibu" (清华女生起诉三部委信息公开意味着公民监督政府朝前迈了一步, A Tsinghua student's lawsuit against three ministries for information transparency marks a step forward in the trend toward citizens' monitoring of the government), Chendi chuanmeiwang (晨笛传媒网), September 16, 2011, http://www.cdcmw.com/show.asp?id=2079.

31. "China: Two Arrested over Hit-and-Run Toddler," *China Digital Times,* October 23, 2011, http://chinadigitaltimes.net/2011/10/china-two-arrested-over-hit-and-run-toddler.

32. Andrew Jacobs, "Chinese Persist in Bids to Visit a Dissident," *New York Times*, October 24, 2011, http://www.nytimes.com/2011/10/25/world/asia/attempted-visits-to-chen-guangcheng-surge.html?_r=1.

FIVE

Han Han and the Public

Yang Lijun

The people who can mobilize the media apparatus today will become tomorrow's negative news; those who operate the state apparatus today will be caught by the state apparatus tomorrow. —Han Han, "The Chongqing American Opera"

The true patriot protects this country and does not let it become the victim of the government. —Speech at Xiamen University, February 5, 2010

I, on behalf of myself, will make a direct donation of zero yuan to the relevant authorities. —Diary, May 15, 2008

Toward the end of 2011, after nearly a half-year silence, the popular blogger Han Han wrote three articles on his blog—"On Revolution," "On Democracy," and "On Freedom"—in which he discussed some of the most sensitive issues in China today in a very direct way:

"Revolution may not be the best option for China." ("On Revolution")
"A revolution makes no guarantee of democracy." ("On Revolution")
"The quality of citizens will not prevent democracy from arriving, but it can determine its quality." ("On Democracy")
"Today, the Chinese Communist Party has 80 million members, and 300 million persons live in families that include a Party member. The Party is no longer just a political party, or even a class. The flaws of the Communist Party on the whole are also the flaws of the people. In my view a very strong one-party system is the same as a no-party system. When the Party organization reaches a certain size, it becomes the same thing as the people. The issue, therefore, is not to deal with the Communist Party in this way or that. The Communist Party is just a name. The system is just a name. If

you change the people, you change everything. That is why popular improvement is so important. Rule of law, education, culture . . . these are the basics." ("On Democracy")

For years, Han Han had been referred to, primarily by thinkers who call themselves China's "New Left," as belonging to the "right," together with the intellectuals who are known as the "liberals." (In fact, Han had no direct connection with the liberals, but that is another matter.) In any case, the lines quoted above marked the first time Han had written directly on the sensitive topic of democracy after he had become famous in China. What he wrote sent shock waves through the Chinese Internet and sparked a lively debate on democracy and revolution among intellectuals and ordinary netizens alike. Does China need democracy? What kind of democracy does China want? Will a revolution bring democracy to China? And so on.

The debate led to detailed examination of Han's personal position on democracy. Why had he changed from a pro-democracy position to one that questions democracy? Does he own an intellect that qualifies him to say anything significant about democracy? The New Left, formerly Han's critics, now found that he had become somewhat intellectually mature; on the other hand, the liberal intellectuals—people who formerly had supported him—now saw him as betraying the cause. Han's new position seemed to break the old molds of "left" and "right." People who attacked his new views on democracy came from both sides; his defenders also came from both sides. Within this great debate, which unfolded on the Internet, a blogger writing as Maitian (literally, "wheat field") questioned whether Han's works were really written by Han. Maitian soon retreated from the debate before long, making apologies to Han, but then Fang Zhouzi, who was already famous in academic circles for his many efforts at disclosing plagiarism, also began to publish pieces that questioned the authenticity of Han's writings. Fang suggested that Han's literary genius was a fraud and that he was not in fact the author of the works of Han Han. The debate, originally about democracy, turned into a widely watched war of attrition between Han and Fang that lasted about two months. Each side had substantial fan support.

From an intellectual point of view, there is little in the way of fresh ideas or arguments in Han Han's three articles on democracy, revolution, and freedom. So why, one might ask, did they spark such a tumult? Why did tens of millions of readers care? The answers lie in Han Han's background and his iconic position in the culture of China's youth.

1999–2009: FROM DEVIANT GENIUS TO YOUNG REBEL TO LEADING VOICE

Born in 1982, Han is a writer, a commenter on current affairs, and a professional race-car driver. As of June 3, 2012, his blog on Sina.com had attracted nearly 570 million visits, a national record, and since the end of 2009 his postings have averaged more than a million readers. His literary talents, good looks, and wealth—as one of the best-paid writers in China today—put him frequently on the covers of fashion magazines.

Many have loved him, calling him "the Lu Xun of Our Age" and "spokesperson for the 1980s generation." Some have even nominated him to be mayor of Shanghai should China ever hold open elections for such posts.[1] But others have disliked Han, saying that his commentaries lack depth and merely hit hot topics in order to attract naive readers.[2] Han has been controversial ever since he became famous in the late 1990s. His public image has gone through a number of stages.

In 1999, during his first year of senior high school, Han won first prize in the New Concept Essay Competition, an annual event organized by several Chinese universities and the prestigious Mengya Literature Press. The aim of the competition was to "promote creative thinking and writing." That same year, however, Han failed school examinations in seven different subjects and was not promoted to the second year of high school. The next year, 2000, he published a novel titled *San chong men* (Three-layered doorways) charging that the Chinese education system has a negative impact on students' personality development. The book became a hit, and as of 2012 it had sold more than 2 million copies. After doing the novel, Han again failed his exams and became a dropout.[3]

The sharply contrasting images that Han Han presented—as China's youngest best-selling writer as well as a spectacular academic underachiever—attracted wide attention in the media.[4] As news of the Han Han phenomenon spread, a heated debate arose over what was meant by "quality education" and the ways in which schools should account for both conventional talent and deviant genius like his.[5] During these years, Han was attracting a huge legion of followers among high school students, especially those who were disaffected with the educational systems they found themselves in. It was they who found greatest resonance with Han's maverick personality.

Meanwhile, in the mainstream of society and media, the young Han appeared as a brilliant aberration but hardly a model for all students.[6] Even his literary genius seemed merely ephemeral.[7] In the 2000s, though, Han continued to publish fiction at the rate of one or two volumes per year and became a race-car driver to boot. This only added to his fame among his following and brought him considerably more income as well, yet the mainstream media continued to ignore him. He stayed generally out of public sight.[8] In 2005, when he began blogging regularly, his many fans devoured his postings. But that attention was only a sliver of what he was getting by 2012.

Han's grand entry onto the public stage came in 2006, when he was twenty-four years old, in what came to be known as "the great Han-Bai debate." That debate was also what marked the shift in his public image from "deviant genius" to "young rebel."

On March 2, 2006, Han posted a blog entry called "Let's Be Frank: The Literary Arena Is Worthless" (*Wentan shi ge pi, shei ye bie zhuangbi*). This was in direct response to an article by literary critic Bai Ye titled "The Current Status and Future of the 1980s Generation" (*80hou xianzhuang yu weilai*). Han and Bai then locked horns on questions of who qualifies as a real writer, what authentic literature is, and the true nature of literary expression on the Internet. Distinguished figures, such as the writer Lu Tianming, the film director Lu Chuan, and the musician Gao Xiaosong, joined the battle on Bai Ye's side. Han fought back against this daunting opposition and generated a glowing hot spot on the Internet. His young fans swarmed onto the blogs of his adversaries, flooding their commentary sections with calumny. The war ended when Han's critics closed their blogs to avoid incessant bombardment. When the smoke had settled, netizens were left with deep impressions not only of Han Han's stunning rebelliousness but also of the amazing solidarity, belligerence, and feistiness of his fans.[9] Five years earlier, when *Three Layered Doorways* had been in vogue, Han's main theme was the lives of high school students, and his readers were also largely restricted to that group. Now, five years later, the Han–Bai debate had made Han known to a much wider circle, including opponents as well as supporters.[10]

Han's sudden rise to fame in 2006 had much to do with the expansion of the Chinese Internet at the time. But it also had to do with intrinsic features of the Han–Bai debate: its two famous antagonists and its language. On one side stood literary authority and orthodoxy, on the other youth and rebellion. Some people were turned off by the caustic language and personal attacks to which Han and his fans resorted, but many were also attracted by Han's untamed character and the cleverness he showed in verbal combat.[11] In addition to the Han–Bai debate, Han stimulated a second round of polemics by publishing a piece called "Why Are Modern Poetry and Poets Still with Us?" and three other articles that contained sharp critiques of modernist poetry and poets, and with this the poets also became his adversaries.[12] These controversies fixed Han's image in the public mind as an uninhibited young rebel who happened to write well.[13] It was his dominant image until 2008.

That year, 2008, was particularly eventful in China. First came the Tibetan uprising in March, then the Sichuan earthquake in May, then protests arising from Western media reports that were critical of the pre-Olympic torch relay,[14] then the Olympics themselves, then the great fire at the CCTV Tower,[15] and finally the scandal over the Sanlu company's tainted milk.[16] The massive crowds that were mobilized to welcome the Olympics became Han Han's cue to begin his career of blogging on current events. His public image turned into one of "commentator" on public affairs and "public intellectual." These changes brought a sharp increase in his popularity and the number of his readers, who now included not only disaffected youth and the "1980s generation" but many older people as well and many other sectors of society. Increasing numbers of young people in the elite, including members of the Communist Party, joined in following him.[17] The year 2008 was also the one in which Han Han's name began to appear with frequency in both the domestic and the international media. He won a number of prizes, and *Time* magazine named him one of the 100 most influential people in the world. In the remainder of this chapter, I focus on this third stage in Han's career, after 2008, and especially on his "voice" as a public intellectual.

HAN HAN'S VOICE

As of the end of May 2012, there were 296 articles in Han's Sina blog: six from 2006, twenty-three from 2007, 105 from 2008, seventy-eight from 2009, thirty-six from 2010, twenty-three from 2011, and twenty-five for January through May 2012. Originally, there were more than these, but some were later deleted either by the authorities or by Han Han himself. The year 2008 was clearly a watershed, both because of the number of blog posts and because of the change in their nature. Before 2008, most of Han's posts were still on literature and car racing; after 2008, most were critical commentary on topics in society and public affairs. Han had strong new appeal, but what exactly was he saying? What made him unique? Most of the themes of his blog pieces can be organized into three categories, discussed in the following sections.

The Problem of Radical Nationalism on the World Stage

In April 2008, young Chinese in several cities and abroad organized protests against what they perceived to be biased Western media reports on the uprising in Tibet the previous month. These "angry youth" established a website that they called Anti-CNN. Patriotism and anti-CNN feelings came into fashion among them, and their positions took on a strong flavor of moral self-righteousness. Anyone who expressed skepticism toward set views on Tibet or Western media bias was viewed as unpatriotic, and to be unpatriotic was equivalent to "betraying" or "selling out" one's country. Almost overnight, the founder of Anti-CNN, Rao Jin, became a national hero in the 1980s generation.

Amid this surge of hypernationalism, Han Han published a contrarian piece on his blog that he called "They're Afraid! They're Afraid!"[18] In it, he wrote,

> I have heard many people say that the Western media did this [biased reporting] because they are fearful. They fear the fact that we are growing powerful; they fear the sight of a powerful China and cannot accept the fact; and their behavior exhibits their fear. Never think in this way. Never. Just take it as a joke. We have quite a dilemma. This is a country where people have no right to watch CNN, yet also a country where we have the right to boycott CNN. Please carry on, you patriots. I will be just an onlooker.

Han's views provoked an anti-Han campaign in the "comments" section of his blog. The more moderate voices said they never would read his blog again, while the more radical ones, delivered anonymously, spewed invective such as "traitor," "un-Chinese,"[19] and "pretending it is cool to be ignorant."[20] But Han also maintained his core of staunch supporters, who praised him with words like "you represent liberty and independence."[21] There are signs, too, that Han's views had a certain effect in changing minds—in mollifying, for example, the nationalist boycott of Le Carrefour, the French supermarket chain, which had been scapegoated for an incident involving the procession of the Olympic torch through Paris.[22] The final sentence of Han's piece—"people have no right to watch CNN, yet . . . have the right to boycott CNN"—drew special praise and seems to have led quite a few people to reconsider their unquestioned commitment to the anti-CNN movement.[23]

The abusive language that was heaped on Han Han for "They're Afraid! They're Afraid!" seems only to have fed his rebellious tendencies. Without flinching, he went on to publish additional articles that were critical of radical nationalism.[24] In these, he stressed two themes: that pluralistic nationalism is preferable to "one-dimensional" nationalism and that "rational nationalism" is preferable to radical nationalism.

In a piece called "Going to a County Fair," Han cast doubt on the claims of radical nationalists that they were "fighting for beliefs they held in their hearts" when they boycotted Le Carrefour.[25] Han saw a recreational element in their protests:

> At this supermarket, some boycott, some erect banners, some seek to organize processions, and some just look on, while others aim to exhaust the change in cash registers by paying for inexpensive items with 100-yuan notes; still others pull the Chinese national flag halfway down at the front entrance of Le Carrefour and then take a photo so that they can accuse Le Carrefour of lowering the Chinese flag. . . . I really doubt whether these people are in fact so angry, or whether they simply have not been in a protest march or demonstration for a long time. Isn't it fun to join a procession? Isn't it fun to go to a county fair? How very safe to do these things under the mantle of nationalism! To

be sure, if you really cannot contain your patriotic sentiments, if you feel our country is critically at peril, as it was when the Eight-Nation Alliance invaded in 1900, and if you feel that the only solution is to protest in front of a supermarket, then I respect your choice and will eventually understand your feelings.

In a piece called "If You Were a Student," Han wrote,

Processions and gatherings are addictive. Today we do them in the name of patriotism and against foreigners; tomorrow we might do them in the name of patriotism and against . . . [you know who]. It follows that we will not always be supported. . . . Patriotism is not a certificate of blanket exoneration; on the contrary, it could well push you closer to . . . [you know what].[26]

In "An Urgent Demand That the World Imitate North Korea," he wrote,

While we aim our guns toward Western governments, we should bear in mind that people in the West can erect banners and their media can freely express their opinions without fear of government regulation. . . . We must accept differing voices. We should not fear dissenting voices. We should assume neither that the Chinese people will behave like Americans nor that the whole world will follow North Korea.[27]

When the American actress Sharon Stone, in reflecting on the repression in Tibet in March 2008 and the Sichuan earthquake that happened in May, wondered aloud whether "karma" was involved, the Chinese media spelled her meaning out as "the earthquake is an interesting act of retribution against China." After that, a wave of nationalist protest against Stone swept through China. On June 1, 2008, Han Han published a piece called "She Spoke at the Wrong Time, in the Wrong Place, and to the Wrong Media," in which he criticized the media for their distorted reports on Stone's remarks and urged netizens to make more rational judgments.[28] As in his earlier blogs on the Le Carrefour boycott, here again he was deliberately contrarian and stimulated a wave of abusive remarks. But comments on his blog also show that he led netizens to reflect on the issue in a less emotional way.[29]

In 2010, a clash between a Chinese fishing boat and a patrol ship from the Japanese coast guard in the area of the Diaoyu Islands in the East China Sea reignited a territorial dispute between China and Japan. Tensions mounted as radical nationalist passions emerged in both countries. In a blog piece called "Protecting Illegal Signs," Han criticized the Chinese government's manipulation of public opinion and reiterated his preference for "rational nationalism":

This indeed is a big event. The Ministry of Foreign Affairs even made the exception of granting overtime work on a weekend in order to launch the criticisms. If all of us Chinese are doing well and business is prospering, and wives, children, cars, houses, jobs, leisure and health care are all secured, and if we enjoy life, embrace a nationalist spirit and are no longer willing to follow [Deng Xiaoping's stratagem of] "lying low to wait for a chance to emerge," then we can of course go out to reclaim the Diaoyu Island region. But if you cannot even protect your rights and property at home, it would be better to attend to those first.[30]

Money Worship, Lack of Empathy, Corruption, and the Environment

The Sichuan earthquake of 2008 elicited an outpouring of sympathy for its victims and sparked a nationwide donation drive to help them. But the drive involved some pernicious patterns as well. People in many state-run offices and enterprises were obliged to donate via deductions from their pay, and there were questions about whether the funds actually reached victims. People on the Internet began to compare the sizes of the donations that artists and celebrities made, claiming that the numbers were measures of their patriotism. Those who donated relatively less were jeered and subjected to verbal abuse. On May 15, 2008, in satire of this practice, Han Han wrote on his blog that "I, on behalf of myself, will make a direct donation of zero yuan to the relevant authorities." At the time the blog appeared, Han had already arrived in person at the Sichuan earthquake zone to join in rescue efforts. In blog posts called "News," "Diary," and "Goodbye, Sichuan," he gave firsthand reports of rescue activities and used his huge personal influence to urge people to make donations for desperately needed items like tents and medical supplies.[31]

In November 2009, China was shocked by a news story about a salvage company that had refused—on grounds that the proposed payment was insufficient—to recover the bodies of several students who had just died trying to save drowning children in a river. In a blog piece called "People in the Same Boat," Han lambasted China's money-above-all mentality, showed how it could lead to chilling insensitivity, and traced its causes to the circles of power and money that dominate society.[32] In other pieces, Han addressed China's food safety problems (see also chapter 12 in this volume),[33] the pervasiveness of fraud and artificiality across different sectors of society,[34] environmental pollution (see also chapter 10 in this volume), and widespread resentment of the wealthy among common people.

Flaws in Government

In 2008, Han began producing articles that criticized corruption and incompetence in government at several levels.[35] In a speech at Xiamen University, he archly suggested that "true patriotism is to protect this country and not to let her become the victim of the government."[36] In January 2009, he wrote several pieces pointing to government use of earthquake rescue funds for kickbacks and the purchase of luxury cars.[37]

In July, he published a piece called "I'd Love to Use Them" in which he lampooned the expenditure of 1,491,234 yuan—after what were apparently politically corrupt bids—to renovate the toilets on the first and second floors of the Great Hall of the People.[38] In pieces called "Here Is the Country That Observes National Day, and Here Is the City That Hosts the World's Fair" and "Don't Offer Your Hand or They Will Arrest You for Sure," Han exposes illegal law enforcement measures that authorities use to make their cities look better by sweeping bad-looking people out of sight.[39]

In "Superhighway G8," Han exposed a Shanghai city government project to spend 200 million yuan to change all the highway signboards in the city. "40,000 yuan per sign," Han observed.[40] His point was not signs but corruption. His widely read blog gave rise to popular demands to investigate the sign replacements, and eventually the authorities who were in charge of the *Xinmin Evening Post*, which had first reported the story, ordered *Post* staff to correct its report and make proper explanations. The staff complied, now explaining that there were 250,000 highway signboards to be changed, so 200 million yuan was a reasonable amount. Han, typically astute, answered in another blog that there could not possibly be that many signboards on the 600 kilometers of Shanghai highways. For this to be true, there would have to be four signs every ten meters. The government's correction could be nothing but a new lie to cover up an old one.[41]

"Give Us a Few Pickles to Eat" was a sharp criticism of new government limits on the speed and weight of battery-powered bicycles. The rules, in Han's view, showed callous disregard for the lives and needs of low-income people.[42] "The City Makes People Die Early" tells of a girl whose legs were crushed in a traffic accident. It should have been a nonfatal injury, but the girl died when the ambulance bringing her to the hospital became trapped in traffic gridlock.[43] "Han Feng Is a Good Official" mocks the "you're fine, we're fine" ethic that masks the endemic corruption in Chinese officialdom.[44] Two pieces, "Where Am I Going to Find Somebody as Good as You?" and "Letters from Strangers," show how hard it is for ordinary people to get justice from courts that are not independent of political authority.[45] They can rely only on the "letters and visits" system to appeal to higher authorities, but that seldom gets them anywhere. In "Who Are You and Why Are You Asking about This?," Han takes on the city government in Chengdu, Sichuan, which apparently told citizens that it had auctioned off government buildings in order to raise funds for earthquake relief. Then, after the buildings had been handed over, a pledge of 120 million yuan was never honored.[46]

It was blog posts like these, in the period after 2008, that caused Han Han's readership to soar into the millions and that drew much more media attention, both domestic and foreign, than he had had before. During the same period, Han's blogs began to draw special attention from government censors of the Internet. His more outspoken pieces began to be deleted shortly after they appeared. His pace of posting blogs also went into sharp decline—although it is unclear how much this was due to censorship and how much because he simply wrote fewer of them. But in any case, the content of his blog posts grew ever sharper.

HOW GOVERNMENT, THE MEDIA, FANS, AND DETRACTORS HAVE ALL HELPED TO SHAPE HAN HAN

When Han Han began his writing career in 1999, government censors largely ignored him because his fan base was small. Ten years later, a much larger fan base helped Han stay the hand of the censors—who were now paying him a good deal of attention—because they now had to worry that obvious repression of a popular figure would make them look bad to millions of people in China and even to some people overseas.

As Han's fame grew, his relations with the media might be called mutually exploitative. In the hypercommercial era that arose in the 1990s, the media have been interested primarily in commercial advantage. For them, a personality like Han Han's—and the issues that he raises—generate news stories that in turn generate profits. Han Han's side of the bargain is that the media help to expand his reader base, which provides him vital support.

Han's relations with his readers—both those who love him and those who do not—has often been interactive. His sharp views tend to cause readers to take sides, either pro or con, and even to switch back and forth in their sympathies. He challenges readers, listens to them, makes adjustments or rebuttals, then comes back to them again, listens again, and so on. A dramatic example of this appeared on October 9, 2010, when Han published a blog piece titled "October 8, 2010." The whole piece consisted of a single pair of quotation marks: " ". Thousands of fans rushed to the comment section of Han's blog to speculate on what their idol had meant. Had he suddenly become lazy? Was "nothing" a kind of "something"? Or what? Eventually, the message was deciphered and generally accepted to mean "Liu Xiaobo won the Nobel Peace Prize" (which had been announced in Oslo on October 8).[47] It was an officially "unspeakable" event that had occurred on that very day. In addition to saying something by saying nothing, by publishing open quotation marks, Han Han had essentially invited netizens to discuss—by indirection, if they liked—the life and achievements of Liu Xiaobo, his Charter 08, and other related topics that the government had for months been repressing.[48] Someone writing from the *Apple Daily* in Hong Kong wrote on Han's blog that "the Internet police, dressed for battle, keep deleting posts, but there is no way they can stem the tide of thousands of short comments, and this is why it happens that, thanks to Han Han's fans, many young people who did not even know Liu Xiaobo's name are getting their first lessons in democracy and human rights."

The fans commenting on Liu Xiaobo included many who, four years earlier, had already been at work during the Han–Bai debate flooding Bai Ye's blog with defenses of Han Han, who had been back-and-forthing with them ever since. They had continually pressed him to comment on an ever-widening range of political and social issues and especially did so during the debates that followed his provocative blogs on the anti-CNN website and the Beijing Olympics. Han explicitly commented on these pressures from readers in his famous piece called "They're Afraid! They're Afraid!," which I have cited above. Readers may have demanded more political commentary partly as a way to divert him from certain other topics, including Japanese porn videos. Han had recently been engaged in a polemic over whether such videos do or do not actually poison the minds of youth. When he began writing blogs, topics related to sex had helped to attract attention. But now it was turning some people off. One netizen (who apparently did not know about the sex in Han's early blogs) commented anonymously,

> I find it hard to express my feelings. I don't really know why you suddenly changed like this. You indeed have changed. You are not as clean as you used to be. Still I am happy that many people support you, because you have been my favorite writer for the last two years. I still remember your writings back then. But now . . . I don't love you anymore. As you have said, you are an idol and your behavior has wide influence. So what should we make of this kind of behavior? Does it measure up to your responsibilities? [49]

Another wrote, "You really are bored, brother, to write so many articles on Japanese women. It's time to get down to real business and write on something more important." Another asked, "Is this what you mean by 'worrying about the nation'?" [50] Others piled on, some calling Han's articles "rubbish" [51] and some saying that they would abandon him.

When he listened to these criticisms and did turn more toward political and social criticism, which involved his treading on politically sensitive turf, his followers showed their loyalty by expressing concern for his safety and praising him for his courage and outspokenness. [52] Some said they wished to see him become mainland China's Li Ao (a famous government critic and essayist in Taiwan). [53] From the comments on Han's blog that followed the government's detention of the famous artist Ai Weiwei in the spring of 2011, it is clear that many of his fans worried that Han's daring might land him in the same trouble that befell Ai Weiwei. Some urged Han to stick with the coded expression that he was so good at; others thought he should avoid "sensitive" issues entirely. Here again, it is apparent that the public figure of Han Han was an artifact not only of his own unusual talents and personality but of guidance from his readers as well. Many readers sent stories of their own troubles to Han, appealing to him to find justice for them by publicizing this or that unfairness. In "Letters from Strangers," Han comments on the many letters of this kind that he receives.[54]

Some of the people who follow Han are not fans but critics. The same traits that attract fans—his unique points of view and his zest for intellectual debate—are what attract and also frustrate his detractors. While his fan base grew during 1999–2000, a significant base of detractors also started to grow during the 2008 debates and tended to center in certain places like the ultraleftist website *Utopia*. When debate grew hot, as it did over the series of pieces Han published on "rational patriotism versus nationalist extremism" in 2008, verbal jousting with adversaries came to preoccupy Han. In that sense, his opponents have also contributed to shaping him.

WHY DO HAN HAN'S FOLLOWERS LIKE HIM (OR NOT)?

The core of Han Han's following has been the high school fans who began reading him in the late 1990s. They are the people who follow him (even adulate him), call him *"lao da"* (big number one—our leader), and see the world through his eyes. Although many began as naive, wide-eyed followers, some gained in maturity as they went along.[55] The influences between Han Han and his readers have been mutual, as we have just seen. But more important than who has influenced whom, what binds Han Han and his readers most tightly are the values they share. Han speaks for these values even though he did not create them single-handedly.

A perusal of the comments on Han's blog makes it fairly clear that a majority of his fans are about his age, born in the 1980s, mostly urban, and in some cases well educated. This "post-80s" generation has benefited from China's rapid economic growth but also feels the pressures of an extremely competitive social environment. They struggle for jobs and money, are anxious about dating (see chapter 9 in this volume), and have trouble affording the soaring costs of urban housing. Their values depart in significant ways from those of their parents, and, as Shuyu Kong makes clear in chapter 6 in this volume, they enjoy limited "public space." Han Han opens a channel for them and serves as their megaphone. Han's attention to prostitutes, migrant workers, ordinary urban people, and other social underdogs created considerable resonance with readers. More specifically, though, just what do they find attractive? Here are some reader testimonies attached to his blog piece called "The Cost of Love":[56]

- Netizen 1: Young people like his coolness; thinkers like his depth and acuity; young girls like his looks and image; the wronged like him for speaking out on their behalf; rights-defenders like him for his defense of the victims of injustice; old men like him for his lovely courage as a young man.

- Netizen 2: His incisive comments—like "there are two kinds of logic: the first is logic; the other is Chinese logic"—are the lifeblood of his commentaries on current affairs. He is quick-witted, humorous, and able to expose the absurdity of things with a simple logic that makes it plain to people who have suffered decades of brainwashing that something they hold as self-evident may just not be the case. *News Weekly* in Guangzhou remarked at the end of 2008 that Han has met the standard for a public intellectual and that "his rational thinking makes us feel a sense of hope for the 1980s generation."
- Netizen 3: He speaks truth to power. When the powerful are harsh in repressing free speech, people venerate Han Han for daring to voice things that we have in mind but cannot say.

Most comments praise Han for being frank, sharp, combative, witty, and brilliantly terse; his sympathy for underdogs; and his good looks. In my own view, however, his biggest advantages are his inner qualities. His carefree outlook, independence of thought, willful authenticity, and aloof attitude toward the rich and powerful would be virtues at any time or place but are especially rare and important in China's current social environment.

Han is valuable to his followers for exemplifying a successful path through life that flouts the expectations of mainstream Chinese society. He forged this route without a college degree, an overseas credential, a rich or powerful father, or a state-sector job. He has earned a lot of money from book royalties and car racing but does not flaunt that wealth, preferring to live the ordinary life of a young person in suburban Shanghai. He could easily capitalize on his fame, for example, by attending opening ceremonies or speaking at public events, as many famous Chinese, even artists and scholars, often do. But he chooses not to and seems to abide by this choice as a way to preserve his independence, which allows him to avoid the entanglements that commitments to social events inevitably bring. It is a choice that very few others make in the money-rules-everything society of China today. In November 2009, Han was invited to give a speech at the World Expo Forum and the Fourth Jiading Auto Forum. When the organizer asked him to deliver a speech titled "Chengshi rang shenghuo geng meihao" (The city improves living), he changed the title to "Chengshi rang shenghuo geng zaogao" (The city screws up living) and said, among other things, that "this is the nature of the Chinese metropolis: it destroys the dreams of millions in order to produce one or two *nouveaux riches*."[57] This is typical Han Han. He prefers personal authenticity to cooperation with the powerful. When he describes himself, he protests that he is only telling it like it is. But it is exactly his frankness that is so rare in China today and therefore is so admired by others. Lu Jinbo, a friend of Han's, sees his honesty as contagious and describes him as "exporting values."[58] Han himself has observed that "if I lose my popularity some day, that will be because everybody is thinking and speaking like me, and therefore doesn't need me anymore. Society will have progressed. I await that day."[59]

But Han Han also has several kinds of detractors. Some parents and high school teachers, even if they like what Han Han writes, worry that his record of dropping out of school is a bad model for young people. Some in the intellectual elite also express dislike for Han even while sharing many of his opinions. Although they may not have read much of what he writes—viewing it as mere commercial activity—they nevertheless doubt his qualifications to make critical judgments on political and social issues simply on grounds that he has not attended college. The liberal columnist Xu Zhiyuan, for example, has written that "the popular craze for Han reflects the inner emptiness, shallowness and insecurity of a rising national power. A smart young man dares to speak some truth in public and thereby rattles the nerves of a whole generation? Is this a victory for Han Han, or is it a victory for mediocrity and a failure of the Chinese nation?"[60] There are, in addition, government workers at several levels who fear Han for his quick, sharp, and stout social criticism. Still others, especially China's New Left, dislike him for ideological reasons. In their eyes, Han is too pro-West because his essays are consistently critical of the Chinese government while speaking well of the American and other Western governments. The leftist website *Utopia*, for example, hosts a column called "Critical Analysis of Han Han" (*Han Han pingxi*) devoted to critiques of Han that attribute "rightist populism" to him.[61] Some of these articles do concede that Han's rise springs largely from pent-up anger at authorities among ordinary people and from resentment of the extremely limited space for social criticism. But they still attribute Han's popularity to a kind of anti-intellectualism that results from youthful frustration and disaffection that they regard as a natural by-product of China's modernization process. The phrase "worship of holy children" (*shenghai chongbai*) was invented to name this phenomenon.

WHAT MAKES HAN HAN DISTINCTIVE?

Many different voices are audible in early twenty-first-century China. Social critics, professional and amateur, impinge from many directions. Why, in this context, does Han Han's voice attract such a large audience—arguably the largest of all? How can we explain this phenomenon, and what are its consequences?

Jeremy Brown, in chapter 1 in this volume, attributes Han's broad influence to his concentration on political and social issues that are central in popular thinking: political corruption, a widening income gap, injustice for weak social groups, and corruption that results from the government's monopoly on political power. Han's candor on these topics has earned him "public intellectual" status, and yet, because these issues are highly sensitive from the government's point of view, he has sometimes made strategic retreats from them. In my judgment, Han has often faced hard choices among taking on more political risk, remaining silent, or settling for issues of lower risk.

Compared to other prominent voices, Han's stands out for addressing concrete problems and events rather than abstract "isms." Most other voices fall into one or two of the camps called the New Left, which advocates "back to state socialism," and the "liberals," who push for human rights and democracy. Both camps speak in terms of "isms," which, for the great majority of ordinary Chinese, are just words on paper. Before the appearance of Han's essays on democracy, revolution, and freedom at the end of 2011, his writing did not mention such terms. He wrote only about specific social problems. He has drawn a line, too, between criticizing the government and criticizing the Communist Party. He addresses problems in government without mentioning the difference between one-party and multiparty systems. Perhaps these are only tactics, but they work better in attracting audiences than anything the New Left or the liberals have been doing. Elites have a bent for ideological struggle, but concrete analysis resonates much better with the public. Such a focus also protects Han. People in the establishment might dislike his inveterate attention to the government's shortcomings and to the "dark side" of the Chinese society, but his focus is concrete, and the problems that he addresses just stay there, unsolved, and their existence remains hard to deny. They do not disappear by invoking any "ism." There is, in addition, the problem that many mainstream intellectuals have been co-opted through material rewards into roles of advising the state. Han's essays would not have had such a major impact were it not that intellectuals have chosen to abdicate their critical roles, preferring instead to focus almost entirely on serving the government by offering "wise policy prescriptions."

Another factor in Han's broad popular appeal is his ability to stay loyal to a largely voiceless majority in China even as he bobs and weaves among shifting political currents, taking criticism from the New Left and sometimes from the liberal camp as well. On May 28, 2011, he published an essay called "Guide to the Game" in which he supported the idea of allowing independent candidates to run for positions as people's representatives. Here, Han seemed to be impatient with China's slow progress toward reform and to be pushing for democratization. But then, after "Guide to the Game," he suddenly fell silent on the topic of democracy, leading many of his fans to suspect that the government was blocking him. Near the end of 2011, however, he startled his readers with his three articles on the highly sensitive issues of democracy, revolution, and freedom in which he seemed to slow down and take a more incremental approach to political reform. In January 2012, he published a piece called "My 2011" in which he acknowledged this change of gear, noting wryly that "I will no longer try to please anyone but my daughter."[62]

The shift was costly for Han. Many of his followers, including some Chinese liberals, saw it as a betrayal, and some even voiced fears that Han had been bought by the Communist Party's Propaganda Department. It is more plausible, though, to see the change as part of Han's characteristic pattern of speaking for a silent majority. The Arab revolutions had fueled spirited debate in China over what the nation's basic direction should be—democracy? revolution? reform?—and the debate had led to some vitriolic extremism, especially between the two poles of New Left and liberal. In Han's view, although most people are not happy with the performance of the government and burgeoning social problems, they also are wary of this or that radicalism that might destabilize society. People of this view, although a majority, were largely not heard within the cacophony of voices. Anyone who might say something for an incremental approach could be severely attacked by both New Leftists and liberals. Han, accordingly, thought he should give such people voice. At the same time, though, he did not abandon his satire of government misbehavior, as shown two pieces: "The Chongqing American Opera," which uses the Wang Lijun incident to satirize top-level power struggles that happen inside black boxes,[63] and "Let Some People Have the Vote First," which mischievously plays on Deng Xiaoping's famous phrase, in inaugurating special economic zones more than thirty years earlier, that said "let some people get rich first." Government censors quickly deleted both these pieces from the Internet.

From deviant genius to public intellectual, Han has grown and matured, and his fans have undergone a similar transformation. He has had relations of mutual influence with both of his major partners—the Internet and his fan base. Some say that the Internet made Han, but it is also true that Han has helped shape China's Internet. He has influenced many fans, but they have influenced him as well. Han's unique approach to political issues has gained him wide recognition as a public intellectual but at the same time put him precariously at the brink of political risk. The mainstream of his fans have been liberals who share most of his values. Still, in his essays on revolution, democracy, and freedom, Han showed that he could be independent of his liberal backers. In retaliating against Han for his waywardness, the liberals showed in turn that they could retrieve him to what they view as a more appropriate position. In any case, although what Han thinks seems to be very stable, what he chooses to put into words can ebb and flow with the political climate.

Temporary silence, when it occurs, has its logic, and sometimes he makes his points metaphorically, but we can hope there will never be a time when he chooses not to make them at all.

NOTES

1. "Du Han Han boke" (Reading Han Han's blog), March 11, 2010, http://www.zaobao.com.sg/forum/pages2/forum_lx100311f.shtml (accessed June 27, 2011).

2. Comments on "Tamen haipa le! Tamen haipa le!" (They're afraid! They're afraid!) http://blog.sina.com.cn/s/blog_4701280b010091cn.html#comment8 (accessed July 4, 2011).

3. "Han Han: Baidu baike," http://baike.baidu.com/view/5972.htm (accessed June 27, 2011).

4. "Zhengyi Han Han, linglei tiancai chulu hezai?" (The Han Han controversy: What is the way out for a deviant genius?), http://edu.sina.com.cn/focus/hanhan.shtml (accessed June 27, 2011); "Piancai shaonian Han Han he biaozhun youdengsheng Huang Silu" (Han Han the deviant genius and a standard good student Huang Silu), http://edu.sina.com.cn/job/2000-11-26/15889.shtml (accessed June 27, 2011).

5. "Zai zhengyizhong chengzheng: Han Han dang'an" (Growing up in controversy: Han Han's profile), http://info.edu.hc360.com/2009/02/011645167201-3.shtml (accessed June 20, 2011); "80hou, linglei shaonian Han Han" (The generation of the 80s: Han Han the atypical youth), http://www.beelink.com.cn/20040709/1624541.shtml (accessed June 27, 2011).

6. "Piancai shaonian Han Han he biaozhun youdengsheng Huang Silu."

7. "Zhiyi 'Han Han yizu': Chushu dilinghua zhishi shangye yunzuo xianxiang" (A skeptical view of "the Han Han type": Publishing books by juveniles is only a commercial maneuver), http://edu.sina.com.cn/i/18876.shtml (accessed June 27, 2011).

8. "Han Han: Baidu baike."

9. On the Han-Bai debate, see "Dang zhengguijun yudao shandawang Han Han" (When a formal army encounters Han Han, the king of mountain bandits), http://book.sohu.com/s2006/dbyydhh (accessed June 26, 2012).

10. http://book.sohu.com/s2006/dbyydhh (accessed June 27, 2011).

11. http://book.sohu.com/s2006/dbyydhh.

12. "Xiandaishi he shiren weishenme hai zai?" (Why are modern poetry and poets still with is?), http://culture.163.com/06/0930/16/2S9HN8DH00281MU3.html (accessed June 27, 2011). This article and Han Han's polemical articles attacking Bai Ye were later deleted by Han Han himself.

13. "Dajia zhi wendou" (Fighting with letters), http://alexbaby1.blog.sohu.com/1192403.html (accessed June 27, 2011); see also the comment by Datoucheng in the commentary section of Han Han's blog, http://blog.sina.com.cn/s/blog_4701280b01000ce8.html#comment44 (accessed June 28, 2011).

14. See Xinhuanet, "Xifang meiti paozhi bushi Xizang baodao qipian shijie minzhong" (The Western media make false reports on Tibet to deceive the world's people), March 28, 2008, http://news.xinhuanet.com/world/2008-03/22/content_7837849.htm (accessed June 3, 2012).

15. See Xinhuanet, "Zhongyang dianshitai beipeilou tufa dahuo" (A fire erupts in CCTV's north building), http://news.sina.com.cn/c/2009-02-10/021417179629.shtml (accessed June 3, 2012).

16. See Lianhezaobao, "Zhongguo dunaifen shijian zhuanti baodaoji" (A collection of articles on China's poisoned milk events), http://www.zaobao.com.sg/special/china/milk/milk.shtml (accessed June 3, 2012).

17. See the comments of Xiao Qigai ("Little Beggar") on "Youxi zhinan," May 28, 2011, http://blog.sina.com.cn/s/blog_4701280b010183ny.html#comment10 (accessed September 30, 2011).

18. "Tamen haipa le! Tamen haipa le," http://blog.sina.com.cn/s/blog_4701280b010091cn.html (accessed September 19, 2011).

19. http://blog.sina.com.cn/s/blog_4701280b010091cn.html#comment3 (accessed July 4, 2011).

20. http://blog.sina.com.cn/s/blog_4701280b010091cn.html#comment7 (accessed July 4, 2011).

21. Comment by LUCYREN, http://blog.sina.com.cn/s/blog_4701280b010091cn.html#comment2 (accessed July 4, 2011).

22. Comments by Wubie, http://blog.sina.com.cn/s/blog_4701280b010091cn.html#comment7 (accessed July 4, 2011), and by Disiwei, http://blog.sina.com.cn/s/blog_4701280b010091cn.html#comment10 (accessed July 4, 2011).

23. http://blog.sina.com.cn/s/blog_4701280b010091cn.html#comment5 (accessed July 4, 2011).

24. For example, "Ganji" (Going to the country fair), April 20, 2008; "Wen" (My question), April 21, 2008; "Jingzhun duijiao dahanjian, shengdong buzhuo maiguozei, weiyou nikang" (What do we use to capture the traitors and catch the turncoats? Nikon!), April 22, 2008; "Aiguo geng ai mianzi" (Love face more than one's country), April 23, 2008; "Huida aiguozhe de wenti" (Answering the questions of the patriots), April 23, 2008; "Ruguo nishi xuesheng" (If you were a student), April 23, 2008; "Wo yao liangkuai qian" (I want two dollars), April 26, 2008; and "Qianglie yaoqiu shijie he Chaoxian yiyang" (An urgent demand that the world imitate North Korea), April 29, 2008.

25. "Ganji," http://blog.sina.com.cn/s/blog_4701280b010092vq.html (accessed July 13, 2011).

26. "Ruguo nishi xuesheng," http://blog.sina.com.cn/s/blog_4701280b010094qa.html (accessed July 13, 2011).

27. "Qianglie yaoqiu shijie he chaoxian yiyang," http://blog.sina.com.cn/s/blog_4701280b0100964k.html (accessed July 13, 2011).

28. Ta zai cuowu de shijian, cuowu de didian, he cuowu de meiti shuo," http://blog.sina.com.cn/s/blog_4701280b01009j6d.html (accessed July 14, 2011).

29. See, for example, the comments of Kongzhongfei, http://blog.sina.com.cn/s/blog_4701280b01009j6d.html#comment9 (accessed July 14, 2011).

30. "Baozhu feifa zifu," http://blog.sina.com.cn/s/blog_4701280b0100lcum.html (accessed June 3, 2012).

31. "Xiaoxi" (Message), May 16, 2008, http://blog.sina.com.cn/s/blog_4701280b01009cnz.html (accessed June 3, 2012); "Riji" (Diary, May 17, 2008), http://blog.sina.com.cn/s/blog_4701280b01009d42.html (accessed June 3, 2012); "Zaijian Sichuan" (Good-bye Sichuan), May 21, 2008, http://blog.sina.com.cn/s/blog_4701280b01009f7p.html (accessed June 3, 2012).

32. Han Han, "Yitiao chuanshang de ren" (People in the same boat), November 5, 2009, http://blog.sina.com.cn/s/blog_4701280b0100fpjr.html (accessed July 27, 2011).

33. "Texuan wudu naifen gong chukou he aoyunhui" (Selecting untainted milk for export and the Beijing Olympics, September 17, 2008, http://blog.sina.com.cn/s/blog_4701280b0100aor3.html (accessed July 23, 2011).

34. "Zheng Jichao yingshi jidi" (Zheng Jichao's film base), December 14, 2008, http://blog.sina.com.cn/s/blog_4701280b0100bk7c.html (accessed June 3, 2012); "Wumao xianxingji" (Fifty-centers in action), December 23, 2008, http://blog.sina.com.cn/s/blog_4701280b0100bmx2.html (accessed June 3, 2012).

35. See, for example, "Hanlei quan chezhu shu: Liuxia mailuqian" (A tearful entreaty to car owners: Leave behind some money to buy roads), January 18, 2009, http://blog.sina.com.cn/s/blog_4701280b0100bwqu.html (accessed July 23, 2011).

36. "Zhongguo wei shenme bushi wenhua daguo" (Why China is not a great cultural power), speech at Xiamen University, http://www.20ju.com/content/V138906.htm (accessed February 23, 2012).

37. "Zaiqu zhengfu caigou mang, beichuan chushou zui dafang" (Governments in the disaster regions are busy buying things, and northern Sichuan is most spendthrift

of all), January 21, 2009, http://blog.sina.com.cn/s/blog_4701280b0100bxke.html (accessed July 23, 2011); "Huozhe de ren yao genghao de huoxiaqu" (Those who have survived should lead better lives), January 22, 2009, http://blog.sina.com.cn/s/blog_4701280b0100bxug.html (accessed July 23, 2011); "Beichuan zhengfu jixu sahuang" (Northern Sichuan governments continue to lie), January 23, 2009, http://blog.sina.com.cn/s/blog_4701280b0100by9s.html (accessed July 23, 2011).

38. "Wo henxiang shang," July 1, 2009, http://blog.sina.com.cn/s/blog_4701280b0100dva6.html (accessed July 25, 2011).

39. "Zheige guojia jiang yinglai guoqing, zheige chengshi jiang yinglai shibo," September 16, 2009, http://blog.sina.com.cn/s/blog_4701280b0100ey1x.html (accessed July 25, 2011); "Mo shenshou, shenshou bi beizhua," October 26, 2009, http://blog.sina.com.cn/s/blog_4701280b0100fk2m.html (accessed July 25, 2011).

40. "G8 gaosugonglu," October 13, 2009, http://blog.sina.com.cn/s/blog_4701280b0100fc2s.html (accessed July 25, 2011).

41. "Zhe shi yige pangda he fuza de gongcheng" (This is a huge and complex engineering project), October 15, 2009, http://blog.sina.com.cn/s/blog_4701280b0100fej4.html (accessed July 27, 2011).

42. "Gei dian xiancai chi," December 14, 2009, http://blog.sina.com.cn/s/blog_4701280b0100g8zf.html (accessed July 27, 2011).

43. "Chengshi rang renmin side zao," December 23, 2009, http://blog.sina.com.cn/s/blog_4701280b0100gcs5.html (accessed July 28, 2011).

44. "Han Feng shi ge hao ganbu," March 4, 2010, http://blog.sina.com.cn/s/blog_4701280b0100h7b2.html (accessed July 28, 2011).

45. "Wo qu nali zhao, xiang ni name hao?," March 14, 2010, http://blog.sina.com.cn/s/blog_4701280b0100hcf6.html (accessed June 26, 2012); "Moshengren de laixin," http://blog.sina.com.cn/s/blog_4701280b0100hrm2.html (accessed September 20, 2011).

46. "Ni shi shei, wen zheige ganma?," January 20, 2011, http://blog.sina.com.cn/s/blog_4701280b01017hsy.html (accessed August 31, 2011).

47. Han's code was broken by a piece called "Han Han boke 2010nian 10yue 8ri de zhenshi yiyi" (The true meaning of October 8, 2010, in Han Han's blog piece) by someone writing under the pseudonym Paodiao de qingchuan (Youth out of tune), http://blog.sina.com.cn/s/blog_4ee204410100mlf6.html (accessed September 18, 2011).

48. On Liu Xiaobo, see Perry Link, Tien-chi Liao Martin, and Liu Xia, eds. *No Enemies, No Hatred: Selected Essays and Poems of Liu Xiaobo* (Cambridge, MA: Harvard University Press, 2012).

49. Anonymous comment on Han Han's "Yizhong zhongyao dongxi de daotui" (The decline of something important), http://blog.sina.com.cn/s/blog_4701280b010090xs.html#comment16 (accessed September 19, 2011).

50. Comments of Ikscb and Wawa on "Yizhong zhongyao dongxi de daotui," http://blog.sina.com.cn/s/blog_4701280b010090xs.html#comment17 (accessed September 19, 2011).

51. Comment of Sunlight Happy on "Yizhong zhongyao dongxi de daotui," http://blog.sina.com.cn/s/blog_4701280b010090xs.html#comment19 (accessed September 19, 2011).

52. Comment Moonkiss on "Youxi zhinan" (Guide to the game), http://blog.sina.com.cn/s/blog_4701280b010183ny.html#comment19 (accessed September 19, 2011).

53. Anonymous comment on on "Youxi zhinan," http://blog.sina.com.cn/s/blog_4701280b010183ny.html#comment15 (accessed September 30, 2011).

54. See note 45.

55. See the comments of Celuntianxia and Xiaokanrensheng on Han Han's blog, June 30, 2010, http://blog.sina.com.cn/s/blog_4701280b010185jh.html#comment2 (accessed September 30, 2011).

56. "Ai de daijia," http://blog.sina.com.cn/s/blog_4701280b01017iv8.html#comment31 and http://blog.sina.com.cn/s/blog_4701280b01017iv8.html#comment32 (accessed June 3, 2012).

57. "Chengshi rang shenghuo geng zaogao," http://v.youku.com/v_show/id_XMTY4NTM0NjIw.html (accessed October 19, 2011).

58. Lu Jinbo, "Han Han: Yu Shijie baochi juli" (Han Han: Keeping a distance from the world), April 11, 2011, http://blog.sina.com.cn/s/blog_467a4bd101017age.html (accessed September 29, 2011).

59. Lu Jinbo, "Han Han."

60. Xu Zhiyuan, "Han Han shou tuichong shi yongzhong de shengli" (The adulation of Han Han shows the mediocrity of the public), http://yule.sohu.com/20100511/n272049331.shtml (accessed February 23, 2012).

61. http://www.wyzxsx.com/Article/Special/hhgou/Index.html and http://www.wyzxsx.com/Article/view/201104/227484.html (accessed September 30, 2011).

62. "Wo de 2011" (My 2011), January 8, 2012, http://blog.sina.com.cn/s/blog_4701280b0102dzqy.html (accessed February 23, 2012).

63. Wang Lijun, head of the Chongqing police, entered the US consulate on February 6, 2012 in Chengdu, Sichuan, asking for protection even as he leaked word that the wife of his boss, the ambitious "princeling" Bo Xilai, Party secretary of Chongqing and a member of the Political Bureau, was responsible for the murder of a British citizen. Shortly thereafter, Bo Xilai fell from power.

SIX

Are You the One?

The Competing Public Voices of China's Post-1980s Generation

Shuyu Kong

Ma Nuo did not expect to become notorious, even though she was bold enough to take part in *Are You the One? (Feicheng wurao)*, a TV dating program recently launched by Jiangsu Satellite Television (JSTV). With its unusual format of twenty-four young women standing behind a string of podiums trying to decide, based on the performance of a single male contestant, whether they want to become his "girlfriend," the program quickly became the most talked about show in China.

During the January 17, 2010, episode, the highly attractive Ma was identified by Zhao Chen, a twenty-three-year-old freelance fashion magazine writer, as his favorite girl. When Zhao asked, "Are you willing to go out riding bicycles with me?," Ma, obviously unimpressed by this shy and slightly eccentric guy, giggled as she blurted out her cutting reply: "I would rather sit crying in a BMW!" Ma's offhand comment and shockingly materialistic attitude touched a raw nerve with younger male viewers, and she immediately became the most controversial figure on the show.

In March 2010, when Liu Yunchao, a typical "second-generation rich kid" (*fu erdai*), presented himself to the twenty-four female contestants, the enormous sum of 6 million yuan was flashed on a big screen as an estimate of his personal fortune. Liu set his sights on the infamous Ma Nuo, casually mentioning that he had three luxury racing cars and was currently customizing a BMW. He invited Ma to "cry in my BMW!" His shameless flaunting of his wealth caused another firestorm of debate among netizens and reopened the wound caused by Ma's caustic BMW remark.

The Ma Nuo controversy came to a head on April 3, when a tough-looking male contestant from Shanghai, Luo Lei, took the stage. His main attack came soon after the screening of his second self-introductory video clip and was aimed directly at Ma Nuo:

> I am here for those netizens who go online everyday just to write a couple of lines of criticism despite the fact that they are exhausted after a full day's work. Have you ever thought of them? Now I have some words for you, Ma Nuo. You shouldn't stay on this show any longer because nobody can satisfy your picky demands. This program is for women who are sincere about coming here to find a boyfriend. You should leave so there is more space for people who are sincere about looking for their other half. . . . The program that really suits you is a beauty pageant where all the new millionaires will be present. You won't need to worry about crying in a BMW; you could even have a runny nose in a Porsche!

"I am not that kind of person," Ma Nuo blurted out in a trembling voice, then turned away from the podium and stumbled off the stage.

This most dramatic episode of *Are You the One?* went viral and was especially popular among the young netizens whom Luo claimed to represent. On Baidu's *Are You the One?* chat room in the following days, comments were posted at a rate of 500 per minute, reaching over 40,000 posts each day. A single thread, "Do you support Luo Lei or sympathize with Ma Nuo," attracted 26,111 posts. But on the Ma Nuo net bar, a post titled "The man who made Ma Nuo cry and leave is not a real man!" received 103,404 hits and had 1,600 followers (data collected on November 12, 2011).[1] There was a range of opinion: some claimed that Ma deserved what she got for being so contemptuous and materialistic, while others felt that she was at least honest and that her materialistic attitude only reflected the dominant values of society.[2] Some blamed Luo Lei for being self-righteous and misogynist, while others praised him as a hero avenging all males for their humiliations at the hands of these demanding women. Some claimed that it was all just a joke, a cynical way for Luo to stage a show to promote his own career, while still others suspected that it was a scripted drama staged by the TV producers just to boost the show's ratings.

After it was launched in January 2010, *Are You the One?* soon became the most controversial reality TV show in China, thanks to episodes that featured Ma Nuo. With its ranks of fashionably dressed, attractive female contestants; the intrusive and ego-deflating questions thrown at the male contestants; and, most of all, the heated debates on various social topics that it stimulated, both onstage and online, it remained for some time at the top of national TV ratings and inspired a string of copycat shows by other provincial satellite TV channels.[3] Enthusiastic contestants from all over China and even a few foreigners tried their luck at finding a date on the show. In four months, the number of applications to compete on the show eclipsed 170,000, and JSTV had to set up five offices in different cities to process all the enthusiastic candidates.

But after JSTV successfully fought off its competitors and began to sell space to major advertisers, exploiting the market value of its enormous audience, the bright flame of *Are You the One?* just as quickly appeared to burn itself out. In mid-June 2010, it was one of the main targets of the State Administration for Film, Radio, and Television (SARFT), which criticized the show for promoting immoral characters and unhealthy ideas. Its very existence was threatened. Chinese Central Television (CCTV) twice criticized the program and similar dating shows on its News Network (*Xinwen lianbo*, June 12) and on the current affairs program *Focus* (*Jiaodian fangtan*, June 11) with Ma Nuo's escapades repeatedly shown onscreen as negative examples. Only a quick and strategic response from JSTV, coupled with the show's enormous popularity, ultimately saved the day, and the program—in modified form—remains one of China's most popular TV spectacles.

Why is this TV show so popular? Why does SARFT regard an entertainment program as so "harmful"? What makes it stand out from numerous other dating and entertainment shows on TV screens? What does it tell us about China's post-1980s generation of restless young adults and their ways of dealing with "the critical problem of existential anxiety about meaning, identity and moral relativism"[4] at a time of dramatic political, economic, and cultural transformation? And how does this TV show and its associated Internet sites and fan clubs create a public space where individual expressions of personal dreams and private emotions are turned into the competing public voices of the post-1980s generation?

In this chapter, I examine the controversy surrounding *Are You the One?* and locate it within the larger context of China's new media culture and its changing formats and functions in a society where social values are in transition and hotly debated. By analyzing the issues confronted on the stage and in emotional online audience responses among various Internet fan communities, I provide evidence of a new form of civic engagement that has been largely overlooked by scholars of Chinese society and politics, that is, the communication of "lifestyle politics" in public space, especially among the well-networked urban Chinese youth who were born into a globalized communication environment.[5]

By "public space," I mean a real or virtual space where social issues and concerns can be publicly presented and discussed and where a range of social groups and actors can interact.[6] In previous studies of Chinese society and culture, the problem of public discourse and public sphere has been limited generally to discussions of elite cultural production, such as investigative reports, independent films and documentaries, and Internet-based intellectual debates. Few researchers have paid attention to the public space constructed by popular media shows or the interaction between entertainment programs (including TV reality shows) and Internet/social media communities. Examining the public space created by *Are You the One?*—between the rock of commercialization and the hard place of political censorship—provides an excellent opportunity to demonstrate how a popular entertainment show and its new media correlates can unexpectedly give expression to the voices of the post-1980s generation of viewers and provide a platform that this generation can use to articulate its own "lifestyle politics" through self-representations and self-expression in a globalizing society.

THE LOCALIZATION OF AN INTERNATIONAL DATING SHOW FOR CHINA'S POST-1980S GENERATION

Global TV audiences will recognize that *Are You the One?* is an international appropriation of the dating show *Take Me Out*. Developed by Fremantle Media based in London, this pacesetting dating game show had already been licensed to stations in half a dozen countries by early 2010, when JSTV and Hunan Satellite TV (HSTV) began competing to purchase the Chinese license. Ironically, even though HSTV was the successful bidder and soon launched its officially licensed clone *Let's Date!* (*Women yuehui ba*), it was JSTV's slightly adapted, unlicensed version *Are You the One?* that won the biggest audience share and transformed the show into a phenomenally popular indigenous brand.

To understand what makes the program so successful, one has to understand matchmaking in the social context of the emergence of so-called leftover unmarried women and men (*shengnan/shengnü*) who are the product of an accelerated pace of life in China. Intense career pressure, heightened social mobility, and loosened social bonds have caused China's urban generation to experience a trend that one finds in other contemporary international urban environments. Many young people have little time to find a partner, and contemporary urban life patterns have generated few convenient channels for meeting suitable people. Further, given the fact that China's younger generation is a product of both economic reform and the one-child policy, their marriages have become matters of great import and urgency to their families and to society more broadly. According to Tian Fanjiang, the head of a matchmaking website that has developed a partner relationship with *Are You the One?*, "There are 180 million single people in China. . . . They and their parents are worried about the marriage problem."[7] Thus, part of the immense appeal of *Are You the One?* lies in its professed goal of helping contestants meet the right person. And compared with its Western counterparts, where a more casual and flirtatious atmosphere of "just dating" prevails, the show adopts a much more serious and pragmatic approach to matchmaking. One male contestant put it bluntly: "This is the most efficient way to compare twenty-four women at one time and choose the most suitable life partner, and unlike one-on-one dating, you don't even need to pay for dinner when you meet them!" The program's enormous viewership ensures that even those male contestants who are rejected by all the females on the show will generally be deluged with online offers of dates from female viewers who watched and then contacted them using the dedicated e-mail address posted at the end of each episode.

Yet from the perspective of the TV station, the show has an additional agenda. According to Wang Gang, the producer of *Are You the One?*, when the show was first conceived, it was intended "not to be a pure dating or entertainment program, but to concern itself with various hot button topics, including housing issues, children, in-law relationships, income, careers, and DINKs [double income no kids], all the social issues that emerge during the dating process."[8] In other words, rather than simply provide a chance for people to find a life partner, one aim of the producers was to make the show into a platform for exploring the issues that most deeply concern its most important demographic population of contestants and viewers,[9] namely, young people of the post-1980s generation. Wang also noted that when his team carried out initial research for the proposed program, it found that "there was no vehicle offered in the mainstream media for the new generation to freely express its ideas about love, family, and marriage." One could say that *Are You the One?* is framed as a post-1980s generation coming-of-age ritual. In other words, by opening up space for these young people to express themselves in front of a broad national public, the show not only acts as a practical way for contestants to find a partner and proclaim their adulthood but also provides a symbolic stage for them to express their personal values and beliefs and to debate these values with others of their generation and other generations.

Representing some 200 million Chinese born between 1980 and 1989, the post-1980s generation is the new face of postsocialist China, the direct product of China's one-child policy, as well as the beneficiary of Deng Xiaoping's vision of economic reform and opening to the world. They grew up in a period when politics were no longer primary and material needs were placed first, and they have felt pressure to vie with their peers in an increasingly competitive, market-based society and to avoid being left behind in the rat race. At the same time, they are also the first generation to experience China's reemergence in the world economic and political order, and (through modern technology and increasing contact with the outside world as immigrants, foreign students, and media consumers) they have a more cosmopolitan appearance and have received a lot

more material benefits from globalization compared to previous generations. They differ from their parents, most of whom were born in the
1950s and early 1960s and experienced the bitter persecutions of the Cultural Revolution. They also differ from people in their late thirties and
forties who still remember the privations of their childhood and the brief
period of enlightenment and idealism before 1989. Because of this generation gap, they not only find that they have little to inherit spiritually
from their parents and grandparents[10] but also have to search for new
values and moral meanings through "competing and conflicting influences" in an increasingly pluralized society.[11] Older generations typically
view the post-1980s generation as self-centered, overly pragmatic and
materialistic, and ignorant of social responsibility and political issues. Yet
diverse international influences and the increasing pluralization of Chinese society in recent decades reveal that this judgment is an oversim-
plification. This generation is not monolithic. There are plenty of younger
people who engage in serious reflection on the problems associated with
their generation and who are willing to take on social responsibilities in
their own unique ways.

JSTV's effort to take *Are You the One?* beyond superficial entertainment and engage with deeper "hot button" social issues is reflected in its
choice of cohosts. In contrast to "Paddy" McGuinness of the British show
Take Me Out, a comedian whose joking around encourages lighthearted
banter among the contestants, the two initial cohosts of the Chinese program, Meng Fei and Le Jia, were specifically chosen for their weighty
professional backgrounds. Bald, warmhearted "brother Meng" established his reputation as an anchor and reporter for *Ground Zero Nanjing*, a
local news and current affairs program on Jiangsu TV. He proved himself
to be a knowledgeable commentator and a serious journalist of moral
integrity. In *Are You the One?*, he encourages the contestants to discuss
social issues linked to their self-presentations, while his frequently in-
serted personal opinions add social relevance to seemingly trivial topics.
At the same time, his self-deprecating humor and mature, balanced tone
help the contestants relax and defuse some of the tense arguments that
break out among them. Meng is backed up by his equally bald cohost Le
Jia, a psychology consultant who is supposed to give character analysis
and advice to contestants about how to handle their emotional problems.
During his initial appearances, Le seemed sharp and ruthless, never
afraid to give the more outspoken contestants a good dressing-down for
their ridiculous prejudices. But over time, Le proved to be a sensitive
judge of character, able to release his private emotions and share his own
difficult personal experiences with contestants. These two hosts, who
clearly have real affection and respect for each other, create a complementary environment of compassionate, paternalistic concern and
psychological/moral guidance for the contestants and, by extension, for
the viewers. At the same time, they are quick to spot opportunities to

shift the focus to broader social controversies that often surface during the show.

One final feature that helped *Are You the One?* rise to the top of the ratings, as demonstrated in the Ma Nuo controversy, is the enormous communicative network that developed around the show, mainly via social media and Internet fan sites. In the past decade, China has seen explosive growth in Internet usage, and the Internet has transformed the cultural lives and social communication of people in a profound way. By early 2012, China had 513 million Internet users and 900 million mobile phone users, including 355 million who go online via cell phones. Among them, 325 million people went online to consume digital video products.[12] At the outset, *Are You the One?* set up an online registration function and formed alliances with several online matchmaking websites, including Shiji Jiayuan wang (Shijijiayuan.com) and Baihe wang (Baihe.com), to solicit contestants and assist in promotional efforts. Its producers also exploited the huge potential online viewership by making every episode of the program available in archives on the official website of JSTV or on You Ku, China's largest digital video storage site. This made it very easy for viewers to share the shows with their virtual friends through instant messaging and social network services. And through Twitter feeds and personal blogs, viewer comments about the show were immediately distributed to hundreds, even thousands, of potential viewers. This kind of interactive viewing of TV shows (including soap operas) is particularly common among students and young professionals, who make up the two largest groups of the 124 million users of social network services in China, constituting 50.3 and 31.1 percent of the total, respectively.[13] The interactive features provided by the Internet have resulted in an enormous proliferation of fan websites, discussion lists, and personal blogs for various shows and have created new forms of social interaction about and around media texts in a way (instant and multidirected) not seen in conventional print and electronic media.

Several unofficial virtual communities were set up by *Are You the One?* enthusiasts on such popular search engines as Baidu and Tengxun, but the show's producers also actively cultivated online debates, social media, and mobile communications to keep viewers involved and engaged between episodes. The show reached out to online audiences by setting up its own official website listing the personal information of the contestants, providing contact information and video clips of them, and creating a discussion forum for visitors to express their opinions about issues raised on the show. The show's hosts regularly participated. In addition to social issues, popular topics for comments on these various official and unofficial online sites include positive and negative opinions about the participants, analysis of the reasons for male contestant failure or success, and speculation about ways to be invited to the show. It is clear that for many netizens, the virtual community surrounding the program functions as an invaluable classroom for learning about how to present themselves successfully in public and win the heart not only of the young woman but also of potential employers.

THE SURVIVAL ANXIETIES OF THE POST-1980S GENERATION

As many viewers noted online, in the first few months following its launch, *Are You the One?* consciously manipulated its choices of female contestants and its controversial presentations of male contestants to attract viewers and boost ratings. In other words, in order to win in a fiercely contested "eyeball economy," the producers created a staged drama aimed at manufacturing controversy (*zhizao huati*).

The male contestants were initially presented by means of a series of professionally produced self-introduction videos, shown to the female contestants and viewers in several stages—"basic personal information" (*jiben qingkuang*), "life plan" (*rensheng guihua*), "my ideal girl" (*lixiang nüsheng*), and "comments from friends or relatives"—with particular emphasis on the careers and financial situations of male contestants.[14] Indeed, each male contestant's job and monthly income were highlighted on the screen, as was detail about whether he owned a car or a home. The central attention given to financial success points to one aspect of a new set of values among many younger Chinese: one's sense of adulthood and masculinity is associated with career achievements, especially in business, and one's ability to achieve material success is one of the most important factors in winning the heart of the "ideal woman."

The way male contestants presented themselves was closely related to the representation of female contestants, all of which was achieved by careful selection of candidates and judicious editing of each episode. For the first six months, many up-and-coming models, actresses, and performers were chosen partly because of their above-average attractiveness but also, just as important, for their outgoing personalities and willingness to make daring comments. A major part of the controversy the show generated was associated with these so-called material girls (*baijin nü*), women who openly expressed their contempt for losers and their desire to find a wealthy man. Zhu Zhenfang, a migrant office worker in Wenzhou, made it clear that men who want to date her must have an income of at least 200,000 yuan a month (far higher than the average provincial-city monthly salary of about 2,000 yuan). She frequently made outrageous comments when rejecting male contestants, including "I didn't smell a luxurious mansion on him." Yu Xia called herself a "three-good female" (*sanhao nüsheng*)—good figure, good style, and good character—and she claimed to be looking for a "man with the four haves" (*siyou nanren*)—good shape, quality, money, and assets. And, of course, there was Ma Nuo, whose cutting remarks included the following put-down of an inexperienced admirer: "The number of girls you have dated is not even a fraction of the men I have dated!"

To be sure, some of these "outrageous comments" were hyperbolic gimmicks that some of the contestants, both male and female, employed to turn the program into an effective platform for self-promotion both in their personal lives and in their careers. Their instant fame was subsequently utilized to publicize their own businesses, to sign contracts to become spokespeople or models for various consumer products, or to join the entertainment world as performers or TV hosts themselves. [15]

But if everyone knew that it was "just a show," why did the comments from Ma Nuo and others strike such a raw nerve among young viewers and generate such heated online debates among netizens? A good example of the popular uproar elicited by the show involves Zhu Zhenfang, who was quickly punished for her outrageous comments by netizens determined to locate her personal information and to harass her by sending hostile and insulting messages to her place of work. As a result, Zhu had to quit the show to avoid losing her job.

To understand the overwhelming reaction to the declarations of these "material girls," it is useful to take a broader look at the dreams and current predicaments of the post-1980s generation. These are vividly encapsulated by two TV dramas that gained extreme popularity and became hot topics of discussion among younger viewers in recent years. The first was *Struggle* (*Fendou*, 2007), which depicts a group of recently graduated classmates who must find their place and establish their careers in the competitive Chinese market economy. As this drama demonstrates, unlike their parents' or grandparents' generation, the "struggle" of the post-1980s generation is a highly individualistic enterprise aimed at improving individual "quality" (*suzhi*), seeking self-optimization, and gaining material rewards. Intriguingly, the maturing process of the young male protagonist, who also happens to win the heart of the most beautiful woman, is depicted as a "struggle" to choose between his two fathers. One (the biological father) is a wealthy multinational capitalist, a returned Chinese American who invests in China's booming real estate development. The other (his stepfather) is an idealistic Party member who is an uncorrupted local official in charge of city planning and development. This ironic plotline glaringly encapsulates the mixed emotions felt by China's younger generation during the current transformation, which awkwardly attempts to balance socialist and neoliberal imperatives.

The second TV drama, *Narrow Dwelling* (*Woju*, 2009) depicts the disillusionment and despair of the young urban middle class through the experiences of two sisters who adopt contrasting strategies as they settle in a big city. The older sister works extra hours and saves every penny to gradually create a better life for herself through her own painstaking efforts. But the younger sister decides to take a shortcut by becoming the mistress of a rich and powerful official who gives her an apartment and numerous other expensive gifts. The younger sister's abandonment of her boyfriend for an older, richer, more powerful (and, of course, corrupt) man evoked a heated online debate among viewers. The discussion reflected the constant fear of many young men: without a certain level of wealth and possessions, they will never be able to attract a suitable wife. As one viewer of *Narrow Dwelling* put it, "Society will not force you to succeed, but it will tell you clearly what it is like to be a failure."[16] This pressure to "succeed" is a real threat to the sense of masculinity and adulthood of many young Chinese men. It is a society in which financial inequality and even sexual frustration seem directly linked to poor family backgrounds, undesirable native places, and age, a place where the disadvantaged cannot compete with corrupt officials, rich entrepreneurs, and their "official kids" and "rich kids" (*guan erdai* and *fu erdai*).

Thus, the current generation of aspiring middle-class youth is experiencing a sense of inner conflict that connects two powerful interlocking emotion—a desire for the kind of affluent life they see or imagine others to be leading and a fear of losing everything in the extremely competitive social environment that China has become. More often than not, this frustration of young Chinese males is directed at the objects of their desire—materialistic young women who ignore them and instead use their looks and charms to attract richer men and to take a shortcut to wealth and fame. Such women have become symbols of the social and moral degeneration of contemporary Chinese society, something that is repeatedly emphasized in online debates about TV personalities, including those on reality shows like *Are You the One?* Seen in this context, it is no surprise that the comments by Ma Nuo and other female contestants and the show's relentless focus on the income and material assets of male contestants would lead to online controversies and ultimately to Luo Lei's public attack on Ma Nuo.

But by looking deeper, we can see a major "struggle" between contradictory values here, with Ma Nuo symbolizing both the temptations and the dangers of a society in transition. On the one hand, she and other attractive female contestants are desired for their modern lifestyles and career ambitions, their beauty and fashionable dress, and even their confident, outspoken personalities. Many female viewers want to become one of these lucky women. And many male contestants choose such women as their "Favorite Gals." Some even come onstage to express their admiration. On the other hand, this very modern and highly material femininity poses a threat to the traditional ideal of a virtuous wife and good mother. As Luo Lei's statement made clear, he wants someone with feminine beauty, but she must come home to him every night. These young women are placed on a pedestal, treated almost like revered figures, yet at the same time they must be publicly punished when necessary and "tamed" so that certain ideals of feminine purity and absolute good are not compromised. And the female contestants are certainly not free of inner contradictions themselves, with many of them apparently unsure of what kind of man to choose and how to judge success in today's society.

COMPETING VOICES: THE LIFESTYLE POLITICS OF THE POST-1980S GENERATION

Are You the One? entailed an exaggerated focus on shameless materialism and tended to fan the flames of young viewers' emotions. This led to extremely heated debates online and in the media, which in turn drew the skeptical attention of official censors. SARFT soon issued notices to several TV stations, including JSTV, criticizing the unhealthy tendencies of dating programs and setting out detailed restrictions on their content:

> Such programs are currently dominated by models, actors, and rich young people. They should broaden the range of their contestants. Controversial public figures who are morally suspect and have alternative values and unorthodox views about marriage should not be invited to participate. These programs cannot be broadcast live, and [producers] must make sure they comply with this regulation and delete any problematic content and incorrect points of view. [17]

Are You the One? was now facing a crisis. The show was temporarily halted, and JSTV had to find a quick solution in order to avoid a cancellation disaster—a fate that greeted many reality shows that had pushed the envelope too far in the past ten years. [18]

JSTV's response to SARFT was compliant yet strategic. The most inventive change to the program involved an invitation to a female professor from the Jiangsu Provincial Party School to sit alongside Le Jia and function as an additional psychological adviser and commentator. Her approachable manner and commonsense perspective helped to balance the occasional sharpness and emotional extravagance of Le Jia, and her Party School background made her an ideal establishment figure, someone who could "supervise" content and demonstrate the "sincerity" of the TV station. Changes were also made to the contestant lineup, with some of the sharper-tongued women removed and the content of the men's self-introductions adjusted. Most important, video material no longer displayed the personal income of male contestants, and the show invited the participation of a much greater variety of men and women representing a broader range of career paths. The producers even staged two special programs on July 18 and August 1, 2010, in which all contestants, male and female, were migrant workers. This was to showcase the program's "media responsibility" (*meiti zeren*) since these workers often find it particularly difficult to meet life partners.

With all these format and content adjustments and promises to do better, *Are You the One?* managed to get permission to continue broadcasting and has maintained its top spot in the ratings for almost two years. Indeed, despite toning down some of its controversial content, *Are You the One?* has managed to further develop its basic function as an "intimate public forum," and its "lifestyle discourse" has engaged legions of young viewers and evoked myriad responses online and elsewhere. The public voice of the show and its various associated network forms are both active and generative.

An exploration of the hypercharged debates generated by *Are You the One?* shows how coming-of-age Chinese consumer-citizens express their individual consciousness and how these individual expressions have been transformed into public discussions about social responsibility and the need for public participation. Of special note are the ways in which the show's hosts allow contestants to raise issues that range far beyond the typical dating format and how dominant assumptions are challenged by alternative voices both on the show and online. In this way, the show became a curious hybrid of popular entertainment and incisive social commentary.

One distinctive example is the recurring debate about the relationship between contemporary lifestyles and environmental awareness. Most contestants on *Are You the One?* display little overt concern for the environment. Their focus is much more on material concerns, career prospects, and physical/psychological attributes of their potential partners. But there have been several conspicuous exceptions involving male contestants who enthusiastically embraced a "green" and sustainable lifestyle. The reaction of many female contestants to these "exceptional" men demonstrates a dominant assumption of the post-1980s generation in China: environmental issues are not central concerns in their lives. Contestant reactions also show that there is a great deal of ignorance about such issues among younger Chinese. The fact that the show consistently gives these "environmental boys" plenty of time to explain their alternative viewpoint indicates that the program's producers and hosts are eager to promote a more mature and socially aware outlook on the issue.

The first environmental enthusiast to appear was a British contestant with the Chinese name Wang Doufu. Although good-looking and personable (complete with an excellent sense of humor and relatively fluent Chinese-language skills), Wang Doufu was rejected by many female contestants when he declared his monthly income to be only a few hundred yuan (he was obviously a foreign student on a small stipend) and revealed that his hobby was serving as a disc jockey at nightclubs—an interest insufficiently respectable or stable for a life partner. Finally, all the remaining lights went off when he said that his other hobby was recycling abandoned objects that he found on the street. The host, Meng Fei, was charmed by the young British man and gave him a chance to explain why he used recycled objects. Wang said that these objects could be given a new lease on life and would not be wasted. It was not good for the environment to mindlessly throw things away. When Meng Fei asked the contestant what his parents did for a living, Wang replied that his mother was an artist and his father an investment banker. "In other words, your family is not short of money?" Meng added. By making sure that these points were clarified, Meng was emphasizing that the environmental issue was one that people should take more seriously and that this was a positive decision made by a thoughtful young man about recycling and avoiding pollution. It was not a sign of poverty, contrary to what most of the female contestants seemed to assume.

This emphasis on sustainability was strongly reinforced in a subsequent episode (October 3, 2010) when an intriguing male contestant appeared onstage. Lu Hongyi was Chinese but had spent some of his childhood in the United States and had graduated from Harvard Law School. He had worked in an American law firm for a few years but then became highly committed to the environmental movement and gave up his secure job to return to China to work in a nongovernmental organization (NGO) dedicated to improving environmental awareness in China. He was a very active person and enjoyed riding a bike, as it not only was healthy but also fit with his "low-carbon" lifestyle. This was the reason he did not own a car. He also mentioned several other ways that he tried to reduce his "carbon footprint," including the rather radical suggestion that he did not want to father any children because the world population is already too large. Instead, he wanted to adopt one or more abandoned children and give them a loving family.

One imagines that many women would be bowled over by this brilliant, articulate, decent-looking young man with his lofty ideals. Once again, Meng Fei gave him plenty of time to state his views and highly praised his idealism and appeals for more people to dedicate themselves to solving China's serious environmental problems. But most of the questions from female contestants focused on material issues. For example, one asked how he would support his family in what she assumed was his low-paying volunteer job. Another contestant asked if he would be willing to reconsider his decision not to father children. While Lu Hongyi did better than Wang Doufu, reaching the final stages and selecting one woman as his date, it is surprising how many of the female contestants rejected him after finding out about his environmental lifestyle despite his apparently excellent personal attributes. However, following this episode, a major debate broke out on the Internet, and many viewers of the show were obviously impressed by Lu's willingness to give up a high-paying job to work for an NGO and his commitment to improving China's natural environment. For example, a Chinese search on Google of the phrase "Feicheng wurao, Lu Hongyi" generated 32,700 items related to this episode, many of which are discussions by fans praising Lu's admirable character and environmental awareness.

During the July 2, 2011, episode, the environmental issue once more took center stage when Wang Sheng appeared on the show. He was an environmental inspector whose job was to test waterways for industrial and other types of pollution. But his "green" attitudes were not just restricted to his job. He declared that he wanted to devote his whole life to environmental sustainability, and while he may have been looking for a life partner on the show, in fact he spent much of his video segments and self-introduction (encouraged by Meng Fei and the other two hosts, of course) suggesting methods that people can use to reduce pollution and emissions, such as recycling old batteries and picking up litter. In his first video, he explained that he would regularly pick up trash dropped by other people and put it in litter bins, and the video showed him doing this and using a plastic bag to pick up dog poop left by someone else's dog. One female contestant was obviously concerned. She said she could not stand her boyfriend picking up dog poop because people would look down on them. She turned off her light. Meng Fei cuttingly asked the woman, "If you saw someone who is not your boyfriend disposing of dog poop, would you look up to him?" The woman said she would but not if it was her boyfriend. Meng Fei then concluded the discussion by saying that she was entitled to have such a muddled opinion but that he was also entitled to look down on her for having such an opinion. Although only one female contestant expressed her opinion so directly, all the others soon turned off their lights, and Wang went off without a date. The general assumption among the show's contestants seemed to be that environmental awareness and commitment is a very good thing in theory, but if it requires a real change of attitude and lifestyle, then it is not something they want to bother with.

One could argue that in encouraging the show's contestants to promote environmental awareness, *Are You the One?* is simply following current Chinese government policy. And it is certainly true that since its run-in with the official censors at SARFT, the program must continually show that it is playing a positive role in promoting "healthy," socially responsible values, and its hosts must make it crystal clear where they stand. Yet such a criticism would be unfair because some discussions of this issue (including the Wang Doufu episode) were broadcast before the censors got involved in June 2010. Second, in terms of the format, two sides of the debate are always presented, and the hosts do give the female contestants who are not impressed with environmental activists the opportunity to explain why they opt to reject. In some cases, their doubts may be legitimate. For example, it is relevant to ask how an environmental activist might support his family if he is not getting any income from a volunteer position. This is one reason why the discussion of such social issues on *Are You the One?* can be so vivid and engaging: each issue has at least two sides to it, and we see real people (who viewers can identify with) taking both sides of the issue and justifying their decisions. The other important difference that sets the program apart from government propaganda are the debates about show content that continue on various online forums. These are less closely monitored and therefore much less likely to be influenced by the official viewpoints embraced by the show's hosts.

Another important feature that helps *Are You the One?* generate open and productive public discourse is its intentional recruitment of non-Chinese contestants. These have included people from Korea, America, Great Britain, Vietnam, Russia, Egypt, and elsewhere. Even more common is the participation of Chinese contestants who have spent many years working or studying abroad, the so-called overseas returnees (*haigui*). In fact, in more recent programs, *Are You the One?* went so far as to stage special programs exclusively for Chinese contestants who live in the United States (October 9 and 16, 2011) and the United Kingdom (January 29 and February 5, 2012). These contestants often have ideas and values that viewers consider unusual or alternative and in some cases superior to what they see as mainstream Chinese values. Their comments provide many fruitful opportunities for discussion among the show's contestants and hosts and among online fan groups. They force Chinese viewers to confront their own entrenched worldviews and value systems and to consider life from a fresh perspective.

This brings to mind Lu Hongyi, the Harvard Law School graduate who returned to China to join an environmental NGO. Many of the online comments about Lu compared his socially responsible outlook to the views of another male contestant on the show, Zhang Fan, who graduated from one of China's top medical schools but who was concerned mainly with getting ahead in his job and seemed to have little awareness of broader social issues. Netizens debated whether this was due to the superior moral education provided by American universities or was a problem associated with the materialistic worldview of Chinese society as a whole.[19]

Yet it was not until another overseas returnee, An Tian, appeared on the show on March 26, 2011, that this particular online debate really exploded. At first, An appeared to be a buffoon, making funny faces and joking as he walked onstage. Some female contestants were critical of his lack of "seriousness" and "respect." But then they found out that he had an undergraduate degree from Harvard and an MA from Oxford, was finishing a PhD at UC Berkeley, and that he had returned to China to contribute to society by researching agricultural economics. Immediately, those who had kept their lights on (twenty-one of twenty-four women) became highly interested though still suspicious of his "eccentricity." But it was not until the final moments that the true drama played out. Two willing female contestants remained in play, and An was given an opportunity to ask them a final question before making his choice. He asked them, "If it happened that you won US$10 million in a lottery, how would you choose to spend the money?" Suddenly, it was clear that despite his joking around, An was very serious about testing the values of the women who might become his life partner. The first woman said that it would not change her life at all; she would just continue to buy things that are necessary. The second woman gave a slightly better answer, saying that she would use the money to make her mother happy and that her mother would not have to work anymore. But An Tian was not satisfied with these responses. He explained to Meng Fei that he would have suggested setting up some kind of foundation and giving the money to a worthy cause like orphans or education rather than just spending it on themselves and their families. "Maybe if it was just $1 million, you could spend it on yourself, to buy a house, car, etcetera, but $10 million is such a lot of money! . . . We have to think about serving the people." He decided not to choose either of the women and left the stage alone. Backstage, he explained to the camera that he did not believe it was possible to change someone's basic character. This is why he was looking for a woman with a vision similar to his own, in other words, someone who wanted to give back to society.

This incident triggered an unprecedented surge of responses by fans and other commentators, with over 700,000 posts on the topic over the next few weeks. The online debate was then picked up by the official media, with newspapers reporting on the incident and adding their own editorial commentary. The main thrust of the debate revolved around the question of whether foreign values were superior to Chinese values because they supposedly led to more socially responsible people who really care about giving back to society ("serving the people," or *wei renmin fuwu*, as An Tian put it, echoing the Communist ideal) as opposed to contemporary Chinese values that stress financial benefit ("serving the people's currency," or *wei renminbi fuwu*, as one wag put it). Some educators reflected on what had been lost from China's current education system despite the fact that people still pay token lip service to lofty socialist slogans.[20]

The An Tian incident is perhaps the clearest example of how *Are You the One?* facilitates public debate on serious social issues through its dating show format, yet it is the deep social emotion that it evokes and restless questioning by young people online regarding the moral uncertainties and social problems in a transitional society that turned this entertainment show into a true public arena. Of course, many other issues have emerged during the show. For example, despite their fashionable dress and contemporary image, many of the contestants seem to have old-fashioned values when it comes to family. Particularly noticeable is a fixation on their mothers among both male and female contestants. Some men have brought their mothers onstage to help them select a partner, and one mother even joined the show as a female contestant alongside her own daughter, not to find her own date but to make sure her daughter did not make the "wrong" decision. Even when mothers are not there in person, their influence is clear from the comments of contestants. For example, men ask women whether they mind if their mother-in-law lives in the same house, and women sometimes prefer men who portray themselves as helpful to their mothers. Monologues by contestants about motherly love provide many of the more sentimental moments in the show, with contestants and audience weeping freely as they think of their relationships with their own mothers. Although there may be some residual influence of customary Chinese concepts of filial piety, this fixation on mothers seems to result largely from the fact that a majority of young people are only children because of China's one-child policy, and there has been a tendency for parents to indulge these "little emperors and empresses." Some young people have become quite dependent and are unwilling to break away from their mothers when they grow up. Yet even here, there is diversity of opinion, with some contestants declaring that they do not want to live with their parents because they never had a good relationship with them and their values are different.

Another frequently debated issue is the career and life challenges faced by young people when they migrate from one place to another and the impact of these choices on one's ability to lead a balanced life. Indeed, one sees an ongoing contradiction between a materialistic focus on making more money, buying possessions, and getting ahead and a desire to enjoy a more balanced lifestyle with fewer material rewards but broader interests (culture, sports, traveling, and so on) and less stress. We have already discussed the fierce disputes that arose from the Ma Nuo incident and the associated attacks on "material girls" and "second-generation rich kids," which are examples of this conflict. In its postcensorship phase, *Are You the One?* has attempted to invite a broader range of male and female contestants, including some who do not agree with the extreme materialistic viewpoint of some of their peers. The show's hosts have also made a point of questioning contestants who are too narrowly focused on careers and getting ahead to the exclusion of other aspects of the good life.

The debates on *Are You the One?* clearly display the diversity of opinion among the post-1980s generation. In turn, these competing voices contribute to a public discourse on lifestyle choices as important aspects of identity and social responsibility. As Rheingold has pointed out, "The public voices of individuals, aggregated and in dialogue with the voices of other individuals, become the fundamental particles of public opinion. When public opinion has the power and freedom to influence policy and grows from the open, rational, critical debate among peers posited by Jürgen Habermas and others, it can be an essential instrument of democratic self-governance."[21] In this process, the passively associated networks of people online and using social media become active public citizens raising and debating some of the most pressing social and emotional issues that deeply concern restless Chinese youth today.

What, then, can we learn about Chinese media and society from popular entertainment shows? The popularity of the TV show *Are You the One?* and the online debates that it evokes point to an understudied yet very crucial phenomenon in Chinese media. With the growth in media commercialization and a corresponding shift in emphasis from news to entertainment, "the responsibility of the media for informing, educating and providing moral guidance to Chinese citizens is now increasingly being fulfilled by entertainment programs produced at the local and provincial levels."[22] Because of the far-reaching influence and broad popular appeal, we should give greater weight to the public space created by them in our efforts to understand public discourse and social emotion in contemporary China.

It may seem strange that a dating show like *Are You the One?* has such a major influence on public discussions of serious social issues like the education system, moral behavior, and family values. But this results from a confluence of several factors, including (1) the willingness of the show's producers and cohosts to encourage detailed discussion of serious social issues that emerge during the dating process; (2) the willingness of both male and female contestants to talk about such issues and give their frank opinions in public, something that older people may not be so keen to do; (3) the extremely rapid development of the Internet and other social media over the past few years (especially among the target audience for the show) and the impressive popularity of authorized and unofficial online netizen fan clubs and bulletin boards that allow the discussion of issues to continue after each episode is broadcast, a practice that is facilitated by the availability of all episodes online, where they can be viewed and exchanged among friends; and (4) the show's conscious selection of some particularly outspoken contestants and hot-button topics. Added to these factors, one could argue that even the official censorship of *Are You the One?* (moves that prohibited overreliance on shock and outrage and forced programing to be more "serious" and "socially responsible" in tone) indirectly influenced its role as a public forum for the discussion of social issues in mature yet still vivid and entertaining ways.

Perhaps the most crucial factor about the impact of the show is the fact that there is a real thirst among restless and self-contradictory young people in China today for public debate and discussion of issues that deeply concern their lives, yet there are not many venues available for them to do this because of restrictions on civil society organizations and state control of official media. While the Internet does allow people more freedom to debate social issues without interference, such debates have tended to be dispersed over many unrelated sites and have had little impact beyond a small group of netizens. What *Are You the One?* has done is to provide a focal point for many of these debates by linking them with dating and romance, a topic that appeals to almost all young people (and to their parents and grandparents) and thereby creates a central forum involving huge numbers of contestants (and viewers) in which discussions of social issues can become broadly meaningful and influential. In fact, some issues that were raised on *Are You the One?* generated so much interest and emotional discussion among viewers that they began to shape national public discourse in the official media, as witnessed in the An Tian incident.

It is in this sense that *Are You the One?* has created a public space for debating competing values in contemporary Chinese society. Certainly, this public space is limited since the show would immediately be censored if it strayed over the line between legitimate discussion of social issues and challenges to the political status quo. Furthermore, it is not the case that all interactions among contestants and netizens constitute serious public debates. Many are extremely trivial. But despite these constraints and the show's obvious focus on ratings and commerce, it does play a crucial role in mediating public discourse. It has clearly encouraged younger people to think about some of the conflicting values that are on display in China today. The program has demonstrated that there are diverse voices challenging mainstream materialistic assumptions, and it has given these voices an opportunity to participate in public discussions with both like-minded and different-minded peers. It is impossible to say what impact this will have on the future development of Chinese society, but, at the very least, it can provide young people with a sense of variety when it comes to lifestyles and diverse values and perspectives that go far beyond the limited experiences of young viewers.

The "intimate public forum" of *Are You the One?* also challenges simplistic assumptions about the allegedly passive, disengaged, and self-centered ways of the post-1980s generation. This case study should cause us to reflect on the frameworks that we use to discuss civic engagement and citizenship among younger generations more broadly. For increasing numbers of Chinese citizens, like citizens in the West, "politics in conventional (collective, government-centered, electoral) forms has become less salient."[23] Thus, we need to look beyond the conventional forms of civic action and political participation that center around party, state, or other political institutions and organizations and pay more attention to the kinds of "lifestyle politics" that make their presence known through popular culture and virtual communities. These individual expressions about lifestyle-related political issues are a crucial aspect of the sort of civil society and democratic life that is emerging in the process of China's modernization and globalization. It is likely that expressions of this sort will become "increasingly forceful features of state-society relations"[24] in twenty-first-century China.

NOTES

1. Baidu, "Support Luo or Sympathize with Ma" (你更支持骆磊还是同情马诺), http://tieba.baidu.com/f?z=741491320 (accessed October 10, 2011).

2. Baidu, "Is There Anything Wrong with Ma Nuo?" (马诺错了吗), http://tieba.baidu.com/f?kz=702641120 ; "Don't Let Beijing Lose Face" (马诺 你能别给北京人丢脸了吗), http://tieba.baidu.com/f?kz=709076808 (accessed October 10, 2011).

3. According to the Fans Network, on May 17, 2010, ratings for *Are You the One?* reached their highest point of 4.23 percent, surpassing *Citadel of Happiness*, the most popular Chinese entertainment show of the past decade, and its fees for a fifteen-second advertising slot during the show almost quadrupled, from 40,000 to 140,000 yuan. See Yu Xiang, "*Feicheng wurao*'s Ratings Go through the Roof, and Its Advertising Rates Quadruple" (非诚勿扰"收视率暴涨 广告价格翻四番), *Fans Network Entertainment* (粉丝网娱乐), February 23, 2011, http://media.ifeng.com/pk/special/xuanxiupkfuqizhenrenxiu/yingxiangli/detail_2011_02/23/4813762_0.shtml (accessed October 10, 2011).

4. Zhu Ying, "Critical Masses, Commerce, and Shifting State-Society Relations in China," *China Beat*, February 17, 2010, http://www.thechinabeat.org/?p=1526.

5. "Lifestyle politics," as explained by W. Lance Bennett, indicates a tendency whereby "individuals increasingly organize social and political meaning around their lifestyle values and the personal narratives that express them." It is used by social scientists to describe "a shift from traditional civic life and political participation to a new age of 'lifestyle politics' driven by values articulated at the level of individual behaviour and popular action in consumer choices, online exchanges, demonstrations and other informal forums." See Bennett, "Branded Political Communication: Lifestyle Politics, Logo Campaigns, and the Rise of Global Citizenship," in *Politics, Products, and Markets: Exploring Political Consumerism Past and Present*, ed. Michele Micheletti et al. (New Brunswick, NJ: Transaction, 2004), 103. See also Anthony Giddens, *Modernity and Self-Identity: Self and Society in the Late Modern Age* (Stanford, CA: Stanford University Press, 1991).

6. I use this critical concept in the way Chris Berry suggested, both related to yet distinct from "public sphere." In his article "New Documentary in China: Public Space, Public Television," Berry chooses to use the term "public space" instead of "public sphere," which is more commonly used in media studies. He argues that the latter is too focused on the power of the state over society and fails to allow that other social actors "also exert power and produce, constrain, and shape public space and activity as well as civil society." See Chris Berry et al., eds., *Electronic Elsewheres: Media, Technology and the Experience of Social Space* (Minneapolis: University of Minnesota Press, 2010), 108.

7. Calum MacLeod, "China Smitten by TV Dating," *USA Today*, May 17, http://www.usatoday.com/news/world/2010-05-17-china-dating_N.htm?csp=34 (accessed October 10, 2011).

8. Mei Zixiao, "*Feicheng wurao*'s Producer Wang Gang: We Will Restrict the Number of Contestants from the Fashion Model World" (非诚勿扰》制片人王刚：将限制模特圈嘉宾比例), Wangyi Entertainment Special Column Network, May 24, 2010, http://hi.baidu.com/%D3%F1%ED%FE%D0%C4%BE%AA/blog/item/1da8cf89c51c75dffd1f1007.html (accessed October 14, 2011).

9. According to my own observations supported by published statistics, the vast majority of contestants are in the age range of twenty to thirty-five years, in other words, young adults born after 1976. These are conventionally referred to as the post-1980s generation. The concerns about giving the post-1980s generation a public space are both practical and political. Young audiences are the keenest audiences and participants in reality TV shows, especially talent shows and contest programs. To exploit this niche market and make its content and format appeal to this group and engage them at a deeper level through Internet delivery and discussion is one thing that distinguishes *Are You the One?* from its peers.

10. James Fallows, quoting Shi Hongsheng, in "Voices from China #1: The Post-1980s Generation," http://www.theatlantic.com/international/archive/2011/04/voices-from-china-1-the-post-1980s-generation/236968 (accessed October 14, 2011).

11. Stanley Rosen, "Chinese Youth and State-Society Relations," in *Chinese Politics: State, Society and Market*, ed. Peter Hays Gries and Stanley Rosen (New York: Routledge, 2010), 161.

12. Data from the China Internet Information Center, "第29次互联网发展统计报告" (The twenty-ninth statistical report on the development of Chinese Internet, January 2012. http://www.cnnic.cn/research/bgxz/tjbg/201201/P020120116330880247967.pdf (accessed March 31, 2012).

13. Data from the China Internet Information Center, "2009年中国网民社交网络应用研究报告" (2009 research report on social network service use of Chinese netizens, November) http://www.cnnic.cn/research/bgxz/spbg/201102/t20110222_20351.html (accessed May 25, 2011).

14. Sometimes the self-introduction videos may also include "self-evaluation" (*ziwo pingjia*), "hobbies and interests" (*xingqu aihao*), and "past romantic experience" (*qinggan jingli*).

15. Ma Nuo appeared to be thriving despite her exit from the show. She was given a contract as a guest judge on another show titled *It's You!* (Anhui TV) largely on the basis of her notorious reputation and her ability to generate a large, if polarized, following among viewers.

16. Quoted in Ruoyun Bai's research, "Snail House as a Middle-Class Construct," unpublished workshop paper presented at the Chinese-Language Television Drama Workshop, Chinese University of Hong Kong, January 22, 2011.

17. SARFT, "SARFT Notice on Further Regulation of TV Programs about Marriage, Love and Friendship" (广电总局关于进一步规范婚恋交友类电视节目的管理通知).

18. Previous reality shows that were canceled because of government regulation include *Perfect Holiday* (*Wanmei jiaqi*, 2000), *My Hero* (*Jiayou hao nanhai*, 2007), and *Spiritual Garden* (*Xinling huayuan*, 2009). Other shows, including *Super Girl*, were forced to tone down their content and format in order to continue broadcasting. See "SARFT Strictly Regulates TV Programs on Human Feelings; *Soul Garden* Goes Off the Air" (广电总局严管情感类电视节目 [心灵花园] 停播), *Dongfang zaobao*, January 3, 2009, http://news.hexun.com/2009-01-03/113022806.html (accessed October 10, 2011). After the SARFT order in June 2010, Anhui TV edited the already produced episodes of its dating show so that Ma Nuo was no longer given a central role and terminated her contract for future shows.

19. One example is a posting that was copied by many bloggers titled "Character Analysis of Zhang Fan and Lu Hongyi from *Are You the One?* (对于非诚勿扰男嘉宾张帆和陆弘毅的性格解析). See one reproduced version on a blogger's Web page at http://blog.sina.com.cn/s/blog_4bcc84ea0100m7jr.html. What is most interesting here is that this blog also copies and pastes the different responses to the original post.

20. See, for example, a post on the *Feicheng wurao* net bar on Baidu titled "The Wisdom and Honesty of An Tian: A Slap in the Face of the Chinese Education System" (安田的智慧与诚实给了中国教育体系一记响亮的耳光), which attracted thirty-six responses in just one day, with a great variety of opinions expressed about the Chinese and American education systems.

21. Howard Rheingold, "Using Participatory Media and Public Voice to Encourage Civic Engagement," in *Civic Life Online: Learning How Digital Media Can Engage Youth*, ed. W. Lance Bennett (Cambridge, MA: MIT Press, 2008), 101.

22. Wanning Sun, "From Central News to Regional Entertainment: The Manufacture of Illusion," unpublished workshop paper, Australian National University, March 2, 2012.

23. Bennett, "Branded Political Communication," 103.

24. Zhu, "Critical Masses Commerce, and Shifting State-Society Relations in China."

Part III

Values

SEVEN

The Sacred and the Holy

Religious Power and Cultural Creativity in China Today

Richard P. Madsen

A famous chapter in Tocqueville's *Democracy in America* asks, "Why the Americans are often so restless in the midst of their prosperity?" Tocqueville observed a nation of materially prosperous individuals who nonetheless seemed filled with anxiety, always looking for more. "An American will build a house in which to pass his old age," said Tocqueville, "and sell it before the roof is on . . . he will take up a profession and leave it, settle in one place and soon go off elsewhere with his changing desires."[1] China today is restless in many of the same ways and for the same reasons as was the America that Tocqueville observed in the mid-nineteenth century. There is a negative side to such restlessness, as Tocqueville noted, but also a positive side. The American restlessness has sometimes led the United States into tragedy, but it has also driven it to become one of the most economically and culturally dynamic societies in world history. The same might be said of Chinese restlessness in the early twenty-first century. Restlessness leads to creativity as well as, sometimes, to chaos. Perhaps the most important source of such creativity — and sometimes of chaos — in Chinese history has been China's religious practices. In this chapter, I will give some examples of how the restlessness of contemporary religious practice carries on, in new forms, a long tradition of grassroots cultural creativity.

THE RECONSTRUCTION OF RELIGION

Millions of local temples have been built or reconstructed in the past two decades, and connected with this rebuilding are hundreds of thousands of communal temple festivals (*miaohui*) held each year. A good festival is *renao* ("hot and noisy").[2] There are thousands of firecrackers and noisy crowds, torch lit processions, dramatic performances, oracles and visions, and sometimes spectacular acts of self-flagellation—behavior that in ordinary daily life would be considered crazy. The opposite of "hot and noisy" is *lengjing* ("cold and quiet"). In popular discourse, cold and quiet is bad. If a festival (or any important celebration, such as a wedding or even a funeral), is cold and quiet, it is a failure. Indeed, a cold and quiet life is a bad life. In the hard years of famine after the Great Leap Forward, the people of Chen Village described their community as *lengjing*.[3]

The Chinese government today does not like the dynamism of *renao*, hot and noisy; it prefers the stability of cold and quiet. In imperial times, the great state religious rituals were dignified and stately, orderly representations of a well-ordered universe. In the modern era, the Guomindang (GMD) government tried to eliminate all temple festivals, and the Communist government, heir to the same culturally iconoclastic, modernizing May Fourth tradition, followed suit (even more ruthlessly and comprehensively than the GMD in the 1930s), although it eventually failed and now has to come to terms with a range of grassroots religiosity.

In imperial times down to the present, Chinese governments tried to co-opt and control hot and noisy festivals. Emperors and their governments were sacred (*sheng*); they not only administered people but also were the mediators between Heaven and Earth. They connected this world to the order of the cosmos and provided a sacred canopy that legitimated orthodox (*zhengjiao*) local cults while ruthlessly persecuting heterodox (*xiejiao*) ones. They gave a particular interpretation to orthodox cults—such cults were good because they promoted the proper virtues delineated by Confucius-Mencius and thus ensured the development of a harmonious society.

For their part, local practitioners were happy enough to tell the officials that their celebrations were indeed sacred representations of the virtues that anchored a harmonious cosmos. And in part this was true. But local cults—at least the good hot and noisy ones—were also *ling*—a word hard to translate but meaning "holy" (in the Rudolph Otto sense), full of charismatic power. The realm of *ling* is the realm of the powerfully unpredictable, the ecstatic, and the awesome. It is the realm of visionaries, seers, and miracle workers—the realm of creativity.[4] Contrary to some stereotypes, in imperial times local culture was never static. In his studies of religion in Fujian, Kenneth Dean has shown how the ritual innovation constantly going on at the local level in the Ming and Qing dynasties was a complicated dialectic between *ling* and *sheng*.[5]

Such creativity continues in the present although in different forms and under different circumstances. Here are a few examples from my own fieldwork.

Exorcizing Evil

The thousand or so villagers in a remote community in the foothills of the Taihang Mountains in the southern part of Hebei province have been reviving their community's *nuo* drama, which they had been performing at least since the early Ming dynasty.[6] The *nuo* drama is an exorcism rite, the purpose of which is to punish the Yan Wang, the King of Hell, who, like the Western Lucifer, is pretty much responsible for all the evil things that people do. The festival takes at least three months to prepare, and all of the thousand villagers are involved in the preparation and performance. The coordination is carried out by a village religious leader, who serves on a rotating basis. By tradition, different sections in the village (defined by lineage) have different jobs in the preparation and performance. A large stage is set up in front of the village on which are performed a continuous series of dramas for the three days leading to the Night of the First Principle (*yuanxiao*) festival, the end of the fifteen-day lunar new year celebrations. The characters in the opera wear masks, some of which were hundreds of years old before being destroyed during the Cultural Revolution and reconstructed in the 1980s. Almost every male member of the village has a part to play in the dramas, and they have to spend considerable time memorizing their lines. Inevitably, though, they cannot remember them exactly, and they do a lot of improvising. The roles evolve through this kind of creativity. Even the Party secretary has a part, albeit a fairly minor one. But he says that as long as he is performing, he is no longer the Party secretary but has *become* the deity he is portraying.

The culmination of the drama is the evisceration of the King of Hell. The person who plays this devil is not a local villager—no local would dare take on such an evil role. The King of Hell is dragged through all of the narrow lanes of the village and then, the people following along, brought to the big stage. Smoke bellows out of specially constructed fire pots. Drums roll. The crowd erupts in a hot and noisy frenzy. The King of Hell is clothed in a light robe under which is a bag of chicken entrails. In the dramatic culmination, the robe is slashed open, and the bloody guts are pulled out. The Devil is dead, at least until next year.

The festival was stopped during the Cultural Revolution, and many of the ritual implements were destroyed, except for one occasion when they were able to perform it with Liu Shaoqi being portrayed as the Devil. Finally, in the 1980s, the festival was revived. People uncovered old scripts for the dramas that had been hidden away. Old people met with craftsmen from the city and told them from memory exactly how to design and paint the masks. The local government was wary at first but in recent years has been willing to see this kind of performance as part of China's "nonmaterial cultural heritage" (*feiwuzhi wenhua yichan*), and some of the festival is even videotaped and presented as a spectacle on local television. Somewhat like the imperial governments attempting to frame such rituals as *sheng* (sacred), the secular PRC government thus portrays the festival as a quaint way of teaching people to avoid evil and thus contribute to a harmonious society. But for the local villagers, it is *ling*, a moment of power breaking into the monotony of "passing time" (*guorizi*) in ordinary life.[7] A powerful ancient tradition that has been revived in face of political obstacles, it is a space where many mysterious and exciting things happen and people become gods and wrestle with evil itself. And even though it has ancient roots, the play keeps evolving through the playful creativity of its participants.

The sacred (*sheng*) likes things cool and quiet, harmoniously arranged under an orderly centralized authority. The holy (*ling*) likes the hot and noisy, the restlessness of crowds, the spontaneity of charismatic outbursts, and the loosening of passions. Before the revolution, there was usually an uneasy balance between the *sheng* and the *ling*, and one can still see this today. The *nuo* dramas are not anarchistic; they follow a traditional framework, albeit with considerable improvisation, and they are confined to particular times of the year (festival time, which itself is pregnant with *ling*) rather than the ordinary time of workaday activity.

Healing the Sick

The *ling*, however, does not necessarily manifest itself in the context of large public mobs. It finds expression too in private one-on-one encounters, such as those of the Healing Woman of a village in the same backwater region as the *nuo* drama village we have just described. After she married into the village in the mid-1950s, she discovered that she had extraordinary healing powers. By listening and talking with afflicted persons and by the laying on of hands, she could transmit a powerful *qi* energy that could cure illness. The work of such "magicians" (*wu*, which could possibly also be translated as "witches") was supposed to be strictly prohibited by the Communist government because it was nonscientific and carried on outside the framework of approved medical organizations. Nonetheless, the woman quietly carried on her healing, and those whom she had cured spread the word about her powers. The healing continued all the way up through the Cultural Revolution, and the woman amassed a large network of followers, not organized in any form of group but connected through her in a loose skein of personal relationships.

Each member in this network had a debt to pay, however. The woman never charged for her services, claiming that her powers were gifts from various deities in China's vast pantheon of gods. But by the principle of "cosmic recompense," when one receives a blessing from a deity, one is obliged eventually to give something in return.[8] Thus, in the new period of reform and opening after the Cultural Revolution, people who had been healed started to donate money to build a temple to the gods that had stood behind the Healing Woman. Over the past thirty years, therefore, an immense temple has arisen up the side of a hill. There are currently sixteen pavilions, and the woman hopes to eventually add ten more. The pavilions house images of many different gods, including the Unborn Eternal Mother, whose promise of an apocalyptic coming traditionally inspired peasant rebellions like the White Lotus. The latest pavilion is devoted to a deity who cures eye problems, a gift from a follower whose eyesight was restored by the Healing Woman.

Throughout the year, on major auspicious dates in the lunar calendar, large, hot, and noisy temple festivals are held at the site, attended by tens of thousands of participants who must travel along narrow rural roads to get there. None of the healing activities, temple building, and festivals have been supported by the state. But local officials appreciate some of the benefits that the Healing Woman has brought to the area. In particular, her temple has planted many evergreen trees on the barren, deforested hillside adjacent to the temple, thus arresting serious soil erosion. Visitors bring in money to the impoverished local economy. Because of such benefits, the local government turns a blind eye to the religious activities at the temple, and some of them even have pride that the temple has put their remote part of the world on the map.

You will not find the map in any official atlas, however. Knowledge about the temple and its holy powers is spread through word of mouth. Nonetheless, the word has spread as far away as Australia, and at least one seeker has come to this remote village to find relief after every other therapy had failed. People's ears are attuned to stories of people or places that are especially *ling*, where mysterious creativity breaks through the stifling cracks of bureaucratic apparatus and scientifically rationalized systems.

None of this is really in opposition to the state. The Healing Woman does not see herself as any kind of rebel against the government, and her son, who manages the temple's affairs, maintains good relations with local officials. But the popularity of this healing temple is an example of a long tradition of indifference to the state. From the Ming and Qing dynasties to the PRC, Chinese governments want to produce order and predictability. Ordinary people appreciate this (sometimes more, sometimes less) but find it stifling and boring, cold and quiet. What makes life interesting and tolerable is *renao*, hot and noisy, the eruption of the *ling*.

Almost by definition, the state cannot provide this, and it is found only in the restless creativity of ordinary people with extraordinary powers.

Inspiring the Masses

A third example, which combines public performance and private, personal *ling*, is that of the "Confucian religion" movement in northern Fujian province.[9] This is not to be confused with philosophical Confucianism or with the state Confucianism that some want to replace Marxism as the Chinese government's official ideology. These are in the realm of the *sheng*, ways for the state to justify its order-producing authority. The Confucian religion movement in Fujian reveres Confucius as a god and appropriates some ideas from the Confucian canon. But it is a mishmash of symbols and rituals, led by a charismatic figure who claims powerful healing powers. He cures by giving the ill a drink of water on which he has chanted an incantation based on sayings from the Analects. (He told me that if I got sick and wanted his services after returning to the United States, he could phone the incantation into a glass of water in my house.) Unlike the Healing Woman, whose ministrations produce a far-flung loose network of grateful followers, the Confucian religion produces a more compact regional organization whose leaders wear special uniforms and take part in regular ritual and educational activities. The movement gains protection from the government because it can claim to be embodying just those Confucian ideals that some in the government are now promoting. But it is clearly acting on its own and restlessly refashioning those ideas in creative new ways. As proven by its miraculous healing, it is powerfully *ling* under the mantle of *sheng*.

Receiving the Spirit

The religious and therapeutic practices I have been describing here are based on a mix of Daoist, Confucian, and Buddhist cosmological ideas. But one can find the same dialectic between *ling* and *sheng* and the same tension between *renao* and *lengjing* in popular Christianity. Protestant Christianity has undergone a spectacular expansion in the era of reform and opening, from fewer than a million believers in 1949 to around 50 million now, with most of the acceleration in growth occurring after 1979. Only a small percentage of this expansion has taken place within the officially supported Three Self Protestant Movement. Until recently, the most rapid growth has been in the countryside, in unregistered "house churches" with a strongly Pentecostal flavor.[10]

Whether they admit it or not, for Pentecostal Christians, the Holy Spirit seems very similar to the *ling*. Somewhat in contrast to Pentecostalism in the United States, the Chinese version has a great emphasis on miracles of healing—real physical healing, not just healing of moral problems like alcohol addiction—and exorcism of demons. A Christian minister whom I interviewed in Hong Kong described going on an evangelical trip to rural China. He has an advanced degree in psychology and says he does not believe in faith healing, but in one of the villages, a woman suffering from a badly abscessed tooth approached him and asked him to lay hands on her. When he did, he felt a tingling energy leave his hands, and the woman proclaimed that her abscess had been healed. Other miracles include the granting of preternatural powers to uneducated people, like the case of the woman in Henan without any training in music who has now produced hundreds of hymns that are now used in worship services throughout China and even in the West.[11]

Accompanying the singing there is often a lot of emotional praying and shouting and even speaking in tongues. Rural Christian services are *renao*. In contrast, the officially approved Three-Self churches are usually decorously staid. There are pleasant hymns and edifying sermons, but the overall effect is *lengjing*, cold and quiet. As the government would desire, religion is presented as an earnest effort to build the harmonious society.

Witnessing Visions

It is similar with Catholics. The part of the church that accepts the official supervision of the Catholic Patriotic Association (most of whom are nevertheless in communion with the Vatican) shies away from reports of visions and miracles. But the so-called underground church, unregistered with the government, is under fewer constraints, and it has been involved in extremely *renao* events, such as the Marian apparition in the small Hebei town of Donglu. The Donglu church was destroyed during the Cultural Revolution, but in the 1980s, after it became possible again to worship in public, local Catholics put up a picture of our Lady Queen of China—a picture they believed to have holy power—on the place where the church had stood, and as many as 20,000 pilgrims came each year to worship in front of the picture. In the late 1980s, the local Catholics began to build a huge cathedral that now can hold several thousand persons. On the Feast of Mary Help of Christians in 1995, tens of thousands of underground Catholics gathered for a Mass concelebrated in Donglu by four underground bishops and 110 underground priests. At that time, participants claim that the sun changed colors and moved across the sky. They said that "Holy Mother this year has come to comfort her children in Donglu, rewarding them for their enormous sacrifice and risk in taking this pilgrimage, with a spectacular, supernatural statement in the sky." The underground bishop of the area, Su Zhimin, expressed his belief that the Holy Mother has "reaffirmed that the Church who is allegiant to the Pope is the true Catholic Church supported by God." Soon after, the bishop was taken to prison, and the following year, a unit of 5,000 soldiers of the People's Liberation Army sealed off the area, closed the church, arrested a number of underground Catholics, and took away the picture of Our Lady of China. No one is allowed to go to Donglu on pilgrimage now.[12]

But even though the government cadres who supervise religious affairs want Catholic worship to be *lengjing*—and even though the Vatican may largely agree with them on this matter—Mary will probably reappear whenever she wants. Such apparitions come out of the realm of *ling*, deeply embedded in even the most politically tamed symbolism and never completely repressible. Indeed, it may well be that the greater the attempts to repress religious belief, the more there will be reports of miracles. Henrietta Harrison nicely demonstrated this in her study of Marian apparitions in a small Shanxi village during the lead-up to the Cultural Revolution.[13]

MODERN TRANSFORMATION OF THE *SHENG* AND THE *LING*

Whether it erupts within the context of popular Christianity or traditional deity worship, *ling* shares the following contrasts with *sheng*. Basically the opposite of bureaucratic, it is nonstandardized. The Healing Woman does not follow any standard medical protocol that could be reproduced by properly trained physicians. Her powers are unique to herself. Indeed, she is facing a crisis because she is eighty-four years old and having a hard time finding a successor. Moreover, *ling* is fundamentally unpredictable. There are certainly places (mountaintops especially) and times (festivals determined by the traditional calendar) that are inherently *ling*, but the exact way this is manifested always contains surprises. Thus, *ling* contradicts the aspiration of modern science toward standardization and replicability.

The existence of *ling* is predicated on the existence of a realm of reality that lies beyond the ordinary world and cannot be investigated through the tools of modern science. Its reality is thus found in the realm of the creative imagination. Unlike the modern Western notion of imagination, however, the imagination that produces *ling* is not based simply in the head; rather, it engages the whole body. One accesses *ling* through public rituals and more privately through bodily exercises (what Daoists call "inner alchemy"), control over breathing, and meditation.

Finally, *ling* is beyond good and evil. Some of the people and events produced through *ling* are very bad by any conventional morality. The King of Hell, after all, is very *ling*—that is what makes him so awesomely powerful and dangerous—and can be subdued only through rituals that are themselves very *ling*. Much of Chinese popular religious ritual indeed involves struggles between good and bad spiritual forces, which are all very *ling*. The Boxers at the end of the nineteenth century got their violent energy through such spiritual forces. For many people, Mao Zedong was very *ling*, and he is indeed elevated to the status of a deity in many newly built temples. Often, though, historical figures who are very *ling* are morally ambiguous, like Lord Guan, the general from the Three Kingdoms, who is worshipped in countless temples, at once violent and cruel and wise and good.[14]

One may even find something *ling* in the disturbing and tragic suicides of Chinese rural women, as analyzed by Wu Fei. As opposed to scholars who (following the classic theory of Émile Durkheim) speculate that these suicides are the result of social isolation or a breakdown of moral norms, Wu Fei finds that they are a powerful way to break from relationships that have become oppressive and norms that have become stifling—a force of creativity against a stifling framework of order. The suicides involve a "gamble with *qi*" (*duqi*), an explosion of impulsive energy against family members whose power has become oppressive. The suicide is thus a form of triumph, leading to a tremendous loss of face for one's domestic or even political oppressors. It is something beyond good or evil, or, to borrow a phrase from Yeats, a "terrible beauty."[15] Very *ling*.

The *sheng*, on the other hand, is about order and harmony achieved through respectable moral and practical action in this world. In the past, the way to such action was exemplified and administered by bureaucratic scholar officials in the service of the emperor who harmonized this world with the cosmos. However, with the Chinese revolution, the *sheng* has become attenuated and its connection with state power changed.

From the early 1900s to the present, all Chinese governments have been opposed to "superstition," in which they include all those ritual and communal activities aiming to tap into energies beyond this visible world. The May Fourth movement propelled this iconoclastic movement forward and led both Nationalists and Communists to be militant secularists. They shared the view that the sole purpose of a modern government was to improve the material conditions of the Chinese people through the application of modern scientific methods. Both Nationalists and Communists tried to destroy most local temples and to wipe out most popular religious practices through a combination of scientific education and political repression. At the same time, both the Nationalists and the Communists carried out great political rituals, like the enshrining of Sun Yat-sen in his memorial tomb in Nanjing, lauding Mao Zedong as the Great Sun That Shines in Our Hearts, and celebrating all the glories of Chinese history (without Mao Zedong) in the opening ceremonies for the 2008 Olympics. There was certainly an attempt to evoke something sacred in all this.

Yet this is not like the old *sheng* that linked local communities through the emperor to the cosmos. First, the Communist government's official ideology is atheist. Second, it is committed to a modern scientific worldview (however much some of its policies might be based on "junk science"). Third, it employs a modern bureaucratic style of management (however dysfunctional the bureaucracy may become), based officially on instrumentally rational rules. The modern Chinese regime is no longer a state drenched in cosmic meaning; it is what Max Weber would have called an "iron cage."

Under such a regime, there is no longer a dialectical interplay but rather a radical disconnect between the spiritual energy described by *ling* and the modern state. The eruptions of *ling* may for practical reasons be tolerated but always contingently and always under suspicion. When, as in the case of Falungong, the power of charismatic force grips too many people, the government can panic and mobilize tremendous power against it. [16]

Yet time and again throughout the twentieth and early twenty-first centuries, the *ling* has resisted all attempts at eradication. It simply, restlessly, changes form. At the beginning of the twentieth century, local temples were the sites for the most powerful ritual. Into the vacuum left by the destruction of temple worship came widespread "redemptive societies," often combining Daoist, Buddhist, Confucian, and sometimes even Christian symbols into a supposedly universalistic message and employing traditional (like spirit writing) and modern means of communication to construct large organizations spanning many provinces and even reaching overseas Chinese communities around the world. During the 1930s, redemptive societies like the Unity Way (Yiguandao) actually had more members than either the GMD or the Communist Party. [17] An important characteristic of the redemptive societies was that they were voluntary associations, with membership open to all who wished to practice their forms of spiritual cultivation. In this way, they were different from village-based worship, which was confined only to those who happened to be born or married into a particular community or lineage. In such organizations, one encountered the *ling* not as a gift given to one through the power of tradition and accident of location but as a benefit achieved through personal practice in a widespread spiritual discipline presided over by a charismatic teacher, full of *ling*. The GMD government did its best to restrict such organizations, and the Communist regime crushed them, although the Unity Way has now become a global organization and is an important force in Taiwanese society. [18]

In reform-era China, the *ling* now manifests itself in new forms. Large-scale organizations, such as the Unity Way, remain banned, but, as mentioned, there are millions of new temples, pilgrimages to holy mountains, local healers, ramifying Christian networks, and syncretistic regional organizations with charismatic leaders like the founder of the Confucian religion in Fujian. It is a partial throwback to the nineteenth century with the power of the *ling* being anchored in localities, local villages, and local temples rather than large organizations, such as the redemptive societies.

Yet unlike imperial times, there is a deep disconnect between these organizations and the Chinese state.

Within the past decade, the state is more tolerant toward popular religious activities than during the Maoist era and even the Deng Xiaoping era.[19] Now, many forms of popular religiosity are being relabeled from "feudal superstition" to "nonmaterial cultural heritage." Temples and festivals are being treated as folklore. Often, they are allowed to be constructed or to be rebuilt as officially designated museums, attracting urban tourists who come to see a quaint part of China's past. Meanwhile, inside the temple, devotees are prostrating themselves, burning incense, seeking their fortunes by casting oracle blocks, and even carrying out séances through "spirit writing tablets" in which they communicate directly with the gods.

The government's tolerance is not due to the melting of its ideologically atheist heart but rather to the practical impossibility of monitoring the hearts of 1.3 billion citizens who are more mobile than ever before. It is a negative tolerance, without acceptance, and it can be instantly revoked whenever officials find a particular manifestation of religiosity threatening.

This does not stop the eruption of *ling* or diminish the creation of *renao*. It actually generates a luxuriant diversity of such breaks in the façade of the workaday world and punctuations in the rhythms of ordinary life. There are now probably more *varieties* of religious experience being cultivated in China than since the nineteenth century. These now include both ascriptive and intentional communities for tapping into the power of *ling* and improvising new rituals to celebrate it. There is spirit writing, inner alchemy, miraculous healing, exorcisms, visionary revelations, and, in some places, an anticipation of the end of the world (when either the Unborn Eternal Mother or the Maitreya Buddha or Jesus will return). Unlike during the Qing dynasty, however, these outbursts of spiritual creativity are not encompassed within a sacred imperial canopy that accepts their ontology even as it tries to isolate and draw on those parts that promote the good virtues necessary for a harmonious social order. But in an era of globalization, they are linked in horizontally rhizomic threads of interpersonal relations with overseas Chinese communities in Taiwan, Southeast Asia, Europe, and the Americas.[20] Money flows from Chinese communities in Singapore to temple-building projects in Fujian.[21] Videos of lectures by spiritual masters flow back and forth across the Taiwan Strait. Pentecostal missionaries from Hong Kong go on secret trips to the mainland to show the faithful how to speak in tongues.[22] Wenzhou immigrants in Paris exchange spiritual testimonies with their relatives back home.[23]

Although restless, Chinese society is thus not atomized, and I would modify Yunxiang Yan's assertion that it is individualized.[24] The grassroots religious celebrations I have described always involve communities and help create social networks. Nor is the society morally empty. The religious groups flourishing throughout the society almost always involve appeals to moral discipline, although this may not be the kind of discipline that supports the interests of the state or even the interests of many others in society. The bravery of Falungong members courting martyrdom to stand up for their beliefs is a case in point.

A DECENTERED CHINA

Yet though not atomized, the society is, in the words of Vincent Goossaert and David Palmer, "de-centered." "Before the twentieth century, Chinese religion was also characterized by diversity, but one with an ordering center of gravity: the religio-political state. The end of the imperial regime and the 1919 anti-traditionalist May Fourth movement ejected this ordering center; the twentieth century was witness to a succession of substitutes, from the New Life Movement to the Mao cult, which did not endure. The result is a de-centered religious universe, exploding centrifugally in all directions. Since traditional Chinese cosmology and society were religiously structured, the result is a de-centered society, a de-centered China: a Middle Kingdom that has lost its Middle."[25]

In this restless, decentered China, there is extraordinary creativity, constant outbursts of *ling*, and explosions of *renao* but also a vast scattering of energy. For Goossaert and Palmer, the religious question is, "Will there ever be, once again, a spiritual center of gravity for the Chinese world?" I would question whether there needs to be a center.

The *Book of Dao* (*Daodejing*) says that the most powerful thing in the world is water, which yields to everything and thus overcomes and eventually engulfs everything. Water is powerful because it has no structure, no center. The Dao is powerful—the source of *ling* and the matrix of all things—because it is an undifferentiated whole, without any articulated form and thus without any center. It is because of this centerless resiliency that, despite the collapse of Chinese political institutions and despite the denunciations of modernizers of all kinds, the Dao has continued flowing like a great subterranean river through the upheavals of the twentieth century to the present day.

The decentered fluidity of this spiritual current may enable it to survive the breakdown of global political economic structures that is now facing us. State socialism as a structure for human flourishing has obviously failed. But the victor in the Cold War, liberal capitalism, seems also on the verge of collapse because liberal democratic political institutions seem unable to contain the restless destructiveness of the global market economy. Uninhibited by Cold War necessity to demonstrate that capitalism could promote general welfare for a mass society, the world's ruling elites are willing to foster vast inequalities of wealth and mass insecurity while allowing the ecological balance of the planet to be destroyed. Meanwhile, democratic political institutions, bought and paid for largely by the ruling elites, seem frozen in indecision. In America, the mores—the "habits of the heart" that Tocqueville hoped would restrain and channel that society's restless creativity—have eroded deeply. As Franz Schurmann once said of the Western political system, the rot may have gone too deep for it to be saved.[26]

If this be so, then the Chinese tragic experience of twentieth-century modernity may yet lead us to hope that centerless, riverine sources of human creativity will continue to flow under the wreckage of political-economic institutions. Around the globe, sparks of creative energy, *ling*, or touches of the Spirit can give birth to new habitats.

NOTES

1. Alexis de Tocqueville, *Democracy in America*, trans. George Lawrence (New York: Doubleday Anchor Books, 1969), 535–36.

2. Robert Weller, *Unities and Diversities in Chinese Religion*. (New York: Macmillan and University of Washington Press, 1987).

3. Author's interview notes.

4. In Western social science, the "sacred" is usually associated with Durkheim's famous definition: a collective representation of the community that unites those who believe in it into a single moral community; see Émile Durkheim, *The Elementary Forms of Religious Life*, trans. Karen E. Fields (New York: Free Press, 1995), 21–44. The Durkheimian definition sees the sacred as the force for social integration. The "holy" was the subject of the German scholar of comparative religion Rudolf Otto's *The Idea of the Holy*, trans. John W. Harvey (New York: Oxford University Press, 1923). For Otto, the holy is an awe-inspiring force that can be disruptive as well as integrative. I think that the contrast between the sacred and the holy is a rough approximation in English of the contrast between *sheng* and *ling* in Chinese parlance.

5. This discussion of *sheng* and *ling* is based on Kenneth Dean, *Lord of the Three in One* (Princeton, NJ: Princeton University Press, 1998), 58–61.

6. Du Xuede, "Wu'an shi, Guyi cun, yingshen jisi ji shehuo nuoxi," in *Handan diqu minsu ji lu*, Fan Lizhu and Daniel Overmeyer, ed. (Tianjin: Guji chubanshe, 2006), 49–91. This account is based on my own interviews as well as the description by Du Xuede.

7. For the significance of *guorizi*, or "passing time," in rural Chinese culture, see Wu Fei, *Suicide and Justice* (London: Routledge Contemporary China Series, 2009), 22–31.

8. See Lizhu Fan and James D. Whitehead, "Spirituality in a Modern Chinese Metropolis," in *Religious Life in China*, ed. David A. Palmer, Glenn Shive, and Philip L. Wickeri (New York: Oxford University Press, 2011), 1–29.

9. Fieldwork conducted mostly by Fan Lizhu and Chen Na, although I also participated in an interview.

10. David Aikman, *Jesus in Beijing* (Washington, DC: Regnery, 2003); Richard Madsen, "Signs and Wonders: Christianity and Hybrid Modernity in China," in *Christianity in Contemporary China: Socio-Cultural Perspectives*, ed. Francis Khek Gee Lim (London: Routledge, 2013), 17–20. For historical background, see Xi Lian, *Redeemed by Fire: The Rise of Popular Christianity in Modern China* (New Haven, CT: Yale University Press, 2010).

11. The song creator's name is Lu Xiaomin, or "Sister Ruth." See Aikman, *Jesus in Beijing*, 108–11.

12. Richard Madsen, *China's Catholics: Tragedy and Hope in an Emerging Civil Society* (Berkeley: University of California Press, 1998), 91–95.

13. Henrietta Harrison, *The Missionary's Curse and Other Tales from a Chinese Catholic Village* (Berkeley: University of California Press, 2013).

14. Richard Madsen, *Democracy's Dharma: Religious Renaissance and Political Development in Taiwan* (Berkeley: University of California Press, 2007), 117.

15. William Butler Yeats, *Easter, 1916.*

16. David A. Palmer, *Qigong Fever: Body, Science, and Utopia in China* (New York: Columbia University Press, 2007).

17. Vincent Goossaert and David A. Palmer, *The Religious Question in Modern China* (Chicago: University of Chicago Press, 2011), 107.

18. Goossaert and Palmer, *The Religious Question in Modern China*, 93–108.

19. Richard Madsen, "The Upsurge of Religion in China," *Journal of Democracy* 21, no. 4 (October 2010): 58–71.

20. Goossaert and Palmer, *The Religious Question in Modern China*, 359–92.

21. Kuah Khun Eng, *Rebuilding the Ancestral Village: Singaporeans in China* (Aldershot: Ashgate, 2000).

22. Aikman, *Jesus in Beijing*, 271–75.

23. Cao Nanlai, *Constructing China's Jerusalem: Christians, Power, and Place in Contemporary Wenzhou* (Stanford, CA: Stanford University Press, 2011), 43–47.

24. Yunxiang Yan, *Private Life under Socialism: Love, Intimacy, and Family Change in a Chinese Village, 1949–1999* (Stanford, CA: Stanford University Press, 2003).

25. Goossaert and Palmer, *The Religious Question in Modern China*, 3.

26. Franz Schurmann, "Is U.S. Suffering from the Same Rot as the USSR?," *San Francisco Chronicle*, op-ed, September 19, 1991.

EIGHT

An Invisible Path

"Urban Buddhists" in Beijing and Their Search for Meaning

David Moser

You don't find Buddhism, it finds you.

I have been living and working in Beijing since 1987, and in the last decade or so, Buddhism may not have found me, but it seems to be stalking me. Many of the secretaries and teachers I work with every day; many of the television producers, artists, and musicians I encounter; and many of my white-collar acquaintances at companies like Nokia and Microsoft—even my daughter's math tutor—have all "come out" to me as Buddhists. Anyone living in Beijing in the years since the turn of the century cannot help but be struck by the proliferation of Buddhist "memes" in the environment, the increasing amount Buddhist paraphernalia on sale in the streets and flea markets, the shelves of Buddhist books and DVDs in bookstores, and an expanding universe of cyber-Buddhism on the Internet. Clearly, vast numbers of Chinese people are exploring—and increasingly embracing—the Buddhist faith.

My subjective anecdotal observations about the increase in the number of Buddhist adherents seem to be borne out by statistics, although it is difficult to obtain accurate estimates. Even the most statistically careful surveys of the number of Buddhists in the PRC vary so widely as to be useless, ranging anywhere from 30 million to as many as 300 million, with some official state estimates averaging about 100 million.[1] Western news outlets and analysts have followed with particular interest the rise of Christianity (under the watchful eye of the government), yet there is good evidence suggesting that the Buddhist revival is actually the largest component of China's growing religiosity.[2]

One of the reasons for the great disparity in survey estimates is the problem of definition. What do we mean by the term "Buddhist"? In post-Mao studies of the revival of Buddhism, the counting usually involved the two traditional categories: the monks and nuns in monasteries (*chujia ren*) and the "lay Buddhists" (*jushi*), who typically participate in temple activities while also incorporating Buddhist observances into their secular lives.[3] However, focusing on these groups gives us only a small part of the total picture. The demographic composition of worshippers at the small number of Beijing temples is predominantly older working-class or retired citizens, and the number of twenty-somethings in attendance tends to be small.

The dramatic increase of interest and involvement in Buddhism is among a diverse group of urban youth, middle-aged white-collar professionals, and the educated elite, whose participation in the religion is largely informal, highly idiosyncratic, and personal—and not necessarily centered in temple ritual. What such new believers have in common is that that their activities tend to involve transient groups that coalesce or dissolve fluidly, all outside the purview of the religious authorities, invisible to the eye of the State Administration of Religious Affairs (SARA) and the various official Buddhist organizations. Unlike the Catholic, Protestant, and Islamic groups, they do not meet in publicly visible houses of worship on fixed days. Very often, even among the most dedicated, their religious participation is kept apart from their professional lives; thus, theirs constitutes a somewhat "invisible" path. And, as such, surprisingly little is known about the extent of this population, their religious expression, and the overall topology of their beliefs. Alison Jones (2010) conducted a groundbreaking study of lay Buddhists in Nanjing that overlaps considerably with this study, but work on this group of believers is scarce.[4]

What should we call this new wave of Buddhist adherents? Terms I have encountered are "weekend Buddhists" and "bedside Buddhists" (suggesting that such people merely read books about these subjects in bed before going to sleep), but these tend to be derogatory terms that misrepresent the seriousness with which most of these believers adhere to the faith. The standard term *jushi* ("lay Buddhist") tends to denote those who have already formally undergone the ceremony of *guiyi* ("seeking refuge") and who take part to some extent in temple activities. This group overlaps considerably with the people I am studying here, but, for clarity, I will refer to my group by the more neutral term "urban Buddhists."

Since the reform and opening period of the 1980s, China watchers have noted and documented the "values crisis" or "spiritual vacuum" in Chinese society. To what extent does this urban Buddhist revival represent a partial fulfillment of this long-standing social need? What is there about Buddhism that is attracting so many people, many of them young, well educated, and highly motivated, toward this belief system? And what form does the religion take in the daily lives of these new converts?

To address these questions, I began to conduct interviews to gain a better understanding of motivations and activities of this group. The information in this chapter is gathered from about thirty hours of recorded interviews with various self-identified Buddhists, interactions and talks with Buddhist masters and Living Buddhas, experiences on weekend temple retreats, and participating in numerous informal Buddhist house meetings or study sessions. My hope is to provide a glimpse into this new world of converts through the voices of the converts themselves. All names are pseudonyms.

THE INITIATION AND CONVERSION PROCESS

Since religious activity of all kinds in China was virtually extinguished during the Mao period, the generation that came of age during the period of Deng Xiaoping's reforms was essentially the first generation to participate in the lay Buddhist revival. Although virtually everyone in China has some rudimentary familiarity with the Buddhist religious tradition, with rare exceptions the belief had not been passed down in families but had to be rediscovered and absorbed by most of my respondents. Thus, there is a question about how these people converted to Buddhism.

The reasons given by my informants for adopting Buddhism were varied and multidimensional, but in sifting through their stories and accounts, some themes emerged. The following are rough (and overlapping) categories I found useful:

Problem solvers. These were people who sought out Buddhism to solve a crisis or serious life trauma. Usually, they could point to a specific event or phase in their lives that prompted their turn toward Buddhism: a traumatic event, a death, a serious illness, a divorce, or a sudden loss.

Seekers. These described their conversion as part of a long-standing search for spiritual or religious meaning or as a general interest in metaphysical and philosophical questions. It was common for such people to have tried a number of religions or spiritual movements before deciding on Buddhism.

Lifestyle Buddhists. These seemed to have approached their involvement with Buddhism as if it were a passionate hobby, having begun with influence from the media, the Internet, their peers, or examples of the conversions of famous pop singers and movie stars and moving in curiosity from there. The religion became part of their self-image, and they often exhibited their belief in displays such as distinctive dress, ornaments, home shrines, and so on. This approach contrasts with the existential concerns or long-standing spiritual quest of the other two categories.

These conversion modes are not mutually exclusive, and no doubt most initiation experiences involve a combination of two or more of them.

PROBLEM SOLVERS

The "problem solver" conversion story often involves traumatic events of various kinds, leading to a desperate search for alleviation of suffering. The most common account involves a sudden troubling or life-threatening illness. Lay Buddhist websites are filled with testimonies of people miraculously cured of cancers, tumors, paralysis, and other ailments, usually through reading scripture, reciting mantras, or praying to the Buddha. It is also a familiar trope in tracts, brochures, and collections of Buddhist tales. Chen Yu, a secretary in a law firm, told me why she had converted to Buddhism:

> Three years ago now, I woke up one morning and found that I had great difficulty swallowing anything. It was painful to eat anything like meat or bread, and even tea hurt to swallow. I went through every test, but they couldn't find what was wrong. I lost so much weight I looked like a ghost. . . . My mother had a friend who took me to see her master [*fashi*], and he asked me about an abortion I had had years before. He said the soul of the unborn child was in torment, and that's why my throat was blocked. He performed a *chaodu* ritual [a ceremony to help the soul of a deceased person find peace] and had me read the *Jinggang-jing* [*Diamond Sutra*] out loud. . . . Very soon after that my throat suddenly opened up, and I've been perfectly healthy ever since.

Believers who lack personal stories of illness volunteer anecdotes about the experience of their friends or acquaintances:

> There was a friend of mine who had a disease, one of those *guaibing* [unexplained illness] that left her totally paralyzed. It was like the disease that [Stephen] Hawking has. She couldn't move, could only sit there all day. The daughter started doing Buddhist activities like *fang-sheng* [liberating of animal life] and such, and the woman was soon completely healed. The entire family was overjoyed and converted to Buddhism. I can introduce you to these people if you'd like; they're all friends of mine.

Such accounts perhaps have the familiar ring of the testimonials at Christian faith-healing sessions. The difference is that there is seldom any account of a change of spiritual consciousness or any of the emotional conversion experiences that we associate with the Christian context; rather, the conversion event involves the mere adoption of formulaic ritual behavior—the reciting of mantras, prostrations, and reading of scriptures—that actuates the miracle. The emphasis is less on interior faith conversion than on the problem-solving efficacy of the ritual behavior itself.[5]

Physical ailments are not the only domain aided by Buddhist intervention; in many cases, the "problem" to be solved is the uncertainty and existential question about ultimate meaning triggered by a psychologically troubling experience. Problem solvers also speak of the efficacy of Buddhism in alleviating psychiatric disorders such as depression and schizophrenia. One informant even told me that his father had reversed the course of Alzheimer's disease through Buddhist meditation and prayer. Converts also talk of difficult life changes, traumatic divorces, or emotional crises. Xiao Wu, a recent college graduate, recounted a conversion experience that is typical:

> You know, many people in my family have died, but to be honest, the first time I really felt the pain of losing someone was when our dog died. This was when I was in high school, and my grandfather bought me a dog, Xiao Bai, and we had him for maybe four or five years, I think. He got very sick, and it was the first time I had seen death firsthand, happening every day right before me. Have you ever had a dog? Then maybe you can imagine how it felt to watch him die. I remember seeing him struggling with each breath to hold on to his life, and I thought, "Though he's just an animal, he feels the strong desire for life and wants to hold onto it." I was so moved by seeing him this way, and I tried hard to understand it. I thought about it night and day, and in the end, seeing him struggle in death made me realize that he had a soul, just like all of us. There is no difference in our souls, animals and humans, I thought. So it struck me then, all I had heard about Buddhism, it all made perfect sense to me, I had seen what Buddhism teaches us right before my eyes. And of course I became a vegetarian instantly. I knew I had to devote my life to this.

Xiao Wu's introspective account seems to indicate that, when confronted with a traumatic event that cries out for a framework to provide meaning and spiritual comfort, the indigenous belief system of Buddhism, embedded in his culture, presents itself as the self-evident solution to the existential puzzlement. Indeed, some of my interviewees talked of Buddhism as a background process in their lives, waiting to be inevitably activated when a crisis or urgent need arose. Han Mei talks about how she was drawn to Buddhism when her mother became bedridden:

> When I look back, I realize that the Buddha was always there in my life as a hidden force in the background. I never had to think about the Buddha, but now when I remember back then, I realize he was always there. So that when I was so upset about my mother, I sent out a *gan* [stimulus], and without me even knowing it, the Buddha sent a *ying* [response]. That's why I said, "You don't find Buddhism. It finds you."

This image of Buddhism as suddenly presenting itself at a time of crisis is a common theme among problem solvers, who often tend to conceptualize Buddhism not as a path of mental cultivation or spiritual development but rather as an ever-present safety net. Whatever the short-term physical or emotional trigger, the result is often a more long-standing, fully integrated adoption of the religion into the daily life of the believer.

SEEKERS

It is not uncommon for those in the seeker category to have tried several different religions, spiritual activities, or philosophical obsessions before coming to Buddhism. The Buddhist revival in urban China comes in the wake of a vast wave of post-Mao interest in *qigong*, yoga, occult mysticism, and indigenous folk religion. When asked, many of my "seeker" informants could produce a list of cults, religions, or spiritual domains that they had investigated or sampled. In retrospect, the believer usually identifies the former pastimes as part of a larger search for overall "spiritual solace" (*jingshen jituo*).

Yuan Bo is example of such a seeker. He has been interested in religion since the 1980s, when he encountered two Christian missionaries on his campus. Yuan Bo and his brother formed an informal Bible study group, and he considered himself to be a Christian for almost a decade. He audited a religious studies class at his university and has experimented with drugs such as "ecstasy" (widely available in China since the early 2000s) in a quest to better understand the phenomenon of consciousness. In 2004, he began reinvestigating Buddhism and converted after a year or so of study. His home bookshelf is filled with Buddhist books and tracts:

Me: So back in the 1980s, Buddhism was not as trendy or common as it is now. Did you even know much about it back then?

Yuan: Oh yes, you have to realize, even though there were not so many "weekend Buddhists," as you call them, we all knew about Buddhism. It was all around us, if you were a boy reading *Journey to the West* or the comic books that have the stories of ghosts and monks. We knew all the concepts and the words so well, of course. It's just a part of Chinese life. But for whatever reason, maybe because of this influence, I was always interested in metaphysical matters. I read a lot of books before, including that book *Dianetics* when it came out in the 1980s in Chinese, though I found it very strange at the time. So even though, since I was a Christian then, I had to exclude all the other religions, actually I already knew and accepted Buddhism, in some way. The way I came to Buddhism was through my own brother, who is still taking part in a Christian Bible study. He said to me, "I have to understand Buddhism; because it is a part of the culture, we must understand it." So I began to study it with him because I felt I should know it, maybe even so I could show how Christianity was superior. That's when I was able to really understand Buddhism in a deep way. . . . Later I realized that this was what I had been looking for.

Clearly, for Yuan Bo, Buddhism was just one of many options on a menu of possible belief systems that he had been exploring since his youth.

Comparing the problem solvers to the seeker category of believers, I noted a socioeconomic class difference. The seekers are more likely to come from a higher, more well educated and connected class that includes professors, professionals, and businessmen—the beneficiaries of Chinese economic modernization. Those whom I perceived as problem solvers tended to be people without a college education, working at lower-paying jobs. This difference may reflect a rather obvious state of affairs, namely, that it is members of the privileged, educated class who tend to have the time and luxury to explore such spiritual domains, whereas the less economically well off resort to religion only when faced with crisis situations that force metaphysical considerations on them. For the affluent, Buddhism is a choice to explore; for the lower class, Buddhism is often simply the most readily available lifeline.

Some members of the seeker category may not have explored various other belief systems yet still speak of a long-term, latent interest in metaphysical issues that was awakened by exposure to Buddhism. Ma Rui, an information technology consultant, is such an adherent. He has not yet committed himself to a Buddhist master, but he meditates every day, reads constantly, and attends informal Buddhist house meetings. Although Buddhism was the first religion he seriously explored, he remembers himself as always asking questions about spiritual matters:

> There was no event that triggered my interest. I was always curious about it. It may seem natural for you Americans to be interested in religion because it's so much a part of your daily life; God is even on your money. But maybe you know, in China we were seldom encouraged to talk about such things, and it was never in my school or textbooks. I can't remember my parents ever even mentioning it to me. But to ask, "What is the meaning of life?"—it's a natural question, isn't it? So throughout my youth, I always would wonder about life and whether there is some kind of spiritual world. But I did not find it in the books I read and never on television except in *Journey to the West* stories, but that's not real Buddhism; it's just an empty phrase or idea here and there. But now, with all the bookstores and websites, there's so much information about Buddhism everywhere that it's easy to learn about it on your own. . . . So to answer your question, I was always thinking about these matters, but I saw there are answers to these questions all around me. That's when I really began to explore this particular thing, Buddhism.

One gets a sense from such accounts that, as the PRC government shifted its general stance on religious practice from "discouraged" to "permitted but not encouraged," the effect was an opening of the floodgates to latent spiritual seekers such as Ma Rui.

LIFESTYLE BUDDHISTS

For young urban elites in the PRC today, Buddhism has become cool. And these new believers have taken advantage of the greater personal autonomy in daily Chinese life to explore Buddhism as a lifestyle choice. The attraction is to a certain extent due to the allure of Buddhism in the popular press and the Internet. Just as actor Richard Gere's Buddhist associations give him a certain cachet in the West, Buddhism's trendiness in part comes from the host of media figures who embrace the religion. Pop celebrities such as singer Wang Fei (Faye Wong), actor Jet Li, and a host of other stars on the mainland and Hong Kong are professing Buddhists. Chinese entrepreneurs, billionaires, and famous chief executive officers take time off from their schedules to commune with Buddhist masters at secluded monasteries. After Steve Jobs's death, the Apple chief's Buddhist leanings were a topic of great interest on the Chinese Internet.

Zhao Ran, a magazine graphic artist, became part of a circle of Buddhist adherents in about 2008 at the invitation of a workmate. She has since filled her living space with Buddhist paraphernalia; there is a statue of Guanyin in her car; she wears the *fozhu*, the Buddhist prayer beads, looped on her wrist; and various statues of the Buddha sit in her living room. She explained to me the attraction of Buddhism this way:

> I always had a good feeling about Buddhism, even when I knew almost nothing about it. I liked going into the temples, the statues, the incense, and all that. It just felt good to me, very natural, like it was my fate to find it. And when so many of my friends started studying it, I asked them whom I should study first, and they said Master Jin Kong. His DVDs were everywhere, so I bought some and began to gradually learn what Buddhism really meant. . . . Even when I found out more about other religions, Buddhism always seemed more *comfortable* I guess. I asked my friend at work, who studied religions, and he had a metaphor; he told me that Taoism is like a pharmacy—all the teachings are like medicine. And Confucianism is like a food store, a place where you could get your daily food. But Buddhism is more like a giant supermarket that sells anything you need for life; it's all-encompassing [*baoluowanxiang*]. I heard that even Einstein, just before he died, said that all the truths of physics he was looking for could be found in the Buddhist scriptures. When I heard that, I said, "This is the religion for me."

One can notice how Zhao Ran's description of Buddhism's attraction resembles the language of product branding, evocative of the identification and loyalty that one feels toward one's Apple computer or Starbucks latte. She speaks of Buddhism almost in terms of a product that delivers more than the other brands and that feels congruent with her own lifestyle and tastes. While her religious conviction may be very real, there is none of the existential urgency of the problem solvers and little of the metaphysical preoccupation of the seekers.

In part because of this trendy fascination with Buddhism, there has arisen a certain type of undesirable practitioner in the urban Buddhist landscape, labeled a *foyouzi* ("Buddhist charlatan/slippery character"). Such a person typically acquires his knowledge of Buddhism by perusing popular books and websites, crashing study sessions, and perhaps ingratiating himself with a Buddhist master or two. With this rudimentary knowledge, he begins to appear at lay Buddhist activities flaunting his supposed enlightenment, adopting the outward pious purity and serene wisdom of seasoned *fashi*, all while possessing none of the dedication, self-sacrifice, and true experience of a spiritually mature believer. This type of annoying individual is the subject of numerous complaints in the blogs and bulletin-board sites. Such persons tend to flit from one master to another, making their presence known in various urban Buddhist circles. Often such people succeed in attracting naive disciples themselves or establish their own study groups, taking in less experienced novices.

BUDDHISM IN CYBERSPACE

There are many thousands of Buddhism-related websites freely accessible within China. Some of these are administrated by major Buddhist organizations, others by the various Lay Buddhist Society branches throughout China, and others by private individuals or groups. If we add to this the numerous personal blogs and "microblogs" and Weibo (the flexible Twitter-like social networking platform that has revolutionized many social domains in China), the number of sites containing Buddhist content is truly enormous. Sina Weibo is by far the most popular, with more than 250 million people registered on the service, and the new medium has become a powerful—and some in the government fear dangerous—medium for connecting like-minded communities of people all over China.[6]

Virtually every major *fashi*, or Buddhist master, has a personal microblog or website. (Even the Dalai Lama has an account on Twitter, which is blocked and inaccessible within the PRC without a virtual private network). Most of these sites are set up and updated by disciples, but a good many of the *fashi* are very media savvy and manage the site and blog entries on their own. These *fashi* use the microblog site to announce gath-

erings and lectures, pass on news and updates, and provide daily homi-
lies, poems, bits of wisdom, and humor. Some of these microblogs have
millions of followers (or *fensi* ["fans"], the new Weibo social network
technical term for "follower") on a scale comparable to movie stars and
pop singers.[7]

While a few urban Buddhists I talked to expressed disdain for the
various Buddhist Internet sites, most of my respondents voiced no objec-
tion or negative reaction to the various Buddhist *fashi* having a presence
in cyberspace. While not all lay Buddhists make use of Weibo and blogs
to the same degree, virtually all seem to approve strongly of this new
niche in cyberspace. "It's just a new medium," they say, "no different
from using the television or radio to get the message out."

In the fast-paced urban environment, Buddhist "memes" must compete with all the other commercial and entertainment information that
fills the airwaves and cyberspace. The bite-sized bits of wisdom or solace
that these blogs provide can be an enticement to explore further and can
lead to more significant involvement and life-changing realizations. Giv-
en the immense amount of cybertraffic that such sites elicit, it is clear that
a great many people are getting their initial introduction to Buddhism
through these channels.

THE CHOICE OF SECT

Although Buddhism is divided into numerous sects (*menpai*), I have
found that, for those in the early stages of involvement, this does not
seem to be an important consideration. Most urban Buddhists begin with
a very general interest, reading a wide variety of literature on the subject,
much of which does not delve into the doctrinal specifics of any particular sect. There are so many books and DVDs produced by individual
Buddhist masters that many of my novice interviewees assumed that
each master had his own school. Also, since the Buddhist temples are by
and large no longer associated with any particular branch of Buddhism,
the salience of sects is even more attenuated in the minds of the general
population.

Many times, I have asked a particular Buddhist master or urban Buddhist which sect he or she follows, and, surprisingly, my question is most
often greeted with polite amusement or mild impatience. "It doesn't matter!" "Why ask that? All the sects lead to the same goal, so don't worry
about it." Even among many of the more dedicated believers I talked to,
the decision of adopting a particular school of Buddhism seemed to be of
surprisingly little importance.

Where the question of sect finally becomes important is when a decision is made to formally "take refuge" (*guiyi*) and to enter into a perma-
nent dependent relationship with a *fashi*. At this point, the believer must

take into consideration more specific questions of the doctrines of each school, the required daily regimen, and the degree of commitment. But even in this case, the particulars of dogma and ritual are given much less importance for the average urban Buddhist, who may explore many different sects, perhaps never settling permanently on any one of them.

And even among those who decide to follow a certain sect, its adoption does not constitute a commitment to the "truth" of the sect or the belief that the sect "provides the best explanation of ultimate reality." Rather, the potential follower tends to talk of the doctrine as merely a "path" or "process" toward a common goal of *jietuo* ("release [from suffering]"). It is assumed from the outset by both the master and the disciple that any number of different paths might be possible, and each person merely selects the one that is more suitable to individual personality and needs.

An analogy I encountered many times in discussions about the efficacy of various sects was that of choosing a marriage partner. Ma Luo, a middle-aged volunteer at the Beijing Lay Buddhist Association, provides such a characterization:

> [Choosing a sect] is like getting married. You can't stay single your entire life; you have to choose a wife at some point. And if you're lucky, you find a wife you really love. But that doesn't mean you couldn't have loved another woman. And it certainly doesn't mean that the other man's wife is no good or that yours is the best one. It's just that you have to choose one woman eventually and be dedicated to her. For me, choosing Pure Land was like that. I was attracted to it, so I married it. Really that's all it is. Zen can be wonderful for other people, and it has many good things about it. Pure Land has been good for me. So I know what you're asking, but it's not a matter of right or wrong.

Of course, the process of settling on a specific school and one particular master is often indecisive and circuitous. The experience of a former student of mine, Wu Di, is representative and worth presenting in some detail.

Wu Di is the son of an officer in the People's Liberation Army (PLA), and when he began to get involved with Buddhism, his parents strongly disapproved. "They were strict materialists, atheists, and I was raised to believe only in science and materialism," he told me. "I realized the only way to convince them was to show some real improvement in my personal life."

After a few months of practicing Buddhism, Wu Di felt he needed to decide on a particular Buddhist sect and devote himself completely to it. He started with Zen, thinking that it would be an easier path and that he could make progress more quickly. He soon found, however, that Zen did not provide him with any systematic means to achieve his spiritual goals. "Zen requires a very high level of cultivation," he told me. "I found

I wasn't at that level. I was quite stupid, in fact. So I thought it better to try a method more suitable for a stupid person." He began to seek a master to help guide him, and within a couple weeks he encountered a Living Buddha (*huofo*) from Tibet who was happy to take him on as a disciple.

The Living Buddha was a master of the "red sect" (*hongjiao*) of Tantric Buddhism. One of the requirements of the master was that Wu Di first perform 100,000 prostrations before an image of the Buddha and recite each of four mantras 100,000 times as a preliminary regimen. "I could never have imagined myself kowtowing to the Buddha in this way," Wu Di reported. "Before this, I would have thought 'Why should I bow to a piece of wood?' But I found it was really a good way to rid myself of my pride and stubborn nature."

Wu Di's conversion brought changes to his family life as well. His wife soon converted as well, and both of them took the "oath of abstinences" (*shou jie*) pledging to obey the "five abstinences" [*wu jie*: killing living things, stealing, lewd behavior, slander or lies, and alcohol]. This was not easy, as Wu Di recounts: "It was hard enough to give up alcohol, but the injunction against stealing was really hard. This includes buying bootleg DVDs and downloading illegal mp3 files! That was really difficult!" The couple has an eight-year-old boy, and although he is too young to understand Buddhism, they began to buy him simple books on Buddhism and to download Buddhist children's parables and stories. They canceled their cable television hookup and no longer watch television.

After a few months, Wu Di found that the daily prostrations and rituals were impractical in the context of his daily life and work. Wu Di began to doubt if this particular set of techniques was right for him. At some point, a friend recommended the Pure Land school (*Jingtuzong*), the simplest of the Mahayana sects, which emphasizes salvation by faith in the Amitabha Buddha and requires only the reciting of *amituofo*. After some consternation, he screwed up his courage and asked the *huofo* if he could switch to the Pure Land discipline. "To my surprise, the *huofo* agreed," he said. "The *huofo* said 'Sure, the Pure Land sect way is really great for some people, go ahead and proceed with that discipline.' I was really relieved." At that point, Wu Di took Pure Land master Jing Kong as his second *fashi*, placing his photo next to the photo of the *huofo* on his informal shrine at home.

Wu Di now recites the mantra *namoamituofo* thousands of times a day. He finds this simpler, more streamlined approach to be just as beneficial in his life. Both Wu Di and his wife, who also has entered into the Jingtu sect, must keep track of how many times a day they recite the chant, and rather than use the traditional string of prayer beads (*fozhu*) to keep track of the number of their recitations, both of them wear Casio digital counters on their wrists, although there are also several Buddhist iPhone apps for this purpose.

The majority of urban Buddhists never settle on any particular sect, and even for those who do, it is fairly common for these more dedicated urban Buddhists to try one or another sect before settling on one that suits them. The general consensus here is that the choice of sect is a practical, methodological issue, not a crucial spiritual or doctrinal matter. In fact, in all the interactions and discussions between various urban Buddhists that I observed, I have never witnessed a dispute or serious disagreement about some intersectarian point of doctrine.

THE ROLE OF THE BUDDHIST MASTER (*FASHI*)

The Buddhist networks in urban settings cluster around a fluidly shifting group of Buddhist masters, all from various sects, regions, and backgrounds. Even the casual "weekend" variety of Buddhists will seek out a master and become part of their particular circle of disciples. Initiation into the group always involves word-of-mouth and personal recommendation, and the sphere of followers is always amorphous, fluid, and informal. Masters who gain a large number of disciples will often form an inner circle of more dedicated and motivated disciples who then become the core of a small hierarchy that begins to organize meetings, manage publicity, and maintain the network of communications between members. The relationship between the master and disciple can range from that of an informal follower who sits in on lectures to a dedicated lifetime disciple entirely devoted to the master's goals and well-being.

Most urban Buddhists do not have regular access to a *fashi*; in fact, the shortage of qualified masters for the vast number of new adherents is considered a mild crisis among the community of believers. Without access to direct instruction, most believers spend a great deal of time reading books, watching DVDs, or accessing blogs of some of the more famous Buddhist masters.

To fill the gap, many talented or charismatic lay Buddhists develop a following of disciples, conducting study sessions and even *fahui* activities, all completely outside the temples and established Buddhist centers. I even encountered one of these lay Buddhist masters who had shaved his head, donned monk's robes, and renovated his northwest Beijing apartment into a quasi-temple environment. His followers speak glowingly of his knowledge and enlightenment, although a few outside his circle express doubts about the qualifications of this "pseudomonk."

Just how important is it to have a master to guide one's studies? I found some strong consensus that, if one is to become serious about studying Buddhism, it is essential to settle on a teacher to guide the process. Liu Haitao, a music producer, gives his reason for seeking a master to study with:

Back when I first decided I wanted to be a Buddhist, I read a lot of books on Buddhism. Since I've always been a good student, I was able to learn a lot in a short time from what I was reading and was feeling proud of myself. I could answer every question, or at least I thought so. I didn't think I needed a teacher because who could teach me? And you know, pride is the worst sin for a Buddhist to commit. So I was chatting with the *fashi*, the master of one of my friends. And I was trying to impress him with how much I knew about Buddhism. He listened very politely because he was clearly a very advanced practitioner, and after I had spoken for a while, he said to me "Well, you seem to know a lot; you've really mastered it. So see that picture of a cow on the wall there?" He was pointing to a picture of a cow. "Surely then you know how to get milk from the cow in that picture. So please show us the milk." And then I realized what he was saying. All my learning from books was like trying to get milk from a picture of a cow. I needed to go to a living being, to the source, to get real milk. And that's when I decided to find a teacher.

"Master shopping" is also fairly common, as adherents encounter a different circle of Buddhists and want to try out a different approach from a new master.

One problem is that the Buddhist masters vary widely in background and qualifications. The pool of *fashi* can include individuals with university backgrounds as well as monks who spent most of their lives in a Tibetan monastery, far away from computers and cell phones. Thus, I have heard that some gurus are ultimately not well educated enough to give the educated disciples the kind of systematic and rigorous instruction they are looking for. (One disciple of a Living Buddha confided in me that he had asked his teacher some questions about Buddhism and evolution, and to his astonishment, his living Buddha had never heard of Darwin's theory.) Many of the urban Buddhists I spoke to expressed great affection for their masters, although sometimes this was mixed with condescension or frustration. Many told me that their master had an understanding that was "natural" and "intuitive," but for specific doctrinal issues, they often resorted to books on the subject. Zuo Wen, a television host and practicing Buddhist with a master's degree in Buddhist studies, voiced his concerns:

I, too, think it's important to have a master, but in some sense I have several of them. What I mean is, I consult with different *fashi* at different times, but I really don't think you can get everything from just one. And some of these monks—you know, every day there must be ten monks who come in from outside of Beijing, and there are so many people looking for masters, so they eventually find each other. But some of these monks, really how much do they really know? Some are quite young, and they haven't studied that much. But many of my friends just dedicate themselves to one of these masters, and some even just become his slave, almost. And I'm thinking, "How much can they really learn from this one monk, he's only one person?"

There is also the accusation that some of these masters are merely taking advantage of the "sacred cash cow" of the Buddhist craze to attract elite followers and bolster their own careers, a notable example being Shi Yongxi, the head of the Shaolin Temple, dubbed "the CEO monk" for his marketing activities involving the temple.[8] Whether such charges are always valid or not, as the *fashi* moves out of the cloistered temple environment and into the big cities to take disciples, the required Buddhist skill set expands from study and meditation to include other abilities, such as networking, public speaking, Internet familiarity, and even fund-raising.

ACTIVITIES OF THE URBAN BUDDHISTS

With the increasing government tolerance of religious faith, the urban Buddhists in Beijing are free to participate in a range of religious activities. Such people may or may not go to the temples. They may or may not meditate. They may or may not become vegetarians. Their involvement may involve quiet personal study and thought, reading books, and accessing websites, or it may intensify to full-time involvement and devotion. One finds believers positioned at various points on a continuum, between the dedicated, conventional religious patterns of the lay Buddhists and a much larger mix of people who are seeking their own idiosyncratic—but no less heartfelt—involvement with the religion.

The traditional options are rather straightforward. Temples such as the Longquan Temple or Guanghua Temple or Buddhist centers such as the Beijing Lay Buddhist Society (*Beijing Jushilin*) are open at regular hours, and the faithful are welcomed to worship, take part in *fahui* activities ("dharma sessions," usually involving a group of worshippers perambulating in a circle while chanting), or consult with a monk if one is available. There are usually regular Buddhist group study classes offered at a reasonable tuition fee and the occasional guest lecture by a famous master or expert.

There are countless informal Buddhist study sessions in homes, with fluidly shifting membership. Many vegetarian restaurants also serve as unofficial meeting places for lay Buddhists. There are numerous ongoing charitable activities, such as volunteering at old-age homes or schools for disadvantaged children, and these tend to be arranged and mediated via websites, microblogs, and text messages.

One of the most common group activities is *fangsheng*, literally "liberating life," the releasing of animals (most often fish or turtles) meant for slaughter back into the wild. This is a practice with a long history; lay Buddhists in the Ming and Qing times formed "animal life liberating societies" (*fangsheng hui*) to promote the freeing of animal life, and they even constructed special fish-releasing pools (*fangsheng chi*), some of which can be found in front courtyards of temples in China today. The spiritual goal of the *fangsheng* activity is to improve one's karma in this life to ensure a better rebirth, and it is also a way to bring about miracle cures and healings. Numerous personal testimonies of the benefits of the practice of *fangsheng* in the Buddhist literature can be found on websites and Buddhist audiovisual materials. This is a popular activity among the world Buddhist community, sometimes carried out in conjunction with alliances of PRC and Hong Kong Buddhist groups and animal rights groups, such as the American Society for the Prevention of Cruelty to Animals; in addition, numerous networking websites and Facebook pages are dedicated to these rituals.

Most informal *fangsheng* activities in the urban areas, however, are more modest in scale and usually involve believers buying up large quantities of fish at seafood markets and then releasing the animals into a local lake or river. (Rescuing animals like chickens or pigs is obviously more problematic because there is no viable environment to release them into.) These activities are common, and restaurant clerks and salespeople are often used to the requests of these lay Buddhists to buy up all their stock in order to liberate it.

Mei Qi is a young secretary in a foreign company and says she has been a Buddhist since high school. Although she does not claim to have experienced any miraculous results of the practice, her first experience at a *fangsheng* activity left a powerful impression on her:

> When I first went to a *fangsheng* activity, I must say I was not sure I could participate fully. To tell the truth, I was looking at the fish in the blue plastic buckets, and I thought, "These are just fish; what do they know of life and death? If we didn't release them, they would just end up on a plate in a restaurant, and no one would care or know the difference." But when I was there at the lake and the prayers and rituals were said, I felt something inside of me. I felt a deep connection to the fish, and for the first time I saw them as life, with a soul even. Oh, how strange; it was the first time I ever felt emotion and affection for a fish! I tell you, I actually cried! [*laughs*] How could this be? I must say it does change your consciousness. Now I can't go into a restaurant without being aware that these fish, and these animals are all living things. It's hard to explain, but it was a powerful feeling for me.

In consideration of the busy workday schedules of so many urban Buddhists, many group events, such as *fangsheng* activities, are scheduled on weekend mornings so that believers can more easily take part. Another important activity, temple retreats, are also scheduled on weekends for this reason. Virtually every urban Buddhist I spoke with acknowledged the importance and usefulness of meditation yet talked of the difficulty of finding peaceful spare time to meditate. Places like the Chaoyang Temple, a Zen monastery outside Huairou, north of Beijing, offer urban Buddhists various weekend retreat options where they can meditate and study in the more tranquil environs of the temple.

RELIGIOUS FAITH VERSUS RATIONALISM

In my conversations with urban Buddhists, issues of faith, metaphysics, and spiritualism versus scientific rationalism came up occasionally. Raised in an environment where the default position is scientific atheism, these new believers very often are in the uncomfortable position of justifying their newfound religious convictions to family and friends. Some had also clearly wrestled with some cognitive dissonance in the process of incorporating Buddhism into their scientific worldview. There seemed to be a range of solutions to this problem, from unquestioning adherence to the prescribed practices ("I can't explain why, but it works") to a highly intellectual and analytical approach to understanding and justifying the beliefs. Alison Jones (2010), in her study of Nanjing lay Buddhists, refers to this continuum as the "spectrum of ritual to rationalism."

Chen Guoming, an editor at a newspaper office, had this to say when asked about the claims of miracle healings resulting from *fangsheng* activities:

> I don't openly dispute the claims of some of my friends who say *fang-sheng* has changed their luck or cured them of some disease. But in my heart I don't really believe it. From what I know of Buddhism, the advantages are not that immediate and direct. I think this is very close to superstition. Plus, I think most of those fish or snakes or whatever are just going to die anyway, even if you release them. It seems pointless. So what else are you going to do: set free a chicken or a pig? It wouldn't last long anyway.

Wen Jie is a medical doctor and a dedicated practitioner (although, as with many urban Buddhists, her busy work schedule keeps her from meditating and practicing as much as she would like). When I asked her if she believed the stories of miraculous healings, she responded this way:

> I'm trained in medicine, so perhaps I know more about these kinds of things than others, though it's still a mystery to me at times. We learned about the placebo effect in medical school, so I understand that many illnesses can be cured by state of mind. But there are still many cases of curing that we can't explain. And you can ask some doctors at my hospital, they aren't religious, and they admit they have no explanation. We doctors deal with the physical part of a disease, but there is a mental part that we have no control over. And some even believe there is a soul [*linghun*] that can have control over the body. I believe that, actually. I think some of the stories are exaggerated sometimes, maybe often. But there are some I think are true. I've never had a

serious illness, but I know my health has improved since I began practicing Buddhism.

Wen Jie's response strategy, somewhere in the middle of the ritual–rationalism spectrum, might be characterized as a kind of pragmatic
agnosticism: "I can't reconcile it with my scientific understanding, but I
also can't deny the results."

Some urban Buddhists suggest a compromise, namely, that the supernatural phenomena associated with Buddhism are a part of some not-yet-
understood laws of nature. Wu Haoming, a graduate of Beijing Normal
University, explained this to me:

> I said this at a meeting the other day, but some people disagreed with
> me. What I said was that I think that Buddhism is just science. What I
> mean is that we don't yet understand how the soul is related to the
> body, and perhaps we don't know everything about cause and effect
> and if there is such a thing as fate [*ming*]. Actually, we really don't
> know much about anything! [*laughs*] But what I said to them was,
> when we do understand everything, we will see that everything in
> Buddhism can be explained by science, and everything in science can
> be explained by Buddhism. That's what I meant.

Wu Haoming identifies himself as a Buddhist yet does not literally believe in aspects such as reincarnation and miracle cures. Rather, he holds
that Buddhism is a system of time-tested techniques for cultivating the
mind and developing traits such as compassion and empathy. Urban
Buddhists, like adherents of other religions, can and often do pick and
choose, in a smorgasbord fashion, from the many doctrines and beliefs of
the tradition and incorporate them in a seamless way into their rationalist
picture of the world.

POLITICAL ISSUES

While Tibetan Buddhism has, for obvious reasons, been subject to restrictions and crackdowns, the Chinese government seems to have adopted a
relatively tolerant attitude toward the informal practice of Buddhism
among the Han, who make up by far the majority of Buddhist adherents
in China. The Dalai Lama is a touchy subject, and most of the urban
Buddhists I talked to avoided taking a stance that might put them need-
lessly in a politically precarious situation. Most also recognized a need
for prudent avoidance of politically sensitive topics and activities in order to preserve the ability of Tibetan monks and Living Buddhas to move
freely within Beijing. The various Buddhist temples and SARA-sanc-
tioned religious centers are careful to emphasize in their materials that all
their activities are in accordance with law and are patriotic in essence.[9]

For the majority of urban Buddhists in Beijing, the religious thaw in
China has opened a space for their religious expression. Most report that

they feel quite safe when taking part in religious activities in homes and temples and that they are able to talk freely about their religious beliefs with others. Since most of their activities involve informal interactions in private homes and spaces, their religious observances seldom come to the attention of police or neighborhood committees (*juweihui*). Many spend much of their time interacting with fellow believers online through blogs and message services like QQ, which so far has remained a relatively safe, anonymous interactional domain.

Madsen (2010) analyzes how the Chinese Communist Party's religious policy stemming from "Document 19" formulated by the Central Committee in 1982 (titled "The Basic Viewpoint on the Religious Question during Our Country's Socialist Period") effectively conceded religious activity to the private sphere ("the crux of the policy of freedom of religious belief is to make the question of religious belief a private matter, one of individual free choice for citizens"), and the seemingly laissez-faire approach of the central government may be merely this policy in action. Madsen also notes that the government's surveillance and control mechanisms have been overwhelmed by the upsurge of religious activity in the PRC, much of it outside the jurisdictional scope of SARA in any case.

Many of my Buddhist friends have even gained the strong impression that the government welcomes their religious activities.[10] Party leaders such as Jiang Zemin and Jia Qinglin have given public support to Buddhism by making public appearances with temple abbots. In a recent speech, President Hu Jintao suggested that Buddhism, as well as other religions, might help to ease tensions between the haves and the have-nots in China. Some scholars even suggest that the Chinese government is tacitly encouraging the growth of Buddhism in order to counteract the spread of Christianity (Laliberté 2001).

While urban Buddhists may not as a group experience any significant restrictions, often the pressure is self-imposed, as many Buddhists feel the need, for various reasons, to keep their religious activities sequestered from their job and daily life. I have met professing Buddhists in government-run work units or organizations such as the Chinese Academy of Social Sciences, CCTV, and the Centers for Disease Control who prefer to keep their religious activities secret. One of my respondents is a PLA soldier (albeit merely a trumpet player in the PLA Army Band) who told me he could not "come out" as Buddhist to his superiors.[11]

BUDDHISM AS A FORCE IN CHINESE SOCIETY

Despite the variety of their opinions, the urban Buddhists I talked to were unanimous in the general conviction that China, in its process of economic strengthening, had fallen into a state of moral emptiness and materialism and was in need of a spiritual foundation. Ma Yang is an urban

Buddhist who is doing well financially. Forty years of age, he works at a multinational accounting firm, lives in a plush apartment inside Beijing's Second Ring Road, and has just bought a house for his parents to live in. He meditates every day and attends informal Buddhist study sessions occasionally. He reflected to me on the material progress of China in recent decades:

> When I was younger, we all thought, "If China can just become more economically powerful, and we can raise our standard of living, our big problems will be solved, and we will be happier." Looking back, was that true? Look at China now, you've been here all this time, you can see it. It's incredible, the opportunities and wealth we have now. Look over there—I have my choice of Starbucks, Costa Coffee, or UBC Coffee. Great! So many choices. Yet what is our biggest problem? It's not our physical condition; it's in the mental state of the people. Depression is common, and you have crazy people going onto a school campus and stabbing little children. You have old people falling down in the street and no one helping them. For someone like me, who went through the 1980s and thought that prosperity was the solution, it was eye-opening to find that we had this new Olympic city, but the people were still frightened, worried, and angry. I remember thinking, "Why aren't we any more satisfied than we were in the 1980s?" No matter how rich we get, there's an empty feeling. I think this is one reason so many of us are turning to Buddhism.

As for what form that spiritual foundation should take, I heard a variety of responses. Surprisingly, only a handful of my interviewees were unabashedly evangelical about Buddhism as the exclusive cure for China's ills. One of these, Fan Zhiyong, is a middle-aged former businessman who now freelances as a computer technician. He is one of the few I encountered who openly tries to convert others (including me), and he is explicit about Buddhism's future:

> I think only Buddhism can save China. And this isn't just my opinion. Even the British historian [Arnold] Toynbee said that only Theravada Buddhism and Confucian thought can save the world in the twenty-first century.[12] Many Chinese intellectuals and Buddhists, including Master Jing Kong, have strongly agreed with this statement. Only China has an uninterrupted 5,000 years of history, so the master thinks only these Chinese traditional forms of thought can really create stability. I think only Buddhism can solve the root problem [*genben wenti*]; other systems can only solve the surface problems. For example, my head hurts, so I take some aspirin. My stomach hurts, so I take some pain medicine instead of taking a look to see what the real source of the problem is. You can change behavior—that's the symptom—but if you can truly change people's perception, as Buddhism does, then the problems will achieve lasting solutions.

Most urban Buddhists, however, are more realistic about the prospects of Buddhism for accomplishing a universal spiritual revolution in China and do not see the religion as a panacea for China's social ills. One respondent answered cynically that "Buddhism has been around for thousands of years; if it were going to fix China, it surely would have been fixed by now!" Nevertheless, all of the respondents felt that China was in need of something like a religious revival, one that Buddhism could certainly be a part of but need not be the only component. Annie Chen, a hotel singer and a new convert, put it this way:

Chen: Personally I think any type of religion does more good than harm at the end of the day. So I don't mind Islam or Christianity even. I think Buddhism is more openhearted in this way—more than Catholicism or Christianity or anything, you name it. All the other religions, all the established religions of the world, they teach people to be good. And there's so much vice going on in China right now, and one of the reasons is this vacuum of religious values. I seriously think this contributes a lot to the current situation. Did you see the recent news about a man stabbing all those schoolchildren? That's just horrible, sickening and saddening at the same time. And I think religion coming in here at this juncture, it's really crucial. The more people believing any type of religion, the better.

Me: So as a Buddhist, you're not concerned that it be Buddhism; it could be any kind of religion?

Chen: Yes, it can be. However, given the background of Chinese mentality and culture, I think Buddhists will always outnumber followers of Christianity or Western religions. I think it will just happen that way. But I'd love to see them all join up together, like a joint venture. Or maybe like "Chinglish," we could have, what? . . . "Buddhi-anity" or "Islam-o-Buddha" or something [*laughs*].

As someone growing up in a predominantly Protestant Christian environment, I was struck over and over again by how discussions tended to focus on pragmatic issues—what "worked" and what did not and what was "suitable to the Chinese context," was "right for the particular person," and so on—rather than issues of "absolute truth" or "universal right and wrong." In the context of a religious tradition I was raised in, such attitudes would be labeled as extreme "relativism," as lacking in any objective moral grounding. In fact, throughout the process, I found the responses of my interviewees refreshingly ecumenical and broadminded in nature, free of the dogmatic assertions of ontological and moral certainty that mark much religious discussion elsewhere.

How has Buddhism changed the lives of these believers? The answers I received, while surely heartfelt and sincere, were also rather predictable. Respondents answered with testimonials about increased empathy, greater tolerance for the faults of others, improved ability to cope with the problems in their lives, and so on. One intriguing theme I encountered was the notion that adopting Buddhism correlates with a strengthening of traditional core Chinese—even Confucian—values. When I asked Wu Di, the son of the PLA officer whose conversion story I recount above, how Buddhism had changed his life, he responded this way:

> How has Buddhism changed my life? [*laughs*]. You, know, in a way, it has made me more Chinese! You know we Chinese have this traditional value of *xiaoshun* [filial piety]—I don't know how to say it in English. I have to say, I was never very good to my parents, especially my father, whom I was always fighting with. I don't think I ever really respected them when I was growing up. Only when becoming a Buddhist did I really start to act *xiaoshun* to my parents. And not only in this way but also in my attitudes toward nature and respecting others and children and so on—the Chinese values they tried to teach us in school—they've all become strengthened by my Buddhism.

While Buddhism may be changing China, it also emerged from my interviews that these new "urban Buddhists" are changing Buddhism. "Adaptation" was a theme I heard often, especially from the more educated respondents who had studied Buddhism as an academic subject. Xu Hao, who lived for more than a decade in the United States and who teaches at an overseas study program in Beijing, had this to say:

> Buddhism has to change to fit the twenty-first century. The way it is now, it doesn't fit the modern lifestyle, the modern world. You say your mother is a Christian? I can imagine her life because I knew so many Christians in the US. It's mainly a private matter, between her and God. What does her church require of her? Just go to church on Sunday and pray and maybe read the Bible, right? The rest is up to her. I think Buddhism has to become simpler in that way if it is going to be a truly national religion here. You can't say, "Okay now if you claim you are a serious Buddhist and you've 'taken refuge,' now you have to recite *amituofo* a million times and remodel your living room to make an altar and do such-and-such activities" and so on. I think there are too many rituals and too many outmoded requirements; it really makes no sense in the modern world. It has to be primarily a personal, transformative relation, without so many exterior requirements.

The confluence of various factors have led to the creation of a relatively open social space wherein the urban Buddhists shape their religious expression with a freedom unprecedented in modern China. The decentralized, apolitical, and cyberspace-mediated nature of their spiritual activity seems to guarantee that this group can continue to evolve in an organic, bottom-up fashion, outside of government supervision and control. It will be interesting to see how this dynamic religious demographic develops in the future and what effect it might have on China's troubled soul.

NOTES

1. Madsen (2010) has a useful summary and analysis of various estimates. Three surveys in 2005, 2006, and 2007 by the group Horizonkey produced results between 11 and 16 percent of the population (Pew Forum Online 2008), and a 2005 survey by Liu Zhongyu at East China Normal University suggested that the number of adherents may be has high as 300 million (cited in Zhang 2009). I strongly suspect that such a high number reflects the fact that many nonreligious Chinese, when asked for their religious affiliation, will often provide "Buddhism" as a default answer.

2. Yang (2010), for example, conducted surveys suggesting that Buddhism represents by far the largest religion in China today, with 18 percent of Chinese identifying themselves as Buddhist, while only 3.2 percent were classified as Christians.

3. There has already been much excellent work done on the rebuilding of temples, the revival of lay Buddhism in post-Mao China, and the activity of lay Buddhists and temple life in Beijing and elsewhere (see Fisher 2010, 2011; Sun 2010).

4. I became aware of Jones's thesis after finishing the first draft of this chapter. Although the scope, subject pool, and methodology of our work differ, I was gratified to see that our results and observations have a great deal in common. This chapter has been greatly strengthened and enhanced by reading her excellent thesis.

5. The recurring theme of catastrophic or incurable illness in these conversion stories is perhaps a reflection of the uncertainty and fear of living in a country with limited and increasingly costly access to medical care. There has been much anecdotal evidence suggesting that the wide appeal of the *falungong* movement among middle-aged and older demographic groups was due to the common insecurity surrounding health care and the "doctor-free" health claims of the cult.

6. There are several other popular microblogging platforms in China, such as Sohu and Tencent, but Sina has captured the market to such an extent that the once-generic term "Weibo" now in everyday parlance simply refers to Sina's microblog.

7. A politically active *fashi* who has mastered the use of media is Xuecheng Fashi, a standing member of the National Committee of the Chinese People's Political Consultative Conference, vice chairman and executive secretary of the Chinese Buddhist Association, and chairman of the Fujian Buddhist Association. He was one of the first monks to engage in blogging and microblogging and still has a strong online presence.

8. Anderlini (2001).

9. For example, in educational materials offered by the various temples, the phrase "love of country, love of religion" (*ai guo, ai jiao*) is stressed, and believers who undergo the ritual of "taking refuge" (*guiyi*) in the temples are required to read the articles on religious affairs in the PRC constitution.

10. SARA and the China Religious Culture Communication Association (CRCCA), working in tandem with numerous Buddhist organizations, organized the World Buddhist Forum in 2006 and 2009 and the International Daodejing Forum in 2007. Yet neither SARA nor CRCCA has granted permission for similar conferences for Christianity or Islam.

11. The Horizonkey survey of 2008 estimates that one in six Communist Party members had some religious belief, which would represent roughly 13 million people, the majority of whom are Buddhist.

12. Apparently, Fan Zhiyong is referring to a spurious quote attributed to Toynbee found on many Buddhist sites: " The coming of Buddhism to the West may well prove to be the most important event of the twentieth century. "

REFERENCES

Anderlini, Jamil. 2001. "Lunch with the FT: Shi Yongxi, the 'CEO Monk.'" *Financial Times*, September 9.

Fisher, Gareth. 2010. "Fieldwork on East Asian Buddhism: Toward a Person-Centered Approach." *Fieldwork in Religion* 5, no. 2: 236–50.

———. 2011. "Religion as Repertoire: Resourcing the Past in a Buddhist Temple." *Modern China* 38, no. 3 (May): 346–76.

Jones, Alison Denton. 2010. "A Modern Religion? The State, the People, and the Remaking of Buddhism in Urban China Today." PhD diss., Harvard University.

Laliberté, André. 2001. "Buddhist Revival under State Watch." *Journal of Current Chinese Affairs* 2: 107–34.

Madsen, Richard. 2010. "The Upsurge of Religion in China." *Journal of Democracy* 21, no. 4: 58–71.

Pew Forum Online. 2008. "Religion in China on the Eve of the 2008 Beijing Olympics." Pew Forum on Religion and Public Life. http://www.pewforum.org/Importance-of-Religion/Religion-in-China-on-the-Eve-of-the-2008-Beijing-Olympics.aspx.

Sun Yafei. 2010. "Religions in Sociopolitical Context: The Reconfiguration of Religious Ecology in Post-Mao China." PhD diss., University of Chicago.

Yang, Fenggang. 2010. *The State of Religion in China: The First Glimpse through a Survey.* http://www.purdue.edu/crcs/itemAboutUs/newsLetters/CRCSNewsletter%20V3N2E.pdf.

Zhang Xueying. 2009. "Buddhism in China." *China Daily*, June 19. http://www.chinatoday.com.cn/ctenglish/se/txt/2009-06/19/content_203310.htm.

NINE

Chinese Youth

Hot Romance and Cold Calculation

William Jankowiak

The relationship between sex, romance, and companionship love is seldom smooth or long lasting. These relationships need to be continuously renegotiated within and between the specific partners involved. Whatever an individual's personal dilemmas, the negotiations never take place in a vacuum. For example, romantic love and a higher degree of sexual interaction are more typical of the beginning than they are of the middle phase of a relationship. Moreover, companionship feelings tend to follow romantic passion crushes; seldom does a passionate love crush grow out of a companionship love bond. Further, the love bond always has a social component and thus wears an ethical face. The intertwining of love, sex, and ethical issues ensures that a couple's negotiations follow a pattern and are not the simple by-product of an idiosyncratic impulse. In this way, love and sex are as much about ethical considerations as they are about an emotional experience.

The discourse of love and sexual expression has moved out of China's urban shadows and into its commercial arteries. It was once forbidden to express it in public, but now it is the currency by which individuals seek to demonstrate their continuing commitment and mutual involvement. In contemporary China, love is hot.

This chapter explores the cognitive models of love and rules for sexual expression as they were found in urban China twenty years ago and how they are being redefined in recent times in terms of commitment and mutual involvement. China's demographic identity as a rural society or-

ganized around the production of the family unit as a collective enterprise is giving way to a new image of family that is organized around
conjugal intimacy and intergenerational emotional bonds. Thus, I explore
the significance of China's shift from a more formal courtship to an informal dating culture. I do this by analyzing the results of my dating survey,
in-depth interviews, and public observations that involve urban males
and females responding to a series of questions concerning intimacy and
marriage. My sample population is China's youth (ages seventeen to
twenty-five). I also rely on a variety of impromptu conversations with
men and women concerning their expectations of what to do in a dating
setting as well as how to respond once love arises. By comparing the two
cultural eras, I can assess the presence of cultural continuities and
changes across space and time.

THE CULTURE OF COURTSHIP

Courtship cultures are organized around a family's interest more than
individual interest.[1] Based in an ethos of duty and thus social obligation,
public performance is the preferred idiom of conversation and social
script used for moral evaluation. Within this cultural milieu, an individual's reputation is critical, and thus shame is regarded as more important
than private remorse or guilt. Moreover, mate selection criteria are organized around explicit material factors that range for men from political
and social position to income. For women, they range from sexual inex-
perience, including virginity, to degree of physical beauty and personal-
ity-oriented willingness to sacrifice self for the family.

Courtship cultures, which may or may not include a chaperone, are
organized around a process of negotiation that involves various family
members who are concerned with finding an appropriate person who
meets most if not all of these socially prescribed criteria. The primary
goal of courtship negotiation is marriage. It differs from dating in its
emphasis on normative rules, social judgment, and conventional standards for articulating romantic involvement. It is conducted according to
rules that organize a couple's meetings into a semiritualistic sequence of
private and semipublic meetings, characterized by incremental increases
in the public expression of commitment, usually resulting in marriage.

Throughout China's work unit era (1949–1992), there was a strong
cultural consensus concerning what constitutes appropriateness and thus
proper conduct. Maoist China, like villages and small townships around
the world, remained grounded in a shared code of public conduct. The
totality of public consensus contributed to fostering uniformity in outlook and conduct. The agreement over the meaning of propriety ensured
a standardized presentation of self. The existence of cultural consensus
did not mean that everyone always followed the rules. Many did not.

There was always some fudging at the margins. The presence of a courtship culture did mean, however, that when a deviation became public knowledge, everyone, including the deviator, attempted at first to deny the relationship; if that failed, all agreed that the transgression was inappropriate.

Within this setting, courtship was characterized by its semiritualistic sequence of private and semipublic meetings and incremental increases in the public expression of commitment that usually results in marriage, all of which constituted a clear pattern. Although Chinese courtship practices shared similarities with courtship practices in other societies, there were differences too. Unlike Spain in the 1960s, where courtship practices were chaperoned and organized around double-standard ethics that allowed males greater freedom of behavior within the courtship ritual,[2] this was less so in urban China. Chinese women did not have to grant sexual access if they did not want to. Moreover, men were also constrained by courtship norms and wider conceptions of decency. Throughout the 1980s, neither gender had greater freedom. For example, if a man got a reputation as a philanderer or was simply known to have had a few previous "girlfriends," his reputation as a virtuous and steadfast fellow would be damaged. Consequently, men and women equally strove to hide their personal involvement through denial. The strength of the ethos of emotional/sexual chastity was a powerful incentive, and it resulted in restraining personal behavior and thus personal appetite.

In Hohhot during the 1980s, I found that there were two distinct styles by which men and women sought to become more familiar with one another. Each style or approach involved different conventions (both formal and informal) and were complementary. Both were entered into with the intention of realizing either an immediate practical gain (enjoyment) or marriage. Formal dating, or courtship, differs from informal dating in its emphasis on normative rules, social judgment, and conventional standards for articulating romantic involvement. Informal meeting was pursued according to very practical rules, based on shrewd common sense and situational standards, that constitute solutions to particular problems that arise from dating in Chinese society. Sometimes these rules are provisionally formed by the parties in order to avoid the pressure of social expectations or the disapproval of one's community. Informal meeting may or may not culminate in marriage. Informal meeting begins in secrecy, appears to be ad hoc or accidental, and is characterized by public denial of any intimate involvement. In general, informal meeting is conducted by individuals who are emotionally involved but are restricted by prior obligations (including marriage, parental or work unit disapproval, and so forth) from publicly acknowledging or expressing their involvement. Within this formal style, there can exist what is often referred to as courtship (or a relationship oriented toward marriage) or just plain "going out" with no stated intent to marry. In the case of a formal meeting, although an individual may use the services of an introductory agency or friendship network to find a suitable mate, it should not be assumed that this style is devoid of romantic excitement. Once a person decides that a particular individual fits his or her "ideal" or comes close to most of his or her criteria, there is a pronounced tendency to fantasize about the other, often resulting in one's becoming overwhelmed with romantic anticipation. Romantic infatuation may arise in either form of courtship and is characterized by emotional intensity (and a tendency to quick shifts), by a kind of anxiety, by expressions of romantic endearment, and by the idealization of the other. The two styles differ only in the domain of public expression but not necessarily in the intensity of involvement or the intensity of attraction.

Discussions with Hohhotians revealed that arranging a meeting or the attraction phase, whether formal or informal, was remembered with mixed emotions. Some people called it a pleasant, enjoyable, though somewhat anxiety-filled experience. Others were more ambivalent and expressed relief that the stage did not last forever. Moreover, I found that more women than men felt that the experience was enjoyable. The women who did not enjoy the informal dating process were involved in situations they did not control: they were involved with a married man or someone who could not make a commitment. In these instances, the courtship process was remembered as an acutely painful experience.[3]

Whether individuals fell in love or never loved at all, everyone strove to adhere to the conventional wisdom that denied the public expression of passionate feelings, whether voiced in the idiom of love or sexual desire. By the late 1990s, this would all change rather abruptly for urbanities living in midsize and large cities.

REFORM CHINA: THE RISE OF INDIVIDUAL EXPRESSION

The abandonment of the work unit (*danwei*) as the primary means to organize society along with the state's retreat from actively monitoring citizen behavior provided an opportunity for greater individual experimentation. Individuals, no longer contained in a web of earnest social surveillance, found that the market economy provided greater anonymity. Late-night restaurants, entertainment clubs, and dance halls provided a privacy zone in which individuals could engage in behaviors that had previously been deemed inappropriate. For example, the singleton generation (the generation raised within the framework of the one-child policy) adopted a more open attitude and increased tolerance of all of the following: bodily decoration (e.g., tattoos), career mobility, foreign travel, casual dating, spontaneous sexual trysts, true love, divorce, cohabitation, the distribution of pornography, conjugal intimacy, and hands-on parenthood. Further, singletons are more introspective than their parents' generation and thus are more comfortable talking about themselves.

This cultural and corresponding psychological shift has given rise to an emergent dating culture that is ideally organized around individual rights and autonomy with little or no parental involvement. The end goal of dating is not marriage per se but the vigorous pursuit of personal happiness. The date is conducted according to very practical rules, based on shrewd common sense and situational standards. It consists largely of expressions of sympathy and kind regard. That is, potential partners try to prove how compassionate they can be.[4] Unlike the informal, or secret, meetings common to the socialist work unit era, contemporary dating is conducted explicitly and publicly. It is flaunted more than it is denied. For example, when I asked a high school student who was at a Western-style restaurant if her male companion was her classmate, she burst out, saying, "No! We are lovers." In this way, dating constitutes a profound transformation in generational authority away from the senior generation's desire to control the sexuality of its youth in favor of the junior generation's determination and ability to ignore parental suggestions and recommendations.

Within this new milieu, lovers fight less with their parents and more among themselves. Moreover, personal reputation or shame becomes more of a secondary consideration in contrast to weight given to feelings of regret or guilt over actions that contributed to harming another. Mate selection criteria shift away from frank statements of material factors in favor of more emphasis on idiosyncratic personality attributes. This does not mean material factors, such as a potential mate's social status, income, or, in the case of a female, relative physical attractiveness, are no longer valued. They clearly continue to be positive attributes. But they are no longer the most important or only factors when deciding who to "go on a date" with, let alone select as a marital partner. The shift from a courtship to a dating culture, however, is not without its dilemmas. The explicit rules readily understood in a courtship culture have given way to a more tacit and thus vaguer set of rules that are not readily understood even by the participants themselves, much less by the public. The transformation in the rules of the game has made what was explicit now tacit.

China's singletons are the pioneers whose social experimentation is reshaping public and personal behavior. No longer constrained by social convention, China's youth are increasing pushing the boundaries of social propriety. The shift in China's generational outlook, much as in the case of American baby boomers, is remaking Chinese society. Courtship rituals stand in direct contrast to dating that is more open ended and less precise in its meaning and consequences for those involved in this type of arrangement. It was not until the mid-1990s that urbanites started to explicitly "date." Previously, dating was conducted in secret and thus through continuous denial. For example, individuals preferred to characterize their "dating" relationship as nothing more than the relationship enjoyed by classmates, workmates, or neighbors. People often knew or expected otherwise but out of politeness seldom questioned a couple's characterization of their relationship. By the late 1990s, however, even people in China's more provincial interior cities readily admitted that they had a boyfriend or girlfriend. The shift in the normative order is indicative of a deeper shift in the local meanings of romance, sexual expression, and marriage in contemporary China.

To better illustrate the significance of the cultural shift in meanings, I will explore emerging normative features of a typical date in urban China. First, a word on methodology is in order. My initial research was conducted in Hohhot, the capital of Inner Mongolia Autonomous Region, in 1981–1983 and again in 1987. In this research, I focused on seventy-five key families (forty-five Han, thirty Mongol) on a variety of different aspects of their lives and also visited, observed, and interviewed other residents of the city. My 2010 data were obtained in part through the use of a survey given to 132 individuals between the ages of nineteen and twenty-five, with 102 being in their twenties. The vast majority were college graduates and primarily Han Chinese, with seven urban-born Mongols who spoke only Mandarin. In 2000 and again in 2006, I conducted personal interviews with Hohhotian men and women about their attitudes and behavior toward a variety of acts that range from who kissed whom first, how long they dated before they kissed, frequency of weekly contact, frequency of sexual intercourse, attitudes toward premarital sex, informing parents about having a boyfriend or girlfriend, and intentions of marrying their current boyfriend or girlfriend. Hohhot, unlike many of China's larger cities, does not have an active gay scene, and thus I was unable to include homosexuals in my sample. Also, I conducted a survey on local notions of hierarchy and found that as late as 2010 no class differences in the assessment of occupational prestige, images of proper love, and dating preferences. Urbanities from every occupational stratum continue to exhibit a remarkable agreement about most things found in their local moral order.

THE DATING EXPERIENCE: SOCIAL PATTERNS AND PSYCHOLOGICAL THEMES

Who Asks Whom Out?

When it comes to attracting a "date," both sexes are active. There is no set rule that the female should wait for a man to call. I found that both sexes actively seek each other out. Moreover, unlike in the 1980s, when classmates associated only with each other, there is now an expansion of the social arena of possible dating partners. My Hohhotian survey found that 41 percent of dating couples include someone who was not a class-mate. This suggests that the expansion of social contacts and thus dating opportunities are now extended well beyond one's immediate social cir-cle. It is further evidence of the collapse of the work unit system and its social insularity that has resulted in an expansion of a person's social network.

Where to Go to Eat?

One of the more important choices is not whether to go to a Western or Chinese restaurant but rather to select the table size. In the 1980s, the preferred table was large and round and seated friends (mostly of same sex or a mixed-gender group of students). Today, the preferred table is smaller, and it is square, requiring a couple to focus only on each other. If the table is the metaphor for what society values,[5] then twenty-first-cen-tury China's preference for the square table is further evidence of its embrace of dyadic or conjugal intimacy.

What Do Young People Talk About?

What do men talk about on the date? The consensus from interviews of females and some men is that men tend to talk about their futures (money they will earn, type of car they will buy, and size of the apart-ment they want, while other men, the minority, talk about the importance of saving for the security of the family) and just chat and offer funny insights and provide perpetual commentary on life and people. In a way, young Chinese men have much in common with young American men—both are insecure about not having a good occupation or wealth to pur-chase expected and desired objects. All young men have is their imagina-tion, dedication, social skills, and bravado, which they hope will lead to a more prosperous future. This is not unique to Chinese males. Research on American conversational patterns found that men tend to spend twice as much time talking about themselves as women do.[6] For some Chinese and American women, a man's ability to sell his future prospects can and does attract and hold her interest.

Who Talks More?

The response depends less on a person's age than on the level of intimacy desired. For the most part, young men talk more than women, who initially prefer to listen and actively encourage their dates to present themselves in the best possible light. Eibl-Eibesfeldt points out that among nonhuman primates, voice tone plays a role in courtship with the males signaling interest through the rising or lowering of voice tone.[7] In Hohhot, I did not dwell on this dimension. Instead, I focused on who talks to whom the most. I found that young couples who were not married and who were at the earliest stage of dating strove to create an environment in which the man either spoke more often or assumed the posture of an attentive listener ready to respond to a query or support his date's observation.

Personality differences, more than gender expectations, can distort this pattern. I found that more extroverted females talked more than introverted men but that overall, in an early dating setting, men tended to talk more but not always more than females. By contrast, among couples in their thirties and forties, women overwhelmingly talked more often. In a way, dating men are trying to attract a woman's interest and thus commitment, while after marriage, men, in a public setting, tend to withdraw from active engagement with their spouses. Chinese women are aware of men's shift in behavior. An insightful twenty-six-year-old unmarried woman noted that "men hustle to attract a girl's interest and then, once they have it, lose interest in keeping her interested." Men do, however, continue to engage their spouse in conversation within the home.

After the First Date, How Many Days Should a Person Wait before Calling?

There is no agreed-on rule. Some people call immediately, and others wait. Both men and women agree that it is important not to seem too eager or too indifferent. If people agree to continue going out together, physical touching becomes more frequent. When this happens, who touches whom the most? Early in the dating cycle, the man tends to be more assertive in grabbing his date's hand or placing his arm over her shoulder as he leads her out of or into a restaurant. In a way, the man is signaling to others that his date is taken. Once the two individuals agree to become a couple, the woman tends to take the man's arm or elbow (the most commonly touched areas of the body) whenever they stroll down a street.

Because the initial stages of dating are a discovery process during which women and men look for signs of commonality and trustworthiness, it is a time to see if there are shared values. For example, a young man discovered that it is important to agree with your date, at least in the beginning. He offered the following account: "We went to see the film *Poseidon*, and we discussed who should have died, the older man or the younger man. I thought the younger man but she thought the older man. So we quarreled, and she got so angry she walked quickly away and turned and said she was taking the bus home alone. I learned from the experience that it is important to just agree with a woman." Dating is also a time to learn about another's life goals and notions of what makes a good marriage. A female college senior, for example, had a first date over dinner during which she learned that the man thought that he should be the leader of the family and that she should be obedient. She argued for an equalitarian relationship, but he insisted on becoming the family's patriarch. She never returned his calls.

Women and men often look for evidence of a potential partner's ability to demonstrate consideration for the other. For example, a twenty-six-year-old man told me he is concerned about his girlfriend who has a crush on him and wants to marry him, but he adds, "I am not sure she lost ten pounds for me, but I find she talks too much about everything. I usually talk a lot and then listen. But with her all I do is listen. This worries me." Other people look for signs of a person's willingness to make a commitment. The ability to make a personal sacrifice in terms of time or resources is seen as proof of a person's willingness to make a long-term commitment. For example, a Hohhotian woman meets a young man who lives near the airport while she lives in the center of the city. She always meets him (only a thirty-minute bus ride) near his home, and they have dinner and walk around the nearby park. When she asks him to come to the center of the city, he always makes excuses. After a year of seeing him, she broke off their relationship. She told me that if he could not make a small concession and compromise over this small matter, what would he do if a major issue faced them? She felt it was not worth pursuing the relationship any further.

The new money economy increases the potential within the sexual encounter for misunderstanding. In the 1980s, men and women earned essentially the same salary, and families did not see much of an income gap. There is now an income gap, and this gives the person with the larger salary potentially a greater ability to manipulate women. An astute seventeen-year-old college student admitted that she fears rich men because they have resources she desired and they might be able to get her to do things she does not want to do. To this end, she admitted, "I fear men with money." A thirty-year-old added the following qualification: "I do not fear men with money. I fear being cheated."

Who Touches Whom?

Eibl-Eibesfeldt notes that "most emotional communication is nonverbal. Gestures are the language we use not only to express our feelings but to constitute them—by making a gesture people often produce a desired internal state."[8] This is an insight echoed in Stendhal's observation that the "greatest happiness love can offer is the first pressure of hands between you and your beloved."[9] It is a point on display whenever couples touch in public. In the case of China, the expansion of heterosexual touching in public is astonishing. Throughout my field research in 1981–1987, I observed well over 1,000 couples walking together in public, and I counted only four couples who lived at Inner Mongolia University (all married) holding hands during an evening stroll through the campus neighborhood. By contrast, in 2000 and then again in 2008, I found that 55 percent of all couples observed prefer to hold hands while walking down a street. To put this cultural shift into a wider context, in 1983, I witnessed around 35 percent of all females walking down a street touching each other and 35 percent of all men walking down a street touching. In 2000, I counted 25 percent of females touching but less than 1 percent of males touching. Over the past twenty-five years, urban China has shifted from a culture that embraced same-sex physical solidarity to a culture that prefers heterosexual physical intimacy.

When it comes to a dating relationship or an ongoing marriage, the question of when and how to touch or not touch is part of a couple's dance of intimacy. I often witness, for example, a young man stand and turn his back to his girlfriend, who then gently and with some hesitation pushes the small of his back. He leads forward, and she then steps back and once again pushes gently on his back before quickly walking ahead of him. After a pause, he joins up with her. Both smile at each other. They say something. He grabs her hand tightly. They walk together, holding hands for about twenty feet, then she suddenly pulls her hand away from his and smiles. Together they walk away together, no longer holding hands. This dance has a recurrent theme of "come here/go away" or, from a psychological perspective, "I am interested in you and then again maybe not." It constitutes, as such, a kind of nonverbal flirting. It is found primarily among newly dating couples, but I also observed a similar behavior among middle-aged men who were dating their mistress or a new, younger girlfriend. Although this is a type of mutual teasing, it is clear that it is the woman who controls the pace, degree, and frequency of the nonverbal physical flirt.

There are two distinct styles of touching with each variety determined by a couple's level of intimacy. At the beginning of a relationship, the man usually grasps a woman's hand or her elbow or drapes his arm over her shoulder. Once the relationship is ongoing, it is the woman who tends to grasps her boyfriend's or husband's elbow or arm. From the woman's perspective, she wants to signal that she is in a serious relationship.

What is particularly significant is the change in the use of the public as a means to signal intimacy. It has changed from a "wall around us" whereby male and female tend to demonstrate, especially in public, lack of interest in the opposite sex to a "wall around us" whereby couples use the indifferent gaze of the public as a way to signal to each other their exclusive union. Young couples in urban China, much like young American couples, use the public arena to exclude others and thus make "an open declaration of unity" to each other.[10] In reform China, most couples prefer to be autonomous islands of privileged privacy.

Frequency of Contact: Texting

Once a relationship begins, the interaction intensifies in its frequency. In 2000, it was understood that men called women's dorms more than women called men's dorms. The popularity of texting as the preferred medium of communication altered this sex difference. I found that young men and women text their partners on average three to five times a day. The texts vary from a simple "Hi" to "Where are you?" to "What are you doing?" to more sexually intimate words. For example, a twenty-three-year-old man told me that his girlfriend sent him the following text: "Last night I had a beautiful dream. I saw you walk toward me. I felt your hug and your passionate kiss on my face. I saw your smiling eyes look at me." A twenty-nine-year-old woman texted her new boyfriend this romantic message: "I had a beautiful dream. We walked hand and hand to a small café and ordered dinner. The smell of the food makes us hungry, and we eat. The candlelight is romantic, we dance, and everyone dances with us. After dancing, we drink rose tea and sleep in a big bed."

Analysis of female texts found more effort directed toward invoking from a boyfriend an emotional response that suggested commitment:

1. "Did you think about me with a silly smile?"
2. "Did you dream about me tonight?"
3. "Do you want to hold me when you feel lonely or happy?"
4. "I am totally enchanted with you."

Male's texts range from the mundane to the romantic and the sexually explicit:

1. "Where are you?"
2. "I want to show the world."
3. "I miss you."
4. "Kiss me!"
5. "I want to sleep with you."

There are sex differences in the frequency with which men and women text each other. Once a "dating" relationship is established, females send more texts than males. A man pointed out that "if you go out with a male friend who has a girlfriend, he is always answering the phone or sending a reply to a text query." "It seems," he adds, "that girls like to tell their boyfriend about what they are doing right now, but unless the girl asks, a boy seldom tells his girlfriend what he is doing." Young females assume that a man's response time is evidence of his dedication to her. If he is slow in responding, she often assumes that he is losing interest in her, and this often results in an angry outburst that leads to the man striving to placate or reassure his girlfriend that he is still interested in her and her alone.

A man's reluctance to express his attachment feelings is a constant source of disappointment. Women agreed that it would be lovely to have a partner who expressed his feelings. But, alas, this is something that most girlfriends and wives seldom get, or, if they do, they feel it is insufficient in quantity. A twenty-four-year-old female revealed that the number one complaint among her friends is that their boyfriends do not communicate often enough their desire or love for them. She admits, "We all complain that our boyfriends never tell us they like us. We tell them, but they say they show it though their behavior but not with words. We prefer words."

Who Controls Sex?

Western women overwhelmingly control the frequency and timing of sexual intercourse.[11] The Chinese also concur. The following comment by a twenty-seven-year-old woman is representative. She acknowledges, "I am not an easy girl to have sex with a man. I only have sex with a man I love." Another twenty-eight-year-old female nurse told me, "I had a boyfriend but never slept with him. He always wanted my body. I refused, as I was not sure how sincere he was." A twenty-four-year-old college student seconded her reluctance immediately to sleep with a man. She thought that sex without love is not fulfilling: "If there is love, there is sex. Any normal person wants sex. But love should be first, then sex." A forty-two-year-old women agreed, stressing that "feelings are very important. Deep feelings are best. I think sex is good but only if there is love. Without love, sex has no feeling. It makes no sense." Men, for their part, invoke love thoughts more quickly than women. It is part of a strategy that may involve attachment or simply serve to reassure the women that they are interested in them and not just sexual release. Women report that men are forever pleading to have sex more often. To this end, some men argue with their girlfriends that they "are old fashioned" in wanting to withhold sex. Other men use a different tactic. They argue that their girlfriends are not in touch with contemporary trends. They stress, "Shanghai girls [a symbol of high modernity] have sex quicker, so why don't you?"

The fact that Hohhotians continue to place a value on female virginity also contributes to a woman's reluctance to become sexually intimate. In the 1980s, everyone, especially males, stressed the importance of virginity and told stories from the countryside and in Chinese history of the lengths to which people went to protect a female's virginity. The strength of this ideal is evident in numerous surveys published on the changing sexual attitudes of Chinese youth. A 1990 survey found that 70 percent of students believed that a woman's virginity is more important than her life.[12] In 2003, 60 percent of men admitted that they wanted to marry a virgin.[13] A 2010 Shanghai undergraduate survey found that around 30 percent of Shanghai college women are virgins. [14] This is nearly identical to the percentage reported for American women. Today, virginity remains a salient ideal continuously challenged by the emotional and pragmatic realities inherent in a dating culture.

Notwithstanding the value many Chinese continue to place on the desirability of virginity, Hohhotian youth are becoming sexually involved more quickly and at an earlier age. The erotic female is celebrated in public media, and it is an image that Chinese women have adopted to attract and hold a man's interest. Today, half of all abortions are on unmarried women. This is true in metropolitan Shanghai, where health clinics advertise that abortion is easy, painless, quick, and inexpensive. I never saw these hospital ads in provincial Hohhot. However, my discussions with local doctors found that 50 percent of all abortions at the city's major hospital were conducted on unmarried women. The doctors admitted that they could not determine how many abortions were on single women in a dating situation compared to women who are engaged to marry but whose economic or social conditions make it inconvenient to have a child. What is clear is the increased frequency of urbanites in a dating situation that involves sexual activity. The national survey conducted by William Parish and his colleagues found that premarital sex is "one of the most conspicuous markers of the degree of liberalization towards sex." [15] His survey found that among China's youngest cohort, those who turned twenty around 1995, more than 40 percent of the males and 25 percent of the females admitted to having premarital sex.

The ability of Hohhotian men to convince their girlfriends to have sex sooner than they prefer stems from a woman's deep-seated concern that is readily expressed and almost borders on a paranoid fear: if the man does not have access to sex, he may leave. This concern is voiced in the remarks of a twenty-year-old college student who told me that her friends are always talking about this subject in the dorm: "Can we hold our boyfriend, or will we lose him to someone else?" It is significant that the two examples noted above where women denied their boyfriends access to sex were cases in which the women were certain that their boyfriends loved them and would not leave. Hohhotian women, like men (discussed below), are anxious about becoming involved in a nonreciprocal relationship. They do not want to make an emotional commitment that involves sexual intimacy, only to be dropped and abandoned.

Chinese women are caught in a bind. They want a boyfriend, and they want to please and not lose him to another woman who is more willing to sleep with him. To this end, women often use smart sex as a means to attract, hold on to, and ultimately induce a commitment. In this way, early sexual involvement may result in a greater payoff. It may engender an emotional commitment that might not have resulted otherwise. But it can also have a downside. It can result in a stronger albeit one-sided emotional attachment and thus a more painful separation. Women often express their anxiety over a lover or potential mate's dedication to sexual fidelity by asking her partner if he is "a one-woman man" or, if he thinks it is acceptable "after marriage to travel with a new girlfriend." The pervasiveness of this concern is readily apparent among college students who share stories of friends who fell in love with a man and moved into his apartment, only to be abandoned later for another woman. These stories are repeated and over time transformed into morality fables that serve as warnings of potential disasters for anyone who rushes to act on their feelings of love. Moreover, there is often some truth in these tales. I found in my conversations with females (but less so with males) who had been in an intimate relationship that ended badly a reluctance to become sexually involved with a man without a promise of marriage. A woman's reluctance to begin a sexual encounter does not mean that she does not also want to be sexually desired. Most Chinese women want to be perceived, especially by their lovers or husbands, as sexually attractive. When a man they are interested in fails to show sexual interest, women can quickly become annoyed. For example, a twenty-six-year-old admitted that "my boyfriend only put his arm around me for three months, but that was all. What is his problem? I simply lost sexual interest in him." Another twenty-six-year-old woman complained, "At first we had hot passionate sex. But lately we have less and less sex. He is younger than I. Why do I have to do all the relationship work? It is a Chinese tradition that the man should be older and thus make all the plans for the relationship. I wonder why I have to do all the work." Another young woman was disappointed that her boyfriend showed a lack of excitement about being with her. She told me, "I text a lot; my boyfriend does not. In fact, he seldom says, 'I like you.' He told me this once. I tell people I have no boyfriend. I have a distance boyfriend. I notice that if I am distant or aloof, he wants me, but if I come closer, he does not want me." Another woman acknowledged that her boyfriend is always too busy for her: "He has no time to care of me. He cannot remember my birthday. After a painful year, I said good-bye to him. Although he is indeed a man of potential, he lacks basic responsibility, which is an indispensable quality in a good husband." A twenty-five-year-old educated woman expressed annoyance at her soon-to-be ex-boyfriend: "All he does is fall asleep after sex. Lazy pig." Other women in long-term relationships repeatedly told me that they are troubled by their boyfriends' reluctance to express positive feelings. A twenty-four-year-old female readily admitted, "We all complain that our boyfriends never tell us they like us. We tell them, but they do not tell us." However, she adds, "My boyfriend shows his concern and love through behavior, not through words." Left unspoken was her clear desire to hear his affectionate endearments.

Is It Good to Live Together before Marriage?

In the courtship culture of the 1980s, this question would have been seen as preposterous because no one lived together before engagement. As China has grown more prosperous, the age of puberty has declined, and women and men are delaying marriage and reproduction. In addition, men and women spend more time away from home and thus out of their parents' immediate observation. This cultural shift has contributed to more openness in terms of appropriate sexual practices. There is now an increased willingness to experiment with new forms of sexuality that range from oral sex, use of sex toys, and experimentation with different sexual positions in a couple's erotic play.

When Do You Tell Your Parents?

Chinese parents believe that the most important thing an offspring should do is study hard. They ban their children from dating in high school. Therefore, their offspring must keep any relationship they develop a secret. My survey found that 31 percent of college students (twenty-two out of seventy-two) admitted to having a boyfriend or girlfriend in high school. Because parents believe that their teenagers are too young to understand love and thus cannot select proper partners, they try to protect their offspring from making a mistake. Particularly in the case of a daughter, they instruct her to be careful in love and not make a random commitment to a boy. Their efforts have instilled in most Chinese young women the notion that dating is a serious encounter.

China's singleton generation shares the belief that, in the words of an eighteen-year-old youth, "Your parents should not have too much control over you—it is your life!" But I found that Hohhot mothers who have developed a strong emotional bond with their daughters are able to undermine, if they choose, a daughter's selection of a marital partner. In 2003, five out of fourteen men I interviewed about love and dating said that they or their previous girlfriends had ended the relationship because the mother strongly objected to her daughter's choice. This increase in parental authority differs from what I found twenty years earlier when the negative opinion of parents, if voiced, was completely ignored.

Why the shift in the strength of parental influence? I suspect this stems from the singleton generation's stable life. Present-day singletons have never been sent to the countryside, a place where the earlier generation had to learn to deal with complex social situations and thus developed a greater sense of psychological autonomy that could and did lead to resistance of parental influence. In terms of gaining an independent emotional life, the singleton generation, especially daughters, has been slower to break away from parents.

1980S CHINA: LOVE NOT AN ESSENTIAL CRITERION FOR
MARRIAGE

An individual falling in love and confounding parental expectations is nothing new. Chinese literature is filled with fatal love stories that serve as a cautionary tale about what happens when one follows individual feelings instead of listening to parental wishes. Socialist China did, however, weaken the power and authority of parents over their children. Within this new social milieu, urban youth often rejected the mate suggestions of their parents. Furthermore, during that era, I found that status considerations remained a key consideration. Affection, while acknowledged, was put on hold until after material considerations were addressed. Once an agreement was reached with respect to engagement, the power of romantic anticipation engendered behaviors typically associated in Western countries with those of a love crush. A main difference was that, in the West, love ideally came first, while in China in the 1980s, apart from instances of an illicit and hidden romance, love arose after more pragmatic concerns had been addressed. In brief, the relationship had been successfully negotiated and the individuals provided with the belief that he or she had found the ideal mate or "true love." The engaged individual then relaxed enough to experience passionate love. The vividness of the romantic experience was strong and deeply memorable. For example, in 1982, a thirty-three-year-old male intellectual fondly recalled the early stage of his informal dating or courtship: "At first it was terrible: I didn't know what to do. I though my wife was the most beautiful girl I'd ever seen and that she wouldn't want me. I worried and worried about this. Then I asked her if she wanted to see me again. I truly believed she would refuse. But she did not. I was so happy for days and days and thought of nothing else but how much I loved her."

In romantic love, the line separating anxiety and excitement is thin and easily crossed. A twenty-eight-year-old female worker who had distantly admired her future husband for some time readily recalled the initial phases of her formal courtship: "After being introduced, I was not disappointed but feared that I wasn't pretty enough for him. When he didn't call on me for several days, I sunk into a deep depression that only lifted when he asked to see me again. After a few more encounters, we were all but married. It was a wonderful time. Everything was easy and happy. Although I am satisfied with my marriage, we seem more distant and busy."

Another female worker, age twenty-four, remembered slowly responding to her future husband's overture for emotional involvement: "He came to see me every other day and gave me a few small but thoughtful gifs. At first I didn't have any excitement in my heart, but slowly I found myself starting to like him. After a month or so, I found myself becoming excited in anticipation of his arrival. In fact, I might have dreamed of him. When he asked me to be his girlfriend, I was very happy. I knew that I loved him very much and that I wanted to marry him."

Not every romantic experience results in entering into a more formal courtship arrangement. For example, a twenty-five-year-old woman explained how she developed a secret but intense infatuation for her former instructor: "When I was eighteen years old, I knew a man who was thirty-eight. He helped me study. I was too young to start seeing men, so I had to keep my feelings secret. I remember that whenever we studied together, I was acutely aware of his presence, especially his smell. He smelled like a man. When he talked, his saliva would hit me, and I liked the sensation. I didn't think about having sex with him, but I was aware that I was very interested in him and that I wanted to be associated with him. I still think of him."

But courtship does not always involve romantic attraction. For example, a forty-two-year-old divorced male was courting a woman who was not particularly interested in him. He explained how he felt when he discovered that his "girlfriend" refused to become emotionally involved: "I wanted this girl. She was thirty-four years old and kind of pretty. We had been writing for a few weeks, and I asked her if she wanted to see me. After a few weeks she wrote back and asked me to come see her in another city. I agreed. We spent the week together going to different places. But I knew she wasn't interested in me when she refused to have her picture taken with me in the park. I think I am doomed to live alone and be sad." (In 1992, I learned that he had left Hohhot and married a thirty-six-year-old woman and was reported to be happy.)

In 1983, a thirty-four-year-old female, who first met her husband when she was thirty-two and desperate to marry, admitted that she never felt anything special for her husband. For her, formal courtship was "a necessary path to marriage and to do what was expected of you." The courtship did not by itself engender romantic infatuation or companionship love.

LOVE IN TWENTY-FIRST CENTURY CHINA

During the 1980s, adulthood could be achieved only through marriage and parenthood. Thus, there were appropriate reasons to marry even when love was not involved. This does not mean that the 1980s self-arranged courtship was devoid of romantic excitement or expectation. As noted above, "falling in love" was also expected and valued in China's courtship culture. It was not the primary reason, however, for entering into a marriage. People married for many reasons, and love was only one reason.

In recent times, Chinese youth, much like their parents, continue to marry for a variety of reasons that range from a desire to gain material resources, fulfill a social expectation, or achieve self-fulfillment. The conception of love articulated by singleton youth is similar to that expressed by their parents' generation. For example, a 2008 focus group, much like my 1987 Hohhotian focus group, listed the following attributes found in a romantic love experience: "It is maddening, a hot feeling, crazy feeling, amazing feeling, it makes us happy, it makes us worried, it makes us excited, and you do not want to share."

Then how do you know you are in love? The following comments were made: "You feel a hurt in your heart when he is not around." "He is my only one, without him I cannot live." "Love is determined. I will obey this arrangement till I die." "I cannot sleep without her." "I miss her, I think about her constantly."

How should one behave when in love? The focus group stated, "You show you care," "You do everything for the person," "You help one another," and "You want your lover to be happy." A twenty-two-year-old, not a member of the focus group, added, "When I feel in love, I want a lot of affection and want to give a lot of affection. It involves simple things like holding hands, sitting close together, snuggling up on the sofa to watch a late-night movie. It also means speaking and acting kindly and with respect to one another."

Love in the 2000s, as in the 1980s, inspires an idealization of the beloved. But in the 1980s, youth were more circumscribed in voicing their love. When it was voiced, it was done tersely and awkwardly: "I miss you," "I love you," "I think she loves me." In the 2000s, I found less awkwardness and more confidence, combined with greater boldness in a person's willingness to express his or her love.

The single-child generation is clearly more comfortable declaring love. It is now voiced loudly and elaborately. For example, a thirty-year-old woman wrote a note to her much older albeit highly successful lover: "I want to be your angel with beauty, empathy, patience, family, community, home, strength, fortitude, kindness, warmth, endurance, courage, sustenance, power, passion, and love. . . . I look forward every day to the time when I can show you in our lives together how much you mean to me. It is dangerous in my view to go through life shunning the blessing that this kind of love brings us. Such a love can indeed be a sanctuary from all the hardships that life can bring to us, and I am ready, my love, to travel this path with you . . . I believe that we can conquer any obstacles that come our way. You are the only man who can accompany me and fulfill me in my life. I think I am so lucky because I can always share anything with you and never worry you would judge me, be angry, or dislike me. I think you are the person who can accept me for who I am. I am lucky to find you!"

Falling in love also involves inclusive thinking about a lover, as evident in a twenty-seven-year-old woman's e-mail to her boyfriend: "Since the very first time I gazed my eyes upon you, I have had a peculiar feeling toward you and am glad we've grown and evolved to this stage. At this very moment in time, I too feel strange and have never experienced anything like it. I love you and only want to continue to love you. Is everything well with you? I hope so. My love, you have been in my heart day and night. My dearest, today I am very upset because I have received no letter from you. Are you angry with me because I write you so many letters? My love, take care of yourself, dearest, and let me know if you are well there, okay? Darling, it is warm here, and today I don't feel well. My dearest, would you like to be here with me and show me your sweetness?" On receiving this message, which was a tacit request to immediately reply, he did so.

Love is highly valued, and when those in love do not keep their promises, it can produce lifelong anger toward anyone who betrays that trust. A twenty-three-year-old woman gave the following account: "I once had a great love. It only lasted one month. We decided to go to college together, but then he went to study in Singapore. He was an outstanding person (*youshou*). He wrote me a lot, but I never returned his letters. Five years have passed, and he wants to see me, but he will only be here for one month and then leave. I want to keep my memories. I will not see him."

In another case, a twenty-four-year-old man told me he had learned to be more careful because his decision to enter into a relationship had consequences for the other person. He did not want to hurt that person. He admitted, "I have had many girlfriends and slept with most. In retrospect, many of them were good people. They loved me. But I did not appreciate them. I now have an eighteen-year-old girlfriend to whom I am very considerate. I think I have learned to be a more responsible lover."

For contemporary Chinese, romantic love, as an idiom, is perceived as a deep-seated subjective experience that also carries with it understood social obligations. It has become a desired experience that many want to embrace but, once experienced, does not necessarily result in a decision to enter marriage. The singleton generation, like the generation of their parents, continues to value a strong commitment to an ideal image of family, one that is seen as greater than the immediate notion of coupleness. In this way, the family, not the conjugal dyad, remains China's basic social unit. To this end, many young people in China have two understandings of what makes for a good marriage. One image is based on a romantic ideal of transcendence that involves the couple, and the other is grounded in the ordinary life of family practicalities. The romantic ideal holds that husband and wife should have conversational intimacy, feel close, and enjoy warm feelings of being together. On the other hand, they also believe that while a marriage begins as a pure love, it must be transformed by other, more pressing pragmatic concerns, such as career demands, housework requirements, child care duties, and the schooling of offspring. In effect, couples understand that they will need a certain amount of privacy and their own space to accomplish different goals. This will produce a border between husband and wife as each person lives in separate albeit overlapping spheres.

A number of singletons I talked with, however, now expect more opportunities to share time together after work, activities that will strengthen the relationship. They hope to mute the emotional distance that often arises within a complementary division of labor. For example, a twenty-year-old female told me, "My [natal] family is a warm place to be, though we have to do our own things. When we are off to work, we are [psychologically] together. When we are at home, it is the best place to relax." Her sentiment is echoed in a twenty-two-year-old Tianjin woman's elaboration on the qualities of a good marriage. Her comments are similar to those expressed by urbanities living in Shanghai in the 1920s and 1930s. She admitted that a good marriage involves "being polite, respectful, and considerate. These values are essential to sustain a marriage." She noted that couples often refer to this as "being respectful to each other since both are guests." She then added, "We should stay together till we grow old together." Today, both images are present in most people's view of a good marriage. In short, most Chinese youth accept that there will be various stages of intimacy within the marriage, each having different tasks and responsibilities that will impact a couple's sense of intimacy.

In sum, an individual's private experience of love in the 1980s courtship culture does not appear to differ from the love experience in the dating culture. The two eras differ primarily in the following ways. First, there has been a muting of material considerations voiced as essential criteria for finding a mate. Second, loving sentiments are voiced earlier and more frequently throughout the dating sequence. Third, displays of erotic desire have become an expected part of being in a relationship; it is now mentioned in casual conversation and readily expressed in the bedroom. Fourth, love is considered best experienced before rather than after marriage. Fifth, the settings for the expression of loving feelings have shifted from the umbrella used in public parks to block nosy viewers to a more explicit and more open public setting that serves to heighten the identity of the two people as a couple.

Today, twenty-first-century Hohhotian singleton youth are kissing earlier, sleeping together sooner, and having more dating partners than any other generation in Chinese history. The newfound personal freedom, typical of an emergent youth phase, is not without its ambiguities. The appropriate time to date, marry, and start a family is less clear. Still, some patterns remain. First, dating does not signal in and of itself an intention to marry; it is something that is not entered into lightly. Females compared to males are more cautious about becoming sexually involved. Second, the single-child generation is more sexually open compared to the generation of its parents, but this openness has not transformed China into a libertine culture.[16] It remains a deeply pragmatic, intensely romantic, and sexually flirtatious culture. Further, the criteria for assessing maturity have changed along with the criteria for establishing a responsible sexual self. This even includes the frequency with which young men and women misunderstand one another. Third, the single-child and smaller-family norms have resulted in strong emotional bonds between parents, especially mother and daughter, that have given parents more influence over their daughter's selection of an "appropriate" marriage partner.

A dating culture implies by its very nature that emotional involvement with a dating partner may or may not be long term. There are, as a consequence, increasing expectations, anxieties, and reservations when young people think about whether they should remain involved. For most, the challenge is not so much to figure out how to play the game; the challenge is to figure out what game they are playing.[17] To this end, the restlessness that has become characteristic of contemporary Chinese life is most acutely experienced within an emergent youth phase that is filled with restless happiness, joy, and contentment as well as disappointment, regret, and anger over the ability or inability to find and hold on to a lover.

NOTES

1. Beth Bailey, *From Front Porch to Back Seat: Courtship in Twentieth-Century America* (Baltimore: Johns Hopkins University Press, 1988); Jane Collier, *From Duty to Desire: Remaking Families in a Spanish Village* (Princeton, NJ: Princeton University Press, 1997).

2. Collier, *From Duty to Desire*.

3. For a more in-depth discussion of 1980s courtship's public and hidden faces, see William Jankowiak, *Sex, Death and Hierarchy in a Chinese City* (New York: Columbia University Press, 1993).

4. David Brooks, "Social Animals: How the New Science of Human Nature Can Help Make Sense of Life," *The New Yorker*, August 2010, 30.

5. Massimo Montanari, *Food Is Culture* (New York: Columbia University Press, 2006).

6. Brooks, "Social Animals," 30.

7. Irenäus Eibl-Eibesfeldt, *Human Ethology* (New York: Aldine de Gruyter, 1989).

8. Eibl-Eibesfeldt, *Human Ethology*, 122.

9. Brooks, "Social Animals," 30.

10. Susan Weitman, "Intimacies: Notes toward a Theory of Social Inclusion and Exclusion," in *People and Places: The Sociology of the Familiar*, ed. Arnold Birenbaum and Ed Sagarin (New York: Praeger), 222.

11. Donald Symons, *Human Sexuality* (Oxford: Oxford University Press, 1979).

12. Harriet Evans, *Women and Sexuality* (London: Hurst, 1997), 108.

13. Joanna McMillan, *Sex, Science and Morality in China* (New York: Routledge, 2006).

14. James Farrer, *Opening Up: Youth Sex Culture and Market Reform in Shanghai* (Chicago: University of Chicago Press, 2002).

15. William Parish, Ye Luo, Ross Stolzenberg, Edward O. Laumann, Gracia Farrer, and Suiming Pan, "Sexual Practices and Sexual Satisfaction: A Population Based Study of Urban Chinese Adults," *Archives of Sexual Behavior* 36, no. 1 (2007): 5–20.

16. William Jankowiak and Robert Moore, "China's Emergent Youth: Gender, Work, Dating and Life-Orientation," in *Adolescent Identity: Evolutionary, Cultural, and Developmental Perspective*, ed. Bonnie Hewlett (New York: Routledge, 2013), 277–300.

17. Susan Pinker, *The Sexual Paradox: Men, Women and the Real Gender Gap* (New York: Scribner, 2008).

Part IV

Global Standards

TEN

A Collapsing Natural Environment?

Su Xiaokang and Perry Link

During Mao Zedong's Cultural Revolution, Huang Wanli, a US-trained hydrologist at Tsinghua University, was sent to a reform-through-labor camp in Jiangxi province near Lake Poyang. In 1970, his daughter Huang Xiaolu visited him there, and the daughter recalls a morning when the two were walking along the lakeshore, admiring the natural beauty. Huang the father recited a famous line from Wang Bo's "Teng Wang Pavilion" that had been written near the same spot in 675 CE, nearly thirteen centuries earlier:

> A lone duck wings its way through rosy clouds at dawn
> The colors of the autumn water reflect an endless sky

Huang the daughter was impressed that what she and her father were gazing on in 1970 was virtually identical to what Wang Bo had seen in 675. But by 2010, a mere forty years, the whole lake had nearly disappeared.

This observation is a poignant but not unusual example of how China's "economic miracle" has affected the natural environment in recent decades. Environmental damage has had cultural and spiritual costs in addition to the costs that are measurable in numbers, such as the depletion of natural resources and the human health problems that have resulted from pollution. The World Bank has estimated that 350,000 to 400,000 people died in China in 2007 as a result of air pollution, but this estimate accounts only for "outdoor" pollution. The World Health Organization, estimating numbers for both indoors and outdoors, has put the figure at 656,000.[1] A full accounting of the costs of what environmental damage of all kinds has been adding up to, if possible at all, will likely

215

not be feasible for many years. Meanwhile, most government leaders in China, at all levels, continue to pursue policies that press for economic growth without calculation of environmental costs. The normal practice is to pass costs to the general public—and to future generations—with no attempt to estimate their size.

Chinese people of many kinds have been noticing the damage and expressing their worries. Their voices have been disparate, though, and have had little effect on basic policy. Some scholars and environmental specialists have issued passionate appeals, one warning that the current development model "eats the legacy of the ancestors and cuts off the road for the descendants."[2] Ordinary people have noticed ever-worsening problems of polluted air and water, water shortage, poisons in food, and mounting piles of garbage. There have been many popular protests, and local officials, feeling threatened, have often detained or punished protest leaders. The case of Wu Lihong, a farmer in Jiangsu province, received national and even worldwide attention. In the early 1990s, Wu began complaining about the dumping of industrial waste into Lake Tai. Local authorities told him to stop, but he repeatedly refused to do so. In 2007, they decided to send him to prison for three years on charges of "extortion." Similarly, in 2008, a man named Tang Zhirong complained about the effluent of an aluminum-processing facility in Hunan province and received an eighteen-month prison sentence for obstructing official business. Sun Xiaodi, in Gansu province, complained for years about pollution from a uranium mine and finally accused local officials of fraud; in July 2009, he was sentenced to two years in a labor reform camp for "illegally providing state secrets overseas" and "rumormongering." Near Chengdu, in Sichuan province, a crowd gathered in early May 2008 to protest the construction of a chemical plant in their neighborhood. Chen Daojun, a freelance journalist who reported on the demonstration, was later sent to prison for three years for "inciting subversion of state power."[3]

Some environmental problems have earned popular nicknames. People in Beijing call the fierce winds that carry dust from Central Asia onto the northern China plains the "wolf of the north." Historical records from 300 to 1950 CE show that, on average, dust storms of this kind caused trouble about once every thirty-one years. In recent times, by contrast, they have arrived nearly every year, blowing away seeds and topsoil, killing seedlings, knocking fruit from trees, and burying culverts and wells. Together, dust storms, droughts, desertification, and the loss of arable land to construction projects have made food production in China more difficult.

Moreover, the food that does get produced has led to increasing worries over whether people can eat it. Contaminants have seeped into food products or, in some cases, have been added deliberately by manufacturers who seek easy profit by substituting artificial ingredients for real ones (see chapter 12 in this volume). Air pollution in some cities has turned breathing into a health risk. Are Chinese cities, with their concomitant health risks, the best place for raising families? This question has crept into the thinking of some of the rising middle class. One resident of Beijing—a person who has done well in China's economic boom—wrote in a microblog in 2011 that "I've noticed for some time now, when I get together with friends, that just about everyone has family members abroad or is looking for ways to get them there. Deep in their bones, beneath the frenetic surfaces, there is melancholy, insecurity, and lack of trust in the system."

The issue of environmental dangers is different from many others in China because it spans the political spectrum. People who have spoken out about the environment are not limited to liberal intellectuals, democracy advocates, oppressed farmers, or people who choke on smog. Some in the government write about it, too. A 2006 report from the Ministry of Environmental Protection lists six "chronic plagues" of environmental pollution.[4] And even people on the ultranationalist left—people who fault the government for its alliance with global capitalism and feel nostalgia for a rosified version of Mao—join in decrying environmental devastation. They see China's environmental losses as the result of exploitation by foreign capitalism: the air of Guangzhou is polluted in order to supply toys to places like Akron, Ohio.

WHAT ARE THE ISSUES THAT CREATE ANXIETY?

Any list of the environmental problems that have caused concern in China in recent times would have to include (but not be limited to) air and water pollution, water shortage, garbage accumulation, loss of arable land, the effects of "megaprojects," and global climate change. We look briefly at each in turn.

Pollution

The "six pollution plagues" in the 2006 government report referred to above are the following:

1. Urban air pollution. Surveys of 522 cities showed that in only twenty-two is air quality "good." The air in another 293 counted as "acceptable for residence," and in the remaining 207 it falls below that standard. Of those, fifty-five cities have air that is "seriously unacceptable."
2. Acid rain. Of 696 surveyed cities, acid rain falls on 357, or slightly more than half.
3. Pollution of surface water. Thirty-six percent of China's surface water is "good," another 36 percent is "polluted," and the remain-

ing 28 percent is "severely polluted." Major pollutants include ammonia, petroleum, and permanganate.

4. Red tides in the East China Sea. The main pollutants in red tides are active phosphate and inorganic nitrogen.
5. Urban noise pollution exceeds acceptable levels in many parts of many cities. Sixteen percent of the urban populace, or 34 million people, live with unacceptable road-noise pollution.[5]
6. Extraordinary energy consumption has led to a loss of control of sulfur dioxide emissions. In 2005, China emitted 25.5 million tons of sulfur dioxide, which exceeded acceptable limits by 7.5 million tons and was 27 percent more than had been emitted five years earlier.[6]

Water Shortage

Chinese civilization arose in the basins of two great rivers, the Yellow and the Yangtze. These two rivers lie deep within China's conception of itself, so when a "water crisis" affects them, it seems somehow to strike the civilization at its roots. Over the vast area of China as a whole, the unusually large population makes it true that the per-capita supply of freshwater is only about one-quarter what it is in the rest of the world. Wang Hao, director of the China Water Resources and Hydropower Research Institute, cites the following data to illustrate China's water shortage in the early years of the twenty-first century:[7]

The basins of the Yellow, Huai, and Hai rivers, taken together, amount to 15 percent of the area of China, contain about a third of the nation's arable land and population, and produce about a third of its gross domestic product (GDP). But their water supply is only 7 percent of the national total.

Rivers in northern China have been running dry. In 1997, the main current of the Yellow River ran dry during 226 of the 365 days of the year, and the length of the dry stretch was nearly 500 miles. The Yangtze, in Wang Hao's view, is in danger of becoming "a second Yellow River."

Two-thirds of China's largest 600 cities have water shortages, and in 110 of them, the shortages are "severe." The shortage in Beijing has become worse than experts imagined just a few years ago, and the city survives only because of the ever-deeper mining of underground water.

The volume of water in China's five largest lakes is in sharp decline.

On the pollution of water, Wang Hao reports the following:

All seven of the nation's major river systems are polluted, with the waters of Lake Tai and the Hai River being in the worst condition.

Hundreds of factories crowd the deltas of the Pearl River and the Yangtze River. They are much more densely packed than in other industrial areas in the world, yet China continues—absurdly, in Wang's view—to apply "pollution effluent standards" that are used in the less crowded conditions of Europe and America. The resultant gush of pollutants is more than China's rivers can bear.

The stock of fish in Bohai, the sea between eastern China and Korea, has dwindled to near zero; pollution and overfishing have rendered Bohai an "empty sea."

Garbage

The changing lifestyles of China's expanding middle class have created severe problems of refuse and how to dispose of it. The problem has begun to stir public anxiety. One of the more audible public outcries occurred in November 2009 in Panyu, a large suburb of the city of Guangzhou in southern China. Panyu's population of 2.5 million was producing about 600,000 tons of garbage per year when authorities proposed building a new garbage incinerator that would burn 2,000 tons of garbage per day. But there was a problem. A few years earlier, a similar project in nearby Likeng Village had caused illness among local people. Now, in Panyu, hundreds of protesters took to the streets to oppose a similar incinerator. Authorities called in police to break up the demonstration.[8] Police, following normal procedure, looked for the protest "leaders" in order to single them out for control and punishment, and this led demonstrators to hold up signs, deliberately crafted to frustrate the police, that read "we have discipline, but no organization" and "no one represents us." One protester, withholding his name, told a reporter that "the matter did not directly concern us, but we were pursuing the public interest and wanted to show our friends and other people what was going on. So we took pictures and used all the modern technology we could in order to show the protest in real time. The police videotaped us, so we must be prepared for consequences later."[9]

Lang Xianping, a distinguished professor of finance at the Chinese University of Hong Kong, wrote in 2010 that the two greatest environmental menaces to the lives of ordinary Chinese people are "shortage of clean water" and "siege by garbage."[10] (By comparison, Lang listed the stylish concern with "low-carbon lifestyle," often touted in the Chinese press during the 2009 climate-change summit in Copenhagen, as "mere fluff.") Lang sees Beijing in particular as headed for crisis: there are already more than 400 garbage dumps outside Beijing's Fifth Ring Road, and these are proving insufficient. Two-thirds of China's other major cities are suffering siege by garbage as well, and in many places garbage is polluting water and crops. Lang cites, in particular, the danger of the batteries that are discarded from China's cell phones and computers. (In early 2012, there were about 900 million cell phone users in China.) The battery of one cell phone can pollute 60,000 liters of water, Lang writes, and one computer monitor contains between four and eight pounds of lead. Lead from "electronic garbage" helps to explain why tests on the blood of 60 percent of Chinese children show excessive levels of lead and why cases of "systemic lead poisoning" have popped up in Hunan, Gansu, and elsewhere. The concentration of lead in the blood of urban residents of China is double that in other parts of the world.[11]

Depletion of Farmland

Chinese farmland is being lost to desertification (see the section "Climate Change" later in this chapter) but, more important, to confiscation for commercial development. Between 1997 and 2009, China lost about 6.3 percent of its arable land (more than 20 million acres) and came close to a "red line" that government agronomists have said cannot be crossed without fearful consequences.[12] In theory, all land in China is publicly owned. Farmers, home owners, and others can get long-term leases to land and in most cases can use it just as owners would. But a crucial fact about "public ownership" is that when the government wants to build things like roads or rail lines or when developers who have connections with officials want land for shopping malls, apartment complexes, or other moneymaking enterprises, the government can evict people at any time. Well-established patterns of corruption that bind wealthy developers and officials put government power reliably on the side of developers. People who are forced to move normally are compensated but are obliged to accept whatever compensation is proposed by their local power elites. Protests have occurred in many places, but they seldom win the day. In any case, "development" has become the major cause of loss of farmland in China. Level, irrigated land in river valleys, the kind that is best for farming, unfortunately is also the land that developers most covet, especially when it is near urban areas.[13]

Megaprojects and Ecological Systems

In the 1990s, the Chinese government began seriously pursuing a number of huge construction projects. A number of them are the largest in the world of their kinds. Chinese scientists have repeatedly warned of environmental perils, yet the projects forge on. The two best known—and most controversial—have been the Three Gorges Dam and the South-to-North Water Diversion Project.

The Three Gorges Dam on the Yangtze River, the third-longest river in the world, is nearly a mile and a half wide and almost 600 feet high and impounds a reservoir that stretches 370 miles. The turbines installed next to it generate about eighty terawatts (10^{12} watts) of electricity per year. It cost nearly $30 billion to build and required the relocation of millions of people. The environmental concerns of scientists have included the danger of erosion, landslides, and earthquakes (the dam is near a seismic fault); loss of forests and wildlife; and decreased sedimentation downstream, where the city of Shanghai in particular relies for its physical base on a continual arrival of Yangtze River silt, much of which the dam now blocks. In 2006, the year after the dam was finished, popular worries about the dam mushroomed because of an unusual heat wave and accompanying drought in the Sichuan Basin, upriver from the dam. That summer, the city of Chongqing experienced more than ninety days of scorching heat, with daytime temperatures reaching as high as 112 degrees Fahrenheit. The next year, 2007, the Yangtze ran dry in some places, and its average water level reached the lowest that had been seen since 1892, when records were first kept. Lake Dongting, which is a flood basin for the Yangtze River in Hunan province, began to dry up. During the first months of 2011, severe drought visited southern China once again. Meteorologists cannot pin these episodes of drought specifically to the dam, but the way in which the dam has loomed as a cause in the popular imagination is beyond doubt. People have even theorized that the towering dam was blocking the natural flow of water vapor *upstream*, thus cutting off downriver moisture from the Sichuan Basin and choking its patterns of rainfall and its network of streams. The dam got a reputation for bad *fengshui*.

While this dam is the largest dam in the world, its twin megaproject, the South-to-North Water Diversion Project, is the largest irrigation project in the world. It is designed to channel 44.8 billion cubic meters of water annually from the Yangtze River and its tributaries northward to the Yellow and Hai rivers, which supply the water-starved northern China plain. The project has "eastern," "central," and "western" routes and is estimated eventually to cost around $60 billion and be completed by 2050.[14] Jiang Zemin, China's president from 1993 to 2003, pushed for parts of the central route to be completed in time to provide an additional billion cubic meters of water for the Beijing Olympics in 2008. Beijing's future viability has been tied to completion of the central route by 2014. Scientists have criticized the massive undertaking for its exorbitant cost, dislocation of people, and destruction of pastureland as well as for spreading pollution and causing loss of water to increased evaporation. Wang Weiluo, a distinguished Chinese hydraulic engineer, has argued that the reason why the middle and lower reaches of the Yangtze River have recently been so short on water, especially in Hubei, is that the area suffers the dual effects of both the Three Gorges Dam and the South-to-North Water Project. Wang notes that a single canal in the South-to-North Project requires, on average, the disruption of 700 natural streams or creeks and that this upsets the natural flow of water throughout the plains of central and northern China.[15] The American scholar Jared Diamond, in his book *Collapse: How Societies Choose to Fail or Succeed*, includes a chapter on China's environmental crisis called "China, Lurching Giant" and cites megaprojects like the Three Gorges Dam and the South-to-North Water Diversion Project to explain why he chooses to describe China with this phrase.[16]

Complaint about megaprojects has extended beyond scientists to the Chinese public at large, where people object to environmental damage, forced relocation, and enormous outlays of money that they feel could better be spent elsewhere. In 2011, a list titled "China's Megaprojects: Designed to Make Foreigners Gape" appeared on a popular website called "Cadillac."[17] The list includes the Three Gorges Dam, the South-to-North Water Project, and 104 other items, including the "West-to-East Electricity Project," which is the world's largest electrical project with a price tag of more than $84 billion; the "Five Vertical and Six Horizontal" superhighway system, the world's largest superhighway network with costs ranging to $144 billion; plans for rail networks that have budgets totaling $320 billion; and the "connecting all villages" (*cuncuntong*) project to link villages with roads, electric lines, water resources, telephone, television, and Internet, whose budget is $160 billion or more.

The point of the popular complaints about these projects is not to say that they do no good; it is to say that much *more* good—and less damage—would result from projects of more modest size. Some critics see megaprojects as grounded in an arrogance toward nature—"playing with nature like a child playing with sand on the beach," as one has put it. The megaproject that the government calls "Western Development," whose projected budget is $136 billion, aims to develop China's vast western region, where 29 percent of the population inhabits 71 percent of the land but where the giant project puts highly fragile ecosystems at risk. In 2010, Beijing built a dam on the Brahmaputra River (which flows across southern Tibet and into India and Bangladesh) to supply power for six eighty-five-megawatt electrical generators. The government of India objected but to no avail.

Climate Change

The part of the Chinese population that feels anxiety over climate change is an extremely small elite. Natural scientists, a few writers, and some officials in the Ministry of Environmental Protection are concerned about the issue, but most people, when they think about environmental problems, are preoccupied with the topics of fetid air, polluted water, contaminated food, and piles of garbage—not global warming. This is understandable. When a child is sick with lead poisoning or from having breathed the air or drunk contaminated milk or water, can a parent be asked to worry about a rising sea level? Worries over climate change seem remote, even a luxury. Yet we need to raise the issue in a volume like this, because the reasons to worry are considerable even if they are not yet widely recognized. China is deeply involved with the problem as both cause and victim.

Over the past century, temperatures on the surface of the globe have risen by about 1.33 degrees Fahrenheit, and meteorologists have calculated that, even if emission of greenhouse gases were to stop tomorrow, the gases that have already been released will likely cause an additional rise of 4.3 degrees Fahrenheit over the next century. If emissions continue at their current rate, the rise for the century could be as much as 7.7 degrees Fahrenheit.[18]

China's economic boom has been an important factor in global warming. In 2006, China passed the United States as the world's number one emitter of carbon dioxide (although it remains far down the list on a per-capita basis). In 2010, China accounted for about a quarter of the world's total carbon emissions.[19]

China has also begun to be a major sufferer of the consequences in such areas as desertification, sea-level rise, and the melting of glaciers. In 2012, deserts, mostly in western China, made up about 27 percent of the nation's land, and slowly rising temperatures were making the battle to reduce their spread more difficult. China also has many coastal cities that are vulnerable to sea-level rise. Shanghai, with a population of more than 23 million in 2011, rested an average of ten feet above sea level, and scientists estimate that melting ice caps (at the two poles, on the Tibetan Plateau, and in Greenland) will cause the seas to rise about three feet during the rest of the twenty-first century. Sang Baoliang, deputy director of the Shanghai Flood Control Headquarters, in 2009 declared the issue of sea-level rise to be "extremely complicated."[20]

Yet the largest and most immediate danger from global warming in China is rapid melting of glaciers on the Tibetan Plateau, whose icy heights have been called, next to the Arctic and the Antarctic, the world's "third pole." Forty-six thousand glaciers cover 17 percent of the land area of the Tibetan Plateau, and glacial melt supplies water to ten great rivers (the Yellow, Yangtze, Mekong, Salween, Irrawaddy, Brahmaputra, Ganges, Indus, Amu Darya, and Tarim) that flow out of the area. Glacial melt is vital to agriculture in downriver areas because it serves to keep water supply in balance as rainfall varies from season to season. Glaciers serve as reservoirs that maintain steady flows during dry seasons.[21]

For reasons that meteorologists have not yet identified, average annual temperatures have been rising even faster on the Tibetan Plateau than elsewhere. When Wang Yongcheng, organizer of Green Earth Volunteers in China, visited the area of the Jianggu Diru glacier in 1998, she saw more than 700 glaciers; eleven years later, in 2009, she saw no glaciers and noted that "many of the tributary streams of the Yangtze had simply dried up."[22] Scientists estimate that 43 percent of Tibet's glaciers could disappear by 2070, and a World Wildlife Fund report warns that in China, Nepal, and India, the loss of glacial melt "will affect freshwater flows with dramatic adverse effects on biodiversity, and people and livelihoods, with a possible long-term implication for regional food security."[23]

HOW DO PEOPLE SEE THE CAUSES?

We have noted that, except on the issue of climate change, environmental problems in China have drawn attention from many people in different parts of society. If this is so, one might wonder why solutions have been so difficult. Why do the problems just seem to get worse if there is broad consensus that everyone needs things like better air and water? The answer is that environmental problems are deeply embedded in other issues—economic, political, and social—that can frustrate reform efforts. Chinese people have their views about these complications, and we review some of them below.

One of the larger problems is that the economic enterprises that consume resources and produce pollution are controlled by elites over whom there is little if any effective public supervision. Until recently, censorship of the news media prevented accounts of environmental abuse from spreading very far. With the rise of the Internet in the 2000s, news began to spread more easily, and popular opinion began to gain some leverage. Police and the courts, however, remained within the control of the political and economic elites. The formula of "greed plus corruption" still worked, and environmental abuse could continue even if the number of people who knew about it was much greater.

For enterprises, the costs of installing equipment to comply with pollution laws has often been far higher than the costs of the bribery or fines one needs to pay in order to ignore them. Wang Hao, the hydrology official we cited above, writes that "when some enterprises receive notices from the Environmental Protection Bureau about exceeding pollution limits, they just celebrate with a big party, as if it were the New Year."[24] Netizens take note, however, and their indignation at abuses only compounds their anxiety over the environmental problem itself.

The pattern might be best shown by looking at an example in detail. In August 2011, Dong Rubin, a writer in Kunming, Yunnan province, together with some fellow writers, posted a story on the Internet about how the driver of a truck that dumps waste products for a chemical plant on the Nanpan River in Yunnan surreptitiously offloaded 140 truckloads (more than 5,000 tons) of factory waste products that were heavily contaminated with chromium on the banks of a reservoir that supplies water for the town of Yuezhouzhen. Rain runoff and seepage carried chromium into the reservoir itself, from where it leaked into the Nanpan River, which is a tributary of the larger Pearl River that flows through Guangzhou into the South China Sea. News of the environmental calamity at Yuezhouzhen created a furor throughout the Pearl River delta. The outcry only got louder when a reporter for the evening newspaper in Guangzhou inquired about the matter with the Yunnan provincial authorities who were charged with environmental protection and received, he reported, the answer that "our monitoring of water quality shows nothing unusual."

Furious netizens took to their keyboards. "Our home is at the mouth of the river," wrote one, "and we have always drunk its water. How are we supposed to tolerate this?"[25] Others advised storing mineral water. One went into the medical science of exposure to chromium: "Inhalation of hexavalent chromium compounds in relatively high concentrations can lead to runny nose, sneezing, itching, nosebleeds, ulceration or perforation of the septum, and even cancer. Skin contact can produce allergic reaction. Prolonged exposure can damage genes." Another explained what a cleanup would have to entail: "When heavy metal ions enter water, and especially after they undergo sediment adsorption and settle, even thirty years is insufficient to return a river to its original state. Even after 10,000 complete transfusions of water, heavy metals continue to be released slowly from contaminated sediment. In order to achieve what the officials are referring to as 'harmless levels,' one would have to scrape all of the silt from the entire Nanpan riverbed." Another netizen went into detail on the Hollywood film *Erin Brockovich*, which was made in 2000 and based on the true story of an unemployed single mother in California in 1993. While working as a file clerk in a law office, Erin happens across an inactive file that shows Pacific Gas and Electric, California's huge utility company, offering to purchase a person's home. Something about the file seems odd to Erin, so she investigates and eventually reveals a thirty-year cover-up of the contamination of an entire town's water supply by hexavalent chromium (the very chemical that now had poisoned the Nanpan River in Yunnan). Erin ties the pollution to illnesses among the California town's residents and in the end wins a judgment that the utility compensate 634 plaintiffs a total of $333 million. The title of the film, in Chinese, was *Yongbu tuoxie* (Never Compromise!). Ma Zhihai, a well-known blogger in Guangzhou, wrote,

> The Guangdong media need to get involved. Industries in the advanced areas along the coasts are focusing more and more on "upgrading" what they do, and that means shipping the more primitive technologies—the ones that pollute more and that waste more energy—to less-developed and more vulnerable areas up rivers, in the hinterland. Guangdong is hardly innocent in this regard.

One of the more poignant comments within the hubbub was that "the last drop of water to survive on this globe may be a human tear."

The Nanpan River case may have struck netizens with special force because of the cumulative effect of a number of other recent cases. In March 2004, a company called Sichuan Chemical Co., Ltd, dumped industrial waste that contained ammonia into the Tuo River in Sichuan, temporarily depriving nearly a million people in five cities of usable water. Seven months later, residents of Puyang City on the Yellow River in Henan had lost their water supply in a similar event. Three months after that, in January 2005, Strength Fertilizers, Ltd, in Chongqing dumped wastewater into the Qi River, leaving 30,000 citizens without water, and near the end of the year, the Shaoguan Smelting Factory in Guangdong dumped chromium-tainted wastewater into the North River, a tributary of the Pearl. On November 13, 2005, an explosion at the No. 101 Petrochemical Plant in Jilin City in the northeast caused about 100 tons of pollutants, primarily of benzene and nitrobenzene (exposure to which reduces white blood cells and has been linked to leukemia) to fall into the Songhua River, creating an eighty-kilometer-long toxic slick in which the benzene level at one point was recorded to be 108 times above national safety levels. Then, in February and March 2006, dead fish started floating to the top of Lake Baiyang in Hebei, China's largest freshwater lake that had long been regarded as a scenic resort. Six months later, in September, three chemical plants in Yueyang county in Hunan dumped so much industrial waste into the Xinqiang River that the water began to turn viscous. Tests showed that it contained arsenic. Next, in May 2007, after a heat wave and sparse rainfall, the water level in beautiful Lake Tai in Anhui province fell to a fifty-year low, and the lake produced effusive algae growth that compromised the water supply of Wuxi, a city of 6 million. Two months later, the Huaishu River in Jiangsu province was declared to be "severely polluted," and 200,000 urban residents were affected.

It would be a mistake to imagine that China's polluters do not know what they are doing but perhaps also not quite right to say that they simply do not care. The psychology is more subtle. The rush to make money during China's "reform" years has left other values far behind and has induced a mind-set whereby all costs other than immediate profit can be handed to someone else—to people who live downstream, to people who breathe the air, or to future generations. This psychology of "buck-passing" applies in another sense as well. Everyone can acknowledge that pollution is a bad thing and that there should be rules about it but at the same time look to see the rules applied to others, not oneself. In this sense, pollution control rules generate the same kind of dilemma that population control rules have generated. A person can agree that population controls are good for the society as a whole even while trying to avoid their application to him- or herself. The difference between the two cases is that the state does enforce family size but, because corruption in commercial affairs is so pervasive, cannot or will not enforce pollution controls.

It is important to understand why central authorities choose to be less firm in combating environmental degradation than they are in areas such as population control or the crushing of dissent. The soft-pedaling of environmental policy follows from the more fundamental policy of "GDP above all," which has been crucial to the maintenance of power by the Chinese Communist Party (CCP) ever since the early 1990s. After the June Fourth massacre of 1989 had brought popular respect for the CCP regime to an unprecedented low, Deng Xiaoping looked for ways to recoup the Party's prestige and settled primarily on two: nationalism and economic growth. Thus, a galloping GDP became not only an economic target but also a key to keeping a huge populace satisfied and therefore docile. Without steady GDP growth, the CCP's rule might wobble or even crumble. Moreover, power at the center depended on the maintenance of working alliances with power elites in the localities, so when local elites ravished the environment in pursuit of ever-more GDP, there was little incentive at the center to crack down. It became easier to pass the accumulating debt to air breathers, water drinkers, and future generations. Many Chinese people, both inside the regime and outside, have decried this policy of GDP *über alles*.

Some have tied it to a kind of great-leader hubris whose origins lie in the Mao era. When Mao Zedong put forth the slogans *chao Ying gan Mei* ("pass England and catch America") and *ren ding sheng tian* ("man is certain to conquer nature") in the late 1950s—and around the same time began to speak of a great dam on the Yangtze—he established an association in CCP culture between "great leaders" and megaprojects. Then in the 1990s, when money became available, the megaprojects began to bloom. Big leaders could now build the biggest examples of things—the biggest dam, biggest irrigation project, biggest high-speed rail network, and so on. Grandiose names reflected the Olympian perspective: south-to-north water, west-to-east gas, west-to-east electricity, "five vertical and six horizontal" roadways, and so on.

From another point of view, however, some in China have pointed out that the fundamental problem has to do with a large population and rising living standards, not just a corrupt political system. Even under a democratic system (or an authoritarian system more willing to enforce environmental rules), with many Chinese people beginning to demand "first world" living standards, any state will need to pursue a "high consumption" development model, and any such model inevitably will strain the environment.

The strains that China's human population have exerted on its natural environment in fact are a very old story. Take today's loess plateau in northwestern China, for example. In the "Tribute of Yu" section of the ancient *Book of History*, where soils are ranked for their quality, this area of China is rated "upper upper first" (*shangshang yideng*). It is described as bearing dense forests and rich, beautiful plains. But in the twentieth century, after more than 2,000 years of human incursion, it had turned into an expanse of barren hills and bald ridges, subject to severe soil erosion that deposited sediment in large volumes into the Yellow River, which carried so much silt downstream that dikes were needed to hold the water as much as thirty feet above the North China Plain. The highlands of the Yunnan-Guizhou area are another example. People in ancient times knew this area as "the region of plagues" and generally avoided it, which may be one reason why it survived for many centuries with its tropical rain forests intact and as home to a startling array of species. In Qing times (1644–1911), after large influxes of human population, which led to "reclamation" of mountainsides in which virgin forests were destroyed for agricultural land, forest cover fell by a third, and here, as in the loess plateau, bleak hills and bald ridges also began to appear. These trends appeared before human beings had come across "modernization"; today's pressures are dramatically increasing the threats.

HOW ARE PEOPLE REACTING?

"Rights awareness" has been on the rise in Chinese society since the late 1990s. The Internet—both as a medium for expression and as a platform for organization—has hastened the spread of a *weiquan* ("support rights") movement, and the number of what the police call "mass events" (demonstrations, protests, and strikes) has increased more than tenfold in official statistics. The government's budget for "stability maintenance" (*weiwen*, a direct answer to *weiquan*) grew in 2010 to exceed even its military budget.

Many of the popular protests have concerned environmental issues, and in the early 2000s there has been a subtle but important shift from seeing environmental questions as public policy to seeing them as matters of personal rights. In 2008, for example, the phrase "guarding the home front" (*baowei jiayuan*) spread on the Internet as a way to describe popular demands for environmental safety. Here are some examples.

In late 2006, a Taiwan-backed company called Dragon Aromatics got permission to build a chemical plant that could produce 800,000 tons of paraxylene annually at a site less than six miles from the center of Xiamen city in Fujian province. The company was said to have ties with Jiang Mianheng, a son of Jiang Zemin, China's former president, and this may or may not explain why the plant was privileged to be part of the government's Eleventh Five-Year Plan. In March 2007, Xiamen University professor Zhao Yufen pointed out the environmental dangers in the plan. Bloggers and journalists took her side, and on the Internet the plan came to be called "an atomic bomb" over Xiamen. In the summer of 2007, popular protests grew large enough to force a relocation of the plant inland. In early 2008, authorities in Shanghai announced the extension of a maglev train line westward from the South Shanghai Station toward Rainbow Bridge. People who lived along the route, especially in the Dianpu River section, where the line was going to be only about thirty yards from their residences, began to worry that radiation from the line would harm their health. On January 6, more than a hundred residents gathered along the route shouting slogans such as "Oppose the maglev!" and "Protect our homes!" They later moved their protest to downtown Shanghai, where, in the evenings, for many days in a row, they engaged in "strolling demonstrations." (Strolling demonstrations emerged in China around this time as a countertactic to the police policy of quelling protests by detaining their leaders. In strolling demonstrations, crowds gather and mill about, everyone knowing the reason but no one standing out as organizer.) In 2009, authorities revised their plans to convert parts of the maglev line to underground construction.

Zhuanghe, a coastal city of 900,000 in Liaoning province, relies on fishing. In the 1990s, its tidal flats began to recede, red tides of phosphates and nitrogen encroached, and seafood harvests plummeted. Meanwhile, the Zhuanghe Party secretary, Liu Qinglian, was making money by selling swaths of nearby mountainsides to developers. Both these events stoked popular resentment, and on April 13, 2010, hundreds of people knelt in a mass protest at the government office building.

In July 2010 in Jingxi county in Guangxi, pollution from the Shandong Xinfa Aluminum Plant drew resentment from the local populace and led to a confrontation between protesters and authorities. After police beat some protesters, on July 11 more than 1,000 villagers gathered on the streets. On July 13, almost all the residents in the nearby village of Lingwan joined to block the road to the county seat and also blocked the plant's gate and damaged some equipment. In the ensuing clash, three people were killed and eighteen wounded. About 1,000 police were called in to quell the protests.

In 2009, the largest paraxylene manufacturing plant in China went into production in Dalian, Liaoning province, without having gotten even pro forma clearance from environmental officials. On July 8, 2011, waves from Typhoon Plum Blossom broke a dike that protected the plant, flooding it and putting two large containers of paraxylene at risk of leakage. Word of the event spread on the Internet, caused panic among Dalian residents, and attracted nationwide concern. Calls went out for Dalian residents to do a strolling demonstration on July 14 at People's Square in the heart of the city. Authorities erased these calls from major Internet fora, but people turned to microblogs to spread the word, and 12,000 people eventually participated. Protesters prepared masks, banners, T-shirts, and placards with messages such as "By international convention, paraxylene plants should be at least sixty miles from a city, but

Dalian's is only twelve miles away," "Producing this kind of superpoisonous chemical is like dropping an atomic bomb on Dalian; our people are destined to a future of leukemia and deformed infants," "We want life! We want an environment! Give us back our Dalian! Kick paraxylene out of our city!," and "Taiwan is no threat, yet we point a thousand missiles at it; paraxylene canisters are a huge threat, but nothing is done." Protesters gathered in front of government buildings, then went to People's Square to "stroll" and sit in. They issued five demands: (1) production of paraxylene must cease immediately, (2) a date for removal of the factory must be set, (3) the person(s) responsible for the decision to locate the factory in the city must be identified, (4) the media must report on the protests, and (5) the mayor must engage the protesters in dialogue. In response, the mayor, Tang Jun, did appear, standing atop a police van and shouting to protesters that the paraxylene plant would cease operation immediately and be removed very soon. In the evening, police reinforcements from Shenyang and elsewhere arrived in Dalian and dispersed the crowds.

After that, nothing changed. The factory continued with its production of up to 700,000 metric tons of paraxylene per year. The protesters had lost their battle, but they did succeed in demonstrating and advertising a new way to engage in "bloodless confrontation" with authorities. They had organized through the Internet, had avoided punishment for particular "leaders," and had garnered broad popular support for their cause in China and even abroad. The authorities, aware of the danger of further inflaming public opinion, had to rely on negotiation and deception—not violence—in response.

The government has called the protests in Xiamen, Zhuanghe, Shanghai, Jingxi, Dalian, and elsewhere "mass" events. In CCP parlance, "mass" actually does not refer so much to numbers of participants as it does to the idea of "originating from below." And, indeed, all these protests came from below, from ordinary citizens acting outside official rubrics. But environmental concerns are by no means limited to ordinary citizens. The ruling elite worries for its safety as well.

One telling piece of evidence for elite anxiety has been the growth of private farms that produce special food for elites. While ordinary citizens have been "guarding the home front," elites have been "guarding their lives with specially produced vegetables" (*baoming tegong cai*). In August 2010, an article titled "State Organs Build Their Own Farms—to Protect Their Own Lives" appeared on the blog of Professor He Bing of the Chinese University of Politics and Law in Beijing.[26] The article was widely forwarded and attracted an unusually large number of comments. In it, the professor recounts a personal experience at a conference in a "western province" that he chooses not to name: "I was eating dinner in the unit's dining hall, and my host said to me, 'Don't worry about the food we serve you; it's all organic. We've rented several acres of land and hired our own farmers to cultivate it; we use no chemical fertilizers or pesticides." Professor He later visited an army unit and a government office in central China, where he heard the same unsolicited message: in both cases, his hosts told him, "Don't be afraid" to eat the food because we have "raised the vegetables themselves" and they are "organic." In his blog, Professor He concludes that "the pattern by which government work units grow their own food as a health precaution seems to be widespread."

He's speculation was reinforced in March 2011 by an investigative reporter named Zhang Lihua, who wrote in the *First Financial Daily* that "because of worries over food safety, a number of province-level government units, large-scale state enterprises, non-state enterprises, market-listed companies, financial institutions, and other autonomous organizations having been renting larger or smaller pieces of suburban land on which to produce food for themselves or for supply to special people. It's as if we have returned to the pre-revolutionary era of self-sufficient small-scale farming. We are no longer aiming for the advantages of industrialized farming and economies of scale. A failure of trust between parts of society is now giving us higher production and transaction costs. The harm, in the end, goes far beyond the simple question of how much food is produced."[27] Zhang Lihua shows how the trend toward private farming by public organs has led to more than one irony. Offices of the Ministry of Environmental Protection have hired people to plant crops for their own people. In eastern China, a company that manufactures herbicides and pesticides has rented land in a wholly different part of the country (the northeast) to raise crops for its employees that are free of herbicides and pesticides. Law enforcement agencies have joined the trend as well. The supreme court in Shaanxi province rented more than five acres of land in the mountains thirty miles from the capital Xi'an and has been hiring a dozen or so farmers to plant vegetables on it.

Some organizations, finding that they cannot grow enough food to supply everyone, reserve their "safe" supplies for leaders or the entertainment of dignitaries. Zhang Lihua writes that an investment conglomerate based in Shanghai that deals primarily in finance and real estate (like He Bing, she withholds specific names apparently for fear of reprisal) cultivated more than sixty-five acres near Suzhou for supply to its main office in Shanghai. That supply, however, was enough to cover only senior management and preferred clients, not ordinary employees. Meanwhile, employees at the company's Beijing office hired a farmer to raise vegetables for a cooperative of their own and in doing so noted that there were already more than a hundred similar "autonomous vegetable cooperatives" nationwide. This led the company, ever astute, to perceive a business opportunity: vegetable gardens and fruit trees could be used as selling points for properties. Their small properties, marketed as residential space, began featuring miniature orchards or gardens. Wealthy people could buy these as vacation homes and hire gardeners to tend the fruit trees and vegetables year-round. In Beijing, a development called "Eastern Sun City" bought a piece of land and divided it into hundreds of miniplots suitable for growing vegetables. Each purchaser of an apartment received a miniplot as a bonus.

While the elite fad for self-supply of vegetables rests on the belief that such vegetables are less contaminated than others, some Chinese scientists have questioned this assumption. He Jiguo, a professor at China Agricultural University, holds that the animal manure used in traditional (now called "organic") cultivation contains elements that present problems that are even more worrisome than chemical fertilizers. Animal manure today contains heavy metals and antibiotics in addition to the potentially disease-causing bacteria that it has always contained.[28] Others see the phenomenon of "self-supplied vegetables" as a social problem more than a health issue. It stands as a vivid example of how "the public good" has retreated as a goal in society, how political power has come increasingly to serve private ends, and how society has begun to disintegrate into an archipelago of "self-protecting fortresses."

In recent years, increasing numbers in the Chinese elite have sought self-protection in another way: by looking abroad. Money is sent abroad for safekeeping, and people are seeking foreign citizenship, especially for their offspring. In Hong Kong, local residents have begun to complain that their hospitals are crowded with mainland women who are willing to pay large sums of money in order to give birth to offspring who will automatically get Hong Kong residency cards, which make travel to the rest of the world easier.[29] It is impossible to say how much of the allure of an emergency exit originates with worry about the environment, but it clearly is a factor, and the elite is especially vulnerable. In early 2012, the Chinese Academy of Social Sciences published the results of a survey that showed that officials are more likely than ordinary citizens to seek foreign residency or citizenship for their children. Among ministry chiefs, provincial governors, and large-city mayors, 53 percent approved of the idea of foreign status for their descendants; among county chiefs, 52 percent approved; and among township leaders, 50 percent did so. Among the general public, 34 percent approved.[30] The survey measured wishes only—not the ability—to access foreign status. It goes without saying that members of the elite have much better chances of access than do ordinary citizens.

We have been looking at some of the practical ways in which Chinese people have been reacting to environmental threats: by protesting, "strolling," growing vegetables, securing the option of moving abroad, and so on. At the level of ideas, the reactions have been even more numerous and varied. Most ideas have been about ways to stop polluters from polluting. We cannot survey all of them here, but it is worth noting how broad their range is. People with very different political and intellectual premises have noticed the specter of environmental collapse. They produce very different interpretations, but the core worry has been the same.

For example, at the "far left" of the political spectrum,[31] there are people who look back at the Mao years (1949–1976) as a time when China was free of corruption and foreign exploitation. They see today's leaders as having sold out to foreign capitalists whose aim is to dominate China and (here is where the environment issue enters) who exploit China's natural and human resources, carry out dangerous experimentation and manufacturing on its territory, and treat it as a waste dump. On Mao Zedong's birthday in 2006, an article forcefully presenting this view appeared on the website "Maoflag," where it drew wide attention.[32] Author Zhang Hongliang titled his piece "The Chinese People Once Again Have Arrived at Their Most Dangerous Hour." Except for the words "once again," this line is taken verbatim from China's national anthem. Playwright Tian Han wrote it to depict China's life-or-death struggle with Japan. Now, Zhang Hongliang implies, China is standing at the brink of an equally fearsome precipice.

Zhang cites destruction of the environment together with "massive corruption" as twin perils that have brought China again to its most dangerous hour. These dangers admit "no bottom line," are "beyond imagination," and "startle people to their bones." During the late nineteenth century, Zhang reminds his readers, European powers "carved China up like a melon"; today, China has been "turned into an 'international milk cow' from which the developed nations of the West squeeze milk at will." China "not only sacrifices the wealth of the present generation but, even more terrifying, hollows out the foundations of livelihood of generations to come." Zhang paints a bleak picture: 80 percent of China's rivers and lakes are drying up; two-thirds of its grasslands have turned to deserts; most of its forests have disappeared; acid rain has fallen on one-third of its land; nearly 100 percent of its soil is hard; 300 million or more farmers do without safe drinking water; 400 million or more urban residents breathe severely polluted air; two-thirds of China's 688 largest cities are surrounded by garbage; the market is already completely permeated with poisoned food; in 2003, the number of work-related deaths reached 136,000, giving China a "bloody GDP" in the literal sense; for every 100 million yuan of GDP, one person dies; and if we add the deaths that private enterprises and foreign enterprises are covering up, the annual deaths reach the level of one Nanjing massacre.

Some of Zhang's numbers are inflated. It is not true that "nearly 100 percent" of China's soil has hardened or that the number of city dwellers breathing "severely polluted air" has reached 400 million. But inflated or not, there is no doubt that Zhang's estimates represent one kind of authentic Chinese opinion. Zhang writes that China is again being "colonized" by the West, that current leaders are "a clique of compradors and traitors," and that the Chinese people, who again face a "responsibility to save the nation . . . can only rely on Mao Zedong Thought."

The Dalai Lama, whose recipe for China's future would be about as far from Zhang's as one could get, has views that nevertheless intersect with Zhang's on some of the fundaments. In Tibetan Buddhism, one of the "three poisons" in human nature is greed. (The other two are anger and foolishness. See chapter 8 in this volume on the current spread of Buddhist ideas in Chinese cities.) Human greed, in the Dalai Lama's view, has long exacted costs from the natural environment; now, with modernization and its skyrocketing demands for energy and other natural resources and its accelerating production of waste, the costs are far greater. They present humanity with daunting technical problems, but at root the problems are much more than technical. The root lies in human greed, and the way out is to see that human happiness does not depend only on material things. The Dalai Lama has written,

> These days we human beings are very much involved in the external world, while we neglect the internal world. We do need scientific development and material development in order to survive and to increase the general benefit and prosperity, but equally as much we need mental peace. No doctor can give you an injection of mental peace, and no market can sell it to you. If you go to a supermarket with millions and millions of dollars, you can buy anything, but if you go there and ask for peace of mind, people will laugh. . . . It is worthwhile to adopt certain methods to increase mental peace, and in order to do that it is important to know more about the mind. When we talk about preservation of the environment, the key point is to have a genuine sense of universal responsibility, based on love and compassion, and clear awareness.[33]

The eminent Chinese historian Yü Ying-shih is not a Buddhist, but in the 1980s, during the general enthusiasm for Deng Xiaoping's "Four Modernizations," Yü astutely observed that Deng's policy aimed at "traditional modernization." It aimed at what Western economies had done during the nineteenth and twentieth centuries: assembly lines, smokestacks, automobiles, and so on. No one could fault China for following these precedents, but Yü had the vision to see that the world of the future would require different patterns—something even more "modern," not "traditionally" modern in the nineteenth-century sense.

There is much space and plenty of room for disagreement between the positions of Zhang Hongliang on one side and the Dalai Lama or Yü Ying-shih on the other. Yet their shared concern for the natural environment illustrates a important common denominator in Chinese public opinion. It shows, too, an implicit skepticism over what the CCP's leaders have sometimes referred to as "the China model" of economic development. Zhang Hongliang calls this model a form of "new colonization" by the West; for Yü Ying-shih, it is not only an authoritarian model but also one built on outmoded notions of "modern." It is impossible to predict what will happen with China's environment. But the crisis it faces—and the very unpredictability itself—are cause for a widespread and deep-seated unease.

NOTES

1. Cited in Sharon LaFraniere, "Activists Crack China's Wall of Denial about Air Pollution" *New York Times*, January 28, 2012, A4, A8.

2. Xiaojin, "Xibu ziran huanjing de bianqian" (Environmental changes in the West), May 21, 2009, http://eco.guoxue.com/article.php/3714.

3. Zhang Zuhua and Jiang Qisheng, "To Help Fix the Climate, Fix Human Rights in China," *Washington Post*, op-ed, November 20, 2009, http://www.washingtonpost.com/wp-dyn/content/article/2009/11/20/AR2009112002972.html.

4. "Liu da huanjing 'wanji' yingxiang shenghuo zhiliang (Six great "plagues" affect the quality of life), *Beijing Evening News*, cited at *Renminwang*, http://env.people.com.cn/GB/4293707.html.

5. Jiao Feng, "Guanzhu: Jiaotong zaoyin wuran keyi fangzhi" (Attention: Traffic noise pollution can be prevented), *Ziran zhi you*, http://www.fon.org.cn/content.php?aid=10486.

6. "Huanbao zongju: Nengyuan xiaofei chao changgui zengzhang daozhi eryanghualiu paifang zongliang shikong" (Central office of environmental protection: Unusual levels of energy consumption cause a loss of control in emissions of sulfur dioxide), *Xinhuanet*, http://news.xinhuanet.com/newscenter/2006-04/12/content_4417256.htm.

7. Wang Hao, "Zhongguo shui ziyuan wenti ji kexue yingdui" (A scientific response to the problem of China's water resources), http://tech.qq.com/a/20110926/000398.htm.

8. http://www.guardian.co.uk/environment/2009/nov/23/china-protest-incinerator-guangzhou; http://www.telegraph.co.uk/news/worldnews/asia/china/6636631/Chinas-middle-class-rise-up-in-environmental-protest.html.

9. http://chinadigitaltimes.net/2009/11/residents-protest-garbage-incinerator-in-guangdong (translation slightly revised).

10. Lang Xianping, "Women de rizi weishenme zheme nan?" (Why are times so tough for us?), chapter 13, "Wei shenme women de laji weiji zheme yanzhong?" (Why is our garbage crisis so severe?), http://read.dangdang.com/content_2209530?ref=read-2-D&book_id=12326.

11. Jared M. Diamond, *Collapse: How Societies Choose to Fail or Succeed* (New York: Viking, 2005), 368.

12. "Shrinking Arable Land Adds Concern on China's Grain Security," *Xinhuanet*, October 18, 2010, http://news.xinhuanet.com/english2010/china/2010-10/18/c_13562418.htm. We have converted *mu* to acres.

13. See Qin Shao, *Shanghai Gone: Demolition and Defiance in a Chinese Megacity* (Lanham, MD: Rowman & Littlefield, 2012). See also "The Land Manifestos of Chinese Farmers" and "State Ownership of Land Is the Authorities' Magic Wand for Forced Eviction" in Liu Xiaobo, *No Enemies, No Hatred: Selected Essays and Poems* (Cambridge, MA: Harvard University Press, 2012), 30–36, 85–93.

14. See http://www.water-technology.net/projects/south_north.

15. "Zhuanfang Wang Weiluo: Bi san xia geng kepa de shi shenme?" (An interview with Wang Weiluo: What is more fearful than the Three Gorges Dam?), *Dajiyuan* (Epoch Times), July 1, 2011, http://webcache.googleusercontent.com/search?q=cache:m_xew-TYAAQJ:www.epochtimes.com/gb/11/7/1/n3302615.htm+&cd=1&hl=en&ct=clnk&gl=us.

16. Diamond, *Collapse*, 367.

17. http://bbs.tiexue.net/post2_3003589_1.html.

18. Summarized in Orville Schell, "The Message from the Glaciers," *New York Review of Books*, May 27, 2010, http://www.nybooks.com/articles/archives/2010/May/27/message-from-the-glaciers. Here we have converted degrees Centigrade to degrees Fahrenheit.

19. PBL Netherlands Environmental Assessment Agency, http://www.pbl.nl/en/dossiers/Climatechange/moreinfo/Chinanowno1inCO2emissionsUSAinsecondposition; US Department of Energy, Carbon Dioxide Information Analysis Center, cited at http://en.wikipedia.org/wiki/List_of_countries_by_carbon_dioxide_emissions.

20. http://www.msnbc.msn.com/id/33368880/ns/us_news-environment/t/rising-seas-threaten-shanghai-other-big-cities/#.TygzZ4Erwtk.

21. Schell, "The Message from the Glaciers."

22. Wang Yongchen, "Qihou biannuan zaocheng changjiang fayuandi bingchuan xiaorong, zhiliu ganhe" (Climatic warming causes glaciers at the origins of the Yangtze River to melt and tributaries to run dry), *Radio France Internationale*, December 5, 2009, http://webcache.googleusercontent.com/search?q=cache:DxovMo5XotsJ:www.chinese.rfi.fr?.

23. Quoted in Schell, "The Message from the Glaciers."

24. Guo Fang, "Wuran zhishui pinkun: Qiye jiedao chaobiao paifang fadan xiang guonian" (Pollution impoverishing water: Enterprises celebrate as if it's New Year's when they receive notices of fines for excessive emissions), http://webcache.googleusercontent.com/search?q=cache:wWNo9OiUjlQJ:news.zynews.com/2011-07/27/content_953282_4.htm+&cd=4&hl=en&ct=clnk&gl=us.

25. This and the other examples of the netizen comment in this paragraph are from "Meiti cheng Yunnan 5 qian dun ge zha bei dao shuiku wuran pai ru Nanpan jiang" (Media reports on the dumping of 5,000 tons of chromium slag into a reservoir and the seepage of contaminated water into the Nanpan River), August 13, 2011, http://news.sina.com.cn/c/2011-08-13/143322985326.shtml.

26. He Bing, "Guojia jiguan wei baoming, kaishi zijian nongchang," http://blog.sina.com.cn/s/blog_486bea1a0100k9jl.html.

27. Zhang Lihua, "Guojia jiguan weihe zijian nongchang guren zhong cai?" (Why are state organs establishing their own farms and hiring people to grow crops?), *Diyi caijing ribao*, March 15, 2011, http://www.1818long.com/viewnews-88.html.

28. Zhang Lihua, "Guojia jiguan weihe zijian nongchang guren zhong cai?"

29. Sharon LaFraniere, "Mainland Chinese Flock to Hong Kong to Give Birth," *New York Times*, February 22, 2012, http://www.nytimes.com/2012/02/23/world/asia/mainland-chinese-flock-to-hong-kong-to-have-babies.html?pagewanted=all.

30. *Southern Metropolis Daily*, February 21, 2012,http://nf.nfdaily.cn/nfdsb/content/2012-02/21/content_38395262.htm.

31. We put *left* in quotation marks because what is called "left" in China differs in important ways from common understanding of the term in the West. A Maoist "left" position in China, for example, favors authoritarianism and tight limits on popular expression.

32. Zhang Hongliang, "Zhonghua minzu zai ci dao le zuiweixian de shihou," http://www.maoflag.net/space.php?uid=36505&op=bbs. Apparently deleted by Internet police, Zhang's piece no longer appears at that website but is available at many others, including http://webcache.googleusercontent.com/search?q=cache:_BzX9sOZz54J:blog.ce.cn/html/92/150592-149791.html+&cd=1&hl=en&ct=clnk&gl=us.

33. Dalai Lama, *My Tibet* (London: Thames and Hudson, 1990), 53–54.

ELEVEN

Awash in Money and Searching for Excellence

The Restlessness of Chinese Universities

Hsiung Ping-chen

While many Western academics are filled with anxiety about the decline in financing for public universities, faculty and students at Chinese universities are restless because of the opposite problem. They are awash in money and perhaps even drowning in it. Through two major government "engineering projects" (*gongcheng*), the government has poured billions of dollars into its universities over the past fifteen years. Besides producing sparkling new buildings and research labs, this money has transformed the academic life of the campuses. Long gone are the days when universities were known for their leisurely pace, the smooth flow of bicycles through landscaped quadrangles, music and theater in the evening, and long, earnest discussions over tea of ancient texts. Now professors have become managers, cell phones in hand, calendars filled with meetings from morning to night, and computers loaded with templates and charts for supporting grant applications. Campuses are noisier, busier, more exciting and anxious, and, at the beginning of the twenty-first century, facing a roller coaster of opportunities mingled with horrendous problems and awesome risks.

On the surface, the best universities in China look like elite public universities in the United States, only richer and, by some quantitative standards, more successful. It is no secret for American academics that the number one institution for producing graduate students for American graduate schools has been Peking University. In terms of producing papers counted in the Scientific Citation Index, China now stands as a formidable number two, second only to the United States. Amidst all of this, however, there remain fundamental problems, leaving observers with the query as to (1) whether much of the money infused into Chinese campuses has been wasted and 2) whether old standards of teaching and scholarship have been abandoned for superficial achievements of dubious quality.

This at least is the impression one gets from reading critical comments from students and faculty alike on the Chinese Internet. But before detailing these complaints, let us first describe how the public money has flowed into the universities.

PROJECTS 211 AND 985

In 1995, China's Ministry of Education proposed to help the country's top 100 universities become world-class institutions by the twenty-first century. Hence, this effort became known as Project 211. Its aim was to spread funding beyond China's most elite campuses and national cities to include all geographic areas and forms of academic expertise. Beneficiaries include Xinjiang University and the University of Inner Mongolia in the underdeveloped northwest; Yanbian University, Jilin University, and Liaoning University in the northeast; Guizhou University and Yunnan University in the southwest; and Hainan University in the southeast. In addition, funding was distributed to many technical schools devoted to applied subjects, such as forestry, aeronautics, geoscience, mining, petroleum, and maritime studies. Support was also given to arts and humanities, even music and ethnography, as well as social sciences such as political science, finance, and law.[1]

Investment in these hundred or so universities amounted to pumping money into 6 percent of leading institutions out of China's more than 1,700 universities. Yet since emphasis was placed on scientific studies and advanced training, Project 211 would have taken care of four-fifths of the nation's doctoral students and 96 percent of the state's key laboratories, with an annual spending of 70 percent of the funds for scientific research. In the first four years, from 1996 to 2000, roughly US$2.2 billion was distributed.

Project 985, on the other hand, was aimed at China's nine most elite universities. It was initiated by Jiang Zemin on the occasion of the 100th anniversary of Peking University on May 4, 1998—hence the name 985. The aim, in Jiang's words, was that with major investments and continuous support, sustained improvements might be expected from a handful of China's best universities so that China "will have a few top-class universities at the international level" before long.[2] The fact that Jiang chose to do this on May Fourth sent an unmistaken signal to those who knew the history of Chinese nationalism.

In the first phase of Project 985, nine elite universities were chosen to receive additional funding jointly from the central and local governments. The nine were divided into three groups. The first group consisted of Peking and Tsinghua universities, which each received 1.8 billion RMB directly from the central government. The next group included five universities with regional acclaim, each of which was given between .4 billion and 1.4 billion RMB jointly provided by the Ministry of Education and the city in which they were located.[3] The third group included two technical universities, Harbin Institute of Technology and the University of Science and Technology of China, receiving 1 billion and .9 billion RMB, respectively, from a tripart contribution from the Ministry of Education, a national-level academy, and local municipal governments. The hope was that the influx of resources would vault these universities into the top tier of international rankings. They are now known as China's C-9, also called "China's Ivy League."

Each of the students in the C-9 comes to benefit from 20,000 to 30,000 RMB per year, which accounts for these institutions' rapid growth and development in infrastructure, research equipment, faculty recruitment, and student body expansion. In subsequent years, another thirty of China's selective regional universities also received funding under this program. These include universities in previously remote areas, such as Lanzhou University and Jilin University, and special schools, such as the Central University for Nationalities, the China Agricultural University, and the Oceanographic University of China.

Especially on these campuses, signs of academic prosperity have become routine over the past decade. Professors frequently traveled abroad for training and conferences and students for exchanges. Lectures by famous international visitors became common. Professors became principal investigators of big projects. The hustle and bustle of Chinese campuses reached a takeoff point even as the rest of the world's universities were plunging into financial disarray and academic depression. China's universities have much to be proud of.

CRITICISM AND CONCERNS

But there are dark sides to this glory. A good place to learn about them is through student and faculty postings on websites. We sample criticisms and complaints from two major websites. Everyone.com (*renren*) claimed 124 million users as of 2011, amounting to a quarter of China's online population (480 million). Together with MutualContact.com (*hulian*), it represents an important network for Chinese students, who use their real names. The most visited site on Everyone.com is called Sharing (*fenxi-*

ang), on which students regularly cut and paste news from other media while posting spontaneous comments of their own.[4] A review of these online exchanges suggests three paramount areas of concern in China's higher education today.

In 2005, Professor Cheng Yao of Taiwan's Tsinghua University wrote an article reflecting on his experiences as a visiting professor for a year at the original Tsinghua University in Beijing. Later posted to Everyone.com, the article inspired thousands of comments, which continued to come in for several years. Echoing the May Fourth author Lu Xun's cry to "save the children," Professor Cheng claimed that students at the Beijing Tsinghua, bright as they might be, had lost the passion for the pursuit of knowledge, for thinking hard and asking good questions, as if their heads had been bound up with some "cursed wire of the mind." All standards of ethics seemed to have collapsed, he complained, as some of the brightest students in China seemed to be worried about nothing except getting good grades.[5]

His remarks hit a sensitive nerve. Some Chinese commentators thought that he had overstated his case, but even more thought that he was absolutely correct. "The facts are indeed like that," said one commentator, "and the problem is getting worse." Others asked the author for more sympathetic understanding. "You want students to study well, but you also criticize them for being too calculating about their grades, and you expect everyone to leave politics behind in search of independent judgments. My dear professor, you're not asking this of the students, you are boasting about yourself."[6] Finally, a netizen wrote, instead of merely saving the students at Tsinghua, "shall we say that we need to save all the children in China."

If it is true that even many students at one of the most elite universities in China seem to be cynical about their education, what would be the causes? Postings on the Internet seem to point to three sets of problems: Party control of the universities, disrespect for the traditional role of teacher, and corruption in research and management.

Party Control

Officially, the leadership of universities is supposed to be jointly shared between the academic president and the Party secretary. But in a recent survey, only 8 percent of students and faculty said that their "real boss" was the university president or that there was a true joint leadership at their university. Among the 92 percent recognizing that the Party secretary is really in charge are many who are frustrated by the lack of intellectual autonomy.[7]

Here is a typical remark from a chemical engineering graduate student from Tsinghua. Venting frustration with the role of the Party—Party school, Party secretary, Party organization, Party publications, Party meetings, and even Party choir—he started his narrative with the university's orientation program.[8]

First thing after registration on August 24, 2011, our informant posted, came a mandatory "Educational Training of the Party School," a school within the school of a university—to inform, some would say inculcate, every new graduate student on the Party organization, Party activities, "thought education," and so forth. "As a university," the complaint continued, "I feel that no one should impose any political views upon the students." It may be reasonable for such a Party school training event to require all Party members to attend, he said, but not every single entering student. In the two-week-long orientation, the university had to cram in compulsory Party training with all sorts of required academic activities, such as visiting the library and English placement test, "very strange indeed."

Then came other "strange" events from the Party office on campus. There was the adviser's e-mail in early September requiring full attendance of all students for a Sunday evening lecture by the university's Party secretary. Now, the student reasoned, in his position as a teaching staff or a university leader, any Party secretary might have the right to speak, but "so should we be given the freedom to attend or not." At the end, this new graduate student confessed that he did not go, nor did anything happen.

In a matter of weeks, similar political gatherings piled up. There was the choir competition for all entering classes that demanded full participation of all entering undergraduates and graduate students. One full Saturday was wasted with fatiguing rehearsals. Similar activities of old cadres' talks, career counseling, or the departmental Party cell's publication projects are all "standard products of Party organizations on campus." Although the student suffered no direct penalty for desultory participation in such events or even skipping them altogether, the pervasive Party control had an effect on his morale. Why take scholarship seriously if the real authorities at the university did not? Why study hard if the political authorities just want to waste your time?

Devaluing Teaching

Another force eroding student morale is the degradation of teaching. In the Chinese tradition, the *laoshi* (teacher) had a near-sacred status, and the teacher–disciple bond was laden with moral significance, warmth, and respect. Now the old role of *laoshi* is being supplanted by the role of research entrepreneur. The sense of loss is conveyed in hundreds of postings about the sad fates of two beloved university teachers in 2005.[9]

Both of them were senior lecturers who failed to get promoted because of lack of publications. One, Yan Caihong from Shanghai Jiaotong University, died without being promoted. Comments flooded into the website when he announced in class that he had been diagnosed with late-stage lung cancer. The students bade tearful good-byes at the classroom and on the Web as their teacher completed his last class, with the parting words that "teaching being an art, you will be my unfinished piece." Hundreds got on the site remembering his short and stocky stature, his oversized glasses, and his disheveled hair as he smoked by the door. Pressed to publish the materials of his lectures for the prospect of promotion, bloggers said, this classroom idol of theirs claimed only that the random notes he had were far from mature enough to be worthy of print. The other lecturer, Zhu Miaohua from Zhejiang University, was sent to early retirement for his lack of publication but, because of public pressure, was later invited back from compulsory retirement to teach at a different campus of the same university.

The question for the students who were continuing to discuss these cases on Everyone.com a good seven years later was the perennial question as to what sort of faculty does any university want—outstanding teachers or researchers. The problem in China, though, has a special bite. The loss of a beloved *laoshi* is especially painful, all the more so when such teachers are not replaced with anything worthwhile. It would be one thing if faculty neglected teaching because they were truly doing world-class research. But "while we seem to be stressing research over teaching, there is little real attention given to scientific studies. The so-called giving weight to research is but a gesture for the manufacturing of a few papers," a Web user from Peking University remarked, "at the end of which both the research and teaching got trashed."[10] A student from Beijing University of Posts and Telecommunications joined in: "If research means fabrication, if it means cutting and pasting things together, then I feel that there is no need for such research anyway. Why does China's higher education fail? It's because fine teachers of such kind are rarer and rarer. Why do such teachers become rarer? This country can think about it for itself! Every human being knows why."[11]

Corruption in Scholarship

It is no surprise to anyone in China that corruption is widespread in higher education, as elsewhere in the society. The only surprise may be that perpetrators seem unashamed about talking about it openly. There are websites devoted to concocting phony grades and Web-based discussion groups about how to forge curricula vitae, how to hack into American university admission offices, how to cheat on exams, and how to game the system.[12] Cheaters are proud to announce their exploits to the world. This would seem to indicate not simply individual human failings or a failure of university surveillance but a profound ethical vacuum, a lack of legitimate rules for professional conduct.

In any case, why should students respect norms of academic honesty when they know that many of their teachers do not? There have been well-publicized scandals involving fabrication of research data. The most notorious was an accusation that Xiao Chuanguo, a professor of urology at Huazhong University of Science and Technology, had fabricated data. Professor Xiao eventually spent some time in jail—not for research fraud but for hiring a thug to beat up Fang Zhouzi, the whistle-blower who was accusing him. After having served his five-month prison sentence, Xiao said that he was always ready to take responsibility: "Yes, I sent somebody to hit him," though "now I regret" that the attack was carried out "with a heavier hand than I expected." He had simply wanted to teach the "unpatriotic" Fang a lesson, "to the point that he might end up with bruises and a bloody nose" but "never to overdo it, to cripple him or anything like that." But the shocking thing about the case was that there was never any professional review on the academic validity of Xiao's claim over against Fang's accusation. There was no clear-cut judgment on the ethics of his conduct or, for that matter, of his accuser. Xiao appealed to his supporters by claiming that not only had his basic rights been compromised by a false accusation but also that Fang's accusations "undermined" China's bid for scientific achievements that can bring international acclaim. Meanwhile, Fang's supporters praised him for his exposure of fraud.[13]

Although the Xiao case is just one of many allegations of recent academic fraud, such misconduct is not as routine as is misappropriation of research funds. In the realm of academic embezzlement, it seems that lawlessness has become the law. It is estimated that only 40 percent of research funds actually go to research. The fact of the matter is that there is no effective auditing, no professional disciplinary measures, and no judicial review, although newspapers are full of complaints about improper use of research funds, including buying private cars or even houses.

How do they do it? An article in 2011 in the *Economic Observer* gives some clues. Titled "Corruption in Technology Research Funding Has Long Been an Open Secret," the article describes how academic corruption is carried out and how institutional flaws that make it easy.[14] First of all, it is common practice to alter budget categories. Every principal investigator knows how to "broaden and adjust budgetary items after projects have been approved. . . . If you don't do it, it becomes odd. No one will believe you anyway."[15] This leads to the hundreds of millions RMB of public money that the National Audit Bureau claimed as uncovered losses in 2010. Not a few principal investigators have proven adept in claiming 8 million to 10 million RMB for equipment that costs 5 million. Extras end up in personal accounts, and after a few rounds of use, automobiles purchased for the project are turned into personal use. Even real estate can be appropriated in this way. Principal investigators have been known to establish companies for money-laundering purposes and turn project grant money into privately owned company shares. The social sciences and humanities have less money to play with, but repeated purchase of computers and endless field trips can still add up to a considerable sum. A research fellow of the Chinese Academy of Sciences, Li Zhi, remarked that many of their advisers "had been to every imaginable place" throughout the world.[16]

The *Economic Observer* noted that there is a geographic and seasonal pattern to academic embezzlement. The activity is especially concentrated in Beijing's Haidian district, the home to its major universities. The peak season is from March to May. A manager in a five-star hotel in Beijing knew the rules of the game well: from March to May, all private rooms in her hotel were reserved by universities and research institutes, spending sky-high money from the "little gold treasure chest" of academia. This is the season for "dashing to the ministries" (of education, science and technology, and finance and the National Development and Reform Commission) to feed at the "financial trough."[17]

Ultimately, what has given rise to this "gray income"? Technicalities and administrative discrepancies aside, people point to the disproportionately low income of Chinese academics and the lack of a professional comptroller and auditing system. When a Chinese associate professor makes on the average 4,000 RMB (US$500) a month, excuses for embezzlement can be strong. In a place where fake accounting is open knowledge and where the going prices for fiscal forgery have become public information—that is, 1,000 to 5,000 RMB per item[18]—the temptation for any project scientist may be too real to pass up. Consider the case of Jiang Qin, who got caught liberally adding 3,100 RMB to the front of the receipt that her principal investigator had habitually signed, so that a mere 20 RMB reimbursement was easily turned into 310,020 RMB.[19]

Such stories have led to outcries for a national cleanup. For the sake of tightening the accounting, China's minister of science, Wan Gang, conceded that the internal auditing system can use some improvement in staffing, proficiency, professionalism, and training. The Ministry of Science and Technology and the Ministry of Finance have jointly issued new guidelines for reform in budgetary management of science projects and nonprofit businesses. However, these drew not only praise but also bitter attacks from scientists themselves. Leading scholars from the Chinese Academy of Sciences and Chinese Academy of Social Sciences complained that the policy was a "useless gesture" to the nation's "open secret" in academic corruption, "which no number of government directives shall fix."[20]

There are many entrenched interests working against change. Principal investigators are "project bosses" who bring in large amounts of money to the universities. Small businesses around the universities—from copy shops to twenty-four-hour convenience stores, not to mention luxury hotels—all stand to profit from the universities' affluence. Most of China's new middle class has learned not only to cope with pervasive corruption but also to reap some degree of benefit from it.

Academic idealism still remains among many university students and faculty, but it is subjected to deep and painful challenges from the university environment. A long article posted on the Web in 2010 and reposted thousands of times lets out a cry representing many: "Am I mad or is this society mad?"[21] The author was a graduate of Wuhan University. Bearing the hopes of "three generations of forebears who had longed to attend university but couldn't," he had dreamed of "studying for the rise of China" from childhood, sleeping over ten volumes of the *Biography of Premier Zhou Enlai* since he was in the fourth grade. But his four years in college filled him with bewilderment, as his rainbow bubbles of idealism burst one after another. The lifestyle of many of his classmates shocked him. They stayed up late partying and slept until noon. Their cynical, vacant expressions clashed with the frantic appeals of their mothers from the countryside who came pleading for a second chance for their failing kids. Even the "good students" were driven to depression and suicide since their hard work was prodded by nothing but sheer terror: fear of not getting into graduate school and fear of not getting good jobs while the rest of the world laughed at their pursuit of "stupid PhDs."

Why should it be that "the more one studies, the more stupid one becomes?" If no one cares at all about scholarship—not the students, not the faculty, not the university—then how should one live? After graduating and getting a leadership position in a Party-affiliated club, the previously mentioned author felt compelled to resign, lamenting his old youthful dream of becoming like Premier Zhou. Later, he got a job with one of China's rising companies but then gave up an opportunity to be sent abroad for training. The gap between career pressures and his own ideals became irreconcilable. The president of his university had lectured on the classical ideals of "great learning" and wanted the university to be great "not because of its big buildings but because of the big minds" that resided on campus. At the end of his ten-page Web post, the author said that he would follow these ideals by joining an old-fashioned Confucian Academy in pursuit of classical learning. Two months into this dramatic turn, he told his Web readers that he now delights in his pursuit, struggling over the Confucian *Analects* and the *Diamond Sutra*. Where this journey shall take him and his fellow dreamers "high or deep in the mountains" no one can tell.

CHALLENGES OF REFORM

The impressive new hardware of China's universities has not been matched by an adequate upgrade of their moral software. The fancy new buildings do not house a culture of independence, mutual responsibility, and integrity. There are certainly many individuals within the universities who have these virtues, but they often have to swim against the tide of the ambient culture. As a result, China's universities—especially the elite ones—are getting world-class funding but are not producing world-class academic excellence. What might it take to achieve such excellence? For answers, we might look to other East Asian countries.

All East Asian societies have built their modern universities to serve state-directed economic development. Funding has been top down and bureaucratically allocated. Learning is seen not as something pursued for its own sake but as a tool for economic development. From Japan to Korea to Taiwan to Hong Kong, the buzzwords in university culture in the early twenty-first century are "world standard," "competition," "targets," "outcomes," and "international visibility."

The approach of the Taiwan government is typical. A project referred to as "5-500" (NTD 50 billion over five years, or roughly US$332 million per year) was allocated by Taiwan's Ministry of Education in the competitive funding for Taiwanese research universities, starting with the year 2005.[22] Now well into its second five-year plan, this supports Taiwan's leading seventeen universities for capacity building and focused investments. Internationally recognized campuses such as National Taiwan University, with over US$120 million per year, have been performing very well with these enhancements albeit under added pressure.[23] As a result, not only leading fields in lab sciences and technology, such as nanotechnology, bioengineering, or earth sciences, received due support, but branded expertise, such as electronics or marine biology, have also been able to advance vigorously. In May 2012, a professor in the medical school of National Cheng Kung University in Taiwan received US$13.3 million from a Danish pharmaceutical company for acquiring her patented research on osteoporosis.[24]

Although this "Taiwan miracle" supports busy laboratories and excited but exhausted graduate students, it also leads to excessive interest in citation indices and key performance indicators. It is the same in the Hong Kong Special Administrative Region under "one country, two systems," where the University Grants Committee generously funds Hong Kong's eight public universities, while subjecting them to bureaucratic oversight to make sure that they are competitive by world standards. When rendered into daily operation, this certainly also means a staggering increase in planning exercises and endless meetings. Corporate efficiency and time pressures have replaced the imagined "care-free zone" of the intellect in or out of campuses. There is too much focus on the instrumental uses of knowledge and not enough on critical inquiry about its meaning and purpose. The difference between Taiwan and Hong Kong and their counterparts from mainland China may be that they have gotten rid of direct political interference with campus affairs, cleared up gross academic corruption, and learned to adhere to international professional standards for research conduct.

It is clear enough what has to be done for Chinese universities to reach the professional standards of peer institutions in East Asia. What is not clear is how to do it. And, if and when Chinese universities do achieve excellence in terms of the East Asian model, basic questions will remain. How will a balance be struck between "Western learning" and "Chinese essence"? What will be the culturally specific form and purpose of Chinese professional institutions? What will it mean for Chinese universities to be internationalized? Will they have to submit to Western standards, or will they be able to develop their own academic style and speak in their own voice? Like China itself, its universities are on a fast track of expansion and will remain so for decades to come. Time will tell whether the negative pressures caused by this expansion will lead to crisis or whether the positive opportunities will prevail.

NOTES

1. Data on funding come the website of the Ministry of Education of the PRC, http://www.moe.gov.cn/publicfiles/business/htmlfiles/moe/moe_94/201002/82762.html, February 5, 2012.

2. Speech of Jiang Zemin in the Centennium of Peking University, May 4, 1998. Jiang Zemin, *Jiang Zemin wenxuan* (Selected works of Jiang Zemin), vol. 2 (Beijing: Renmin chubanshe, 2006), 121–26.

3. These can be further divided into two subgroups: the well-known Fudan and Shanghai Jiaotong universities, with 1.2 billion RMB each, equally shouldered by the Ministry of Education and the metropolis of Shanghai, and the Zhejiang, Nanjing, and Xi'an Jiaotong universities with 1.4, 1.2, and 0.9 billion RMB each shared by the Ministry of Education and the cities where they are situated.

4. http://www.renren.com. The website is a Facebook-like social platform used in mainland China (as a reaction to the blockade of http://www.facebook.com by the PRC government).

5. The article was originally written by Professor Cheng Yao of National Tsinghua University in Taiwan in 2005 and later shared at http://www.renren.com and until January 28, 2012, it has the record of 1,453 shares and 17,641 browsings, http://blog.renren.com/GetEntry.do?id=305501489&owner=3539, January 28, 2012.

6. Comment posted by account user "Zang Wei (臧偉)" on the previously mentioned article, January 18, 2012.

7. Huihua Nie et al., "Xiaozhang he shuji: Shei shi daxue di yi bashou?" (President and Party secretary: Who is the real boss?), in *Jingjixuejia chazuo* (Teahouse for economists), vol. 2 (Jinan: Shandong renmin chubanshe, 2011).

8. Unpublicized Web exchange from the student, made available by a fellow graduate student at the Chinese University of Hong Kong at the receiving end of the electronic communication.

9. The article was originally posted at http://www.xinhua.com as news in 2005 and later shared at http://www.renren.com on January 26, 2012. By January 28, it recorded 203 sharings, 1,115 browsings, and over 50 comments, http://blog.renren.com/share/439509771/11374870589?from=0101010202&ref=minifeed&sfet=102&fin=4&ff_id=439509771, January 26, 2012.

10. Comment posted by account user "Wu Wei" on the previously mentioned article on January 26, 2012.

11. Comment posted by account user "Zhang Keyao" on the previously mentioned article on January 27, 2012.

12. The article was posted on February 2, 2012, in the forum http://bbs.gter.net/bbs/index.php, which aims to serve as a platform of communication for those who are interested in studying abroad, http://bbs.gter.net/bbs/viewthread.php?tid=401278&highlight=, January 26, 2012.

13. "Xiao Chuanguo tanyan xiangrang erfang biqingmianzhong" (Xiao Chuanguo confessed that he just wanted to teach the Fangs a lesson), *Jinghua shibao*, September 29, 2010.

14. Chen Yong, "Keyanjingfei bei siyi qinzhanhuihuo zai keyanquan nei zaoyi bushi mimi" (Corruption in technology research funding has long been an open secret), *The Economic Observer*, November 7, 2011.

15. Chen, "Keyanjingfei bei siyi qinzhanhuihuo zai keyanquan nei zaoyi bushi mimi."

16. Chen, "Keyanjingfei bei siyi qinzhanhuihuo zai keyanquan nei zaoyi bushi mimi."

17. Chen, "Keyanjingfei bei siyi qinzhanhuihuo zai keyanquan nei zaoyi bushi mimi."

18. Chen, "Keyanjingfei bei siyi qinzhanhuihuo zai keyanquan nei zaoyi bushi mimi."

19. Chen, "Keyanjingfei bei siyi qinzhanhuihuo zai keyanquan nei zaoyi bushi mimi."

20. Chen, "Keyanjingfei bei siyi qinzhanhuihuo zai keyanquan nei zaoyi bushi mimi."

21. The article was published on January 19, 2010, at http://www.renren.com, and as of January 28, 2012, it held the record of 2,139 shares, 20,899 browsings, and over 720 comments, http://blog.renren.com/blog/200602053/440403458, January 28, 2012.

22. The "5-500" was first initiated in 2006 with the official name "Project Promoting Academic Excellence and Developing World Class Research Centers." Its first phase funded NTD 50 billion for seventeen top universities in Taiwan for five years, from 2006 to 2010. By 2011, a new phase of the "5-500" project has been granted under the name "Aiming for Top University" and is planned to fund seventeen universities, including thirty-four research institutes, from 2011 to 2015.

23. These include National Taiwan University, National Cheng Kung University, National Tsinghua University, National Chiao Tung University, National Central University, National Yang Ming University, and National Sun Yat-sen University.

24. This news was posted on May 15, 2012, on the website of National Cheng Kung University, http://web.ncku.edu.tw/files/14-1000-92885,r1220-1.php.

TWELVE

Food Safety and Social Risk in Contemporary China

Yunxiang Yan

The safety of the foods that we eat every day, once an ordinary issue too mundane to warrant scrutiny from society or the state, has become a focal point in public opinion, scholarly research, professional management, and government regulations throughout the contemporary world (Jensen and Sandøe 2002; Nestle 2010; Pawsey 2000). In a very literal way, food safety problems and the associated waves of national panic confirm Ulrich Beck's insightful observation that fear of various kinds of risks is a new psychological state among those who live in postindustrial societies (Beck 1992; see also Almas 1999; Buchler, Smith, and Lawrence 2010).

Beck argues that the notion of risk is a product of modernity because in all traditional societies, hazards, dangers, and disasters are perceived as givens or determined by an external force, such as nature or God. Advancements in science and technology during the stage of industrial modernization have led to a belief that one can calculate the probabilities and costs of hazards and dangers, can control or avoid them, and can deal with their consequences through insurance. At the postindustrial stage, however, the potential impact of some incalculable and uninsurable risks—such as pollution, climate change, the threat of nuclear war, or the global transmission of disease—threaten the existence of everyone, rich and poor alike. These risks, ironically, are the unintended consequences of the advances in science and technology as well as the effects of scientism, particularly its logic of control, in modern politics (Beck 2000). Unlike the natural risks in the past, most risks in contemporary times are manufactured and widespread across spatial and social boundaries. The increasing awareness and various perceptions of risks have begun to redefine how we think, behave, and engage in politics in the contemporary world, hence the emergence of a risk society that in turn marks, together with the process of individualization, the arrival of a second modernity (see Beck 1992, 2009; Giddens 1998; for a updated and comprehensive review of the theory, see Ekberg 2007).

Perhaps China is more impacted by food safety scares than anywhere else, as where incidents of food contamination and poisoning have been exposed in succession for two decades and show no signs of declining, even after promulgations of the 2009 Food Safety Law (Zou 2011); China's use of chemical fertilizers and pesticides ranks number one in the world; exported foods from China are often rejected by foreign countries because of chemical contamination (Calvin et al. 2006; Gale and Buzby 2009); and in official surveys, the Chinese public consistently considers food safety a top concern (see, e.g., the annual survey reports by the Ministry of Commerce [2008] since 2004).

Do the frequent and widespread food safety problems also constitute an omnipresent perception of risk in Chinese society? Has China entered the stage of a risk society, thus allowing an examination in light of the risk society theory of Ulrich Beck, Anthony Giddens, and others? Although some scholars answer these questions in the positive (Thiers 2003; Zhang 2007; Zhang and Zhao n.d.), others have serious reservations because many Chinese citizens still regard science and market mechanisms as solutions to their food safety problems and thus seem to be far away from the postindustrial stage of a risk society (Veeck, Yu, and Burns 2008).

This disagreement arises, in my opinion, mainly from the complexity of food safety problems in China that cut across the boundaries of premodern, industrial modern, and postindustrial modern times and therefore present a mix of different types of risks, as will be shown in the present study. In the following, I will first briefly review the development of food safety problems in China from the 1950s to the present, noting that the emergence of poisonous foods is indicative of a shift in the focus of risk from food hygiene to food safety. Next, I take a closer look at the four types of poisonous foods that continue to cause national food scares and are perceived by ordinary people to be the most serious and highly possible risks (see, e.g., Zhang and Zhao n.d.). In the third section, I distinguish the current food safety problems at three levels—food hygiene, unsafe food, and poisonous foods—arguing that their coexistence constitutes a unique challenge of mixed risks. In the fourth section, I further analyze the nature and ramifications of food safety problems in light of Ulrich Beck's theory of risk society. I argue that food safety problems not only affect the lives of Chinese people in harmful ways but also pose a number of manufactured risks that are difficult to calculate and control. Yet, conditioned by a number of social factors embedded in China's transition to a modern society, such as the disjunction between economic development and political reforms, the unequal distribution of food safety problems across social groups, and the dominance of scientism, technocracy, and materialistic understandings of modernization, food safety risks have become entangled with premodern dangers and modern industrial hazards. More important, food safety problems in China have contributed to a rapid decline of social trust, thus posing a risk of distrust that has far-reaching social and political ramifications. In this sense, a risk society has already arrived in China, but it comes with certain local characteristics.

The present study is based on a mixed body of data that include case studies by medical and public health professionals, surveys by government agencies and researchers, investigative reports in printed and online media, and ethnographic evidence that I gathered during in-depth interviews and participant observation in longitudinal fieldwork.[1]

FROM FOOD POISONING TO POISONOUS FOOD: A BRIEF HISTORY

The notion of food safety (*shipin anquan*) is relatively new in Chinese discourse, emerging in the 1990s in Chinese media and becoming a household term by the turn of the century. To obtain a basic understanding of the evolution of food safety problems, I collected 356 case studies of food poisoning from 1950 to 2002 through a key word search of the published journal articles contained in the China Academic Journals Full-Text Database of the China National Knowledge Infrastructure (http://www.cnki.net). In table 12.1, I classify these cases into eight types based on their major causes, with the earliest cases occurring in 1950. I divide the five decades into two periods, comparing conditions before and after the 1982 Provisional Food Hygiene Law, a law that indicates official recognition of the prevalence of food-borne diseases. I end the review in 2002 because thereafter there was an explosion of reports on food scandals in the Chinese media, social surveys, and government documents. The major cases of food scandals after 2002 will be examined in the next section.[2]

Several features of food safety problems during the first period (1950–1982) are noteworthy. First, during the period prior to the Provisional Food Hygiene Law, forty-nine out of the 139 cases of food poisoning were caused by public canteen problems (type D in table 1), which include poor sanitation, unsafe storage of leftovers, lack of hygiene regulations, improper cooking methods, and the use of spoiled foods (Wang 1975). The concentration of food-poisoning cases in public canteens is related to the fact that during the pre-Reform era, most urban employees ate at least one meal per week in their work unit canteens, and rural collectives offered lunches in canteens to peasants during the busy sea-

Table 12.1.   A Comparison of Food-Poisoning Cases during Two Periods

Type	Major Causes	Number of Cases, 1950 – 1982	Number of Cases, 1983 – 2002*
A	Meat of diseased animals	26	18
B	Spoiled foods	27	18
C	Pesticides or other chemicals	23	15
D	Problematic canteens	49	55
E	Toxic plants	4	1
F	Improper food preparation	6	0
G	Unsafe food in restaurants or markets	4	87
H	Food with toxic additives in restaurants or markets	0	23
	Total	139	217

* Food-poisoning cases that involved 100 or more victims.

sons. But the causes of food poisoning in public canteens are not much different from those occurring in private homes, such as spoiled foods (type B in table 1) or poor sanitary conditions. Second, the consumption of diseased animals (type A) caused food poisoning in both public canteens and private homes during this period, such as the case of workers in a Shanxi factory who ate diseased pork (Zhang and Chen 1961). Third, under the planned economy, staff members in state-owned or collective food stores perfunctorily performed their duties at assigned jobs, with no profit-making incentives. When they sold substandard food products, such as meat from diseased animals or spoiled foods, they made no effort to cheat the customers—they merely used the lower prices to attract buyers, and the customers or public canteens willingly and knowingly purchased substandard, contaminated, or even spoiled foods to save money.[3] Fourth, food-poisoning cases caused by pesticides or other harmful chemicals (type C) began to occur in the 1970s. A close reading of the reports, however, shows that in most cases pesticides had been mistakenly directly or indirectly consumed. The most common occurrence was the use of pesticide containers to store food; in several cases, public canteen staff accidently put pesticides or other chemicals into the foods (Hu

1982). Interestingly, none of the type C food-poisoning cases were attributed to pesticide residues; this might be due to the fact that in the 1960s and 1970s, growers used only a limited amount of pesticides and did not apply them repeatedly.

Most authors in the public health literature attribute these cases to problems of backwardness, namely, the lack of modern scientific knowledge and regulations, and they identify education and hygiene regulations as the main solutions (see, e.g., Sun 1980; Wang 1975; Zhou 1958). Their argument seems to be well grounded to a certain extent because all of the previously mentioned features changed in the second period (1983–2002). When peasants became more familiar with the use of pesticides, the number of type C food-poisoning cases among farmers declined. Health concerns increased among Chinese consumers because of both the spread of scientific knowledge, as the health professionals had hoped, and improvements in living standards. Consequently, the number of types A, B, and D food-poisoning cases also declined.

Two new types of food-poisoning cases emerged in the second period, namely, those caused by foods purchased at markets and/or consumed in restaurants (types G and H). In these cases, the contaminated foods were traced to the restaurant owners or the producers and retailers of the processed food who deliberately added poisonous chemicals to foods for the sake of profit-making. Since the late 1990s, toxins such as nitrite have frequently been the primary cause of food poisoning because they are regularly used to lower the costs of processed foods. Food poisoning has also been caused by the harmful chemicals contained in animal feed. These developments have motivated Chinese health professionals and food experts to think beyond the conventional boundaries of food hygiene. By the turn of the century, a new Chinese phrase was coined to describe the contaminated foods that caused types G and H food poisoning, that is, *youdu shipin*, which literally means "poisonous food."

THE NEW CHALLENGE OF POISONOUS FOOD

Poisonous food in recent Chinese history can be broken down into the following four major types.

Food Adulteration

The first and perhaps most common type of poisonous food is adulterated food. Seeking higher profits, food processors and/or producers resort to cheaper, inferior, or less desirable materials to produce or cook foods. On their own, these are not necessarily dangerous. In most cases, however, the inferior foods need to be polished with chemicals, such as coloring unripe strawberries or cherries with carmine dye so that they appear to be of good quality and can be sold at higher prices. Using toxic chemicals to preserve processed foods is also common; for example, formaldehyde (*jiaquan*, 甲醛) or sodium formaldehyde sulfoxylate (*diaobaikuai*, 吊白块) are widely used to whiten seafood and grains (see Zhou 2007, 87–123). The Chinese media frequently expose scandals of food adulteration, especially the use of toxic agents in the process of adulteration. The most disgusting yet perhaps the most widely consumed adulterated food, however, is adulterated cooking oil that is extracted from oil in sewage pipes or from leftover foods collected in restaurants. Chinese food safety expert He Dongping, who led a research team in a multiyear project to investigate the large-scale production and circulation of sewerage cooking oil, asserts that the tainted cooking oil was widely found in eateries and food-processing factories as well as in private homes, probably used to prepare one out of every ten meals in China (Barboza 2010).

Food Additives

Food additives constitute the second most frequent channel by which a variety of toxins enter the food chain. Antibiotics, colorants, and hormones are widely used as additives to animal feeds and processed foods. Well-known examples include using Sudan dye IV (*sudanhong*, 4 hao [苏丹红4号]) to feed chicken or ducks so that they produce eggs with red yolks; using ciprofloxacin (*huanbing shaxing*, 环丙沙星), enfofloxacin (*ennuo shaxing*, 恩诺沙星), flavomycin (*huangmeisu*, 黄霉素), or simply contraceptive pills to feed farm fishes; or adding melamine to a number of foods. More often than not, farmers openly use illegal food additives, such as clenbuterol, that have long been banned by government regulation.

Clenbuterol was originally developed to help patients with breathing disorders. It causes central nervous system stimulation and increases aerobic capacity in the metabolism rate. Used in excessively large amounts in pig feed, clenbuterol can reduce the amount of fat in pigs. During the 1980s, it was experimented with but was soon banned in the United States and other Western countries because of its harmful effects on humans. In the 1990s, clenbuterol was introduced to China, reportedly by Chinese scientists returning from a visit to the United States, as a pig-feed additive to increase the production of lean meat. The additive was sold in the market under the Chinese name *shouroujing* (瘦肉精), meaning "lean meat powder." The first case of food poisoning from clenbuterol-contaminated pork was reported in Guangzhou in 1998, followed thereafter by a string of similar cases. In 2001 alone, more than 1,100 people in Beijing, Guangzhou, and Hangzhou were victims of tainted pork, leading the Chinese government to strictly ban the use of clenbuterol in animal feed (Zhou 2007, 68–75). However, pork contaminated by clenbuterol has continued to be found in the market during the subsequent decade, with recent cases reported in late 2009 (CNN 2009) and early 2011. The 2011 outbreak of clenbuterol contamination, well covered by the key state-owned media outlets, such as CCTV and Xinhua News, led the central government to convene an emergency meeting (McKenna 2011).

Pesticides Used as Food Reserves

The third type of poisonous food results from the direct application of pesticides, especially in the course of food processing. For a number of food producers, pesticides serve as a cheap yet strong preservative, as in the well-known cases of pickled vegetables in Sichuan province and Jinhua ham in Zhejiang province. In Xianghe county, Hebei province, farmers used a strong pesticide called 3911 to soak the roots of chives so that the vegetable would grow extremely large and strong. From 1999 to 2004, the pesticide was used on thousands of acres of chive fields. This was an open collective action; when the pesticide was applied, there was a very strong acrid odor in the entire area. Yet until an investigation team from a journal sponsored by the General Administration of Quality Supervision, Inspection, and Quarantine in the central government exposed this illegal operation, no local government agency had bothered to question this harmful practice (Wang 2004).

Modern farming relies heavily on the use of chemical fertilizers and pesticides, making pesticide residues the most common threat to food safety throughout the world. The problem of pesticide residues widely exists in China and has become worse as farmers are using an ever-increasing amount of pesticides and shortening the nonspray time before harvest to avoid infestations of insects from neighboring farms, thus creating a vicious cycle of pesticide residues. It should be noted that the abuse of pesticides by food-processing companies differs from the problem of pesticide residues because in the former, food producers and processors intentionally violate the laws and regulations, directly adding toxins to foods and resorting to chemicals and other techniques to make sure that the consumers are not aware of them. This is why Chinese consumers carefully distinguish between pesticide residues and the abuse of pesticides, calling the former *nongyao canliu* (pesticide) and the latter *youdu shipin* (toxic foods).

Fake Foods

The last type of poisonous food is a challenge to the imagination—it is simply fake or counterfeit food, such as the 2004 case of fake milk powder made out of starch in Anhui province. The earliest and perhaps also the most common practice is the production of fake medicine. As early as June 1985, an investigative report was published in the Party's mouthpiece, the *People's Daily*, exposing a large business scam of fake medicine that involved more than 1,000 participants and various local government agencies in Jinjiang county, Fujian province. When more details were revealed in other reports, provincial Party boss Xiang Nan resigned, the highest-level political casualty of food safety problems in China to date. However, fake medicines did not disappear along with the fall of Xiang Nan. Counterfeit drugs still constitute a large share of the Chinese market, and they are also exported to foreign countries, with serious medical consequences. Describing this as a sign of the weakness of the Chinese state, Wang Shaoguang (2003) cites some horrifying figures: "In 2001, 192,000 people died after using bogus or poor-quality medications. Despite government efforts that led to the shutting down of 1,300 pharmaceutical factories, or half of the entire industry that year, the first half of 2002 brought an additional 70,000 deaths from fraudulent drugs" (40).

The making of fake foods often involves heavy doses of toxic chemicals and the use of cheaper and inferior substitute materials. For example, fake soy sauce made out of human hair and chemicals was found in 2004 because human hair can be collected as recyclable waste at an extremely low price, fake chicken eggs made out of water and chemicals appeared in different regions between 2005 and 2007, and fake pig-blood pudding made out of water and chemicals caused a new food scare in 2009. Despite government efforts to punish offenders with criminal charges under the new 2009 Food Safety Law, the production and circulation of fake liquor and wine, fake soy sauce, fake beef, and fake milk powder continued throughout 2010, and some of the cases were cited as among the top ten most influential criminal cases (Zou 2011).

THE SPECTRUM OF FOOD SAFETY PROBLEMS AND THE MIX OF RISKS

Food safety problems in contemporary China are complicated because they result from different causes and pose different kinds of risks to consumers and the society as a whole. For the sake of analysis, I classify the food safety problems into three levels and refer to them respectively as food hygiene problems, unsafe food, and poisonous food.

Food Hygiene Problems and Conventional Risks

Conventional food hygiene problems continue to exist but with a shift of their primary site from family kitchens or public canteens to food factories and various eateries. During the past three decades, Chinese consumers have increasingly relied on *fangbian shipin*, or convenience food, that is, processed, precooked, or semicooked foodstuffs. Many urban employees and migrant workers eat out of lunch boxes, another type of convenience food, offered by street vendors or available at small eateries. The demand for convenience foodstuffs is also rapidly increasing in the countryside. In the village where I have worked since the 1980s, the most popular items in the village stores are sausages, instant noodles, and roasted chicken or pork (in order of sales volume). Consumers have little knowledge about the origins, ingredients, and the actual making of the foods they eat. Such disconnection and sense of alienation associated with food has long been regarded as a major cause of the public fears and the actual incidents of compromised food safety (Pawsey 2000; Smith 2007).

Food processing has thus become a booming business. Yet, as many have pointed out, small-scale family workshops, with more than 70 percent of market share, dominate the food-processing industry in China. The highly fragmented and primarily household-based food-processing sector presents a challenge to regulatory agencies in terms of public health, quality control, food processing, and transportation. Furthermore, corruption in these regulatory agencies creates an additional problem of enforcement (Li 2009; Tam and Yang 2005). Many of the family workshops operate under poor sanitary conditions with little modern technology. For example, an investigative report in 2003 revealed that 70 percent of the new food-processing enterprises in Guangzhou had to be closed down because of failure to meet official quality-control standards. Among them, many cooking-oil-processing plants were actually operating in residential apartment units. In Hunan, it was reported that 80 percent of the food-processing workshops lacked production permits and/or business licenses (cited in Tam and Yang 2005, 26). Packaging and labeling procedures are also poorly regulated, and official corruption and counterfeiting are often prevalent. As an informant explained to me, "All you need to do is to buy the good-looking packaging materials, wrap your products, and seal the package. Better yet, you can buy packaging materials with famous brand-names or super-quality labels. This really helps."[4] In 2005, two men were found guilty of making fake brandy under the Hennessy and Rémy Martin brand names. The liquor bottles they used had laser-burned lot numbers and special anticounterfeiting labels, making the fake products appear to be authentic (Lin 2009, 56–57).

The heavy reliance on processed foods has significantly increased the chances of food contamination, thereby keeping food hygiene problems in the limelight. According to the Chinese Ministry of Health, the number of victims of food poisoning by microbial contamination exceeds the number poisoned by farm chemicals (Calvin et al. 2006; Wang et al. 2007). This is why Wu Yongning, a senior scientist at China's Center for Disease Control, argues that media coverage of food scares in China in 2007 misinformed the public. Citing statistical results from a national survey on diet and health, Wu asserts that despite headline news stories about chemical contamination, the main food safety threat remains microorganisms (see Ellis and Turner 2007).

Food hygiene problems are not new. This conventional risk in public health, according to many Chinese medical health professionals and government officials, can be controlled and managed in terms of more education campaigns, food quality control, regulation and integration of the food-processing market, and rigorous and systematic management of public health authorities (see, e.g., Ministry of Commerce 2008; Wang et al. 2007). In this connection, it is noteworthy that food hygiene problems generally are not regarded as key issues in the developed countries and thus do not constitute the kind of modernization risks that risk-society theory helps us to understand.

Unsafe Food and the Arrival of Postindustrial Risks

At the second level, unsafe foods result mainly from the heavy use of chemical fertilizers, pesticides, hormones, steroids, preservatives, flavor enhancers, colorants, and pollution and environmental degradation in the larger context. Nonseasonal growing and intensive factory farming also contribute to the production of unsafe foods. Among other problems, pesticides stand out as the number one cause of food safety problems in China. As a Chinese promoter of organic food has noted, in Shanghai the excessive use of pesticides is profit driven and regarded as a survival strategy by vegetable farmers, who apply four times the recommended amount of pesticides to boost yields (Moore 2010). According to research by Paul Thiers in the 1990s, about one-third of the pesticides sold in China were not registered or tested. Safety information rarely reached down to the level of farmers; consequently, 10,000 or more Chinese farmers died of pesticide poisoning every year (Thiers 1997). The situation appears not to have improved, as one decade later nearly 50 percent of the fruits and vegetables grown in China contain pesticide residue, exceeding China's official standard, and on average more than 100,000 people are poisoned by pesticide residue each year (Yang 2007). It has been estimated that in 2005 only about 6 percent of Chinese agricultural production was pollution free and that only 1 percent was green (Calvin et al. 2006, 20).[5] The only significant progress has been found in the death toll from the improper use of pesticide among farmers, which has dropped to several hundred per year (Yang 2007, 2).

The unsafe-food problems associated with chemical contamination and other modern agricultural techniques are a global phenomenon, and China is merely following the Western path of modern production and consumerism. For example, Chinese dietary patterns have changed rapidly since the 1980s, especially meat and egg consumption. By 2005, China's meat output reached 78 million tons, representing 29 percent of the world's total output; in the same year, per capita meat consumption was sixty-three kilograms. To meet the high market demand, Western technologies of factory farming have increased in popularity in the livestock sector, resulting in a number of food safety concerns (Li 2009).

Because many problems of unsafe food are actually derived from modern farming and food-processing technologies as well as from a modern consumerist ideology, the food safety problems at this level are an inherent and reflexive part of modernity, a typical example of manufactured risk (Beck 1992; Giddens 1998). Moreover, as science and modern technology have proved not to be omnipotent forces and as the global scale of food production and circulation has made it almost impossible to predict and control some of the most serious problems of unsafe food, food safety problems have posed increasingly daunting yet uninsurable risks (see, e.g., Beck 1992, and a number of the studies cited at the beginning of this chapter). In this sense, China has indeed joined the global trend of postindustrial risk-society despite the fact that it is still striving to reach the goals of industrial modernization (see Thiers 2003).

But not all the problems of unsafe food at this level are simply by-products or unintended consequences of modern technologies. Some of them overlap with other types of food risks. For instance, the large number of sick or dead animals is a typical problem associated with factory farming, but how these animals are disposed of depends mostly on institutional regulations and their implementation. According to Peter Li, three out of the eight Chinese factory farms that his research team studied sold dead chickens to employees who in turn resold the chickens to food dealers or restaurants, and five out of the seven pig farms they examined disposed of dead pigs by selling them to vendors who collected the animals for small street food-stall vendors. This practice can be traced back to the 1990s, and even though it has been repeatedly exposed by the Chinese media and food safety professionals, the problem persists (Li 2009, 235–36). In 2007, Chinese scientist Jiang Gaoming and his research team found that nearly 80 percent of the more than 200 million chickens that had died from various diseases or from the harsh conditions of factory farming each year were sold to roast chicken shops and sausage factories or were used as animal feed. Even avian hospitals were involved in these illegal practices. In one animal hospital, for example, twenty-five to fifty kilograms of diseased chicken carcasses were sold daily for $US0.10 per kilogram to pig farmers who then blended the chicken meat into pig feed (Jiang 2007).

This illegal trade in sick or dead animals among farmers and vendors constitutes a different kind of food safety risk in China because it is intentional and calculated, revealing not only the loopholes in market regulation but also the existence of a serious ethical problem. The selling of chicken carcasses by avian hospitals is indicative of the corruption of the professionals who are supposed to be the guardians of food safety. This does not resemble the postindustrial risks in risk-society theory; instead, it leads us to the next level of food safety problems.

Poisonous Food, the Risk of Trust, and the Challenge to Regulatory Governance

At the third level, the poisonous-food phenomenon stands out as a new and devastating development in Chinese food safety problems, with the deliberate contamination of foods as a defining feature. The producers, processors, and traders knowingly add an array of banned toxic chemicals to human foods or animal feed. In order to make profits, they not only violate government laws and regulations but also intentionally hurt consumer health. Moreover, because they are fully aware of the illegality of their actions, the harm to consumers, and the punishment if they are to be caught, the retailers of toxic foods resort to hiding the true nature of their foodstuffs and sell them as normal, healthful products. This distinguishes poisonous food from other counterfeit products that flood the Chinese market, especially fraudulent luxury goods, such as fake cosmetics, watches, bags, and famous-brand clothing, which are sold as an open secret of a defiant lifestyle (for a systematic study of counterfeiting culture in China, see Lin 2009).

Perhaps the most morally disturbing fact is the well-organized and large-scale production and distribution of poisonous food, which often involves various government institutions. Many people, most of whom are ordinary workers on the front lines of production and processing, actively participate in the deliberate contamination of food. Others are the economic or political elite at various levels, such as entrepreneurs, managers, professionals in quality control agencies, and government officials. Poisonous food beyond the household workshop level causes serious damage to public health and the social ethos, easily creating national panics, such as during the 2008 case of the tainted baby formula by the Sanlu Group, a leading joint-venture giant in the Chinese dairy business.

To artificially increase the amount of protein in inferior milk that was either diluted with water or spoiled, melamine, a chemical used to make plastic and to tan leather, was added, and the contaminated milk was then used to produce baby formula, ice cream bars, and other products. By September 15, 2008, Sanlu products had been found manufactured with melamine, and the company recalled 700 tons of its baby formula. But on the following day, a nationwide test conducted by the General Administration of Quality Supervision, Inspection, and Quarantine (AQSIQ) revealed that the milk products of twenty-two out of another 109 inspected firms were also contaminated with melamine, including products made at Yili and Mengniu, two top firms. Although most contaminated products were sold on the domestic market, some were also exported to Hong Kong. The Sanlu Group milk products had enjoyed the privilege of a quality inspection and quarantine waiver by the AQSIQ, and the reports on the Sanlu problematic baby formula were not disclosed by the local government and its agencies until the New Zealand partner company contacted the authorities in Beijing. Obviously, the production and distribution of hundreds of tons of contaminated milk powder would not have been possible without negligence and dereliction of duty by a number of government agencies in charge of the safety and quality of dairy products, including the AQSIQ, the Bureau of Food and Drug Supervision, the Ministry of Health, and the Bureau of Industry and Commerce. The tainted Sanlu milk powder stands out as one of the worst cases of poisonous food, causing six deaths, 51,900 hospitalizations of children with serious kidney problems, and 24,900 cases of children suffering from other problems. The seeking of justice by the families of the victims remains an open wound, even after harsh legal punishments were meted out to a few individuals who played a major role in the scandal (Barboza 2009; Yoo 2010).

In addition to the toxic chemicals that directly harm the physical well-being of consumers, the problem of poisonous foods is socially lethal because of the disregard or even outright dismissal of the health and safety of others, the intention to cause harm to others for the sake of profits, the secrecy and deception necessary for the production and circulation of such toxic foods, and, in the case of organized large-scale production and circulation of poisonous foods, the indifference and failure of the regulatory agencies that are closely associated with the flows of poisonous food. It is true that poisonous food does not enter the food chain on an everyday basis, and it is not produced on a regular or national scale. Thus, statistically, the actual number of people sickened or dying from consuming poisonous foodstuffs is less than the number of those suffering from food hygiene problems or unsafe foods. However, almost every incident of poisonous food after being exposed by the media or on the Internet has caused large-scale panic and nationwide food scares. These food scares have resulted in widespread social distrust of both food sellers and the food industry as a whole as well as a deeply felt sense of insecurity—at any moment and through any imaginable or unimaginable channel, the consumption of foodstuffs may result in food poisoning and even possibly death.

During my interviews, most people cited incidents of poisonous foods as justification for their worries about food safety, and almost without variation my informants wondered why on earth someone would put toxins in foods for the sake of profits. This widely expressed disbelief was regularly followed by a strong expression of distrust because, as many informants told me, "nowadays you never know what is inside a package of food; anything is possible."[6] Outraged and morally disturbed, many informants lamented that they no longer knew what was safe to eat and who could be trusted. "I am so panicked these days that I suspect every food-seller on the street and I only buy expensive and well-packaged foods from supermarket chains," said another informant, "but food scandals come from these supermarkets too. What can we ordinary people do?"[7] "I heard on the news that China has become the number-two most powerful country in the world and our state leaders are even more powerful than the American president, your president!" A village friend jokingly announced to me but then questioned me with all seriousness, "But why do our powerful leaders not protect us from those poisonous foods out there? This society is very dangerous, you know. You could die if you do not carefully watch the foodstuffs you buy in the market. No one can help you."[8] A young mother became so angry during our discussion of food safety that she announced that she would not hesitate to harm the producers and sellers of poisonous foods if she had the chance. "I hate those people who manufacture or sell poisonous foods, especially those who deliberately poison the babies [referring to the 2008 milk powder scandal]. I just want to let them know how painful it is," she told me.[9]

These individual testimonies show that the threat of poisonous food has incited suspicion of strangers, stirred up social resentment, caused a decline of social trust, and posed a risk of trust that China cannot afford to bear during its rush to modernity. Distrust in strangers is a common feature in most traditional societies, and China is by no means an exception. As the historian Chen Ruoshui notes, popular texts on moral teaching for children in late imperial China are full of messages about the dangers of strangers and the wisdom of not trusting anyone outside one's own network; these messages were meant to be memorized during the process of socialization (Chen 2006, 118–55). But distrust of strangers was less harmful in a culture of close-knit communities and kinship organizations where strangers normally were kept at a distant existence or remained simply imagined as nonexistent. However, in a highly mobile and open society, most social interactions occur among individuals who are not related to one another by any particularistic ties, and more often than not people do not expect to interact with the other party again in the future. Consequently, distrust of strangers is socially destructive, and social trust is more important than personal trust.

Social trust is understood as a more generalized trust in social institutions that one expects will act in accordance with the stated rules, in experts who will guard the rules to make the institutions work well, and in strangers who will engage in peaceful and nonharmful social interactions. In contrast, personal trust is invested only in people who are in one's own social web, ranging from the family, kinship, or community to a wider yet still well-defined network of friends. The expansion of personal trust to social trust provides one of the key mechanisms in making a modern economy and society work, and thus it is a necessary precondition for modernity (Giddens 1990, 79–111).

The promotion of social trust has become an urgent issue in contemporary Chinese society as it rapidly becomes more open, modern, and highly mobile. Unfortunately, even though the market economy has developed rapidly, social trust has generally declined. A Chinese sociologist describes the six kinds of distrust prevailing in contemporary Chinese society that contribute to the crisis of social trust: distrust of the market due to faulty goods and bad service, distrust of service providers and strangers, distrust of friends and even relatives, distrust of law enforcement officers, distrust of the law and legal institutions, and distrust of basic moral values (Peng 2003, 292–95). The widespread production and distribution of contaminated and fake foods, as indicated above, has played an especially vicious role in further spreading distrust in strangers and social institutions. The most damaging risk that poisonous foods, together with other food safety problems, present to Chinese society is therefore the risk of distrust. The cases of large-scale and organized production and circulation of poisonous foods, such as the contaminated milk powder by the Sanlu Group in 2008, are particularly lethal in provoking the decline of trust because they expand distrust in strangers to distrust in food experts, to regulatory agencies, and to modern society in general.

Thus far, the Chinese government seems to have little way to promote social trust and consumer confidence other than enacting more regulations and establishing more regulatory agencies in an effort to keep the food safety problems under control (Liu 2010; Tam and Yang 2005). Yet because of the fragmentation and internal competition among regulatory agencies, the developmental preference for employment and growth over safety and health, and, more important, the corruption of government officials and the lack of rule of law, the results of top-down initiatives for food safety regulation are often ineffective and unsatisfactory (Li 2009; Liu 2010; Tam and Yang 2005), and high-profile food scandals continued to surge (see, e.g., Barboza 2010; Watts 2011; Zou 2011).

Consequently, public concerns about food safety and waves of national food fears have become a regular feature in media reports and large-scale surveys. Starting in 2004, the Ministry of Commerce has carried out an annual investigation on food safety conditions and has issued a yearly report. Year after year, the investigation shows that Chinese consumers are highly concerned about food safety problems. Among urban consumers, the rate of concern increased from 79 percent in 2005 to 96 percent in 2008, and among rural residents it increased from 58 percent in 2006 to 94 percent in 2008. The 2008 report admits, quite diplomatically, that the increase in public concern about food safety may be an indicator of the decline of consumer confidence in the government's ability to regulate food safety (Ministry of Commerce 2008). In 2006, the State Food and Drug Administration admitted that more than 60 percent of surveyed consumers viewed food safety conditions in China as bad or very bad. In 2007, an online survey conducted by the official Xinhua News Net revealed that 95 percent of respondents agreed that there are too many problems with the food safety situation in China (cited in Mou 2007). According to a recent study on perceptions of food risks, the greatest fear of Beijing residents is the risk of consuming fake food, and the majority believe that food risks are highly likely to occur (Zhang and Zhao n.d.).

RISK-SOCIETY THEORY AND CHINESE REALITY

It should be noted that the classification of China's food safety problems at three levels is obviously for analytical purposes; in reality, the boundaries between the lack of food hygiene, unsafe food, and poisonous food are often blurred, especially in cases of food adulteration. The recycling of cooking oil from sewage and restaurant waste and the harmful trade of dead animals from factory farms are two prominent examples in this regard. My main point is that food safety problems indeed constitute a mixed body of risks to Chinese people and society, chief among which is the social risk of distrust, which is incalculable and uninsurable, undermining regulatory governance and having far-reaching social and political implications. Risk-society theory can indeed provide us with a powerful conceptual tool both to examine the food safety problems in China and to address their consequent risks. It is even more relevant to the Chinese case because the Chinese government and most scholars in China still view food problems and risks from a modernization perspective, and they do not critically assess the unintended consequences of industrial modernity.

Although many of the food risks in China belong to the category of manufactured risks and are closely related to the rapid advances in science and technology and the control logic of modernity, not all of them — the premodern, natural risks of food hygiene problems — are equally serious and challenging. These counterfacts in Chinese social life to risk-society theory do not necessarily discount the applicability of the theory; rather, they may simply point to cultural specificities that differ from those in the Western societies where the theory was developed. A close look at the differences actually reveals a deeper layer of food risks in the Chinese social context. In the remainder of this chapter, I will highlight two of them.

First, it is common in China for science, technology, and modernization generally to be regarded as the solution to food safety problems and as the proper way to control food risks. For example, Ann Veeck, Hong-yan Yu, and Alvin C. Burns discovered that most Chinese consumers do not attribute food safety problems to the unknowable consequences of scientific advancement, and many consumers turn to the famous brands of large companies and other market mechanisms to minimize their food risks. Such behavior seems to contradict risk-society theory (Veeck et al. 2008). In a similar way, the majority of my informants, both urban and rural, placed the blame for the outbreak of food safety problems on individual farmers, manufacturers, and retailers of toxic foods for being too greedy and for lacking morality, while others criticized the government agencies for regulatory failures or traced the origins of all food scandals to corrupt officials. Moreover, because of the dominance of household workshops in China's food-processing sector, chemicals are used in low-tech and labor-intensive processes. An elderly villager put it succinctly: "No poison can be poisonous without the touch of human hands."[10] These folk explanations and attributions are precisely the same as the explanations offered by Chinese journalists and scholars in media reports and academic research albeit in a much more systematic and sophisticated fashion in the latter.

In other words, the epistemological role of science and technology and modernity in the formation of contemporary food safety problems remains a blind spot in Chinese public opinion and professional discourse. But does the existence of this blind spot cancel out the actual link between modernity and contemporary food safety problems? Does not knowing of this link eliminate the felt risk of poisonous foods among Chinese consumers? Do the counterfacts make the theory of risk society irrelevant in Chinese reality, as suggested by Veeck and her colleagues? In my mind, the answer to these questions is clearly "no." What it does tell us is perhaps the unquestionable centrality of modernity and the much stronger influence of its control logic among Chinese people across all walks of life, which is missing from risk-society theory because it aims to explain postindustrial or second modernity in Western Europe.

The significance of modernization in developing countries tends to be underestimated by Western scholars because modernity has never been a most sought-after objective in Western history: it gradually arrived even before people found a name to call it. In contrast, modernization was the Holy Grail when China was fighting for national survival and nation building, and it remains unchanged to this day as the country is trying to redefine its position on the global stage. It is impossible to review China's spiral path in pursuit of modernity here, but what I want to point out is that in the post-Mao era, this Holy Grail has been interpreted and understood almost exclusively in materialistic terms. Such an understanding was first made possible through the state-sponsored national debate in 1978 that concluded that practice is the sole criterion for testing truth. It was then specified in material terms in Deng Xiaoping's well-known definition of Chinese modernization.[11] Ever since the early 1980s, the promotion of science and technology and the maintenance of political stability have been sacredly guarded by the Chinese state as the secret recipe to realize the dream of modernization, and since the early 1990s, this way of thinking has been widely accepted and practiced by the majority of both the elite and ordinary people. It is not surprising, therefore, that few in China—scholars and ordinary people alike—could (or would want to) attribute the food safety problems and food risks to the unintended consequences of advances in science and technology and modernity's control logic.

The second noteworthy difference between Chinese reality and risk-society theory lies in the fact that food safety problems and the consequent risks are unequally distributed among the Chinese social groups and have resulted in an increase in social injustice. This may contradict the risk-society theory at a surface level because the theory also emphasizes the equalizing effects of modernization: "Reduced to a formula: *poverty is hierarchic, smog is democratic*. With the expansion of modernization risks—with the endangering of nature, health, nutrition, and so on—the social differences and limits are relativized" (Beck 1992, 36, emphasis in the original). This is also known as the "boomerang effect," namely, that people who produce modernization risks will also be caught up by them. However, Beck notes that the logic of wealth redistribution is replaced by the logic of risk distribution because in Western Europe the people's basic material needs are already met and individuals are generally protected by the law, modern regulations and institutions, and a culture of democracy in the welfare state (Beck 1992, 2009).

This boomerang effect of risk distribution has yet to be seen in China, where wealth is accumulated at the upper levels and risks of various kinds are channeled downwardly and the rich and powerful can find a variety of ways to avoid risks (see, e.g., Xia and Wu 2007). This pattern can be found in the food safety realm as well. To deal with food safety problems, wealthy individuals in Shanghai, Beijing, Guangzhou, and other cities have long had their own production bases of safe foods, that is, by hiring a farmer in the countryside to exclusively produce their foods. In most cases, this is practiced by way of the existing *guanxi* ("social connections") network. The most noteworthy development in this respect is the surge of contracted green food production by government agencies and large state-owned enterprises. Typically, these powerful state entities commission a company to produce green foods exclusively for their canteens and for their employees' private consumption. Food safety is the top concern: use of chemicals is banned, nonseasonal growing is limited, factory farming is replaced by free-range farming, and the safety period for pesticide use is strictly observed. In 2010, I took a group of students from the University of California, Los Angeles, to visit a special farm for green food production in suburban Shanghai as part of our outside-the-classroom learning experience in a summer program on globalization. At the farm, we were repeatedly assured by the host that all the farm's produce was organic and absolutely safe because its foods are not for sale on the market; since the farm's establishment in 2001, all its foods have gone directly to the canteen of the municipal government. In recent years, the production site has become a favorite venue for city leaders to entertain important guests and friends because they know the foods are absolutely safe and taste good. My students and I were completely convinced after we were treated to a rather elaborate meal of organic chicken, pork, and fruits and vegetables at the end of our visit.

This practice, serving high-ranking government officials and selected intellectual elite, began in the 1950s when food shortages were a regular part of everyday life. After the Chinese economy took off in the 1980s, the practice temporarily disappeared, but it then resumed as a strategy to cope with the newly emerging food safety problems. In recent years, several investigative reports have been published in the Chinese media (for the latest, see Lü et al. 2011), drawing public attention to this long-existing yet little-known practice. The reports have incited anger among the people because government agencies use the taxpayers' money to fund the production of green foods for themselves, while the general populace must suffer from so many food safety hazards and risks. At the societal level, this practice enhances the power and privileges of government entities and enterprises and at the same time increases the gap in social equality by protecting the privileged and abandoning the powerless.

The unequal distribution of risks, which coincides with the unequal distribution of wealth, is certainly recognized and felt by ordinary people in the lower rungs of society. In different ways, they exercise their agency to protect themselves from the looming food risks (see, e.g., Lora-Wainwright 2009). In some cases, the painful experiences of social injustice are used by individuals in socially disadvantaged positions to morally justify the harm they have done to others. In 2008, I had a rare opportunity to interview a migrant worker in Shanghai who admitted that he used to make fake blood pudding but had stopped doing so by the time of our meeting. When asked whether he was aware that his product would harm the consumers' health, he replied without any hesitation, "I knew but I did not care. Why should I? I don't know them at all." Two more clues emerged as our conversation proceeded. At first, he told me that it was acceptable to sell fake food to people in the cities because urbanities had medical insurance. "If they get sick, they can afford to see a doctor." Then he recalled his painful experiences working in two cities during the last twelve years when how on several occasion he was seriously beaten by the *chengguan dui*, a self-supporting patrol force in charge of maintaining order in urban food markets. "I actually felt good when some of them ate my blood-pudding and I hoped that they would become seriously ill," he admitted triumphantly.[12] In a similar way, chicken farmers do not consume the chickens they raise through factory farming, telling researchers, "We just sell them to the cities" (Jiang 2007).

Is the production of fake blood pudding this man's way of making money, his way taking revenge, or both? What are the social implications of his using his personal suffering of social injustices to justify the harm he does to others? How much have we learned about the motivations and moral justifications among producers, manufacturers, and retailers of poisonous foods who may be victims of food safety problems on other occasions? More important, will the unequal distribution of wealth and the unequal distribution of risks reinforce each other in a vicious cycle and thus generate another risk beyond that of nutrition and health? These are some of the daunting questions that beg for answers, but it is possible that risk-society theory cannot provide a ready answer to any of them in the Chinese case because of differences in social conditions and the mix of different types of risks. In my research, on the individualization of Chinese society, I found that the individualization thesis (which is part of Beck and others' theory of second modernity) in its original form is based on three social premises: the welfare state, cultural democracy, and classic individualism. None of these three premises exists in China; consequently, the Chinese process of individualization has taken quite a different path and has generated unique features and challenges. Nevertheless, the individualization thesis in the theory of second modernity is still critically important and useful to study the Chinese case (Yan 2010). The same is true, I believe, with the application of risk-society theory to study food safety problems and food risks in China.

To conclude, food safety problems constitute a new, urgent, and multifaceted risk to Chinese people, society, and the state, involving a number of social, political, and ethical issues beyond those of food safety, nutrition, and health. The complexity of the looming risk, however, has yet to be fully recognized, as evidenced by the lack of a detailed account of the typology, major features, and wider implications of food safety problems and of food risk perceptions. In an initial effort, I have reviewed the development of food safety problems, identifying the shift from the public hazard of food poisoning to the social fear of poisonous food as a key to understanding the changing patterns of food safety problems during the last six decades. I classify food safety problems into three types—problems of food hygiene, unsafe food, and poisonous food—and note that each of them constitutes a different type of risk. Although the traditional problem of food hygiene persists and calls for continuing attention from health professionals, unsafe food caused by modern modes of farming and food processing has quickly become the dominant and increasingly large-scale cause of the food safety problems affecting the health and lives of Chinese people. Socially and ethically, however, it is the poisonous food that presents the most serious challenge to public trust, regulatory governance, and the general well-being of Chinese individuals, not to mention the physical and psychological damage that each poisonous-food scandal causes at the level of society. The consequent social risk of trust, I reiterate, poses the most serious challenge to China.

The tripartite food safety problems and the mix of natural and manufactured risks also cut through temporal space and reflect a time-compressed feature of modernization in China. Although the unsafe-food problem certainly presents a social risk of second modernity or postindustrial and late modernity, it occurs in the Chinese context in a much fragmented market of food production and processing, where most food safety problems exist at household farms and workshops where food hygiene problems persist. The disregard and distrust of strangers, reflected in the making and circulation of poisonous food, however, is indicative of the ethical tension and crisis during China's transition from a kinship-based society of acquaintances to a highly mobile society in which interactions with strangers are increasingly common. This premodern-to-modern problem, however, has a contemporary twist of increased social inequality and injustices caused by the Chinese model of growth and development that in turn allows many to justify their immoral behavior. In this regard, the food safety problems present a clear and present danger to social solidarity and political stability of first modernity on top of the science-and-technology-induced risks of postindustrial modernity. The food safety problems and the associated risks have indeed demonstrated the arrival of a risk society in China, but they have arrived with a number of Chinese characteristics. More scrutiny of the Chinese case in light of risk-society theory will, as I argue elsewhere (Yan 2010), help to enrich the theory of second modernity and expand it into a cosmopolitan scale.

NOTES

1. In addition to paying attention to food safety problems in my fieldwork since the late 1990s, between 2006 and 2010, I conducted fifty-three in-depth interviews in Shanghai, Beijing, and rural Heilongjiang on individual moral experiences and interpretations of food safety problems, including the personal accounts of several individuals who had been involved in the production or circulation of unsafe and poisonous foods. However, ethnographic evidence plays only a marginal role in this chapter, as my aim here is to map the spectrum of food safety problems at the macro level and to explore whether the notion of a risk-society is applicable to the Chinese case.

2. This review is incomplete for several reasons. First, all the cases I collected and review here are those that have clear indications of the causes and that have been studied by medical and public health professionals whose primary interest is the medical and public health aspects of food-borne diseases. Obviously, not all cases of food poisoning are published in these professional journals; more cases are registered with the authorities but are never studied, and many others are simply not reported or registered. Moreover, the cases between 1983 and 2002 are limited to larger cases involving at least 100 people or one death, a threshold standard for registering a case with the Ministry of Health. The total number of food-poisoning studies contained in the database during this period exceeds 5,000. Furthermore, the Chinese government does not publicize all relevant data because of ideological and political concerns, making it even more difficult to understand the whole picture (Gale and Buzby 2009). It is safe to say that the actual occurrence of all types of food poisoning is much more frequent and widespread than what is reflected in the data I collected from this online search. For example, a recent study indicates that between 1994 and 2005, a total of 12,687 cases of food poisoning were registered with government authorities, resulting in nearly 290,000 people becoming ill and 2,297 deaths (Wang et al. 2007).

3. When I lived and worked in rural collectives in the 1970s, on two occasions I consumed meat from horses that had died of unknown diseases. At the time, many

villagers jokingly commented that we might end up sick or even dead if we ate the horse meat, but it was still worth it because "we will be happy ghosts with meat in our stomachs." During the 1970s, rural people had the opportunity to eat meat only during the Chinese New Year or when the collectives held banquets. Therefore, when a draft animal died of disease or old age, many villagers rejoiced because of the unexpected opportunity to consume meat.

4. Personal interview with a private entrepreneur in the food-processing business, Shanghai, June 2007.

5. The Chinese Ministry of Agriculture has introduced standards for pollution-free food, requiring all agricultural products to be free of dangerous chemical contaminants. However, the notion of green food is used mostly to improve the safety and quality of exported foods that fall under strict standards (see Calvin et al. 2006).

6. My informants most frequently mentioned cases of fake chicken eggs, fake soy sauce, diseased roast chicken, and cooking oil from sewage. These foods may not be the most toxic, but they all contain ingredients that challenge a basic principle of food ethics and thus cause panic and fear (see Jensen and Sandøe 2002; Smith 2007; Zwart 2000).

7. Personal interview with a female accountant working for a foreign company, Beijing, August 2006.

8. Personal interview, rural Heilongjiang, June 2008.

9. Personal interview, Shanghai, 2008.

10. Personal interview, rural Heilongjiang, August 2008.

11. When he met a British delegation on March 21, 1979, Deng Xiaoping brought up the notion of a "Chinese way of modernization," specifying that this was the realization of the modernization of agriculture, industry, national defense, and science and technology. On another occasion, when meeting provincial leaders on July 28, 1979, Deng further defined the specific standards for Chinese modernization: "It would be quite good if we could reach the level of GNP [gross national product] US$1,000 per capita (by the year 2000). [Chinese people] would be able to eat well, dress well, and use good appliances." In 1984, Deng lowered this expectation to US$800 per capita. It should be noted that in the late 1970s, per capita GNP in China was about $300.

12. Personal interview, Shanghai, July 2008. Elsewhere, I examine the scam after a distressed person who is helped by a stranger accuses the Good Samaritan of being the original cause of his distress and attempts to extort money from him. The majority of extortionists are poor elderly women, and the Good Samaritans tend to be wealthy middle-aged men. Poverty and social injustices are frequently used as a moral justification by both the extortionists and some of the public (see Yan 2009).

REFERENCES

Alams, Reidar. 1999. "Food Trust, Ethics and Safety in Risk Society." *Sociological Research Online* 4, no. 3. http://www.socresonline.org.uk/socresonline/4/3/almas.html.

Barboza, David. 2009. "Death Sentences Given in Chinese Milk Scandal." *New York Times*, February 2. http://www.nytimes.com/2009/01/22/world/asia/22iht-milk.3.19601372.html (accessed September 10, 2010).

———. 2010. "Recycled Cooking Oil Found to Be Latest Hazard in China." *New York Times*, March 31. http://www.nytimes.com/2010/04/01/world/asia/01shanghai.html?scp=1&sq=recycled%20cooking%20oil%20found%20to%20be%20latesthazard%20in%20china&st=cse (accessed October 28, 2010).

Beck, Ulrich. 1992. *Risk Society: Towards a New Modernity*. Translated by Mark Ritter. London: Sage.

———. 2000. "Risk Society Revisited: Theory, Politics and Research Programmes." In *The Risk Society and Beyond: Critical Issues for Social Theory*, edited by Barbara Adam, Ulrich Beck, and Joost van Loon, eds., 211–29. London: Sage.

———. 2009. *World at Risk*. Translated by Ciaran Cronin. Cambridge: Polity Press.

Buchler, Sandra, Kiah Smith, and Geoffrey Lawrence. 2010. "Food Risks, Old and New: Demographic Characteristics and Perceptions of Food Additives, Regulation and Contamination in Australia." *Journal of Sociology* 46, no. 4: 353–74.

Calvin, Linda, Fred Gale, Dinghuan Hu, and Bryan Lohmar. 2006. "Food Safety Improvements Underway in China." *Amber Waves* 4, no. 5: 16–21.

Chen Ruoshui. (2006). *Gonggong yishi yu Zhongguo wenhua* (Public awareness and Chinese culture). Beijing: Xinxing chubanshe.

CNN. 2009. "China: 70 Ill from Tainted Pig Organs," February 23. http://www.cnn.com/2009/WORLD/asiapcf/02/22/china.poisonings/index.html (accessed September 22, 2010).

Ekberg, Merryn. 2007. "The Parameters of the Risk Society: A Review and Exploration." *Current Sociology* 55, no. 3: 343–66.

Ellis, Linden, and Jennifer Turner. 2007. "Food Safety: Where We Stand in China," December 18. http://www.wilsoncenter.org/event/food-safety-where-we-stand-china (accessed February 26, 2012).

Gale, Fred, and Jean C. Buzby. 2009. "Imports from China and Food Safety Issues." *Economic Information Bulletin*, no. 52, US Department of Agriculture, Economic Research Service.

Giddens, Anthony. 1990. *The Consequences of Modernity*. Stanford, CA: Stanford University Press.

———. 1998. "Risk Society: The Context of British Politics." In *The Politics of Risk Society*, edited by Jane Franklin, 23–24. Cambridge: Polity Press.

Hu Bing. 1982. "Chi zhimagao yinqi de yichang fengbo" (An incident caused by the consumption of sesame cake). *Zhongguo shipin* (Chinese food), no. 5, 21.

Jensen, Karsten Klint, and Peter Sandøe. 2002. "Food Safety and Ethics: The Interplay between Science and Values." *Journal of Agricultural and Environmental Ethics* 15, no. 3: 245–53.

Jiang, Gaoming. 2007. "The Truth about Dead Chickens," June 14. http://www.chinadialogue.net/article/show/single/en/1096-The-truth-about-dead-chickens (accessed February 26, 2012).

Li, Peter J. 2009. "Exponential Growth, Animal Welfare, Environmental and Food Safety Impact: The Case of China's Livestock Production." *Journal of Agricultural and Environmental Ethics* 22, no. 3: 217–40.

Lin, Yi-Chieh Jessica. 2009. "Knockoff: A Cultural Biography of Transnational Counterfeit Goods." PhD diss., Harvard University.

Liu, Peng. 2010. "Tracing and Periodizing China's Food Safety Regulation: A Study on China's Food Safety Regime Change." *Regulation and Governance* 4, no. 2: 244–60.

Lora-Wainwright, Anna. 2009. "Of Farming Chemicals and Cancer Deaths: The Politics of Health in Contemporary Rural China." *Social Anthropology* 17, no. 1: 56–73.

Lü Zongshu, Zhang Qing, Zhu Yang, and Shen Nianzu. 2011. "Zhongguo 'tegong' shipin gongyingshang buwanquan mingdan" (An incomplete list of suppliers of special [safe] foods in China). *Nanfang zhoumo* (Southern weekend), May 6. http://www.21ccom.net/articles/zgyj/gqmq/2011/0506/34946.html (accessed February 26, 2012).

McKenna, Maryn. 2011. "China Pig Crisis: Drug Residues in Pork," March 26, *Wired* http://m.wired.com/wiredscience/2011/03/china-pig-crisis (accessed April 5, 2011).

Ministry of Commerce. 2008. "The 2008 Report on Food Safety in the Circulation Domain." Beijing: Ministry of Commerce.

Moore, Malcolm. 2010. "China Goes Organic after Scandal of Cooking Oil from Sewers." *The Telegraph*, August 30. http://www.telegraph.co.uk/news/worldnews/asia/china/7971983/China-goes-organic-after-scandal-of-cooking-oil-from-sewers.html (accessed October 28, 2010).

Mou Xiurui, ed. 2007. "Lianghui yu baixing (3): Shipin anquan zhi you heshi chengwei qiren you tian" (Worries about food safety: When is it unfounded?). *Zhongguo shipin anquan wang* (China Food Safety Net), March 14. http://www.ce.cn/cysc/sp/info/200703/14/t20070314_10686083.shtml (accessed August 27, 2010).

Nestle, Marion. 2010. *Safe Food: The Politics of Food Safety*. 2nd ed. Berkeley: University of California Press.

Pawsey, Rosa K. 2000. "Food and Its Safety." *Medicine, Conflict and Survival* 16, no. 2: 192–200.

Peng Siqing. 2003. "Wo ping shenme xinren ni?" (Why should I trust you?). In *Zhongguo shehui zhong de xinren* (Trust in Chinese society), edited by Zheng Yefu and Peng Siqing, 292–301. Beijing: Zhongguo chengshi chubanshe.

Smith, David F. 2007. "Food Panics in History: Corned Beef, Typhoid and 'Risk Society.'" *Journal of Epidemiol Community Health* 61, no. 7): 566–70.

Sun Ruixing. 1980. "Ershinian shiwu zhongdu de qingkuang fenxi" (An analysis of the causes of food poisoning in the past twenty years). *Jiangsu Yixue*, no. 7, 4–5.

Tam, Waikeung, and Dali L. Yang. 2005. "Food Safety and the Development of Regulatory Institutions in China." *Asian Perspective* 29, no. 4: 5–36.

Thiers, Paul. 1997. "Pesticides in China: Policy and Practice." *Pesticide Outlook* 8, no. 1: 6–10.

———. 2003. "Risk Society Comes to China: SARS, Transparency and Public Accountability." *Asian Perspective* 27, no. 2: 241–51.

Veeck, Ann, Hongyan Yu, and Alvin C. Burns. 2008. "Food Safety, Consumer Choice, and the Changing Marketplace in Urban China." In *Papers of the 33rd Annual Macromarketing Conference*, 39-44. Clemson, SC: Macromarketing Society, Inc.

Wang Jinfu. 1975. "Ziboshi shisinian shiwu zhongdu fenxi" (An analysis of food poisoning during the past fourteen years in Zibo city). *Shandong Yixue*, no. 4, 15–18.

Wang Liming. 2004. "Qinli Xianghe dujiucai jinjing" (Experiencing the arrival of poisonous chives from Xianghe). *Zhongguo zhiliang wanglixing zazhi* (Journal of quality supervision in China), no. 4, 22–26.

Wang, Shaoguang. 2003. "The Problem of State Weakness." *Journal of Democracy* 14, no. 1: 36–42.

Wang, Shijie, Huili Duan, Wei Zhang, and Jun-Wen Li. 2007. "Analysis of Bacterial Foodborne Disease Outbreaks in China between 1994 and 2005." *FEMS Immunology and Medical Microbiology* 51, no. 1: 8–13.

Watts, Jonathan. 2011. "Exploding Watermelons Put Spotlight on Chinese Farming Practices." *The Guardian*, May 17. http://www.guardian.co.uk/world/2011/may/17/exploding-watermelons-chinese-farming (accessed February 26, 2012).

Xia Yuzhen and Wu Yadan. 2007. "Zhongguo zheng jinru fengxian shehui shidai" (China entering an era of risk society). *Gansu shehui kexue* (Social sciences in Gansu), no. 1, 20–24.

Yan, Yunxiang. 2009. "The Good Samaritan's New Trouble: A Study of the Changing Moral Landscape in Contemporary China." *Social Anthropology* 17, no. 1: 9–24.

———. 2010. "The Chinese Path to Individualization." *British Journal of Sociology* 61, no. 3: 489–512.

Yang, Yang. 2007. "A China Environmental Health Project Factsheet: Pesticides and Environmental Health Trends in China," February 27. http://www.wilsoncenter.org/topics/docs/pesticides_feb28.pdf (accessed June 1, 2011).

Yoo, Yungsuk Karen. 2010. "Tainted Milk: What Kind of Justice for Victims' Families in China?" *Hastings International and Comparative Law Review* 33, no. 2: 555–75.

Zhang Guining and Chen Shifu. 1961. "Zhuhuoluan shamenshijun shiwu zhongdu ganran de liuxing bingxue diaocha baogao" (An epidemic report on food poisoning caused by salmonella cholerae). *Shandong yixue* (Shandong medical journal), no. 5, 12–15.

Zhang, Wenxia, and Zhao Yandong. n.d. "Beijing Citizens' Perception of Risk on Food Safety." http://www.kent.ac.uk/scarr/events/beijingpapers/WenxiaYandong.pdf (accessed May 31, 2011).

Zhang Xiaofang. 2007. "Shipin anquan yu hexie shehui" (Food safety and harmonious society), MA thesis, Shanxi University.

Zhou Qing. 2007. *Min yi heshi weitian: Zhongguo shipin anquan xianzhuang diaocha* (What kind of God: A survey of the current safety of China's food). Beijing: Zhongguo gongren chubanshe.

Zhou Shunan. 1958. "Nongcunzhong fasheng shiwu zhongdu de yuanyin yu yufang" (Causes of food poisoning and prevention in rural China). *Zhongguo yikan* (Chinese medical journal), no. 1, 25–27.

Zou Wei. 2011. "Gonganbu gongbu 2010 nian quanguo shida shipin anquan fanzui dianxing anli" (Ministry of Public Security publicizes the ten typical criminal cases of food safety in 2010), Xinhua News Agency, March 22. http://www.gov.cn/jrzg/2011-03/22/content_1829610.htm (accessed June 1, 2011).

Zwart, Hub. 2000. "A Short History of Food Ethics." *Journal of Agricultural and Environmental Ethics* 12, no. 2: 113–26.

Index

About the Contributors

Jeremy Brown is assistant professor of modern Chinese history at Simon Fraser University. He is the author of *City versus Countryside in Mao's China: Negotiating the Divide* (2012).

X. L. Ding is professor of social science at Hong Kong University of Science and Technology. A recent book in Chinese is *Debating the Chinese Model* (2011) with Korean and Japanese editions (2012 and 2013, respectively).

Hsiung Ping-chen is professor of history at the Chinese University of Hong Kong, where she is director of the Research Institute for the Humanities. She is author of *Tender Voyage: Children and Childhood in Late Imperial China* (2005).

William Jankowiak is the Barrack Distinguished Professor of Anthropology at the University of Nevada, Las Vegas. He is editor of *Romantic Passion* (1995) and *Intimacies* (2008). He is completing a book titled *City Days/City Nights: Emergent Social Pattern in a Chinese City, 1981–2012*.

Shuyu Kong is associate professor in the Department of Humanities and the Asia-Canada Program at Simon Fraser University. She is author of *Consuming Literature: Best Sellers and the Commercialization of Literary Production in Contemporary China* (2005).

Perry Link is Professor Emeritus of East Asian Studies at Princeton and Chancellorial Chair for Teaching Across the Disciplines at the University of California, Riverside. He teaches about language, literature, popular culture, and human rights in modern China. His latest book is *An Anatomy of Chinese: Rhythm, Metaphor, Politics* (2013).

Richard P. Madsen is Distinguished Professor of Sociology at the University of California, San Diego. He has written extensively on the sociology of morality, religion, and politics in both the United States and Asia. His latest book is *Democracy's Dharma: Religious Renaissance and Political Development in Taiwan* (2007).

David Moser holds a PhD from the University of Michigan, majoring in Chinese linguistics and philosophy. He has been a visiting scholar at Peking University and Beijing Foreign Studies University. He is currently at Beijing Capital Normal University, where he is academic director for CET Chinese Studies.

Paul G. Pickowicz is Distinguished Professor of History and Chinese Studies at the University of California, San Diego. He holds the UC San Diego Endowed Chair in Modern Chinese History. His latest book is *China on Film: A Century of Exploration, Confrontation, and Controversy* (2012).

Su Xiaokang is a Chinese writer who has lived in exile since 1989, when the Chinese government charged him with "counterrevolution" after his television documentary *River Elegy*, which aired in 1988, inspired Chinese students to call for democracy. In the United States, he served for many years as editor of *Democratic China*.

Xiao Qiang is adjunct professor of the School of Information, University of California, Berkeley, and director of Counter-Power Lab, a research group focusing on the intersection of social media, digital activism, and Internet freedom. He is founder and editor in chief of *China Digital Times*, a bilingual China news website.

Yunxiang Yan is professor of anthropology and director of the Center for Chinese Studies at the University of California, Los Angeles. He teaches and writes on family, kinship, the individual, and morality in China and on cultural globalization. His latest book is *The Individualization of Chinese Society*.

Yang Lijun is visiting fellow in the Department of Chinese Studies and research fellow at the East Asian Institute at the National University of Singapore. Her Japanese-language book *Social Structure and the Cultural Revolution in China: Citizenship and Collective Violence* (2003) received the Ohira Memorial Foundation Award.